Medicare Prescription Drug Coverage For Dummies

Quick Facts about Part D You Should Know

Here's the quick scoop on Part D, Medicare's prescription drug program. This book explains the ins and outs of Part D in detail, but the following are the program's key essentials:

- ✔ **Everyone on Medicare can get Part D drug coverage,** regardless of income or health.

- ✔ **If you've been getting your drugs from Medicaid,** you must instead get them through a Part D plan after you become eligible for Medicare.

- ✔ **You don't have to sign up for Part D** — but you may pay more for your coverage if you enroll later than when you first become eligible.

- ✔ **You must join one private Part D plan,** out of many Medicare has approved, to get coverage. You can switch plans each year if you want.

- ✔ **If your income and savings are limited,** and you qualify for Extra Help benefits, you'll pay much less for your Part D drug coverage.

- ✔ **If your drug costs are very high,** Medicare pays 95 percent of them after you've spent a certain amount out of pocket in any one year.

- ✔ **If you have good drug coverage already** — maybe from an employer or union — you may not need Part D at this time. But it's wise to check.

Finding Your Best Deal in Part D

Picking a single Part D drug plan out of maybe more than 50 in your area is a challenging task because each has a different mix of costs and benefits. Ideally you want a plan that covers all the drugs you take and costs the least out of pocket. Here are the most important do's and don'ts for getting there (see Chapter 10 for more details on picking a Part D plan):

- ✔ **Don't pick a plan based only on someone else's recommendation.** Unless the person takes exactly the same set of prescription drugs as you (unlikely!), the plan that's best for him probably won't be best for you.

- ✔ **Don't rely on marketing brochures or a sales agent's pitch.** Their main goal is to make a sale. The plan suggested may not give you the best deal and may not be appropriate for your circumstances.

- ✔ **Don't automatically pick the plan with the lowest premium.** Your main expense in any plan is its charges for your specific drugs, not the premium. (The exception: If you take no drugs right now, the plan

with the lowest premium is the best bet — minimizing your costs but giving you the protection of coverage.)

- ✔ **Don't automatically pick a plan with a familiar name.** It won't necessarily cover all your drugs at the least cost.

- ✔ **Do compare plans carefully.** Finding the best deal means comparing plans head to head — according to your own specific drugs, their dosages, and how often you take them. The most effective way is to use the online plan comparison tool on Medicare's Web site, www.medicare.gov. If you can't do this search yourself, you can get personal help to find your best option.

- ✔ **Do compare plans again each year.** Doing a new search every year (during open enrollment from November 15 through December 31) is well worth the trouble. Every plan changes some of its costs and benefits from one calendar year to the next — sometimes substantially so. The plan that's best for you this year may not be the best next year.

For Dummies: Bestselling Book Series for Beginners

Medicare Prescription Drug Coverage For Dummies®

Cheat Sheet

Steering Clear of the Coverage Gap

If the total cost of your drugs rises above a certain level in the year, you'll fall into the coverage gap (also known as the infamous "doughnut hole"). At that point — unless you have additional benefits to reduce expenses in the gap — you'll start paying full price. Here are ways to lower the cost of your drugs, stretch your Part D coverage, and maybe keep you out of the gap entirely (see Chapters 15 and 16 for additional information about the coverage gap):

- **Find out whether you really need all the meds you now take.** Many people are overprescribed. Ask your doctor to review all of your drugs — for the sake of your health as well as your pocketbook.

- **Switch to less-expensive drugs.** Ask your doctor whether lower-cost versions of any brand-name drugs you take now would work as well for you. This slashes your co-pays, reduces expenses in the deductible (if your plan has one), and staves off the doughnut hole by making your initial coverage last a lot longer.

- **Buy meds by mail order.** Most plans charge less for drugs bought through their mail-order service in 90-day supplies than from retail pharmacies in their networks.

- **Apply for Extra Help.** If your income and savings are limited, it's worth applying for these extra benefits. There's no coverage gap for people who qualify. (Check out Chapter 5 for details about Extra Help.)

Key Sources of Help

These are the main go-to resources for information and personal help on Part D issues (see Appendix B for many more):

- **Medicare:** For information and personal help on Part D, call its help line at 800-633-4227 (TTY: 877-486-2048) or go to www.medicare.gov.

- **Social Security:** For information and personal help in signing up for Medicare or applying for Extra Help benefits in Part D, call 800-772-1213 (TTY: 800-325-0778) or go to www.ssa.gov.

- **State Health Insurance Assistance Program (SHIP):** For free personal help with Medicare and Part D issues, call 800-677-1116, go to www.shiptalk.org, or see Appendix B to get the phone number of your nearest counselor.

- **Medicare Rights Center:** For regularly updated consumer information on Medicare and Part D, go to www.medicarerights.org. For free personal help with Part D issues, including appeals, call 800-333-4114.

For Dummies: Bestselling Book Series for Beginners

Medicare Prescription Drug Coverage

FOR DUMMIES®

by Patricia Barry

WILEY

Wiley Publishing, Inc.

Medicare Prescription Drug Coverage For Dummies®

Published by
Wiley Publishing, Inc.
111 River St.
Hoboken, NJ 07030-5774
www.wiley.com

WILEY

About the Author

Patricia Barry is a recognized expert on Medicare and its Part D prescription drug coverage. As a senior editor of the *AARP Bulletin* — the newspaper and Web site that serve AARP's 40 million members — she's written extensively about Medicare from the consumer's point of view since 1999. That year, she went to a press conference at the White House to hear President Bill Clinton announce his proposal to add outpatient prescription drugs to Medicare and came away thinking: "This story has legs — it'll run and run." For the next four years, she covered the bitter political battles in Washington that finally led to President George W. Bush signing Part D into law in December 2003.

Ever since, Patricia's mission has been to explain the controversial and complicated benefit to consumers. She's written numerous articles and guides on navigating Part D for AARP publications and books. Before and after the drug benefit went into effect in 2006, she invited readers' questions and personally answered hundreds of them. She continues to do so through the *Bulletin*'s Web site (bulletin.aarp.org). Patricia has directly helped many, many people — readers, friends, neighbors, and colleagues' parents — find the Part D plan that suits them best. Those questions and experiences are the foundation of *Medicare Prescription Drug Coverage For Dummies*.

In her long journalism career in Europe and America, Patricia has written thousands of newspaper and magazine articles and three books. A native of Great Britain, she's lived since 1985 in Maryland, where she and her husband raised three adventurous children — Katerina (currently living in Russia), Jessica (in France), and Oliver (in Egypt). In 2006, not without a sense of mutinous disbelief, Patricia became a Medicare beneficiary herself.

Dedication

This book is dedicated to the hundreds of older or disabled Americans who so generously shared their personal Part D stories with me since Medicare prescription drug coverage began. You told me what it was like on the front lines — experiences that were good, bad, and occasionally downright ugly. You prompted me to find answers to questions I hadn't thought of asking. You gave me the motivation to write this book, and I couldn't have done it without your insights. You were the consumer pioneers of Part D. To each and every one — a huge thank you!

Author's Acknowledgments

Writing this book has been a roller coaster grounded by the expertise and wisdom of many people who kept me on track. My thanks go to experts at two key federal agencies, the Centers for Medicare & Medicaid Services and the Social Security Administration, who helped me through the labyrinth of regulations that govern the Part D program and patiently answered hundreds of questions I threw at them. I'm also indebted to experts at the consumer help organizations who daily assist Medicare beneficiaries with Part D issues: the Medicare Rights Center, the Center for Medicare Advocacy, California Healthcare Advocates, and the State Health Insurance Assistance Programs.

I'm especially grateful for the advice and generously shared knowledge of many colleagues at AARP: David Gross, Gerry Smolka, Paul Cotton, Ed Dale, Lee Rucker, Elinor Ginzler, and, above all, Joyce Dubow, a national expert who for many years has been my guru on all things Medicare. I thank my editors at the *AARP Bulletin,* Jim Toedtman and Susan Crowley, for their encouragement and forbearance when I needed to take time out — and my former editors, Elliot Carlson and Bob Hey, who first twisted my arm to take on the *Bulletin*'s Medicare beat.

I'm enormously grateful to my project editor on this book, Georgette Beatty, and copy editors Vicki Adang and Jen Tucci at John Wiley & Sons, who have been a pleasure to work with. Also to Vicki Gottlich, of the Center for Medicare Advocacy, for her profound knowledge of Part D and vigilant eye while acting as technical adviser during the book's draft stages. And to my superb agent, Maureen Watts, who got this ball rolling.

Finally, to my children (who urged me on when I felt daunted by the task) and to my husband (whose devotion ran to cooking dinner every night for months), I can only say: What would I do without you?

Publisher's Acknowledgments

We're proud of this book; please send us your comments through our Dummies online registration form located at www.dummies.com/register/.

Some of the people who helped bring this book to market include the following:

Acquisitions, Editorial, and Media Development

Senior Project Editor: Georgette Beatty

Acquisitions Editor: Stacy Kennedy

Senior Copy Editor: Victoria M. Adang

Copy Editor: Jennifer Tucci

Assistant Editor: Erin Calligan Mooney

Technical Editor: Vicki Gottlich, Center for Medicare Advocacy

Editorial Manager: Michelle Hacker

Editorial Assistants: Joe Niesen, Jennette ElNaggar

Cover Photo: Jose Luis Pelaez, Inc.

Cartoons: Rich Tennant (www.the5thwave.com)

Composition Services

Project Coordinator: Katherine Key

Layout and Graphics: Reuben W. Davis, Melissa K. Jester, Christin Swinford, Stephanie D. Jumper, Christine Williams

Proofreaders: Broccoli Information Management, Caitie Kelly, Susan Moritz

Indexer: Broccoli Information Management

Publishing and Editorial for Consumer Dummies

    Diane Graves Steele, Vice President and Publisher, Consumer Dummies

    Joyce Pepple, Acquisitions Director, Consumer Dummies

    Kristin Ferguson-Wagstaffe, Product Development Director, Consumer Dummies

    Ensley Eikenburg, Associate Publisher, Travel

    Kelly Regan, Editorial Director, Travel

Publishing for Technology Dummies

    Andy Cummings, Vice President and Publisher, Dummies Technology/General User

Composition Services

    Gerry Fahey, Vice President of Production Services

    Debbie Stailey, Director of Composition Services

Contents at a Glance

Table of Contents

Introduction

*I*f you're reading this book, chances are you're baffled. That's okay — you're not alone. Since Medicare prescription drug coverage began in 2006, I've heard from multitudes of people trying to get their minds around Medicare Part D — the program's official name — and most often they call it "confusing." In fact, the crispest verdict came from an exceptionally on-the-ball 93-year-old who'd spent the afternoon swing dancing at a Wisconsin senior center. He asked, simply: "Why did they come up with a program I couldn't figure out myself?"

That's why I've written this book. There's no doubt about it — the Medicare drug program is complicated, largely because it comes with a lot of choices. Sure, choice is a good thing, but having many options also forces you to make more decisions. And to make good decisions — instead of just guessing and hoping for the best — you have to know the angles. That's where *Medicare Prescription Drug Coverage For Dummies* comes in. It takes you step by step through the choices you face and gives you the practical knowledge you need to make informed decisions. Consider it a road map for navigating the twists and turns in the system so you *can* figure it out for yourself — and with confidence.

Part D is a real benefit. Yes, it could be simpler and better, but it has still saved money for millions of people and allowed many to get the meds they need for the first time. For 40 years, Medicare didn't pay for outpatient prescription drugs at all, and during that time, these meds became increasingly expensive and more necessary as a medical treatment. But now there's Part D, and the problems are different. Typical questions I hear include:

- ✔ "There are 52 Medicare drug plans in my area, so how the heck am I supposed to choose one?"
- ✔ "I'll be getting my meds through my retiree health plan. How will Part D affect it?"
- ✔ "I was tricked into a plan I didn't want. How do I get out of it?"
- ✔ "This benefit has saved me a lot of money, but now my plan has stopped paying for my drugs entirely. Why?"

This book answers those questions and many more. Yes, taking a whole book to explain Part D says a lot about the program's complexities. But in these pages, I try to consider everybody's circumstances by covering the widest possible spectrum of issues. In doing so, I draw on the frontline experiences of people like you who've grappled with Medicare drug coverage, my own experience in helping them, and the knowledge of many experts I've badgered for answers to the trickiest questions.

So whatever your situation, *Medicare Prescription Drug Coverage For Dummies* offers strategies to cut through the confusions of Part D, either for yourself or for someone you're helping. It explains the program's ins and outs in plain words. It shows you how to avoid or cope with pitfalls and suggests how you can lower your costs or find a better deal. Best of all, it convinces you that you can — yes, you can — handle Medicare Part D!

About This Book

Medicare Prescription Drug Coverage For Dummies gives you a lot to chew on, but don't worry — you can take small bites. What you personally want to read depends on your situation — and on whether you're using this book to help yourself or someone else. But one matter's certain: If you recognize yourself in any of the following scenarios, you can find help in these pages:

- ✔ You have no insurance for prescription drugs right now (or it's coming to an end), but you'll soon be going into Medicare and know zip about Part D coverage or how to get it.

- ✔ You do have drug insurance now (from an employer or elsewhere) but will soon be eligible for Medicare and need to know whether Part D will affect you and whether you should sign up for it.

- ✔ You're already in Medicare but haven't signed up for Part D and are wondering whether you should.

- ✔ You're already enrolled in a Medicare Part D plan but can use some help troubleshooting problems, finding a better deal, or cutting your expenses.

- ✔ You need to know about Part D because you're helping parents, relatives, or friends find the best Medicare drug plan for them.

- ✔ In your job (or as a volunteer) working with seniors or people with disabilities, you can use a plain-language reference to Part D.

Conventions Used in This Book

As you may expect from a program run by a federal bureaucracy, you're going to meet certain unavoidable jargon in this book. This Part D–speak is worth getting to know, because notices you receive from Medicare or your drug plan — or any to-and-fros you have with either — will be easier to understand. So I use the following conventions:

✔ New terms in Part D–speak are explained the first time they appear.

✔ When you see the word "Medicare" used on its own, it usually means the whole Medicare program. (As in: "When you join Medicare . . .") Sometimes it means the federal agency that runs Medicare. (As in: "Medicare may send you a notice . . .") The agency's official name, the Centers for Medicare & Medicaid Services (CMS), is used as the source of information in some tables.

✔ The Medicare prescription drug program is referred to interchangeably as Part D or Medicare drug coverage. The private plans that provide this coverage are referred to as Part D plans or Medicare drug plans.

I also include a few standard conventions to help you navigate this book:

✔ *Italics* indicate definitions and emphasize certain words.

✔ **Boldface** text highlights key words in bulleted lists and actions to take in numbered steps.

✔ Monofont points out Web and e-mail addresses.

✔ "Quotation marks" generally indicate specific buttons or links you are to click on a given Web site.

What You're Not to Read

Guess what? You can skip the sidebars — chunks of text that appear in nifty gray-shaded boxes. They're not necessary to understanding how to find your way through Part D. Still, you may find them interesting. Ever wonder how on earth Congress dreamed up some of the more oddball bits of this program? You'll find answers in the sidebars scattered throughout this book.

Foolish Assumptions

This book assumes that you don't have any working knowledge of the Medicare prescription drug program — none, zip, nada. But even if you do, you can still find practical insights and useful tips to help you navigate the system more quickly, easily, and confidently.

Another point: This book assumes no political standpoints. Part D has always been controversial, coming under fire from conservatives and liberals alike. If you hold strong opinions, fine — that's your privilege. But in these pages, the only "us versus them" undertone is a bias toward consumers (us) rather than government bureaucracies and insurance companies (them). The aim of this book is to help you understand and deal with the system as it is now. If you want it changed, please tell your members of Congress, not me!

How This Book Is Organized

Medicare Prescription Drug Coverage For Dummies has six main parts with 21 chapters and three appendixes. Just dive into whatever you need to know — whether you're thinking about Medicare drug coverage for the first time, you're already in a Part D plan, or you're in a special situation, such as having a limited income or living in long-term care. You don't need to read stuff you already know, and you don't have to wade through stuff you don't need to know right now. The following summaries of each part include guidance on what you may want to read, according to your own situation.

Part I: The Nuts and Bolts of Medicare Prescription Drug Coverage

This first part begins with a quick run through the essentials of Medicare as a whole. This spot's your first port of call if you'll soon be going into Medicare and need to know if you qualify and how to sign up. Next, I get into the nitty-gritty of Part D itself by first looking broadly at the main rules of the prescription drug program and how it works. Then I take a closer look at the big questions that matter most to your pocketbook and health — costs and coverage. These chapters are essential reading if you're considering Part D for the first time.

In this part, too, I provide detailed information about the program-within-a-program known as Extra Help, which offers much more generous drug benefits to people with limited incomes. Head to this chapter if you think you can't afford the premiums and co-payments required in the regular Part D program, or if you currently get your meds from Medicaid.

Part II: Deciding Whether to Sign Up for Part D

For many people, this crucial question — "Do I really need Part D?" — can cause everything from head-scratching to panic attacks. Read this part if you already have prescription drug insurance, rely on free or low-cost drugs from some other source, or take no or very few meds right now. Here you discover how to find out if your current drug coverage is considered better or worse than Part D coverage and why this distinction matters. You also find help in weighing the consequences of continuing to have no drug coverage when you're eligible for Part D — including hard facts about the late penalty if you don't sign up for Part D at the right time.

Part III: Choosing and Enrolling in the Right Part D Plan for You

Having to pick just one Medicare drug plan — out of more than 50 that are available to you, wherever you live — can bring on an acute form of paralysis, especially because each plan has different charges and covers a different range of drugs than the next one. So this part shows you the best ways to pick the plum — meaning the best plan for you — out of a whole lot of apples, oranges, and pears. It explains how to compare plans properly in the quickest way and why doing so is worth the effort. It also suggests ways to avoid scams and hard-sell marketing tactics. Finally, I show you how to enroll in the plan of your choice. Check out this part if you're joining Part D for the first time *and* if you're already in a Part D plan in November or December and want to know if it'll still be the best one for you next year.

Part IV: You're In! Navigating Part D from the Inside

This part covers a ton of ground — from first receiving your plan's card right through to the end of the year when you're deciding whether to stay with this plan or switch to another. Want to know how to navigate the dreaded dough-nut hole (formally known as the coverage gap)? Need a drug that your plan won't pay for? Want to cut down your out-of-pocket expenses? Wondering how going into a nursing home affects your Part D coverage? Need help in challenging a decision your plan has made that you don't agree with? You can find the answers to these questions and many more right here. Consider reading much of this part if you're joining a Medicare drug plan for the first time. But if you've been in a plan for a while, you may just want to jump into the chapter that directly speaks to your particular concern.

Part V: The Part of Tens

From the Ten Commandments to David Letterman's Top Ten Lists, ten has long been the magic number for snappy lists. This part has two ten-point lists. Check them out for information you can take in at a glance on two key areas — ten ways for boomers to ride to the rescue of loved ones grappling with Part D and ten proposed changes to Part D that you should know about.

Part VI: Appendixes

Appendix A offers sample worksheets you can use when comparing Part D plans — whether stand-alone drug plans or Medicare Advantage plans. Appendix B is your go-to resource for when you need personal help with Part D. Look here for the names and contact info of organizations and agencies mentioned in this book. Appendix C is your guide to safely buying prescription drugs by mail order from abroad. It explains steps you can take to ensure you receive genuine products from reputable pharmacies instead of falling prey to counterfeit medicines and dubious sellers.

Icons Used in This Book

Icons are those cute drawings you see in the page margins now and again. Here's what they mean:

This icon indicates a situation in which you need your doctor's help — for example, when asking your Part D plan to pay for a medicine it doesn't usually cover, or when finding out whether a lower-cost drug would work just as well as the expensive one you're taking now.

This icon signals important info. If you take anything away from this book, it should be information highlighted with this icon.

This icon draws your attention to on-target advice and practical insights that will save you time, effort, and maybe even money.

This icon raises a red flag to alert you to a Part D rule or potential pitfall that may trip you up if you remain blithely unaware of it.

Where to Go from Here

Nobody expects you to read this book cover to cover. *Harry Potter* it's not! But you can jump in anywhere to the bit you need, at whatever point you happen to be in when grappling with Medicare prescription drug coverage. I'm going to whip off the cloak of invisibility to reveal . . . not the Sorcerer's Stone, not the Chamber of Secrets . . . but the practicalities of a system that isn't very mysterious at all — after you know how to navigate it.

Part I

The Nuts and Bolts of Medicare Prescription Drug Coverage

The 5th Wave — By Rich Tennant

"Exactly what kind of prescription medication <u>are</u> you taking?"

In this part . . .

*B*efore you can choose a prescription drug plan, you should understand the basics of Medicare Part D prescription drug coverage — how it fits into the wider Medicare program and, broadly, how it works.

First, for those of you who are just about to join Medicare, I give a quick primer on the different parts of the Medicare program — Part A (hospital coverage), Part B (doctors and outpatient services), Part C (private health plans), and Part D (drug coverage) — as well as how to be sure you're eligible for Medicare and how to enroll. Then I give an overview of the main rules of Part D so you can get a general idea of how Medicare drug coverage works if you're not yet enrolled in the program.

In the remaining chapters of this part, I explain in more detail the two topics that probably most concern you at this stage — how much you're likely to spend and save in Part D (whether you're in the regular program or you qualify for extra financial help in paying for meds) and how your prescription drugs will be covered.

Chapter 1

The ABCs (And D) of Medicare

....

In This Chapter

▶ Getting a grip on Medicare and how to qualify

▶ Checking out Medicare's benefits and costs

▶ Figuring out when and how to enroll in Medicare

▶ Discovering how to decrease your costs and increase your benefits

....

Medicare helps pay for your prescription drugs *only* if you're in the wider Medicare health program. You don't necessarily have to be using its medical services at this time to be eligible for drug coverage; you just need to have your very own numbered file in the vast Medicare system.

So with this info in mind, why not begin at the beginning with a quick tour through the essentials of Medicare as a whole? If you're already well acquainted with Medicare, you can skip to other chapters for the scoop on Medicare prescription drug coverage. But stick around if you're facing the mysteries of Medicare for the first time and need to know whether you qualify, how to sign up, and how the different parts of the program — each with its own benefits and costs — fit together.

This chapter outlines only the basics of Medicare, just enough to get you on your way. To find out where to go for more detailed information, turn to Appendix B.

Knowing Your Place in the Wide World of Medicare

Medicare is a federal government insurance system, begun in 1966, that helps tens of millions of seniors and people with disabilities nationwide pay for healthcare. It's the only national healthcare program — available regardless of income or where you live — in the United States, and it's enduringly popular among people who use it.

Medicare doesn't pay all of your medical bills by any means. Nonetheless, it still gives a lot of protection against today's high healthcare costs if you don't have other health insurance. And unlike other forms of health insurance you may have met in the past, you can't be excluded from Medicare, or pay more for it, because of advancing age or the state of your health. How's that for your tax dollars at work?

To qualify for Medicare, you must meet certain rules, depending on the following circumstances:

✔ **If you're age 65 or older:** You qualify for Medicare as soon as you reach age 65 if you *or* your spouse has worked long enough to entitle you to Social Security or Railroad Retirement benefits, even if you're not yet receiving them. You usually need at least 40 credits (amounting to about ten years of work) to become eligible for these retirement benefits, which are paid through monthly checks. Anyone with enough work credits can claim these benefits from the age of 62 onward, though doing so means accepting lower payments than when starting at or after full retirement age. (For people born between 1943 and 1954, full retirement age is now 66.) But remember — even if you claim these benefits early, you still have to wait until age 65 to qualify for Medicare.

The annual statement you receive from Social Security says whether you qualify for Medicare or, if you're not eligible yet, when you will be. If you lose your statement, call Social Security at 800-772-1213 to ask for a replacement.

✔ **If you're younger than 65 and have disabilities:** You're entitled to Medicare at any age if you have a severe illness, injury, or disability that prevents you from earning more than a certain amount of money each month *and* you've received Social Security disability benefits for at least 24 months. These months need not be consecutive. Anyone diagnosed with Lou Gehrig's disease (Amyotrophic Lateral Sclerosis, or ALS) doesn't have to wait 24 months to join Medicare. If you think you may qualify and want to find out the earnings limits that apply to your circumstances, call Social Security at 800-772-1213 or go to www.ssa.gov.

✔ **If you have permanent kidney failure:** You're entitled to Medicare at any age if you have end-stage renal disease (ESRD) — usually defined as needing a kidney transplant or regular dialysis — *and* if you or your spouse has paid into Social Security through work for a certain length of time. This period depends on how old you are. For specific eligibility information, visit www.ssa.gov or call Social Security at 800-772-1213.

✔ **If you don't qualify for Medicare:** If you're 65 or older but don't have enough work credits, you may be able to buy into the system by paying premiums. You can buy in *only* if you're an American citizen or a legal resident (green card holder) who has lived in this country continuously for at least five years. The premiums for Medicare Part A (hospital insurance) are pretty hefty for people who don't qualify for Medicare — the amount varies depending on how many work credits you have — but they're probably less expensive than insurance you can buy yourself.

> Purchasing Medicare Part A makes you eligible for other Medicare benefits, like prescription drug coverage. If you work long enough to earn enough credits to qualify for Medicare in the future, you no longer have to pay Part A premiums.

Now you know the general guidelines. Of course, the fine print of Medicare rules and regulations deals with many specific situations, but I avoid this nitty-gritty here because you'll find out where you stand when you go to sign up for Medicare. (I explain how to enroll later in this chapter.) If you want more detailed information, contact the sources listed at the end of this chapter.

Examining Costs and Coverage in Medicare's Four Parts

Medicare has never been a single unified program in which you pay just one premium to belong and a certain amount for each medical service you use. Instead, Medicare evolved over time and now has four parts, each covering different types of medical care and requiring different payments. The following sections are a brief overview that outlines what you pay and what you get in return. Here's where you dive into the Medicare alphabet soup and learn your ABCs all over again!

Part A

Part A is insurance that pays most of your costs when you're a patient in a hospital and also, in some circumstances, if you're in a skilled nursing facility or hospice, or are receiving treatment from a home healthcare agency. When you turn 65 and have enough work credits, as described in the previous section, you instantly qualify for Part A.

But wait! There's more good news: If you're eligible for Medicare, you pay no monthly premium charges for Part A. (That's because you, or your spouse, already paid payroll taxes for Medicare in a job.) Services received through Part A, however, aren't free; you pay a share of the costs when using them. For example, when you go into the hospital, you pay the first chunk of expenses until you meet the deductible, an amount set by law that usually goes up every year ($1,024 in 2008).

This amount isn't an annual deductible. Instead, it applies to every *benefit period* — the time you're treated in the hospital for a particular spell of illness or injury. After you've met the deductible, Medicare pays 100 percent of covered costs for a stay of up to 60 days (which need not be consecutive). After that, you pay a share of the costs ($256 a day in 2008) from Day 61 to Day 90. (If you need extra days, you can use up to 60 *lifetime reserve* days that Medicare allows for additional coverage over the rest of your life.

The co-pay for these days, in 2008, is $512.) If you go into the hospital for a *different* illness or injury, you start a new benefit period and again pay the deductible before coverage kicks in and the payment cycle starts over. There's no limit to the number of benefit periods you can use.

Part A covers the following inpatient services:

- A semiprivate room.
- Regular nursing care.
- All meals provided directly by the hospital or nursing facility.
- Other services provided directly by the hospital or nursing facility, including lab tests, prescription drugs, medical appliances, and rehabilitation therapies.
- A temporary stay (up to 100 days) in a nursing home or hospital under the skilled nursing facility benefit. This benefit is available *only* when nursing or rehabilitation care is necessary following at least three days in the hospital with a related illness or injury.

Part A doesn't cover the cost of a private room (unless one is medically necessary), private nurses, or nice-to-have conveniences such as a telephone or television. Except for the skilled nursing facility benefit, Part A doesn't cover the costs of living in a nursing home. (I explain this benefit, and nursing home care, in more detail in Chapter 18.)

Part B

Part B is insurance that helps you pay to see a doctor and use services outside of a hospital or nursing facility. Part B is voluntary, meaning you can choose whether you want it and, depending on your circumstances, when to sign up.

If you're 65 or older, you can purchase Part B coverage even if you don't qualify for Part A. To do so, you must be an American citizen or a legal resident who has lived in the U.S. continuously for five years.

Part B requires you to pay a monthly premium, even if you or your spouse paid taxes for Medicare while working. The Part B premium amount is set annually ($96.40 a month in 2008) and generally goes up from year to year. Most people pay the same premium. However, those with high incomes (more than $82,000 a year in 2008) pay more, and those with very low incomes may receive state help for paying these premiums, if they qualify. Part B also requires you to pay an annual deductible, determined by law ($135 in 2008), which is the out-of-pocket amount you pay for medical care at the beginning of the year before coverage kicks in. You also have to pay a share of the cost of services that Medicare covers — usually 20 percent of the bill, though some services (such as outpatient mental health care) cost more, and some (such as approved home healthcare) cost less.

Wondering what you get for this voluntary coverage? Part B covers

- ✔ Approved medical and surgical services from any doctor who accepts Medicare patients, whether provided in a doctor's office, hospital, long-term care facility, or at home, anywhere in the nation

- ✔ Diagnostic and lab tests done outside hospitals and nursing facilities

- ✔ A certain number of preventive services and screenings, such as flu shots and mammograms

- ✔ Some medical equipment (for example, wheelchairs and walkers)

- ✔ Some outpatient hospital treatment received in an emergency room, clinic, or ambulatory surgical unit

- ✔ Inpatient prescription drugs given in a hospital or doctor's office, usually by injection (such as chemotherapy drugs for cancer)

- ✔ Some coverage for physical, occupational, and speech therapies

- ✔ Outpatient mental health care (copay of 50 percent in 2008 reducing to 20 pecent by 2014)

- ✔ Approved home health services not covered by Part A

A wide range of medical services, such as dental, vision, and hearing care (including hearing aids); routine checkups; and outpatient prescription drugs, falls outside Part B's coverage zone. Fortunately, outpatient prescription drug coverage is exactly what Part D is for!

Part C

In the previous two sections, I outline costs and coverage under *traditional* or *original Medicare,* which earned the name because it follows the basic design of the program originally laid out in 1965. It's also called *fee-for-service Medicare* because each provider — whether a doctor, hospital, laboratory, medical equipment supplier, or whatever — is paid a fee for each service.

But Medicare also offers an alternative to the traditional program in the form of a range of health plans that mainly provide managed care. These plans are run by private companies, which decide each year whether to stay in the program. Medicare pays plans a fixed fee for everyone who joins the plans, regardless of how much or little healthcare a person actually uses. This health plan program is called *Medicare Advantage,* or Medicare Part C.

In most cases, you pay a monthly premium for a Medicare Advantage (MA) plan — with the amount varying from plan to plan — on top of the regular Medicare Part B premium. Some plans, however, don't charge an extra premium, and a few also pay all or some of the Part B premium for their members. You pay a share of the costs of hospital and outpatient services. These co-pays vary from plan to plan and are usually different than those required in traditional Medicare.

MA plans must cover all services covered by Part A and Part B in the traditional Medicare program. They may also offer extra services that Medicare doesn't cover — for example, dental and eye care. Most plans include prescription drug coverage as part of their package.

Unlike traditional Medicare, your choice of doctors and hospitals under most MA plans is likely to be limited to those in the plan's provider network and to the plan's local service area. You also pay more if you go out of network. In a medical emergency, however, the plan must cover the treatment you receive from *any* doctor or hospital.

Part D

Part D is insurance for outpatient prescription drugs — meaning medications you take yourself, instead of having them administered in a hospital or doctor's office — that Medicare began offering in 2006. Like Part C, this program is run entirely through many private plans approved by Medicare, each of which has different costs and benefits. You can get Part D through *stand-alone plans* (which cover only prescription drugs and are used mainly by people in traditional Medicare) or through Medicare Advantage health plans that include drug coverage. But I don't dwell on Part D here, because the rest of this book explores the program in detail.

Comparing different types of Medicare insurance

All the different kinds of insurance under Medicare are enough to blow any-body's mind. (Would you believe there's another? Medicare supplementary insurance isn't a government program, but it can be bought to fill in some of the gaps in Medicare, as I explain in the later section "Lowering Costs and Adding Benefits.") Consequently, it isn't surprising people get confused about what each means and what the difference is between them.

Table 1-1 helps cut through the confusion by briefly describing coverage, provider details, and pros and cons for each kind of Medicare insurance, including the types of Medicare Advantage plans you're most likely to encounter. *Note:* Two types of Medicare Advantage plans aren't included here: Special Needs Plans (SNP) and Medicare Medical Savings Account Plans (MSAs), both of which restrict enrollment to certain groups of people.

Table 1-1	Types of Medicare Insurance and What Each Means			
Type of Plan	**What It Covers**	**Provider Access**	**Pros**	**Cons**
Traditional Medicare (Parts A and B)	Hospital care, doctor services, some other types of outpatient care, some medical supplies and screenings	Any doctor, hospital, lab or supplier that accepts patients with Medicare	Available anywhere within U.S.; charges standard co-pays for each service	Doesn't coordinate care or cover eye, dental, or hearing care; routine checkups; or outpatient prescription drugs
Medigap Supplementary Insurance	Some out-of-pocket expenses of traditional Medicare; some policies cover extra services	Not applicable — except for one type of policy called a "Select Plan" that limits coverage to network providers except in emergencies	Reduces costs of deductibles and co-pays; may help pay for some extra services	Can be expensive; doesn't cover out-of-pocket costs of prescription drug coverage; can't be used with Medicare Advantage plans
Medicare Stand-Alone Prescription Drug Plans (PDP)	*Only* prescription drugs; intended mainly for people in traditional Medicare who have no other drug coverage	Drugs available from pharmacies and mail-order services within plan's network; going out of network costs more	Cuts costs of medications; more generous help available for people with low incomes and/or high drug costs	Gap in coverage in most plans; comparing plans can be confusing because each has different costs and benefits

(continued)

Table 1-1 (*continued*)

Type of Plan	What It Covers	Provider Access	Pros	Cons
Medicare Advantage Plans	Everything that traditional Medicare covers and maybe some extras	Depends on type of MA plan — see the "HMO," "PPO," and "PFFS" entries in this table	Depends on type of MA plan — see the "HMO," "PPO," and "PFFS" entries in this table	Depends on type of MA plan — see the "HMO," "PPO," and "PFFS" entries in this table
HMO	Managed care; may or may not cover outpatient prescription drugs	Providers limited to those in plan's network, except in medical emergencies	Coordinates care; may have lower or higher costs and offer more services than traditional Medicare	Not portable — limited to service area; limited choice of providers; costs, benefits can change each year; costs not covered by Medigap insurance
PPO	Managed care; may or may not cover outpatient prescription drugs	Seeing providers outside network is allowed but costs more; no referral needed to see specialists	Coordinates care; may have lower or higher costs and offer more services than traditional Medicare	Not portable — limited to service area; costs, benefits can change each year; costs not covered by Medigap insurance
PFFS	Private fee-for-service; may or may not cover outpatient prescription drugs	Any provider that accepts the plan's conditions and payments	Available anywhere in U.S. from providers that accept plan	Not all providers accept plans; not easy to find out in advance which ones do; providers may accept plan on a visit-by-visit basis; doesn't coordinate care

Getting with the Program: When and How to Sign Up for Parts A and B

Don't panic if your 65th birthday is looming and you haven't a clue about how to sign up for Medicare — or even whether you should. You're not alone. Remember how you dived into a state of denial when you turned 50? Now you're 15 years further on, but you still haven't given much thought to Medicare, an even bigger psychological milestone — until now. In the following sections, I explain when to sign up at the time that's right for you and walk you through the process of enrolling.

It's all in the timing: When to sign up

You can (and should) sign up for at least Medicare Part A — hospital insurance — around the time you turn 65, whatever your circumstances (even if you're still working, have health insurance from your employer, or haven't yet begun to draw Social Security retirement payments). It costs nothing to enroll, and you have no premiums to pay. But even if you don't need any Medicare coverage right now, simply getting your name in the system as soon as possible may ensure a smoother ride later on if and when you decide you want (or need) to sample more of Medicare's offerings.

When to enroll in Medicare and what services you decide to sign up for depend on your circumstances. This section covers the possibilities.

You already receive Social Security benefits

When I say "Social Security benefits" here, I'm referring to Social Security benefits for retirement, dependents, and survivors — or similar benefits for Railroad Retirement. If you're already receiving any of these benefits and *haven't* yet turned 65, you don't need to sign up for Medicare. In this case, Social Security automatically enrolls you in Medicare Part A and Part B, and you receive your Medicare card in the mail. Coverage starts on your 65th birthday. The same automatic enrollment takes place if you've been getting Social Security disability benefits for two years, regardless of your age.

In both situations, you have the right to cancel Part B coverage if you don't want it (for example, if you already receive medical coverage from an employer or union health plan). But if you're considering canceling because the Part B premium is more than you can afford, you may want to apply for your state's Medicare Savings Program. If you qualify, the state pays your Part B premium, and you automatically become eligible for low-cost prescription drug coverage under Part D's Extra Help program, as explained in depth in Chapter 5.

You don't receive Social Security benefits yet

If you don't receive Social Security benefits by the time you're 65, you need to apply to enroll in Medicare. Timing is very important here because you have a seven-month window, or *initial enrollment period,* to sign up. It begins three months before the month in which you turn 65 and ends three months after your birthday month. So if you're going to celebrate 65 years on June 22, you can sign up any time between March 1 and September 30.

Sooner is better than later. If you enroll early, your coverage starts the month you turn 65. If you wait until after your birthday, it begins on the first day of the month after you enroll.

If you don't sign up for Medicare Part B when you first become eligible, you have to pay a late penalty when you do eventually sign up. (The exception is if you're still working and have group health insurance from an employer or union that's *primary* to Medicare, meaning that your group plan pays your medical bills first.) A late penalty means paying more for Part B in the form of permanently higher premiums — 10 percent higher for every year you could've had Part B but didn't. After your personal deadline for joining Part B has passed, you can sign up *only* during a general enrollment period from January 1 to March 31 each year. Your coverage then begins July 1.

You have no other health insurance

If you don't currently have health insurance, you'll need Medicare for all of your medical coverage. So you'll probably want to sign up for both Part A (hospital insurance) and Part B (insurance for doctor visits and outpatient services). You should sign up for these programs during your seven-month initial enrollment period around the time of your 65th birthday (see the preceding section). If you don't sign up for Part B during this time but decide to do so later, you'll pay a late penalty.

You work and have group health insurance

If you're still working after the age of 65 and have group health insurance from your employer or union, check with your benefits administrator to find out whether this coverage is primary or secondary to Medicare. *Primary* means your own insurance pays your medical bills first; *secondary* means Medicare pays first and your insurance pays for certain services that Medicare doesn't cover. So how does this explanation relate to your specific situation? Here are your options:

- ✔ **If your insurance is secondary:** You should sign up for Medicare Part B within your seven-month initial enrollment period (see the earlier section "You don't receive Social Security benefits yet"). In fact, your employer or union health plan will probably insist on it as a condition for continuing your current coverage. (If your employer has fewer than 20 employees and you are 65 or older, your health plan is automatically secondary to Medicare.)

✔ **If your insurance is primary:** You don't need to sign up for Part B at this time. However, when you sign up for Part A, make sure that Medicare documents that you have primary coverage from elsewhere. In the future, if you lose your employer or union coverage, you'll need Medicare to know that you once had it so you can enroll in Part B at that time without incurring a late penalty. If you do lose your current coverage, you'll have eight months to sign up for Part B, starting from the end of the month in which you lose coverage. As long as you sign up within this period (or earlier), you won't pay a late penalty, and you'll still have guaranteed access to Medigap insurance. (I explain guaranteed access to Medigap later in this chapter.)

You no longer work but have retiree health insurance

After you retire, consider signing up for Part B, even if you still have health insurance from your former employer or union under a retiree plan. Yes, this precaution probably means paying two premiums — and of course you have the right not to join Part B if you don't want to (unless your employer or union insists on it as a condition of your retiree coverage). But if at some future date you lose or drop your retiree benefits and need to sign up for Part B at that time, you'll have to pay a late penalty. You won't incur a late penalty if you join Part B within eight months of retiring from your job.

You don't qualify for Part A

If you don't qualify for Part A's hospital insurance, you may be able to buy into the system by paying a premium for this coverage (see the earlier section "Knowing Your Place in the Wide World of Medicare"). Regardless of what you choose to do with Part A, you can still get outpatient medical coverage under Part B as long as you're 65 or older and an American citizen or have lived in the U.S. as a legal resident for at least five years. To receive this benefit, you simply pay the same premium, deductibles, and co-pays as anyone else. To join the Part B party, and avoid a late penalty, enroll at one of the following times:

✔ During the seven-month initial enrollment period around the time of your 65th birthday if you have no other health coverage, or if your current coverage is secondary to Medicare

✔ Within eight months of losing your current health coverage, if it's primary to Medicare

✔ Within eight months of retiring from a current job that provides retiree health benefits

You live outside the United States

If you have enough Social Security credits to qualify for Medicare, you should file for Medicare Part A (hospital insurance) around your 65th birthday if you live outside the U.S. You can't use this insurance abroad, but, after all, it doesn't cost you anything to sign up. To do so, contact the U.S. embassy or consulate in the country you're living in — or the Department of Veterans Affairs's regional office if you live in the Philippines.

Deciding whether to buy Part B (doctor and outpatient services) may be trickier. If you're still working and have primary group health insurance from your employer, you don't need to join Part B yet. But if you don't have such insurance (or are perhaps relying on the public health service of the nation where you live) or are retired, you have two options:

- ✔ Sign up for Part B when you turn 65 and pay the required premiums — even though you won't be able to get Part B medical services while living abroad.

- ✔ Delay signing up after you turn 65 and incur a late penalty if you join Part B after moving back to the U.S.

Taking the plunge: How to sign up

When you don't automatically qualify for Medicare — that is, if you're not *already* receiving Social Security or Railroad Retirement payments — you must apply for the program. All you have to do is make one toll-free phone call to the Social Security Administration (*not* Medicare) at 800-772-1213. A customer representative will ask for your Social Security number and will give you the choice of signing up for Medicare directly on the phone or making an appointment for you to visit your local Social Security office. Signing up on the phone is simpler, but you need to send important documents (such as your birth certificate or passport and, if you're not an American citizen, proof of legal residence) to Social Security through the mail. If this process unnerves you, you can take the documents with you to an office appointment. The representative you initially speak with schedules the appointment and gives you the address of the nearest Social Security office.

During this interview, whether on the phone or in person, you can discuss your Medicare needs — such as whether you want to sign up for Part B right now — and whether you want to start receiving Social Security payments as soon as you're eligible. The customer representative then answers your questions and enters your information into the computer system. A week or two later, you'll receive your Medicare card in the mail. The card indicates which benefits (Part A alone, or Part A and Part B) you've signed up for. With your card, you'll also receive a copy of your information that's been entered into the Medicare system. If any details are wrong, call the phone number listed in your mailing to have them changed.

Lowering Costs and Adding Benefits

Medicare has a whole slew of out-of-pocket expenses and doesn't cover all medical services. What, if anything, can you do to lower costs and get more benefits? These sections break down your possible options, depending on various circumstances.

Medicare supplementary insurance (also known as Medigap)

Medicare supplementary insurance is *not* a government program offered by Medicare. It's a separate private insurance you can purchase for an additional monthly premium to fill in some of the gaps in traditional Medicare, which is why it's often called *Medigap*. Depending on the kind of policy you buy, Medigap covers out-of-pocket expenses in Medicare, such as deductibles and co-pays, and may cover extra services (for example, at-home recovery after hospitalization and emergency treatment abroad). Medigap features 12 standard policies, designated A through L, each offering a different range of coverage options — the more options, the more expensive the policy. These policies are sold by many insurance companies at varying premiums. You can compare benefits and costs online at www.medicare.gov or by calling Medicare at 800-633-4227.

The best time to buy Medigap insurance is within six months of signing up for Medicare Part B, because this timing gives you significant consumer protections. During the six-month window, you have a *guaranteed* right to buy any Medigap policy sold in the state where you live. In other words, you can't be turned down because of poor health or any pre-existing medical conditions. Nor can you be charged higher premiums based on your age. You get this window, with all of its guarantees, regardless of when you enroll in Part B, even if you sign up late for Part B.

Other factors may affect your decision to purchase Medigap insurance:

✔ You can't use Medigap if you're in a Medicare Advantage health plan. So if you enroll in one of these plans immediately after joining Part B, you lose your right to buy Medigap with guaranteed protections. (However, you may be able to get this right back if you leave the MA plan within your first year in Medicare or if you gave up a Medigap policy to join an MA plan for the first time. I explain the details of these exceptions in Chapter 17.)

✔ No Medigap policies sold after 2005 include drug coverage, and you can't use them to cover out-of-pocket expenses in Part D.

Medicare Advantage plans (Part C)

Medicare Advantage (MA) plans may have lower costs and offer more benefits than traditional Medicare. Depending on the plan, lower costs may include zero premiums, a reduced hospital deductible, a flat co-pay (for example, $10 or $20) rather than 20 percent coinsurance for each doctor visit, and a cap on out-of-pocket expenses in a calendar year. Extra benefits may include coverage for vision or hearing services, emergency treatment abroad, or exercise programs. However, some plans charge higher costs than traditional Medicare for some services and offer only minimal extra benefits. Also, you need to recognize that most MA plans limit the choice of doctors and hospitals and may not cover treatment outside of their service area, except in emergencies. (I compare MA plans with traditional Medicare in Chapter 9.)

Veterans benefits

If you qualify for federal health benefits from the Department of Veterans Affairs (VA), you can use them in addition to, or instead of, Medicare. You can also decide which benefits to use for each medical service you need. If you choose the VA for treatment, you must obtain your treatment at a VA facility. Medicare doesn't pay for care at VA facilities but does pay for Medicare-covered medical services that you obtain elsewhere. If you're a veteran with a low income or a high enough service-related disability rating, you may qualify for free VA care. Whether you're eligible for free care or not, you should consider signing up for Medicare in case you need future services that the VA can't provide or you have to travel too far to get to a VA facility. For more info, call 877-222-8387 or visit www.va.gov/healtheligibility.

Medicaid

Medicaid is a healthcare program for low-income people and is administered by each state, which shares the costs with the federal government. (In some states it has a different name — for example, MediCal in California, MassHealth in Massachusetts, and TennCare in Tennessee.) Eligibility depends on the level of your income and savings and varies among the states. If you qualify for both Medicaid and Medicare, you should pay little or nothing for medical treatment — because Medicaid covers Medicare's out-of-pocket expenses — and you have coverage for broader benefits, such as nursing home care. In addition, you automatically qualify for low-cost prescription drug coverage under Medicare Part D's Extra Help program. (Extra Help is covered in detail in Chapter 5.) To find out whether you qualify for Medicaid and how to apply, call your State Health Insurance Assistance Program (SHIP). See Appendix B for the local number to call.

State Medicare savings programs

If you don't qualify for Medicaid, but the Medicare Part B premiums and other costs are still more than you can afford, you may be eligible for help from your state to pay for them. Getting this assistance depends on your income level and any savings you may have. If you qualify, you also automatically receive the full Extra Help benefit under Part D, which provides prescription drug coverage at low cost. Call your State Health Insurance Assistance Program (SHIP) to find out whether you qualify for a Medicare savings program and how to apply. (SHIP contact information is in Appendix B.)

Chapter 2

The Rules of the Game: How Part D Works

In Chapter 1, I introduce you to the general Medicare program, but from this chapter forward, I focus on the Medicare prescription drug program (also known as Part D). In later chapters, I outline the decisions you'll likely face in getting drug coverage and how to find the best deal that suits your situation. And I delve into a lot of details on different aspects of Part D. But first, here's the big picture — a broad view of how the program basically works. If you're new to Part D, this framework helps you more easily grasp the specific information that you find out later in this book.

Qualifying for Medicare Prescription Drug Coverage

Everyone in Medicare is entitled to Part D drug coverage. As long as you're enrolled in Medicare Part A *or* Part B — it doesn't matter which — or both, you qualify for Part D. That's true whether you're in Medicare because of your age (65 or over) or because you have disabilities.

It doesn't matter whether you're rich or poor or somewhere in between. You're entitled to Part D regardless of your income or how much money you have in the bank or invested in the stock market or stashed under the mattress. However, if your income is low, you may also qualify for a special part of the program known as *Extra Help.* As its name implies, this part offers much more generous drug benefits and lower costs than the regular Part D program. To get Extra Help, your income and savings are taken into consideration and must be under a certain level, as explained in detail in Chapter 5.

The state of your health isn't taken into account to enroll in Part D either. Unlike many other types of private health insurance, there's no such thing as a pre-existing condition in Part D (just as there is none in Medicare as a whole). You can't be denied coverage because of any illness or disability that you have now or had in the past, no matter how severe, or because you take a large number of drugs or very expensive ones right now.

Voluntary Enrollment and All the Strings Attached

You get to choose whether you want Medicare drug coverage. Well, that's true for most people. The exception would be if you're now getting your prescription drugs from *Medicaid,* the federal-state program that pays the medical costs of people with very low incomes. In that case, you'll be automatically switched to Part D (and receive Extra Help) to help pay for your drugs as soon as you become eligible for Medicare, as explained in Chapter 5. For everyone else, enrolling in Part D is voluntary.

The folks who tend to be the most anxious about Part D are those who already have prescription drug insurance from elsewhere, such as an employer or union's health plan, or retiree benefits that cover medications. Let me give some reassurance here. You won't need to join Part D if you have such coverage *and* that coverage is what Medicare calls *creditable* —meaning Medicare considers it at least as good as Part D. But you'd be wise to check that your current coverage is, in fact, creditable. Also, some employers require retirees to take Part D at age 65 and may or may not contribute toward their out-of-pocket expenses. (Chapter 6 goes into all the angles on how Part D fits in with employer- or union-sponsored drug coverage.)

The outlook is different if your other insurance is *not* creditable, or if you have no coverage for drugs at all. Here's where the strings are attached. You still have the right to turn your back on Part D, but doing so means you have to pay more for your coverage if you decide to join Part D in the future. Medicare rules say that people without creditable coverage who sign up for Part D *later than when they first become eligible for the benefit* must pay a late penalty in the form of permanently higher premiums. (I explain the late penalty more fully in Chapter 8.)

The late penalty is a powerful incentive (as Medicare intends it to be) for enrolling in Medicare drug coverage at the right time. What the "right time" is for you depends on when you first become eligible for Part D, which in turn depends on your circumstances. The best time to enroll may be when

✔ You first sign up for Medicare

✔ You lose your current creditable drug coverage, or decide to drop it

✔ You return to live permanently in the United States after living abroad

Each of these situations comes with a time limit for signing up for Part D without incurring the late penalty, as explained in more detail in Chapter 8.

Picking a Plan, Any Plan — but Only One

In earlier sections, I talk about signing up for Part D as though it were a simple one-step operation. It isn't. There's no single Medicare drug plan. Instead, the program is run through many private insurance plans that Medicare has approved to offer drug coverage. To get coverage, you must join one of them.

There are scores of these private drug plans servicing any given area of the country. Some are called *stand-alone plans* because they provide only drug coverage and are mainly used by people in traditional Medicare. Others are *Medicare Advantage health plans* that provide medical services and prescription drugs. Each plan differs from the next in the fees it charges, the range of drugs it covers, and its overall benefit design. So you have plenty of choices. But when it comes to picking a plan, this isn't a straightforward, apples-to-apples comparison. It's more like comparing apples to oranges to pineapples, with maybe a few lemons thrown in. Nonetheless, you have to choose just one.

Not surprisingly, people find this aspect of Part D the most daunting. Even if you've had employer health coverage in the past and are used to comparing plans, it's safe to say that you've never faced such a huge number of choices before — there could be well over 50 plans available to you, wherever you live. But please don't let this put you off. It's possible to drill down and find the plan that most meets your needs in a relatively short time, if you know how to go about it. You can find all sorts of helpful information on how to do this — including a step-by-step guide for comparing plans properly and to your best advantage — in Chapters 9 and 10. Chapter 11 shows you how to be on your guard against scams and hard-sell marketing tactics. And in Chapter 12, I walk you through the process of actually signing up for a plan.

Making Sense of Drug Coverage That Can Vary throughout the Year

Bizarre as it sounds, you may find yourself paying different amounts for the same medicines at different times of the year. That's because Medicare drug coverage is generally divided into four phases over the course of a calendar year. Whether you encounter only one phase, two, three, or all four *depends mainly on the overall cost of the drugs you take during the year.* Here's how it works:

- ✔ **Phase 1, the deductible:** This is a period in which you may pay full price for your drugs until the cost reaches a limit set by law ($275 in 2008, $295 in 2009) and drug coverage actually begins. Many plans don't charge deductibles. But if your plan has one, this period begins on January 1, or whenever you start using your Medicare drug coverage.

- ✔ **Phase 2, the initial coverage period:** This begins when you've met the deductible, if there is one. Otherwise, it begins on January 1, or whenever you start using Medicare drug coverage. You then pay the co-payments required by your plan for each prescription, your share being roughly 25 percent of the drug's cost. This period ends when the total cost of your drugs — what you have paid *plus* what your plan has paid — reaches a certain dollar limit set by law ($2,510 in 2008, $2,700 in 2009).

- ✔ **Phase 3, the coverage gap:** This gap — often called the *doughnut hole* — begins if and when you reach the dollar limit of Phase 2. You then pay 100 percent of the price of your drugs until your total out-of-pocket expenses reach another dollar limit set by law ($4,050 in 2008, $4,350 in 2009). This amount includes your deductible (if any), your co-pays during the initial coverage period, and what you paid for your drugs during the gap.

- ✔ **Phase 4, catastrophic coverage:** If your drug costs are high enough to take you through the gap, coverage begins again. And here, at last, is the good news — your payments then drop sharply. In this period, co-pays are small and set by law: $2.25 per prescription for generic drugs and $5.60 per prescription for brand-name drugs in 2008, or $2.40 and $6.00 in 2009, or 5 percent of each drug's price (whichever is the greater amount). Catastrophic coverage ends on December 31. The following day, January 1, you return to Phase 1 (or Phase 2 if your plan has no deductible), and the whole cycle starts over again.

Table 2-1 is a quick way of looking at the same progression.

Table 2-1	Phases of Part D Minimum Drug Coverage and Dollar Limits, 2008 and 2009		
Phase of Coverage	*What It Means*	*2008 Limits*	*2009 Limits*
1. Deductible (if your plan has one)	You pay 100% of your drug costs before coverage begins, up to a maximum of:	$275	$295
2. Initial coverage	You pay about 25%, and your plan pays about 75% of *total* drug costs until they reach:	$2,510	$2,700
3. Coverage gap (the *doughnut hole*)	You pay 100% of your drug costs until your *out-of-pocket* spending reaches:	$4,050	$4,350
4. Catastrophic coverage	You pay about 5%, and your plan pays about 95% of your drug costs	Unlimited until the end of the calendar year	Unlimited until the end of the calendar year

What you see in Table 2-1 is the basic design for *minimum* Medicare drug coverage that Congress dreamed up and set in law. No drug plan can offer less than this coverage. However, drug plans often vary this design, as explained in Chapter 3. Many charge no, or lower, deductibles. Some plans charge less than 25 percent of the cost for some drugs and more than 25 percent for others. And some plans provide partial or full coverage during the gap, usually for a higher monthly premium. You can find a lot of detailed information about the coverage gap — including how to tell whether you'll fall into it and some ideas for avoiding it or softening its impact — in Chapters 15 and 16.

No plans limit the amount for catastrophic coverage. If you reach that level, you continue paying the same low costs until the end of the year, no matter how many drugs you use or how high the cost becomes.

If your income is limited and you qualify for Extra Help (as explained in Chapter 5), you'll pay far less than the costs shown in Table 2-1, and you'll receive continuous coverage throughout the year. People enrolled in Extra Help don't face the doughnut hole.

Getting Coverage for the Drugs You Take

You may assume that all Medicare drug plans cover any prescription medicine that you need. Well, maybe they do and maybe they don't. No drug plan covers every drug — though every plan has to cover at least two drugs out of several that are used to treat a particular medical condition — and some plans cover a much wider range than others. Each plan has its own *formulary* — that is, the list of drugs the plan will pay for.

What if the plan you choose doesn't cover all of your drugs? You'll need your doctor's help here. She may decide that a different drug that *is* on the plan's formulary will work just as well for your medical condition. Or, if your doctor wants to keep you on your present medication, she can help you ask the plan to cover that particular drug for you as an exception to its policy. If the plan turns down your request, you have the right to appeal against its decision.

I explain all these coverage issues (and more) in detail in Chapter 4.

Paying for Your Drugs and Filling Your Prescriptions

To get drug coverage under Part D you'll likely pay a monthly premium to the Medicare drug plan that you choose. (However, some Medicare Advantage health plans that offer drug coverage don't charge a premium; see Chapter 9 for details.) You may have to meet a deductible, if your plan has one, before coverage starts. You'll also pay a share of the cost of each prescription you fill. Your share may be in the form of a *co-payment* (a flat dollar amount) or *coinsurance* (a percentage of the cost of the drug).

If you compare plans properly — that is, according to the medications you take — you'll notice a lot of variation in the co-pays that different plans charge for the same drug. What's more, even within one plan you can pay different co-pays for different drugs. Why and how this happens — plus tips for using the system to your advantage — is explained in Chapter 3.

You can fill your prescriptions at local pharmacies that are in your plan's *network* — meaning that they have a business relationship with the plan. Going to pharmacies outside the network means you pay more for your drugs. Most plans also give you the choice of getting 90-day supplies from a mail-order service, often for a lower price.

How does the pharmacy know what to charge you? After all, your payments can vary according to

✔ The Part D plan you're enrolled in

✔ What phase of coverage you're in (deductible, initial coverage period, coverage gap, or catastrophic coverage; see the "Making Sense of Drug Coverage That Can Vary throughout the Year" section, earlier in this chapter, for details)

✔ Whether you receive the Extra Help benefit (see Chapter 5)

✔ Whether you have other coverage (for example, from an employer or a State Pharmacy Assistance Program) that coordinates with Part D (see Chapter 6)

The answer is that your plan's ID card is the key that should unlock these mysteries. Scanned through the pharmacy's computer, it accesses a database that tells the pharmacist the amount you're required to pay each time you fill a prescription. These pharmacy issues (including what to do if the system fails to work properly) are explained in Chapter 14.

Being Locked into One Plan for a Year

After you're enrolled in a Medicare drug plan, you have to stay in that plan for the whole year (or the rest of the year if you first join Medicare sometime during the year) except in special circumstances, which are described in Chapter 17.

During the calendar year, the plan can't change its overall design or the amount of its premium and deductible. Those must stay exactly as they were at the beginning of the year. The plan can change the prices it charges for drugs, but it must also conform to certain Medicare rules that give some protection to consumers. Chapter 3 goes into this in more detail.

At the end of the calendar year, plans can change anything they please for the following year — their benefit design, their premiums, the drugs they cover, and their co-pays. Most plans do, in fact, make changes, so it's important to read the notice that your plan must send you each fall (usually in October) informing you of any changes, as explained in Chapter 17.

Being locked into a plan for a whole year makes it all the more critical that you choose the plan that's best for you to begin with, as explained in Chapters 9 and 10. And, if you want to continue being in a plan that gives you the best deal, you should be prepared to compare plans *every* year.

What were they thinking . . . when they made the Part D drug benefit so complicated?

Part D was the result of a bitter political battle in Congress between lawmakers with opposing philosophies. One group (mainly Democrats) wanted prescription drug coverage to be run by the federal government as a simple add-on to Medicare, for which beneficiaries would pay an extra premium and uniform co-pays for each prescription — a proposal that would've cost billions of dollars more than Congress was willing to allow. Another group (mainly Republicans) argued that a drug benefit offered by competing private insurance plans would hold down costs and give beneficiaries more choice. A third group wanted a benefit that would give drug coverage only to low-income people. And a fourth group didn't want a drug benefit at all, arguing that it would add an expensive new entitlement to Medicare that the country couldn't afford.

Underlying all these conflicting views was a more fundamental political struggle that had been going on for decades. Should Medicare continue to be a federal social insurance program that gave all eligible Americans the same deal, as originally enacted by a Democratic-controlled Congress and a Democratic president, Lyndon B. Johnson, in 1965? Or should it become a more "privatized" system with a menu of options offered through private insurance companies? Prescription drug coverage eventually became a bargaining chip in that struggle. Most Republican lawmakers and some conservative Democrats were willing to add drug coverage to Medicare only if the program was overhauled to include many more private options.

In late 2003, after years of stormy debate, a Republican-controlled Congress narrowly voted to pass the Medicare Modernization Act — by only five votes in the House and ten in the Senate — and a Republican president, George W. Bush, signed it into law. The final package contained compromises that provoked howls of rage from both liberals and conservatives. The act established a drug benefit available to everyone in Medicare and gave extra help to people with low incomes or high drug costs. It also gave private insurers a much greater role in Medicare than they'd had before, as well as large financial incentives to participate in Part D, which resulted in far more drug plans entering the market than had ever been expected. These trade-offs created a program so complicated that the original legislation ran to 681 pages, and subsequent regulations that interpreted the law and put it into effect ran to thousands more. Years later, Part D remains controversial, with many lawmakers on both sides vowing to "reform" it, in one way or another, if they get the chance.

Chapter 3

The Big Question: What Will Part D Cost (And Save) You?

In This Chapter

▶ Deciphering the jargon of Medicare drug costs

▶ Getting a grip on how costs are connected

▶ Recognizing how a drug plan's benefits may fluctuate in a given year

▶ Knowing how costs may be adjusted from year to year

It's all about money, right? You're thinking about Part D because you're looking for some relief from the outrageous cost of prescription medicine. Okay, a lot of drugs aren't especially expensive, and some of them allow you to avoid the even steeper costs of surgery and hospital stays. But plenty of meds out there can still take a big bite out of the average retiree's Social Security check, and some cost more than the typical mortgage payment for a house. (Think I'm kidding? The priciest cancer drugs range from $4,000 to more than $10,000 a month.) So you're wondering how much money you'll save in Part D — and, at the same time, how much it'll cost you.

Medicare says that "on average" people with Part D coverage save about half the cost of their medications. But that calculation runs the gamut from people who don't save anything to those who save thousands of dollars a year. Again, your individual savings depend on the drugs you use, how many you take, and — to a degree that may surprise you — the Medicare drug plan you choose. That said, you can't judge a plan on cost alone. Whether a plan covers all of your drugs, or makes you go through hoops to get some of them, is equally important when you're choosing the plan that's best for you (see Chapter 4 for details).

In this chapter, I explain the out-of-pocket expenses you're likely to have in Part D and how those costs add up if you're in the *regular* part of the program. But if your income is low, see Chapter 5. It explains the much greater financial assistance available to people who qualify for the Extra Help part of the program, and therefore pay much less.

Decoding the Jargon of Medicare Drug Payments

As you're well aware, health insurance has its own special language — a whole lexicon of jargon relating to coverage, payments, restrictions, and the like. In the following sections, I explain the meanings of words and phrases used in Part D to describe your out-of-pocket expenses.

Making a commitment: Monthly premium

Here's an easy one: Your *monthly premium* is the amount a plan charges each month to provide drug coverage, in addition to the monthly Part B premium (see Chapter 1 for more info on Part B). Medicare prescription drug plans (PDPs) that cover *only* drugs always charge premiums, which vary a great deal among plans. Medicare Advantage prescription drug plans (MAPDs) that cover both healthcare and drugs usually charge a single monthly premium for the whole package, though some have no premiums at all. If you're married, you and your spouse must each pay a premium to be in Part D, even if you both join the same plan. In other words, there's no price break for married couples.

Forking over the first financial slice: Annual deductible

The amount you may have to spend out of pocket on drugs each year *before* your coverage starts is the *annual deductible*. The maximum amount is set by law and increases each year ($275 in 2008, $295 in 2009). However, many plans charge lower deductibles or none at all. Most people in plans with deductibles spend this amount at the beginning of the calendar year. But if you join Part D later in the year, there's no reduction — you still have to spend the required deductible amount before your coverage begins.

Sharing the pain: Co-payments and coinsurance

Co-payments and coinsurance are what you pay for your share of each covered prescription. Your share may be in the form of a *co-pay,* which is a flat dollar amount — say $20. Or it may be coinsurance, which is a percentage of the drug's total cost — say 25 percent. Some plans use only co-pays and some only coinsurance; others use both, according to the type of drug.

Leveling on costs: Tiers of charges

REMEMBER

You may find that your plan charges you different co-payments (or coinsurance) for different drugs. That's because the plan arranges its covered drugs into three or four levels, or *tiers*, according to price:

- **Tier One:** This tier has the lowest co-pay because it covers the least expensive drugs, usually the generic kind. (*Generics* are low-cost copies of brand-name drugs that have been on the market long enough to have lost their exclusive marketing rights.) A few plans don't charge any co-pays for Tier 1 generics.

- **Tier Two:** This tier has a medium-priced co-pay because it covers the plan's *preferred* brand-name drugs. The plan prefers you to use these drugs because it pays less for them after having negotiated good discounts with the drug manufacturers.

- **Tier Three:** This tier has a higher-priced co-pay because it covers *non-preferred* brand-name drugs. The plan prefers you not to use these drugs because they're expensive, or perhaps because the plan hasn't managed to negotiate adequate discounts for them.

- **Tier Four:** This tier has the highest co-pay because it comprises very expensive or specialty drugs, such as anti-rejection drugs used after organ transplant surgery and drugs used to treat certain cancers. In most cases, plans charge coinsurance — a percentage of the total cost — for drugs in this tier. This percentage is usually 25 percent but can be 33 percent or higher.

These tiers are typical of many Part D plans. However, some plans arrange them differently — for example, putting preferred generics in one tier and nonpreferred generics in another. So a plan may have more than four tiers. Then again, some plans (those that charge the same cost percentage for all drugs) have only one tier.

Getting out your wallet: Full price

You pay full price for your drugs during the deductible (if your plan has one), in the coverage gap (if you fall into it; see Chapter 15), or if you're taking a drug that your plan doesn't cover. *Full price* actually means the price your plan pays for each drug. If the plan has negotiated a decent discount, its price may be quite a bit less than you'd pay retail at the pharmacy. If the full price of your drug is lower than the co-pay for its associated tier, you pay full price, because that's the lesser cost.

Counting the cost: True out-of-pocket costs

True out-of-pocket costs is an odd bit of jargon — which bureaucrats shorten to the acronym *TrOOP* — that relates to the coverage gap (also known as the doughnut hole). If you fall into the gap, you can only get out of it when you've spent a certain amount out of your own pocket for drugs since the beginning of the year. This TrOOP amount ($4,050 in 2008, $4,350 in 2009; it increases every year) includes

✔ Your deductible (if any) before drug coverage starts

✔ Your co-pays in the initial coverage period

✔ Anything you've spent on prescriptions while in the gap, according to certain rules

Are there any "false" out-of-pocket costs? Yes, actually — premiums and some other payments that don't count toward the TrOOP limit. (Wouldn't you think bureaucrats would call these FrOOPs? But they don't!) Details on what counts and what doesn't are in Chapter 15.

Grasping How Costs Fit Together and Add Up

So when it comes to choosing the least expensive Medicare drug plan, you just pick the one with the lowest premium, right? Nope! This approach is a trap many people fall into, and it's why most plans have tried to keep their premiums relatively low ever since the Part D program began. Low premiums are designed to lure you in the door. But if you're smart, you want to know more about what's inside before you cross the welcome mat. No, nothing bad is lurking behind that beckoning door. It's just that — *with one exception* — the premium contributes much less to your overall out-of-pocket expenses than two other items that contribute far more: the medications you take and the way your plan is designed.

So what's the exception to avoiding the plan with the lowest premium? If you take no drugs right now, or only the occasional one, then absolutely opt for the plan in your area that has the lowest premium. Overall, you're still paying more in premiums than you get back in benefits. But what you're buying at this point isn't drugs but *insurance*. You're playing safe because you don't know what the future holds — it may bring some unforeseen illness that requires expensive medications. Choosing a plan with the lowest premium gives you the comfort of having insurance at the least cost (see Chapter 7).

This section focuses on the calculations everyone else — those who already take a number of drugs or a few costly ones — needs to make.

The importance of the drugs you take

If you absorb just one bit of knowledge from this book, I want it to be the realization that *the drugs you take are the most important part of choosing a Medicare drug plan.* Your medications, their dosages, and how frequently you take them are the keys to how much you may spend out of pocket in any plan. Why? Two reasons:

- Huge differences exist among the co-pays for meds in different tiers, even among drugs used to treat the same medical condition. For example, the co-pay for a nonpreferred drug in Tier 3 can be twice as much as a similar preferred drug in Tier 2; a generic version in Tier 1 can cost a fraction of either. So if you're paying a hefty co-pay (say $60) for a Tier 3 drug, and you realize an alternative Tier 2 drug costs $30 or that a Tier 1 generic is available for $5, what are you going to do? Ask your doctor whether a lower-priced drug may work just as well for you. Well, why not? It's your money!

- The co-pays that *different* plans charge for the *same* drug also vary a lot. Plan X's co-pay (or coinsurance) for a particular brand-name drug may be quite a bit higher or lower than Plan Y's. Each plan negotiates the price of each drug with the company that makes it. If Plan X wins a relatively low price for a drug, it will charge you less for that drug (through a lower co-pay) than a plan that doesn't get such a good deal. And if your costs are high enough to take you into the doughnut hole, where you pay full price (see Chapter 15), you're still paying less under Plan X due to the steeper discount it has negotiated. This cost advantage is another good reason for comparing plans carefully before choosing one.

But wait a minute, you may say: What if one of my drugs is least expensive under Plan X, but another drug I take has the lowest price in Plan Y, and maybe a third is cheapest under Plan Z? You need to find out which single plan will cost you the least out of pocket for your whole batch of drugs throughout the entire year — including co-pays, premiums, deductibles, and possible costs in the doughnut hole. Don't worry! Figuring out your potential cost savings isn't as difficult as you may think. Flip to Chapter 10 for step-by-step guidance on how to do so in a reasonably fast and efficient way.

Here's another wrinkle regarding prescription drugs that baffles people. The law says Part D enrollees pay about 25 percent of the cost of their drugs during the initial coverage period. Yet I often hear from folks who say things like: "My plan charges me $28 for one of my drugs, but it only costs $35 full price at my local pharmacy — so I'm paying 80 percent, not 25." In response, Medicare officials say a Part D drug plan can vary its charges and benefits any way it wants, but its total package must be at least *actuarially equivalent* to the standard benefit created by Congress.

Translated into English, *actuarially equivalent* means that the whole amount a plan shells out for all of its enrollees — collectively, not individually — must be about 75 percent of the enrollees' total drug costs, with the remaining 25 percent paid by the enrollees themselves. If you're in the type of plan that exactly mirrors the standard benefit, then you *will* pay a strict 25 percent of each prescription's cost. But if you're in a plan that has tiered co-pays or maybe offers extra benefits, such as a waived deductible or some coverage in the doughnut hole, you may pay more than 25 percent of the price for some drugs — or, in some cases, less. What you pay depends on the plan's design.

The importance of the plan you choose

Each plan has its own mix of costs and benefits. And although this fact may make the plans seem harder to compare, their different designs allow you flexibility in finding one that best meets your needs. Here are some of the different designs Part D plans typically offer:

- ✔ A plan that mirrors the basic design for minimum Part D coverage outlined by Congress features a full deductible, 25 percent coinsurance for each prescription during the initial coverage period, a doughnut hole, and standard catastrophic coverage.

- ✔ A plan that charges no deductible (or a reduced one) and has tiered co-pays for prescriptions during the initial coverage period (probably with coinsurance for drugs in the highest tier), a doughnut hole, and standard catastrophic coverage.

- ✔ A plan that looks like either of the preceding designs, but charges nothing for drugs in Tier 1.

- ✔ A plan that looks like either of the first two designs, but also covers generic drugs in the doughnut hole.

- ✔ A plan that looks like either of the first two designs, but also covers generic and some brand-name drugs in the doughnut hole.

About the only aspect that stays the same in every plan is catastrophic coverage. The federal government heavily subsidizes this level of coverage, and its low co-pays are fixed each year by law. Otherwise, you can find many variations from plan to plan. Plenty have tiered co-pays and charge a full deductible. Some have three or five tiers of charges rather than four, some don't use tiers at all, and a few charge nothing for generic drugs. To make matters even more confusing, plans can be here one year and gone the next. In 2006, one plan charged a straight 30 percent of the cost of all of its covered drugs throughout the year with no doughnut hole — but this plan vanished in 2007. Expect to see other creative plan designs come and go in the future.

Putting together drug costs and plan designs: Three common examples

So in one hand you have all these different costs, and in the other you have all these different plan designs. And you know what? None of it really matters! In this book, I give you a strategy for navigating the prescription drug plan maze that focuses on only the medications *you* take, as well as a few other personal preferences you may have. This strategy can help you whittle your choices down to just a few plans — the ones that will cost you the least out of pocket but cover all (or most) of your drugs. (Hooray!) You may then want to consider these options according to certain conveniences, like being able to buy your drugs at a favorite local pharmacy, receive them by mail order, or purchase them anywhere in the country. In other words, the process of choosing begins with *you*, not the plans.

I explain this strategy in detail in Chapter 10. In the meantime, it may help to know how the different costs and plan designs can work for different people. I provide some examples in the following sections — the people may not be real, but the math sure is!

Hearty Harry: Feeling healthy and happy

Hearty Harry is still in good shape. But years of energetic activity — hoop jumps, rock climbing, and daredevil skiing (not to mention chasing after his grandkids) — have proved tough on his joints, so he's had knee and hip replacements. The only med he needs is something to keep his blood pressure in check. Choosing a Part D plan felt a bit like searching for all the hiders in a 20-person game of hide-and-seek, but he finally settled on a plan with a low premium ($15 a month), a full deductible ($275), and 25 percent coinsurance. Hearty Harry has to pay the plan's full price for his blood pressure pills ($32 a month) until he meets the deductible, and because his drugs don't cost much, he doesn't meet it until halfway through September. At that point, he starts getting coverage, and his drug payments drop to $8 a month (25 percent of $32) for the rest of the year. Here's what he pays out of pocket:

- ✔ **January through August:** $15.00 a month for premiums + $32.00 a month full price for drugs = $47.00 per month.

- ✔ **September:** $15.00 for premium + $21.66 for drugs = $36.66 for this month. (Meeting the deductible on September 20, Hearty Harry's coinsurance kicks in, reducing his drug payments to about $2.66 for the remaining ten days of the month.)

- ✔ **October through December:** $15.00 a month for premiums + $8.00 a month coinsurance for drugs = $23.00 per month.

- ✔ **Grand total:** Over the course of the entire year, he pays just under $482, which includes his monthly premiums ($15.00 × 12 = $180), annual deductible ($275), and coinsurance for the rest of the year ($8.00 × 3 = $24.00 + $2.66 = $26.66).

Hearty Harry likes this deal almost as much as he likes seeing his favorite basketball team lose, because over the year he pays out about $97 more for his coverage than his single drug actually costs ($32 × 12 = $384). However, after a lifetime of close calls on cliff faces and ski slopes, he figures his risk-taking days are over, so he settles for paying the extra to have insurance, just in case.

Normal Norma: Taking some medications regularly

Normal Norma isn't the dynamo she used to be, but she remains in reasonably good health as long as she takes regular meds to control diabetes and a thyroid condition. She takes five drugs (four brand-names and one generic), which would cost her well over $4,000 a year retail without insurance. As a diligent consumer, she compared Part D plans carefully and found the least expensive one that covered all of her drugs. This plan has a premium of $23.50 a month and no deductible, so her coverage starts at the beginning of the year. For eight months she's in the initial coverage period, with medium co-pays. But at the beginning of September, she hits the doughnut hole (the time when she pays full price for medications in the gap before coverage kicks back in), and her drug expenses jump to almost three times as much each month for the rest of the year. Here's what Normal Norma pays out of pocket:

- **January through August:** $23.50 a month for premiums + $92.96 a month for drugs = $116.46 per month.

- **September:** $23.50 for premium + $309.37 for drugs = $332.87 for the month. (The total cost of her drugs that both she and her plan pay reaches the $2,510 limit of initial coverage very early in September, pitching her into the doughnut hole.)

- **October through December:** $23.50 a month for premiums + $312.81 a month for drugs (full price in the doughnut hole) = $336.31 per month.

- **Grand total:** Throughout the whole year, she pays just over $2,273, which includes her monthly premiums ($23.50 × 12 = $282). At the discounted prices this plan pays for her drugs ($3,756 for all of them), she saves $1,483.

Remaining cost-conscious, Normal Norma did some extra research in an effort to bring her costs down further. Unfortunately, no lower-cost versions of her four brand-name drugs exist yet, so that idea didn't work. But she found that if she buys her drugs in 90-day supplies from the plan's mail-order service, she can stave off the doughnut hole for another couple of weeks and pay less — $1,823 over the whole year — saving herself a total of $1,933.

Sickly Sam: Shelling out for expensive specialty drugs

Sickly Sam is hanging in there. He's doing okay after a recent heart transplant, but he needs a cocktail of medicines to prevent rejection and deal with side effects. He chose a Part D plan that covers all of his drugs, features a $26.40

monthly premium, and has no deductible. At this plan's full price, his meds cost a whopping $1,340.77 a month, a tough sum to pay when he goes into the doughnut hole. But he gets through the gap quickly and by mid-May he's into the catastrophic phase of coverage, with low costs to the end of the year. Here's what he pays out of pocket:

- ✔ **January and February:** $26.40 a month for premiums + $371.27 a month for drugs (in the initial coverage period) = $397.67 per month.

- ✔ **March and April:** $26.40 a month for premiums + $1,340.77 a month for drugs (in the doughnut hole) = $1,367.17 per month.

- ✔ **May:** $26.40 for premium + $676.90 for drugs = $703.30 in May. (Halfway through the month, his drug expenses from the beginning of the year reach $4,050, the limit of the doughnut hole, and he begins catastrophic coverage.)

- ✔ **June through December:** $26.40 a month for premiums + $72.64 a month for drugs (catastrophic coverage) = $99.04 per month.

- ✔ **Grand total:** Over the course of the year, Sickly Sam pays just over $4,926 out of pocket, including the monthly premiums ($26.40 × 12 = $316.80). The full price of his drugs under this plan amounts to $16,089 over the course of the year, so he saves $11,163.

Although he has a hard time paying the bills during his two and a half months in the doughnut hole, Sickly Sam feels his low payments for the last seven months of the year are like seven months of opening birthday presents, eating cake, and playing games *without* having to turn any older.

Knowing the Costs That Plans Can (And Can't) Change during a Calendar Year

Since Part D went into effect in 2006, a common complaint among consumers is that they're normally allowed to change plans only once a year, whereas those plans can change their charges any time during the year. This statement is only partly true; some regulations protect enrollees against the whims of any plan that wants to make changes. This section lists the rules on what plans can and can't do during the year, from January 1 through December 31.

The costs your plan can't change

Plans *can't* change these costs during the year:

- ✔ The amount of the monthly premium.
- ✔ The amount of the annual deductible (if any).
- ✔ The overall design of the plan (for example, whether it covers any drugs in the coverage gap).
- ✔ The tier structure of co-pays. So if a plan has three tiers of co-pays rising from $5 to $28 to $60 through the different levels, and charges 25 percent coinsurance in the fourth tier, the charges in each tier must stay the same throughout the year.
- ✔ Any costs set by law. These costs include the maximum amount of the deductible, the minimum dollar limit of initial coverage, the maximum out-of-pocket limit that ends the coverage gap, co-pays at the catastrophic level of coverage, and all co-pays for people who receive Extra Help. (See Chapter 5 for more on this program.)

The costs your plan can change

Plans *can* change these costs during the year:

- ✔ **The *full price* cost of drugs:** A plan can change these prices on a weekly basis (see the earlier section "Decoding the Jargon of Medicare Drug Payments" to understand what this term means). These price fluctuations usually vary by only a few dollars or cents, but they can still add up. Such changes — up or down — may affect what you pay during the deductible period (if your plan has one) and in the dough-nut hole (if you fall into it). These changes *don't* affect you in the initial coverage period if your plan charges tiered co-pays for your drugs. But if you pay coinsurance in this coverage period, any changes *will* affect you because you're paying a percentage of the full price.
- ✔ **The co-pay for different drugs:** A plan can move any drug into a higher or lower price tier, which consequently raises or reduces your co-pay. However, plans can't make this change during the annual enrollment period (November 15 to December 31) or during the first 60 days of a new year.

Being aware of your rights

You have some rights and protections in relation to the costs of your drugs that are worth knowing about:

✔ If one of your drugs is moved up to a higher tier of charges, *you can't be asked to pay a higher co-pay for it during the year.* Say one of your medicines is in Tier 2 and your co-pay is $24. You'll continue to pay that amount for the rest of the year, even if your plan moves the drug into Tier 3 where the co-pay is normally $56. However, if your drug is moved to a lower tier — yes, it can occasionally happen! — your co-pay drops to the lower level.

✔ If your doctor thinks a particular drug is the only one that will work for you but your plan places the drug in its tier of nonpreferred drugs and doesn't offer a generic or a similar drug in its preferred tiers, you can request your plan to charge you a lower co-pay. (You'll need your doctor's help in making this request; see Chapter 4.) You *can't* ask your plan to do this if the drug you need is in the highest specialty tier of charges or if the requested change would put your co-pay in the lowest (usually generic) tier.

✔ If any of your plan's changes will affect a drug you're taking, your plan must notify you in writing at least 60 days in advance, unless the drug has been withdrawn from the market for safety reasons.

What should you do if your plan violates any of these rights? Contact the plan, point to the regulations in question, and ask for the mistake to be rectified by filing a *coverage determination,* which means asking the plan to look into the facts of your case. If that doesn't work, you can appeal the plan's decision. See Chapter 19 for details.

Understanding How Costs May Change from Year to Year

Drug plans have only so much wiggle room to hit you with higher costs *during* the year. But they do have the right to change everything from one year to the next. No, this privilege doesn't necessarily mean raising all charges. But with the price of prescription drugs on the rise in general, Part D costs tend to creep up, not down.

Cost increases for enrollees in Part D aren't solely related to drug plans raising their premiums and co-pays. Medicare, the federal program, also controls several costs and dollar caps that affect all enrollees, regardless of the private plan they're in. These costs change by law each year and generally go up, because they're tied to the rising cost of drugs in the whole Part D program.

Medicare typically changes these costs and benefits from year to year:

✔ The maximum amount of the annual deductible

✔ The limit to the initial coverage period

✔ The limit on out-of-pocket expenses that gets you out of the doughnut hole (if they ever get that high) and into catastrophic coverage

✔ Co-pays at the catastrophic coverage level

✔ Co-pays for people receiving Extra Help (see Chapter 5)

Drug plans can change the following costs and benefits from one year to the next:

✔ Monthly premiums

✔ Annual deductible (no higher than the maximum amount set by law)

✔ Co-pays for each tier of charges in the initial coverage period

✔ Percentage of coinsurance in the initial coverage period

✔ Full-price charges in the deductible or doughnut hole

✔ Covered drugs

✔ Overall plan design

Following are some recent trends in annual cost changes:

✔ **Medicare-controlled costs have gone up steadily.** For example, the maximum deductible rose from $250 in 2006 to $295 in 2009. The out-of-pocket limit that triggers the end of the doughnut hole rose from $3,600 in 2006 to $4,350 in 2009, which means it costs more to get to the catastrophic coverage level. On the other hand, the annually raised limit on total drug costs in the initial coverage period — which went up from $2,000 in 2006 to $2,700 in 2009 — means you get a bit more coverage before hitting the doughnut hole than you did in previous years.

✔ **Drug plan costs are more variable.** Consumers certainly see the effects if their premiums or co-pays suddenly take a jump on January 1. But often changes are much more subtle — for example, more drugs moved to a higher cost tier. From 2007 to 2008, a few plans lowered their premiums and/or co-pays, but most plans raised both, especially through increased charges for brand-name drugs. And in the most dramatic change of 2008, coverage for brand-name drugs in the doughnut hole — which in the previous two years had saved a lot of money for enrollees with high costs — all but vanished.

Your Part D plan must mail you a notice each fall (usually in October) to inform you of any changes it will make in costs and benefits for the following year. This mailing is called the *Annual Notice of Change,* and it's important that you read it, as explained in Chapter 17. If you haven't received this notice by early November, call the Medicare help line at 800-633-4227 (877-486-2048 for TDD users) and complain.

Chapter 4

Delving into Drug Coverage under Part D

*T*he whole point of Part D is to help people with Medicare get the prescription drugs they need to fight disease and maintain their health. The cost of meds under Part D, explained in Chapter 3, is only part of it. The other big concern is *coverage* — that is, which drugs a Part D plan helps pay for. In particular, you want to know if your drugs are covered and how easily you can get them.

Chances are high that your drugs are covered in several plans available to you, or even in most of them. But you can't just assume that all of your drugs are covered in *every* plan. That's because Part D plans are allowed to choose which drugs they cover in any given year, within certain Medicare rules. Just as plans vary in their charges, so do they vary in the drugs they help pay for.

Another aspect of Part D coverage to be aware of is that any plan can require you to ask permission before it will cover certain drugs your doctor has prescribed. You may not encounter this hurdle — again, it all depends on the drugs you take and the plan you choose — but you should know that this obstacle exists and what to do if it happens.

In this chapter, I share how plans vary in their coverage of different drugs and how to find out which plans cover your meds. I also explain the ways that plans can restrict immediate access to some drugs and how to deal with this situation if it arises. I delve into the important role your doctor plays in how to get coverage for drugs that your plan doesn't normally cover or restricts access to. Finally, I explain how the same drug may be covered under Part D, Part A (hospital care), or Part B (outpatient care) in different circumstances.

Finding Out about Formularies

Formulary is a jargon word that becomes very familiar when you're in Part D, because it directly affects your prescription drug coverage. A *formulary* is simply the list of specific drugs that each Part D plan has decided it will cover.

If the drugs you take are on your plan's formulary, the plan will pay its share of the costs during the initial and catastrophic phases of coverage (see Chapter 2 for an introduction to these phases). If any drug *isn't* on the formulary, you pay full price for that drug in *every* phase of coverage — in the initial coverage period and at the catastrophic level, as well as during the deductible period and in the doughnut hole — unless you can persuade the plan to cover it in your case, as explained in the later section "Requesting an exception with your doctor's help."

As you can see, coverage is intimately entwined with cost. The difference in cost between a drug that's on a plan's formulary and that same drug when it isn't on a plan's formulary can amount to several hundred dollars. Consider this example for a drug prescribed to help people sleep when they're in pain. The full price of this drug is the same in both Plan X and Plan Y. But Plan X, which covers the drug in the initial and catastrophic phases of coverage, charges $521 for it over the whole year. In contrast, Plan Y — which doesn't cover the drug at all — charges $1,200 for it over the year. If my math's right, that's a difference of $679 for the identical drug!

Making sure that the drugs you need are on your chosen plan's formulary is essential for another reason, too. If you fall into the doughnut hole (also known as the coverage gap; see Chapter 15), a drug that isn't on the formulary *doesn't* count toward your out-of-pocket limit that gets you out of the gap — unless, again, you've persuaded the plan to cover it for you.

So when you're picking a Part D plan, both for cost reasons and because, darn it, you need these drugs for your health, your goal is to find a plan that covers all of your medications — or, failing that, almost all of them — on its formulary. (I explain how to find out which plans cover your drugs in Chapter 10.)

How many medications do Part D plans cover at any one time? The number varies a great deal among the plans, and some have many more than others. As a general indication, in 2008, the top ten plans (those with the greatest number of enrollees) averaged 2,285 distinct drugs on their formularies, according to an analysis by the health research group Avalere Health.

Despite this variation in the number of covered drugs, each Part D formulary must comply with Medicare rules in the following four areas:

✔ The drugs that plans must cover

✔ The drugs that Medicare doesn't pay for

✔ The tricky issue of off-label drugs that are prescribed for unapproved treatments

✔ The rules on what plans can and can't do when changing their formularies

I provide more info on each of these areas of regulation in the following sections. Later in this chapter I explain what you can do to get needed drugs that are affected by these conditions.

The drugs that Part D plans must cover

Medicare doesn't require Part D plans to cover any individual prescription drug. But it does require plans to cover at least two in each class of medications. A *class* means all the similar drugs that are used to treat the same medical condition. Many plans cover more than two in a class.

For example, about half a dozen brand-name statins — drugs commonly used to counteract high cholesterol — are currently sold, as well as generic versions of some of these drugs. Many plans cover all the brand-name statins, and some don't cover any. But plans that don't have the brand-names on their formularies do cover at least two of the generic statins, which have the same active ingredients and are just as effective at less cost to you. (I cover generic drugs, and why it's worth talking with your doctor about using them, in Chapter 16.)

Every plan must also cover "all or substantially all" drugs in each of the following six classes of medications:

✔ Anticancer drugs (used to halt or slow the growth of cancers)

✔ Anticonvulsants (used mainly to prevent epileptic seizures)

✔ Antidepressants (used to counteract depression and anxiety disorders)

✔ Antipsychotics (used to treat mental illnesses such as schizophrenia, mania, bipolar disorder, and other delusional conditions)

✔ HIV/AIDS drugs (used to block or slow HIV infection and treat symptoms and side effects)

✔ Immunosuppressants (used to prevent rejection of transplanted organs and tissues, immune system disorders, and some inflammatory diseases)

Medicare requires every Part D plan to cover pretty much all drugs in these categories due to the clinical problems that can occur when patients abruptly stop such medications or switch to others.

The drugs that Medicare doesn't pay for

By law, Medicare doesn't pay for certain kinds of drugs. This directive doesn't mean Part D plans are prohibited from covering them — just that, if they do, Medicare won't reimburse its share of the cost. So, although a few plans (typically those with higher premiums) may cover some of these drugs, most plans don't cover any. The types of drugs excluded by Medicare are

- Barbiturates (used for seizures and anxiety, such as Amytal, Nembutal, Seconal, and so on)

- Benzodiazepines (used for anxiety and sleeping problems, such as Serepax, Valium, Xanax, and the like)

- Drugs sold over the counter (nonprescription medicines)

- Drugs used for anorexia, weight loss, or weight gain

- Drugs used for cosmetic reasons and hair growth

- Drugs used to promote fertility

- Drugs used to treat sexual or erectile dysfunction

- Medicines to treat cough or cold symptoms

- Prescription vitamins and mineral products

Sometimes Medicare pays for medications in these categories if they're used for a "medically accepted" purpose. Here are a few examples:

- Drugs to help people stop smoking are excluded when bought over the counter, but accepted if prescribed by a doctor.

- Prescriptions for drugs used to counteract severe weight loss in AIDS patients are accepted because they're medically necessary and not regarded as the usual weight-gain drugs.

- Prescriptions for drugs used to treat skin conditions, such as acne and psoriasis, are accepted because they're not considered cosmetic.

- Cough medicines are accepted when prescribed to alleviate medical conditions such as asthma.

- Drugs normally used to treat sexual or erectile dysfunction (impotence) are allowed if prescribed for a different but approved use, such as the treatment of certain conditions affecting veins and arteries.

If you need any of these drugs for medically accepted reasons, you need to ask your doctor to file for an exception with your plan, as explained in the later section "Getting the Drugs You Need When They're Restricted or Not Covered."

The off-label uses for some drugs

When a doctor prescribes a drug *off label,* she's using that drug to treat a medical condition for which it hasn't received official approval. The U.S. Food and Drug Administration (FDA) approves drugs and allows them into the market to treat specific illnesses. But if scientists find that a drug is also effective for another illness, doctors are legally free to prescribe it off label for the other illness, even if it hasn't received FDA approval for that purpose.

This practice allows doctors to use their clinical judgment and is officially endorsed by the American Medical Association. In fact, it's so common that hundreds of thousands of off-label prescriptions are written every year, especially for patients with cancer, chronic pain, and rare disorders.

Medicare law says simply that Part D plans may only cover drugs approved by the FDA. That's very clear, and it's meant as a safeguard to patients' health. But what if a doctor prescribes a drug that's both on a plan's formulary *and* is FDA-approved — but not for the condition prescribed? Can the plan cover it? Medicare regulations say that it can, but only if the off-label use is included in any of three medical *compendia* (directories of drugs that list their usages).

The snag is that some time may elapse between medical research finding a new use for an existing drug and that usage being listed in the compendia. As a result, Part D plans are prohibited from covering drugs in this twilight zone, and patients who've used them effectively before joining Part D must either pay the cost themselves or do without. However, there's one important exception. Under a recent change in Medicare law, Part D plans are allowed to use authoritative medical literature (as well as compendia listings) to justify off-label use — for anticancer drugs alone — starting January 1, 2009. (The Medicare Rights Center, an advocacy group, is suing the federal government to have the ban removed for all off-label uses.)

The rules of formulary changes

Every plan is allowed to take drugs off its formulary or add new ones to it at any time, subject to Medicare approval. If you're in a plan that discontinues coverage for a drug you take, the plan must inform you of this action in writing at least 60 days before removing it from the formulary. (Here's an excellent reason for reading the mail your plan sends you!) This written notice gives you the opportunity to ask the plan to make an exception and continue coverage in your case, if your doctor confirms that the drug in question is necessary to your health.

This rule doesn't apply when a drug is removed from the market for safety reasons — for example, if new research shows that its risks outweigh its benefits. In this case, you don't receive a 60-day warning, and you can't seek exceptions for coverage.

Making Sense of Special Restrictions on Some Covered Drugs

Perhaps you've found a plan that covers all of your medications. Great! What a relief, huh? But wait a minute. Does the plan require you to ask its permission before it will cover some of your meds? And if so, what's that all about? Well, Medicare allows Part D plans to place restrictions on some of their formulary drugs in the interests of safety or holding down costs.

Here's what these special *restrictions* (which bureaucrats refer to as "utilization management tools") are called and what they mean:

- **Prior authorization:** You're required to ask your plan for permission before it will consider covering a drug placed in this category. These medications are usually powerful ones that may pose safety concerns when used inappropriately or for too long. The plan authorizes coverage for such a drug only if it accepts your doctor's statement that the drug is necessary to treat your medical condition.

- **Quantity limits:** This phrase *doesn't* mean that your plan will cover your prescriptions for a certain time and then stop. It means that your doctor has prescribed a dosage or number of pills per month that's higher than the plan considers normal to treat your condition. For example, if your doctor prescribes a pill to be taken twice a day (60 a month), and the normal quantity is once a day (30 a month), the plan won't cover the prescription unless your doctor shows that the higher quantity is necessary to treat you effectively.

- **Step therapy:** Your plan requires you to try other similar but lower-cost drugs before it will consider covering the more expensive one your doctor has prescribed. This situation can happen if the prescribed drug has a generic or older version (or even one sold over the counter) that's much cheaper. To avoid step therapy, your doctor must show that you've already tried lower-cost drugs that didn't work as well for you as the prescribed drug.

As you can see, some of these restrictions address safety concerns. So you may suppose that all plans restrict the same drugs according to some general Medicare regulation. But no, the system doesn't work that way. Instead, each plan gets to decide which of its formulary drugs requires prior authorization, quantity limits, or step therapy. This fact raises a question: Couldn't a plan use these restrictions to discourage people with certain illnesses and who require expensive drugs from joining the plan? Medicare says no. Officials say the agency reviews each plan's proposed restrictions every year before approving its application to provide Part D services so that plans can't use restrictions to steer the sickest people away.

Getting the Drugs You Need When They're Restricted or Not Covered

Earlier in this chapter, I explain the basic rules about formularies and special restrictions on covered drugs. These restrictions may never affect you. But if they do, what can you do to get the drugs you need? You can start by knowing how to avoid having to jump through these hoops to begin with. Already in a plan that restricts or doesn't cover your drugs? Fortunately, other established rules give you the opportunity to get your plan to cover nonformulary drugs or to set aside its usual restrictions. I touch on all of these possibilities in the following sections.

Sidestepping the hoops

Although restrictions like prior authorization and step therapy may be of benefit in protecting people's health or even saving them money, most Medicare beneficiaries regard them as a hassle — just more hoops to go through to get the drugs they need. But you may be able to sidestep these hoops by avoiding plans that restrict your drugs in the first place.

Each Part D plan chooses which restrictions it wants on which drugs, so these requirements vary a great deal. For example, the same drug may come with quantity limits under Plan W, step therapy under Plan X, both under Plan Y, and neither under Plan Z. This variation gives you a chance to find a plan that doesn't restrict your particular drugs, or at least not all of them, in advance — when you're choosing a plan.

You can find this critical information in any of the following ways:

- ✔ **Compare Part D plans online at www.medicare.gov, as I explain in Chapter 10.** Each plan's details show which of your drugs, if any, have restrictions.

- ✔ **Go to the "Formulary Finder," also at www.medicare.gov.** Here you can find out which plans in your state cover all of your drugs on their formularies, and which cover only some of your drugs. Clicking any plan name shows whether it has restrictions on any of your prescription meds.

- ✔ **Call the Medicare helpline at 800-633-4227.** Ask the customer representative to find the plans that cover all of your drugs at the least cost and, among these, which have restrictions. TDD users should call 877-486-2048.

- ✔ **Go directly to any plan's Web site and look up your drugs on its formulary.** Restricted drugs are designated PA (prior authorization),

QL (quantity limits), or ST (step therapy). You can also call the plan directly and ask a customer representative about drug restrictions, but be sure to keep a record of this conversation. If you enroll and then find you were given wrong information, you may be able to switch to another plan, as explained in Chapter 17.

Understanding the 30-day rule

If you're *newly* enrolled in a Part D plan and are *already* taking any drug that isn't on its formulary or has restrictions (such as prior authorization or step therapy), the plan must temporarily waive its rules and cover at least a 30-day supply of that drug. Medicare requires every plan to do so under a *transition* or *first-fill policy* to ensure that a patient's treatment isn't interrupted when first joining a plan. (People in nursing homes have the right to a 90-day transitional supply, as explained in Chapter 18.)

You can use this rule whether you're joining a Part D plan for the first time or have just switched from one Part D plan to another. Just ask your pharmacist to fill your prescription on a transitional basis. Your pharmacist, or your plan, may contact your doctor to verify that you were already on this particular drug when you joined the plan. If your pharmacist denies you a 30-day fill, call your plan immediately. If the plan doesn't help, complain to Medicare.

The 30-day rule is only a temporary respite, and you must take immediate steps to get the drugs you need when this period ends. Ask your doctor if the plan covers a similar drug that may suit you just as well (see the next section). Or contact your plan for an exception to its policy, as explained later in this chapter.

Trying another drug

Perhaps you *can* use a similar drug — one that's on the plan's formulary and/ or doesn't come with restrictions — that may treat you just as effectively as the medicine you're taking now. The possibility is worth asking your doctor about. A similar drug, which may be an older or generic version of your prescribed drug, will likely cost you less, too. (I explain the meaning of generic and older meds, and how they can slash your expenses, in Chapter 16.)

Requesting an exception with your doctor's help

By law, you have the right to ask your plan to cover a needed drug that isn't on its formulary. You can also ask the plan to waive any restrictions it has placed on any of your drugs. This process is called *requesting an exception* to the plan's policy or, more formally, requesting a *coverage determination*. In the following sections, I explain the process of filing paperwork for an exception request, what your doctor can do to help, how you can help your doctor help you, and what happens when your request is granted or denied.

The paperwork you need

In some circumstances you may not have to go through this process yourself. Sometimes pharmacists resolve the problem themselves — by calling your plan and maybe your doctor — without you ever knowing about it. And occasionally your doctor deals with the issue directly. (In fact, it's essential that your doctor send your plan a statement saying why the drug in question is medically necessary for you, as I explain in the next section.) But in most cases, you need to apply personally, too.

To request an exception, pick up your favorite pen, fill out the appropriate form, and send it to your plan. You can obtain a form by downloading the right one from your plan's Web site, or by calling the plan and asking that one be sent to you. Medicare also provides an acceptable template form that you can download from www.cms.hhs.gov/MedPrescriptDrugApplGriev/Downloads/ModelCoverageDeterminationRequestForm.pdf (so get those typing fingers ready!). This form, titled "Request for Medicare Prescription Drug Coverage Determination," asks you to fill out the following:

- Your name, address, Medicare ID number, and plan ID number

- The name of the prescription drug you're requesting an exception for, the strength of the drug (for example, 100 mg), and the prescribed quantities (for example, 2 pills a day)

- Your physician's name, address, and phone number, and his medical specialty (such as internist, family practitioner, cardiologist)

- What type of coverage determination you're requesting — the form provides a list of possibilities, so check off which one applies to you

- Any other information you want the plan to consider

You can attach your doctor's statement to the form, unless he prefers to send it to the plan independently. Then just sign the form and send it to your plan. If you need exceptions for more than one drug, you can make the request on separate forms and send them all in together.

What your doctor can do to help

To have any chance of succeeding in an exception request, you need your doctor's help. In fact, without his supporting statement, the plan may not even consider your request — or at least, not in a timely manner.

Under Medicare rules, your plan must respond within 72 hours of receiving both your request *and* your doctor's supporting statement. (That's 72 hours by the clock, not business hours.) If your doctor thinks waiting this long would endanger your health or life, he can ask for an *expedited exception,* a request that the plan must reply to within 24 hours (again, by the clock) or even less if your health depends on it. If the plan doesn't respond within either time frame, you should immediately file an appeal, as explained in Chapter 19.

Table 4-1 shows you at a glance the different situations you may encounter, what you can do about them, and how your doctor can help.

Table 4-1	Teaming Up with Your Doc to Get Your Meds	
Situation	*What You Can Do*	*What Your Doc Can Do*
Plan doesn't cover one or more of your drugs	Ask your doc if there's a similar drug your plan does cover	May prescribe similar drug on your plan's formulary
Similar drug(s) on plan's formulary not available or not effective for you	File an exception request asking your plan to cover this drug for medical reasons	Provide statement on why formulary drugs won't work for you or may be harmful
Plan requires you to get permission before covering the drug (prior authorization)	File an exception request asking your plan to cover this drug for medical reasons	Provide statement explaining diagnosis and why this drug is medically necessary for you
Plan requires you to get permission before covering drug in the dosages or quantities prescribed (quantity limits)	File an exception request asking for drug to be covered in the quantities or dosages prescribed	Provide statement and medical records showing you've already taken lower quantities or dosages that weren't effective
Plan requires you to try a less expensive drug before covering prescribed drug (step therapy)	File an exception request explaining that you've already tried less expensive medications	Provide statement and medical records showing you've tried alternatives that weren't effective
Plan won't cover drug because it's off label — not officially approved to treat your condition	File an exception request saying that this drug is the only one effective for your condition	Provide medical literature showing that off-label use is known and appropriate for your condition
Plan requires medical details to determine whether drug should be covered by Part D, A, or B	Supply required information or, if necessary, file an exception request	Provide required information supported by medical records

Situation	What You Can Do	What Your Doc Can Do
Plan sends you a letter denying any of these exception requests	File an appeal against the plan's decision within 60 days	Provide statement and medical records supporting your appeal

How you can help your doctor help you

A doctor's help is critical to obtain a successful exception request. If you think this process is a hassle for you, consider what it's like for your doctor, who may have many patients seeking help for the same reason and who doesn't get paid for providing this assistance. Medicare prohibits doctors from charging patients fees for helping to file for exceptions.

Fortunately, most doctors — even if they grumble about the extra work Part D has imposed on them — put their patients' needs first and are willing to do the paperwork involved in filing for an exception. However, you can score major Brownie points with any doc if you do your part to lessen the work he is doing on your behalf. Your health permitting, call your doctor's receptionist and ask whether it would help for you to provide any of the following materials:

- **A copy of your plan's formulary:** Your doctor needs to know which similar drugs are covered by your plan in order to explain why they won't work for you. You can download the formulary from your plan's Web site or call to have it faxed to you or your doctor. (Some doctors have these formularies in their offices, and some use computer programs that allow them to look up any Part D plan's formulary instantly.)

- **The phone and fax numbers of your plan's Clinical Review Department:** All exception requests must be sent to this department. You can call your plan's customer service number to verify the appropriate contact information.

- **A blank exception request form:** Providing this form for your doctor may make the process a bit smoother. Ask your plan to fax a copy of its own form to your doctor, or visit www.cms.hhs.gov/MLNProducts/ Downloads/Form_Exceptions_final.pdf to download the appropriate Medicare form. This form is useful because it asks doctors precise questions. However, under Medicare rules, no plan can insist that doctors use a form, but must accept any statement written on their letterhead.

- **A set of instructions for doctors unfamiliar with the exception-request process:** Obviously, a doctor who's well versed in the process doesn't need to see pointers. But if you're the first patient your doc has helped file an exception for, you can find useful instructions from the Medicare Rights Center online at www.medicarerights.org/PartD_for_ Physicians_national.pdf.

It's almost inconceivable that a doctor would refuse to help you request a Part D exception, especially if you've gone to the trouble of getting together the information in the preceding list. But it can happen. For this reason, Medicare proposed new regulations in 2008 (not yet finalized as this book goes to press) that allow not only physicians but also other health professionals who are qualified to write prescriptions — such as nurse practitioners and physician assistants — to file Part D exception requests. So if your doctor refuses to help you, ask whether anyone else in his office can. Otherwise, you can't do much — except perhaps report the refusal to Medicare and take your healthcare elsewhere.

What happens when your exception request is granted or denied

In most cases, if you win an exception it'll be valid until the end of the calendar year — especially if the plan grants you an exception to cover a drug not on its formulary or to waive quantity limits and step therapy restrictions. But when plans approve prior authorization for a certain drug, they can (and sometimes do) require another request after an interval of time (like one month, three months, or six months). In this case, you and your doctor must go through the exception-filing process again, and may even be required to do so repeatedly throughout the year.

What happens at the end of the year? If you stay in the same Part D plan, your exception may continue to be valid throughout the following year, so you wouldn't need to request another. However, that depends on the plan's policy. Some plans require new exception requests for the same drug every year. If you switch to a different plan next year, you'd certainly have to file a new exception request — unless you choose a plan that doesn't impose a restriction on your particular drug(s).

If your plan denies your request for an exception, you can pursue the matter further by asking for a *reconsideration* (asking the plan to reconsider its decision) and, if necessary, by taking the dispute to a higher level of appeal. You can also take these actions if your plan doesn't respond to your request for an exception (or reconsideration) within the required time frames. I offer a detailed explanation of how to ask for a reconsideration or file an appeal in Chapter 19.

Obtaining excluded drugs

If you need a type of drug that the law excludes from Part D coverage (as listed in the earlier section "The drugs that Medicare doesn't pay for"), what can you do? The ban on barbiturates and benzodiazepines is especially controversial. These drugs can lead to oversedation (especially in nursing homes), serious side effects, and addiction. But they're also commonly used to treat older and disabled people for conditions such as muscle spasms, seizures, sleeplessness, panic attacks, and other forms of anxiety.

If your doctor says you need an excluded drug, your options for getting it covered under Part D are limited. You can't file an exception request for any of these drugs, unless your doctor has prescribed them for what Medicare considers a medically acceptable reason, as explained earlier in this chapter. Here are some alternative possibilities:

✔ Although hardly any Part D plans pay for brand-name benzodiazepines, a few plans cover generic versions of these drugs — for example diazepam (Valium) and alprazolam (Xanax). These are often enhanced-benefit plans that have higher-than-average premiums. So check plan costs carefully. Generic benzos aren't expensive, and it may be cheaper to pay their full cost each month than to pay a higher premium.

✔ State Medicaid programs often cover prescription drugs that are excluded from Part D; so do many State Pharmacy Assistance Programs (SPAPs). If you're enrolled in either of these programs, and your doctor says you need one of these drugs, contact the program to see whether it's covered. (See Chapter 6 for more info about these plans.)

✔ If you have other drug coverage that wraps around Part D (like coverage from an employer), you may be able to use those benefits to cover these drugs, as explained in Chapter 6.

✔ You may be able to obtain these drugs from the manufacturers through their patient assistance programs, depending on whether you qualify according to the programs' conditions and income limits. To find out, go to www.pparx.org. (Check out Chapter 16 for the scoop on these programs.)

Getting drugs for off-label uses

Unless Medicare regulations change, Part D plans will continue to cover off-label prescriptions only if their usages are included in the specified medical compendia, as explained in this chapter's "The off-label uses for some drugs" section. If the drug your doctor has prescribed as medically necessary doesn't fall into this category, your chances of being able to appeal your plan's coverage refusal are slim.

It may help to contact the Part D Appeals Project of the Medicare Rights Center, which helps Part D enrollees try to get the medications they need and has a special interest in off-label denials. Call the Center at 888-466-9050.

Also, your doctor may agree to argue the case with your Part D plan when requesting an exception by describing how an off-label use is the only means of alleviating your medical condition. She can do so by providing references to scientific research that demonstrates the drug's effectiveness and has been published in authoritative medical journals. Success isn't guaranteed, but the voice of a physician who can quote the relevant research carries weight.

Knowing When Drugs Are Covered by Part D, Part A, or Part B

As confusing as it sounds, some prescription drugs may be covered not only under Medicare Part D but also under Part A (hospital insurance) or Part B (outpatient care), both of which I touch on in Chapter 1. Sometimes an identical drug may be covered by all three but charged under one or the other, according to different circumstances. That's because certain drugs were covered under Part A or Part B before Part D came into existence, and that practice has continued.

Here's the general rule of thumb on the differences:

✔ Part D covers outpatient drugs you administer to yourself at home, or that a caregiver administers to you at your home. (These drugs include self-injected insulin for diabetes, for example.)

✔ Part A covers drugs administered when you're a patient in a hospital or skilled nursing facility.

✔ Part B covers drugs administered in a doctor's office (such as injected chemotherapy drugs), hospital outpatient departments, and, in some circumstances, in a hospice or by a home healthcare professional.

These general rules are more complicated in some situations. For example, if your organ transplant is covered by Medicare, the immunosuppressant drugs you need afterward are covered by Part B. But if your transplant surgery *isn't* covered by Medicare (perhaps because you received it before joining the program), the drugs are covered under Part D.

Part D doesn't pay for drugs covered by Part A or B. So if any of your meds are in question, your Part D plan may require information from you and your doctor before covering them. Usually this info includes details of the related medical treatment (such as a transplant or cancer surgery). For this reason, plans often place a prior authorization restriction on such drugs, to determine whether they should be covered by Part A, B, or D. Your doctor may be able to settle this matter over the phone or may help you file a speedy exception request as explained earlier in this chapter. Either way, your doctor needs to explain why a prior authorization shouldn't apply in this case.

Chapter 5

Extra Help: A Better Deal if Your Income Is Low

In This Chapter

▶ Knowing what you pay and what you get in Extra Help

▶ Qualifying automatically or applying for Extra Help

▶ Seeing whether Extra Help affects other assistance you may receive

▶ Selecting a drug plan, enrolling, and switching

▶ Finding out whether you'll still qualify for Extra Help all year and next year

▶ Figuring out what to do if you're denied or lose eligibility for Extra Help

*P*remiums, deductibles, co-pays, and that huge chunk of change that is the doughnut hole — yes, a lot of consumer costs go along with Part D. And for many people, they're just not affordable. That's where Extra Help comes in. This is the name of the program-within-a-program that's specifically designed for people with limited incomes and savings and has the most generous benefits that Part D provides. If you qualify, you'll receive drug coverage throughout the year, and your out-of-pocket expenses will be much smaller than in the regular Part D program.

Millions of older Americans and those with disabilities are thought to qualify for Extra Help but, for one reason or another, they aren't receiving it. Could you be one of them? It may be worth applying even if you're not sure you'd qualify. Or do you think that someone you know — a relative, a friend, a neighbor — could use some Extra Help? If so, you may want to encourage or help that person to apply.

In this chapter, I explain how Extra Help works, depending on whether you qualify for it automatically or need to apply, and how it could affect other government assistance you may receive. I also explain Extra Help in the context of choosing and enrolling in a Part D plan or switching to another, the all-important question of continuing to receive Extra Help from year to year, and what to do if you're denied or lose eligibility for Extra Help.

This chapter explains the Extra Help program as it works in the 50 states and the District of Columbia. Similar but different assistance is available in Puerto Rico, the U.S. Virgin Islands, and other American territories.

✔ For information and help in Puerto Rico, call the Medicare Platino program at 866-596-4747.

✔ In the U.S. Virgin Islands, call the Department of Human Services at 340-774-5265 (St. Thomas/St. John) or 340-773-2323 (St. Croix).

✔ For contact information for other U.S. territories, call Medicare at 800-633-4227.

Understanding the Value of Extra Help

Millions of people in Medicare have been able to save many hundreds or even thousands of dollars a year on their drug bills under the Extra Help program. Even more crucially, Extra Help has allowed many folks who didn't previously have any drug coverage to fill all the prescriptions they need for the first time. For them, Extra Help has been a godsend.

At the same time, there are many who aren't much better off with Extra Help than they were before — and a few who may be worse off. People enrolled in Medicaid are automatically transferred to Part D for their drug coverage when they join Medicare. Those in states that require Medicaid recipients to pay small co-pays for their prescriptions won't see much difference in their out-of-pocket expenses under Part D. However, people who are used to getting their meds completely free from their state's Medicaid program should expect to have small co-pays for the first time.

Is there much red tape to go through? Compared to many assistance programs, Extra Help is easy to get into. Some people qualify automatically and don't have to apply. Others must apply, but navigating the application is fairly straightforward. On the other hand, after you're in the program, you may have some hoops to jump through in choosing and joining a drug plan and, when you're in a plan, getting all the meds you need. Also, no question, people who receive Extra Help one year but don't qualify the next face big disruptions. I cover these specific topics later in this chapter.

But first, you need to know how you can qualify for Extra Help and, if you do, how it can help pay for your medications. Extra Help benefits are available at five levels, mainly according to income. Table 5-1 explains these levels at a glance.

Table 5-1	The Different Levels of Benefits in Extra Help (Based on Income and Savings in 2008; Costs for 2009)					
Level	*If You Have Medicare and also:*	*Monthly Premium*	*Annual Deductible*	*Co-Pay per Pre-scripttion*	*Cata-strophic Coverage Co-Pay*	*Eligibility*
1	Full Medicaid benefits and live in an institu-tion, such as a nursing home	$0	$0	$0	$0	Automatic
2	Full Medicaid benefits and a yearly income no higher than $10,400 (single) or $14,000 (married couple)	$0	$0	$1.10 for generics; $3.20 for brand-name drugs	$0	Automatic
3	Full Medicaid benefits and income higher than in level 2; **or** Supple-mentary Security Income; **or** your state pays your Medicare premiums	$0	$0	$2.40 generics; $6.00 brand-name drugs	$0	Automatic

(continued)

Table 5-1 *(continued)*

Level	If You Have Medicare and also:	Monthly Premium	Annual Deductible	Co-Pay per Pre-scripttion	Cata-strophic Coverage Co-Pay	Eligibility
4	Yearly income no higher than $14,040 (single) or $18,900 (married couple) and value of assets no higher than $7,790 (single) or $12,440 (married couple)	$0	$0	$2.40 generics; $6.00 brand-name drugs	$0	Must apply
5	Yearly income no higher than $15,600 (single) or $21,000 (married couple) and value of assets no higher than $11,990 (single) or $23,970 (married couple)	Percentage of plan's premium according to income	$60	Up to 15% of the cost of each prescrip-tion after meet-ing the deductible	No more than $2.40 for generics or $6.00 for brand-name drugs or 5% of the cost	Must apply

Source: Centers for Medicare & Medicaid Services.

Checking out examples of Extra Help at work

Here are some examples of how Extra Help works in practice (at 2009 rates):

✔ Louisa is very frail and lives in a nursing home. The little income she has from Social Security goes to Medicaid, which pays her costs in the home, leaving her a small allowance for personal needs. The full price of her medicines runs to $370 a month. But because she gets Medicaid and lives in an institution, she automatically qualifies for maximum Extra Help (Level 1) and pays nothing for her prescription drugs.

✔ Edward and Sue's combined income is $12,750 a year, and they get medical benefits from their state Medicaid program, so they qualify automatically for full Extra Help under Level 2. The total, joint cost of their drugs is $550 a month. Under Extra Help, Edward's four brand-name drugs and two generics cost him $15 a month ($3.20 × 4 = $12.80; $1.10 × 2 = $2.20). Sue's one brand-name med and six generics cost her $9.80 a month ($3.20 × 1 = $3.20; $1.10 × 6 = $6.60). Together, their monthly out-of-pocket expense is $24.80, saving them $525.20 each month, or $6,302.40 over the year.

✔ Cora has many health problems, and the meds her doctor prescribes add up to $1,220 a month, or $14,640 over the year — unafford-able for her without Extra Help. Because her state pays her Medicare Part B premiums, she qualifies automatically for full Extra Help at Level 3. She uses four brand-name drugs (including an expensive one for cancer) and four generics regularly. Her out-of-pocket cost is $33.60 a month ($6.00 × 4 = $24.00; $2.40 × 4 = $9.60) for the first five months of the year. But then, because her drug costs are high, catastrophic coverage kicks in, and from June through December, she pays nothing. Over the whole year, her total expense is $168 ($33.60 × 5), and she saves $14,472.

✔ Carlton is a widower with an income that entitles him to partial Extra Help (Level 5). He pays half ($14) of his Part D plan's regular monthly premium, a $60 annual deductible, and 15 percent of the cost of his drugs. At full price, his drugs would cost $350 a month, or $4,200 over 12 months. Under Extra Help, they cost $52.50 a month (15 percent of $350). His total out-of-pocket expense over the year is $858 ($14 × 12 = $168 in premiums + $60 deductible + $630 share of drug costs). He saves $3,342 over the year.

These examples reflect the 2009 maximum co-pays set in law. People receiving Extra Help can't pay more than these amounts. But in some Part D plans, they may pay less. For example, if a plan normally charges nothing for certain generic drugs, Extra Help enrollees in that plan don't pay anything for them either. (So if Cora were in a plan like this, she'd get her four generics free and save $48 more over the year.) And if a plan has no deductible, people receiving partial Extra Help receive coverage right away and don't have to pay their reduced deductible. (So Carlton would save a further $60 in a no-deductible plan.)

From Table 5-1, you see that

✔ People who receive full Medicaid benefits *and* live in nursing homes or other types of institutionalized long-term care (Level 1) automatically qualify for full Extra Help and pay nothing for their medications.

✔ People who receive benefits from Medicaid or some other government programs that pay their Medicare premiums or provide supplemental income (Levels 2 and 3) automatically qualify for full Extra Help and pay a small amount for prescriptions.

✔ Others who aren't enrolled in any of these programs but whose monthly incomes are still below certain dollar amounts (Levels 4 and 5) must apply for Extra Help.

✔ People in Levels 4 and 5 have their assets (mainly savings), as well as their incomes, taken into account to qualify for Extra Help.

✔ People in Level 4 receive full Extra Help benefits and pay the same co-pays as those in Level 3, but don't qualify automatically. They must apply for Extra Help.

✔ People in the highest qualifying income group (Level 5) receive "partial" Extra Help. They pay a share of their plan's premium on a sliding scale according to income, a reduced annual deductible (about one-fifth of the regular Part D deductible), and up to 15 percent of the cost of each prescription.

✔ People in Levels 1, 2, 3, and 4 pay nothing for catastrophic coverage, which kicks in after their drug costs reach a certain level in the year ($4,050 in 2008; $4,350 in 2009). People in Level 5 have small co-pays after getting to that level. Everything the government contributes toward prescription costs through Extra Help counts toward the spending limit that triggers catastrophic coverage.

✔ Everybody, at all five levels, gets full drug coverage throughout the year. Nobody receiving Extra Help has to face the dreaded doughnut hole.

Income and asset limits increase every year. The Social Security Administration announces the new amounts in February or March, and they become effective immediately. These limits are higher in some circumstances — if you live in Alaska or Hawaii, have dependent relatives living with you, or have some earnings from work that aren't counted. Any of these situations may give you a better chance to qualify for Extra Help than the income and asset limits in Table 5-1 suggest.

Extra Help co-payments (and the amount of the deductible for people in Level 5 who receive the partial benefit) increase at the beginning of each calendar year and remain the same for that whole year.

Qualifying Automatically for Extra Help

You qualify automatically for Extra Help — without having to go through the process of applying for it or answering any questions about your income and savings — if you're in Medicare and also receiving any of the following government benefits:

- ✔ **Medicaid:** This is the program in your state that provides healthcare benefits for people whose incomes are below a certain level. The program is generally known as Medicaid but may have other names in different states — for example, MediCal in California, MassHealth in Massachusetts, and TennCare in Tennessee. If you're in Medicaid, you get Extra Help as soon as you become eligible for Medicare (Chapter 1 explains the eligibility rules). Or, if you're already in Medicare, you'd get it if and when you qualify for Medicaid.

- ✔ **Supplementary Security Income:** SSI is a federal program that provides monthly payments to people in certain categories (blind, disabled, or 65 and older) whose incomes are very low.

- ✔ **Medicare savings program:** Three Medicare savings programs (officially designated QI, SLMB, or QMB) give varying help to people with low incomes and few resources to pay for the out-of-pocket costs of Medicare. If you're in any of these programs, your state pays your Medicare Part B premiums (see Chapter 1 for Part B information).

- ✔ **Medicaid medical spend-down programs:** Some states have a system that allows people whose incomes are above the state limit for Medicaid to become eligible for it when their out-of-pocket medical expenses reach a certain level in a calendar year. If you're receiving Medicaid in one of these medical *spend-down* programs, you automatically start getting Extra Help for drug coverage as soon as you become eligible for Medicare. Or, if you're already in Medicare, you qualify for Extra Help as soon as your medical spend-down reaches the point of putting you in Medicaid. After you're in the Extra Help program, you'll continue to receive its benefits until the end of the calendar year. (See the later section "Determining Whether You'll Qualify for Extra Help All Year and Next Year" for more about these programs.)

Jargon alert: People in any of these programs are known as *dual eligibles* in Medicare lingo, because they qualify for help from both Medicare and Medicaid.

If you automatically qualify for full Extra Help, Medicare should send you a letter telling you so. If you don't receive this notice but are in one of the previously listed programs, call Medicare at 800-633-4227 to find out why.

Be aware that qualifying for Extra Help, even automatically, is only one step in the process. You still have to join a Part D private plan to get prescription drug coverage. You can sign up for a plan of your own choosing — but if you don't do so, Medicare will pick one and enroll you in it, even though that plan may not be ideal for you. You'll find more details about this in the section on choosing a plan later in this chapter.

It could happen that you qualify for Extra Help only after you've been in the regular Part D drug program for some time — for example, if your situation changes and you suddenly become eligible for Medicaid, Supplementary Security Income (SSI), or your state's Medicare savings program. But be aware that it can often take months before the various government agencies get their paperwork sorted out and confirm your eligibility.

You have the right to be reimbursed for the money you spent on drugs dating back to the day you applied for Medicaid, SSI, or the Medicare savings program. Your Medicare drug plan must return the difference between what you would've paid under Extra Help rules during this period and what you actually paid. But you can't rely on your plan to automatically refund that money to you. Instead, you should contact the plan and ask for the appropriate refund, explaining the circumstances. If you still don't get the money, call Medicare at 800-633-4227 and report it. Or, if necessary, file a grievance against the plan, as covered in Chapter 19.

Applying for Extra Help

Perhaps your income and resources are limited but you're not enrolled in one of the programs that qualify you for Extra Help automatically, as I explain in the previous section. In this case, you need to *apply* for Extra Help. You can apply at any time — when you first join Medicare; when you lose a job, become widowed or divorced, or experience any other change that lowers your income; or if you're already in Part D and have only just realized that you may qualify for Extra Help.

Applying involves filling out a form and sending it to the Social Security Administration (not Medicare), which will then decide whether you qualify. I walk you through the process in the following sections.

Obtaining an application form

You must apply for Extra Help in writing on the official printed form or online on the Social Security Web site. Don't use a photocopy or a form printed from the Web site — these can't be scanned by computers, so they'll just delay your application.

You can obtain a form in any of the following ways:

- ✔ **By mail (without requesting it):** You're likely to receive an Extra Help application in the mail soon after you sign up for Medicare. Social Security seems to send them out to virtually all new beneficiaries, even people who are still working and earning far more than the Extra Help income limits.

✔ **By phone:** Call Social Security toll-free at 800-772-1213. (If you're hard of hearing, call the TDD number at 800-325-0778.) Tell the representative that you want to apply for Extra Help to pay for Medicare prescription drug costs. You can ask for the form (in English or Spanish) to be sent to your home, or you can arrange to pick one up at your nearest Social Security office.

✔ **Online:** Go to www.ssa.gov and click "Medicare" on the top panel, then click "Apply for help with prescription drug costs." You can use this form to apply directly online, but only in English. Before downloading the application form, it's helpful to click the link headed "How the Online Application Works." This page explains the process, including instructions on how you can save your work so you can leave the form partially completed and return again later.

You *can't* print out the form and mail it in — but a printout may be useful for a practice run before you make the proper application. (For more information about applying online, see the later section "Signing and sending in the application.")

✔ **In person:** You can obtain a form (and help filling it out, if you need it) at your local Social Security office or State Health Insurance Assistance Program (SHIP) office. (To make an appointment at a Social Security office, call 800-772-1213. To call your SHIP, see the contact info in Appendix B at the end of this book.) Forms are also sometimes available in pharmacies, doctors' offices, and senior centers.

Helpful tips for filling out the application

The Extra Help application contains four pages of questions, mainly about your income and savings. I provide tips for answering them in the following sections.

Don't panic if you can't answer all the questions! Answer as many as you can and send in the form. Someone from Social Security will be in touch to help you complete it. However, if you apply online, you must answer every question before you can submit the form.

Getting instructions

You can get detailed instructions in English and 15 other languages (Arabic, Armenian, Chinese, Farsi, French, Greek, Haitian-Creole, Italian, Korean, Polish, Portuguese, Russian, Spanish, Tagalog, and Vietnamese) by calling Social Security or by visiting its Web site. If you want these instructions mailed to you, ask for form SSA-1020B-INST plus the language you need. But you must fill out the actual application in English or Spanish only.

Gathering information you need

Before you start, pulling together some information is useful. This info includes your Social Security number and recent financial records relating to any earnings, pensions, savings, life insurance, and investments you may have. You need to refer to these records to answer questions about your income and savings. You do *not* have to send in any documents to support what you say about your finances, but that doesn't mean you can be untruthful! Social Security will likely compare what you say with information from tax records and other government sources.

Single or married status

Income levels are for either single people or married couples "who are living together." If you're married and living with your spouse, you can both apply on the same form. If only one of you is applying, you still have to provide your spouse's income and resources. You count as single if

- ✔ You're married but living apart.

- ✔ Your spouse is living permanently in a nursing home or another type of long-term care.

- ✔ You have a domestic partner or are in a common-law or same-sex marriage.

If you're not sure whether you count as single or married for this purpose — for example, if it isn't clear that your spouse will be in a nursing home permanently — call Social Security for clarification.

Income

The income limits for qualifying for Extra Help go up slightly each year and are announced in February or March. The application form doesn't actually say what these dollar limits are, mainly because they're somewhat flexible. For example, the limits are higher if you

- ✔ Have relatives living with you who depend on you for at least half of their support

- ✔ Live in Alaska or Hawaii (where the cost of living is higher than in other states)

- ✔ Have some earnings that aren't counted as income

- ✔ Have certain expenses related to disability that allow you to work

Otherwise, if none of these circumstances are applicable, the upper income limits in 2008 and the early part of 2009 are $15,600 a year for a single person and $21,000 a year for a married couple living together.

You should include the following as income:

- ✔ Pretax wages or earnings from self-employment
- ✔ Social Security or Railroad Retirement benefits, *before* deductions
- ✔ Veterans benefits
- ✔ Pensions and annuities
- ✔ Workers' compensation
- ✔ Net income from rental property
- ✔ Alimony
- ✔ Payments from anyone (other than a government agency) to help pay for certain household expenses, as explained later in this chapter

You can leave out the following:

- ✔ Cash or credit acquired from a loan or through a reverse mortgage
- ✔ Federal income tax refunds and earned income tax credit payments
- ✔ Victim's compensation
- ✔ Education grants and scholarships
- ✔ Help from food stamps or Meals on Wheels
- ✔ Help from a housing agency, energy assistance program, or public relocation program
- ✔ Help paying for medical treatment and drugs
- ✔ Disaster assistance

If you're not sure whether you qualify for Extra Help because your income may be a bit over the top, it's still worth applying. Social Security doesn't count every dollar of income toward the limits, so you may find that you qualify after all. Also, remember that the income limits increase a little each year in February or March. You can find updated levels by calling Social Security or Medicare or by going to the chart in Section 3 of "Your Guide to Medicare Prescription Drug Coverage," available online at www.medicare.gov/Publications/Pubs/pdf/11109.pdf. You can apply for Extra Help at any time, so if a new level suddenly brings your income within the limits, you can apply at once.

Assets

Assets (also called "resources") are the value of certain things you may own, mainly savings. The upper limit of this value increases from time to time. In 2008 and early 2009, it's $11,990 for a single person and $23,970 for a married couple living together.

You should include the following as assets:

- ✔ Bank accounts, including checking, savings, and certificates of deposit
- ✔ Proceeds of a loan if saved beyond the month they are received
- ✔ Cash kept at home or anywhere else
- ✔ Individual retirement accounts (IRAs) and 401(k)s
- ✔ Stocks and bonds
- ✔ Mutual funds
- ✔ Real estate (other than your primary home)

You can leave out the following:

- ✔ Your primary home and the land it stands on
- ✔ Your vehicle(s)
- ✔ Personal possessions, including jewelry and furnishings
- ✔ Property you need for self-support, such as land used to grow your own food
- ✔ Burial plots
- ✔ Up to $1,500 (or $3,000 for a married couple living together) of the cash value of life insurance policies

Social Security rules for Extra Help don't prevent you from spending down or giving away some of your savings to reduce them below the asset limit. Only what you have during the month you apply is counted. However, bear in mind that spending down may affect your eligibility for other assistance programs — especially Medicaid, which has strict rules about this — if you should need them within a few years.

Life insurance

The *cash value* of a life insurance policy means the amount you'd receive if you cashed it in right now. This is less than the *face value* of the policy, which is what you'd receive if it went to term. Most people have no idea what their policies' cash value is, you'll probably need to call your insurer to find out. Some types of life insurance — such as policies that can't be cashed in before they come to term, or burial insurance where the benefit can be used only for funeral expenses — don't count as assets. *Note:* Starting in 2010, life insurance will no longer count as an asset under Extra Help.

Funeral expenses

The application asks whether you expect to use money from your savings or investments to pay for funeral or burial expenses. Answering "yes" simply means you expect to do so, not that you have some amount ready and waiting for that purpose. Answering "no" will reduce your asset limit for qualifying for Extra Help by $1,500 if you're single or $3,000 if you're married and living together.

Dependent relatives

If you have any relatives — related to you by blood, marriage, or adoption — who live with you and depend on you (or your spouse) for at least half of their financial support, be sure to answer the question on household size. Every extra person raises the income limits and increases your chances of qualifying for Extra Help.

Help toward household expenses

The application asks whether anyone else (other than a government agency) helps you pay for food, mortgage, rent, heating fuel or gas, electricity, water, and property taxes. If you answer "yes," a part of the amount you specify will count as income. For example, if you live with someone who pays all these expenses each month, you'd add the amounts together and divide by the number of people in the household — then subtract from the total any contribution you normally make. The result is the amount you report on the application. Social Security will decide what portion of that amount would count toward your income. You don't have to show proof of such help. *Note:* Starting in 2010, this assistance will no longer count as an asset under Extra Help.

Getting a hand with applying

Many circumstances — like being sick or recently widowed, to name just two — may make you feel that dealing with this application on your own is beyond you at this time. In that case, don't hesitate to get help. All sorts of people can lend you a hand in applying:

- ✔ **Someone you know:** Anybody can help you fill out the application, or even apply on your behalf — a family member, a friend, a legal representative, a social worker, or anyone you choose to act for you.

- ✔ **Free, expert personal help:** Counselors at State Health Insurance Assistance Programs (SHIPs) are specially trained to personally assist people in sorting through their Part D options, including helping them apply for Extra Help or applying on their behalf. For the number of your local SHIP, see Appendix B at the end of this book.

- ✔ **Help from Social Security:** If you're filling out the application on your own and need help on how to answer specific questions, you can call Social Security at 800-772-1213 (or the TDD number at 800-325-0778 if you're hard of hearing) or visit your local Social Security office.

- ✔ **Community groups:** You may be a member of a church, senior center, or other community group that can assist you in filling out the form. If English isn't your first language, an organization or group for people of your own nationality may be especially helpful in this regard. (Also, see Appendix B for sources of help in other languages.)

Signing and sending in your application

Signing the form means you're legally declaring that all the information you've given is true to the best of your knowledge. If you're married and living together, your spouse must also sign the application, even if he or she isn't applying for Extra Help at this time. If someone else signs on your behalf, that person should complete the section provided on the form for his or her name, address, and personal or professional relationship to you. Then you can submit the form by

- **Using the printed application form:** After you've completed and signed the form, just put it in the preaddressed envelope and mail it in. If the envelope is missing, send the form to the Social Security Administration, Wilkes-Barre Data Operations Center, P.O. Box 1020, Wilkes-Barre, PA 18767-9910.

- **Applying to Social Security online:** Go to www.ssa.gov and click "Medicare" on the top panel. Then click "Apply for help with prescription drug costs." Remember to look at the instructions, as explained in the previous section "Getting an application form," before filling out the form. You must answer all the questions before signing the form electronically and submitting it.

- **Applying on the BenefitsCheckUp Web site:** You can apply for Extra Help at www.benefitscheckup.org using the same Social Security online form. The advantage of going this route is that the site automatically screens your information and lets you know whether you qualify for other benefits to help pay for prescription drugs and other living expenses. (I give more information about this Web site in the later section "Looking for help to pay other expenses.")

Knowing what happens next

So you've sent in your application and crossed your fingers, waiting for a decision. What happens next?

- **Social Security should send you a notice saying it has received your application and is processing it.** If you don't receive this notice within a couple weeks of applying, call Social Security to let it know you sent in an application for Extra Help, just in case your form has gone missing.

- **You may hear from Social Security by phone or mail if it has additional questions.** The agency will contact you if your application is incomplete or if some of your financial information doesn't match other government records, for example.

How do you know that the person on the end of the line is actually from Social Security and not just some scam artist trying to steal your Social Security number and financial data? If the call is legitimate, the person won't normally ask for your Social Security number — unless the one you've given on your application appears incorrect — or for your credit card or bank account numbers. If you have any suspicions, hang up and call Social Security right away to check that the call was really from someone in that agency. (For more tips on avoiding scams, see Chapter 11.)

✔ **You may receive what's called a "Pre-Decisional Notice" saying that your application is likely to be turned down.** This document specifies what information on your application will cause you to be denied — for example, that your income is too high or that your assets are above the limit. If this information is wrong, receiving the notice allows you time to correct it. You must do so within ten days of the date of the notice, by calling or visiting your local Social Security office at the number or address given on the notice.

✔ **Social Security will decide whether you're eligible for Extra Help.** You should hear within 60 days of Social Security receiving your application, maybe sooner. You'll receive either a "Notice of Award" saying that you qualify for either full or partial Extra Help (see the earlier section "Understanding the Value of Extra Help" to find out how to tell the difference) or a "Notice of Denial" saying that you don't qualify.

If you're told you don't qualify, you can appeal the decision, as explained in the later section "Taking Action if You're Denied or Lose Your Eligibility for Extra Help." That section also looks at alternative ways of reducing costs outside of Extra Help.

Figuring Out Whether Extra Help Affects Other Assistance

You may hesitate about Extra Help if you think it may cause you to lose or reduce other benefits you're receiving. Sometimes it can, but maybe not to your disadvantage. The money you save through Extra Help should far outweigh reductions in other benefits. In other words, you end up better off and with more cash in hand, even if you receive less in other assistance. Take a look at these situations:

✔ **Food stamps and housing assistance:** Medical expenses are taken into account in receiving food stamps and government housing subsidies. So if you pay less for your drugs under Extra Help, your food stamps will be reduced, and you'll pay a larger share of your subsidized rent. But you're still likely to be better off.

Here's an example: Sarah was paying $400 a month out of pocket for her prescription drugs before joining Medicare. But when she began receiving Extra Help, her monthly drug expenses dropped to $40. This meant losing $40 in food stamps. And under the formula used by her housing assistance program to calculate her new benefit — *not* a dollar-for-dollar reduction — she paid $108 more in rent. But what she saved on medicines ($360) was more than her extra expenses for food and rent ($148). Overall she saved $212 a month, making her $2,544 better off over the year.

✔ **Home heating/cooling assistance:** Eligibility for the Low-Income Home Energy Assistance Program is based on income, without regard to medical expenses. So Extra Help does *not* affect it.

✔ **Supplementary Security Income (SSI):** Medical expenses aren't taken into account in calculating eligibility for SSI. So even though Extra Help reduces what you spend in drugs (effectively giving you more cash in hand), you'll continue to qualify for SSI.

Choosing a Drug Plan, Signing Up, and Switching Plans

Qualifying for Extra Help is just one step in the process. You still have to be in a Medicare drug plan to get coverage for your drugs. If you qualify for Extra Help *automatically* and don't immediately sign up for a Medicare drug plan on your own, Medicare enrolls you in one. Medicare does this to make sure you continue to get your medications, especially if you're being moved from Medicaid to Medicare for your drug coverage. Medicare may sign you up with a plan a month or two before you're switched from Medicaid to Medicare — a move that's intended to ensure your details are entered into the computer system and that everything will go smoothly at the pharmacy. (If it doesn't go smoothly, you have a right to a 30-day supply of drugs to tide you over, as explained in Chapter 14.)

However, Medicare enrolls Extra Help people in plans at *random*. This is the computerized version of taking your name out of a hat and matching it to the name of a plan taken out of another hat. In other words, there's no effort to put you into a plan that suits your needs, or even to ensure that the plan you're assigned to actually covers your drugs. So you may find yourself in a plan that's not ideal for you — unless you take action and choose a plan for yourself. You can switch to another plan immediately or whenever you want to, as explained in the next section.

You have the right to enroll in a Medicare drug plan of your own choosing — and you should do so by comparing plans carefully according to the drugs you take — just like anyone else (see Chapter 10 for details). But you should know about some details specific to Extra Help. I give you the nitty-gritty in the following sections.

What were they thinking . . . when they created the asset test?

Well over 2.5 million people on Medicare have incomes limited enough to qualify for Extra Help — yet fail because of the asset test. Not surprisingly, many feel the test is deeply unfair because it penalizes those who, despite limited incomes, have managed to save a small nest egg toward their retirement.

Medicare never had any type of asset test before Part D began in 2006. But Congress created the test for Extra Help as a cost trade-off — without it, the program would've cost $35 billion more.

Lawmakers in favor of the test pointed out that other assistance programs, such as Medicaid, have long taken people's assets into account when deciding eligibility. Nonetheless, consumer advocates have consistently lobbied against the Extra Help asset test from the beginning, and some members of Congress are working to eliminate it or raise its limits so that more people with low incomes can qualify.

Before you choose: Realizing that some plans may cost you more than others

In the earlier section "Understanding the Value of Extra Help," I point out that full Extra Help entitles you to a zero premium. But there's a catch. You can get that benefit *only* if you join a plan with premiums below a certain dollar amount.

Under Medicare rules, you don't pay a premium if you're in a plan with a premium that's generally below the average of all plan premiums in your region in any given year (see Chapter 3 for an explanation of premiums). But if you join a more expensive plan — one with a premium above that regional average — you have to pay the difference between the average premium and the full premium. For example, if the average premium in your region is $30, and the premium in the plan you join is $37, you'd pay $7 each month for your drug coverage. (This rule doesn't affect your low-cost Extra Help co-pays for prescriptions — they remain the same.)

This regional average (which bureaucrats call the *benchmark*) changes every year. That's why, each fall, Medicare sends letters to some Extra Help beneficiaries, warning them that if they stay in the plan they're in for the following year, they'll no longer be able to claim zero premiums, or in some cases, the letter tells them they've been automatically switched to a new plan that has zero premiums. So be sure to read any letters that come from Medicare or your plan during the fall (September to November) so you're not caught off-guard in January having to pay a premium you didn't expect.

Finding a plan with the premium you want and the drugs you need

In general, the process of comparing plans to find the least expensive one that covers all or most of your drugs is the same in Extra Help as it is for folks in the regular Part D program, as explained in detail in Chapter 10. But there are some differences, depending on whether you're receiving full or partial Extra Help.

Using an online comparison tool if you're getting full Extra Help

Under full Extra Help, your co-pays (being set in law) are the same under any Part D plan. But the premium you pay depends on whether you choose a plan with a premium above or below the regional average, as explained in the preceding section. How can you tell which plans have these higher or lower premiums?

Fortunately, you can see this information at a glance on Medicare's online Prescription Drug Plan Finder. (If you don't have access to the Internet, you can get the same info in other ways, which I explain later in this chapter.) Before using the plan finder, you may want to look at the step-by-step instructions given in Chapter 10 on how to navigate it. Here are the variations if you're on full Extra Help:

1. **Go to www.medicare.gov and click "Medicare Prescription Drug Plans." Then click "Find and Compare Plans," and then "Begin General Search."**

2. **Type in your zip code and answer the questions — in particular, the ones at the bottom of the page that establish what kind of Extra Help you qualify for.**

3. **Enter the names of all of your drugs, plus their dosages and how often you take them.**

   You'll then see a list of drug plans, starting with the least expensive.

4. **Look under the Monthly Premium column to the right of each plan's name.**

   A zero dollar amount means you won't have to pay a premium under that plan. A dollar amount shows what part of the premium you'll pay if that plan's premium is above the regional average. Click the name of any plan to see its details — in particular, whether it covers all of your drugs.

Using an online comparison tool if you're receiving partial Extra Help

If you receive partial Extra Help, you pay 15 percent of your drugs' full price under any plan. And your premium is a percentage of the plan's regular premium — such as 25, 50, or 75 percent — calculated on a sliding scale according to your income. How can you tell what you'll pay for drugs and premiums under any given plan?

Again, you can use Medicare's online plan finder to see instantly how much you'll pay for your drugs. (You may want to look at the step-by-step instructions in Chapter 10 on how to navigate it though.) Go to www.medicare.gov and follow the steps outlined in the preceding section. But when you're asked in Step 2 whether you receive full or partial Extra Help, click "Partial." After you've entered the names of your drugs (plus their dosages and how often you take them — this is important in determining the price), you'll see the list of plans in descending order of out-of-pocket expense. The premium you see given for any plan is what you pay, according to what percentage of the regular premium your partial Extra Help entitles you to. Click a plan's name to bring up its details, and you'll see what you'd pay for each of your drugs under that plan. This price is 15 percent of the plan's full price. In other words, your premium and co-pays for drugs are automatically calculated for you.

Comparing plans if you don't have Internet access

Comparing plans carefully is so important that this would be a good time to ask a relative or friend who's savvy about computers to search the Medicare plan finder for you. Or you can get the same info in the following ways:

- **By phone:** Call the Medicare help line toll-free at 800-633-4227. Tell the customer representative that you're qualified for full or partial Extra Help and give the names of your drugs, plus their dosages and how often you take them. (If you're on full Extra Help, say whether you want only plans that will accept you for a zero premium or whether you're willing to consider paying your share of a premium for more expensive plans. You can also ask for a full list of plans that won't charge you a premium.) Ask for printouts of the most suitable three or four plans to be sent to you.

- **In person:** Counselors at your local State Health Insurance Assistance Program (SHIP) can help you find the plan that suits you best. To find your SHIP phone number, see Appendix B at the end of this book.

Moving forward if no affordable plan covers all of your drugs

Medicare doesn't cover all medications. Some Part D plans cover most drugs that Medicare has approved and even some that Medicare doesn't pay for, as explained in Chapter 4. But these are mostly "enhanced" plans that have higher premiums. In general, the lower-premium plans cover fewer drugs — and some of these plans cover brand-name drugs *only* if they have no lower-cost, generic equivalents. So some people on Extra Help who are seeking less expensive plans — especially those needing a zero premium — may find themselves without access to some of the drugs they need.

This won't necessarily happen to you — it all depends on the drugs you take. But if you do find yourself in this situation, what can you do? Consider these options:

✔ If you're receiving Medicaid, your state may pay for the drugs your Part D plan doesn't cover, or even those that Medicare doesn't cover. To find out, and to get help applying, call your State Heath Insurance Assistance Program (SHIP). (See Appendix B for contact numbers.)

✔ If you're in a State Pharmacy Assistance Program (SPAP), it may pay for drugs your Part D plan doesn't cover. Contact the program to find out. (I cover these programs in more detail later in this chapter.)

✔ Ask your doctor whether switching to a similar drug (or drugs) that your plan *does* cover would be just as effective for you. This may lower your co-pays as well as give you coverage, as explained in Chapter 16.

✔ You have the right to ask the plan to cover a particular drug — by requesting an exception to the plan's rules — if your doctor considers it necessary for your medical condition, as described in Chapter 4.

✔ You can choose to pay an extra share of the premium of an "enhanced" Part D plan that does cover all of your drugs.

✔ You can switch to another plan that does cover all of your drugs. In Extra Help, you have the right to switch plans at any time of the year, as explained in the next section.

Joining and switching plans

Joining a plan is easy. After you've picked the plan of your choice, you can sign up by calling the Medicare help line at 800-633-4227 (877-486-2048 for TDD users) or by visiting www.medicare.gov, as described in Chapter 12.

But there are some things to keep in mind about switching plans. Unlike most folks in the regular Part D program, you won't be limited to enrollment periods or locked into a Medicare drug plan for a whole year. Extra Help gives you the flexibility to join or switch to another plan at any time of the year. Table 5-2 shows when you can switch from one Part D plan to another, and when your coverage begins in different circumstances.

Table 5-2	Switching Part D Plans in Extra Help	
Your Situation	*When You Can Switch from One Part D Plan to Another*	*When Your New Coverage Begins*
You become eligible for Extra Help (or become eligible again)	As soon as you hear you're eligible	Usually backdated to the time you applied or qualified automatically
You receive Extra Help	Once a month, any time in the year	First day of the month after you sign up for a new plan

Your Situation	When You Can Switch from One Part D Plan to Another	When Your New Coverage Begins
You lose eligibility for Extra Help at the end of the year	Once, up to the end of March the following year	First day of the month after you sign up for a new plan
You lose eligibility for Extra Help during the year	Within two months after you hear you'll lose Extra Help	First day of the month after you sign up for a new plan

You need to compare plans carefully to find one that suits you to begin with so that you won't want to change, unless it becomes necessary. Why? Because it's possible that switching (and especially switching often) could cause any of these problems:

✔ It may take time for your new plan to be entered in Medicare's computerized record system, which could cause delays in getting your meds at the pharmacy. (But see Chapter 14 for ways to avoid delays.)

✔ If you've requested and received from your present plan an exception that allows you to use a drug not on its formulary — or a prior authorization before the plan agreed to cover a drug — you may have to go through the same process again in the new plan.

✔ If you're paying any premiums at all, and these are being taken out of your Social Security check, you may find yourself paying two premiums for a while — for both the old plan and the new one. Why? Because communication between Medicare (which knows you've changed plans) and the Social Security Administration (which cuts your checks) doesn't always work as rapidly as it should. If this situation happens to you, call Medicare at 800-633-4227 immediately to complain.

An option to consider: Participating in a State Pharmacy Assistance Program

About 30 states have State Pharmacy Assistance Programs (SPAPs) in 2008, though over time new ones are introduced and others disappear. All help people whose incomes are limited (but too high to qualify for Medicaid) pay for prescription drugs. Some SPAPs have income limits above Part D's Extra Help maximums and/or no asset tests.

Benefits vary a great deal among these programs. Some — including the long-established and excellent programs in New York (EPIC) and Pennsylvania (PACE and PACENET) — provide comprehensive services that wrap around Extra Help and offer additional benefits, as well as assisting many Part D enrollees who don't qualify for Extra Help. Other SPAPs focus on drug assistance for patients with a particular medical condition (such as HIV-AIDS or cancer) or offer discount cards to use at pharmacies.

For details on SPAPs, go to www.medicarerights.org/searchframeset.htm or www.medicare.gov/spap.asp. You also can call 800-633-4227 and ask for a brochure to be mailed to you, or you can call your State Health Insurance Assistance Program (SHIP) for this information. (See SHIP phone numbers in Appendix B.)

Determining Whether You'll Qualify for Extra Help All Year and Next Year

I'm going to assume that you didn't just win the lottery or suddenly inherit great riches from some distant relative you've never heard of. So you're hoping you'll continue to get Extra Help throughout this year and next year too. The following sections explain the circumstances that can cause you to lose Extra Help (or get a lesser benefit) and how you'll know where you stand for next year.

How you could lose Extra Help

In most cases, you'll still receive Extra Help until the end of the year — once qualified, you're likely to receive the benefit until midnight December 31 of the same year, regardless of whether your financial circumstances changed during the previous 12 months. But there are some exceptions. If any of the following marital events happen during the year, you're expected to report them immediately so your eligibility for Extra Help can be reviewed:

- ✔ Your spouse dies.
- ✔ You and the spouse you've been living with start living apart, divorce, or have your marriage annulled.
- ✔ You and your spouse start living together again after being apart.
- ✔ You get married.

These events wouldn't necessarily result in losing Extra Help during the year. In fact, they could mean that you qualify for *more* Extra Help than you received before, if your income reduces. Any benefit changes — whether a decrease, increase, or loss of Extra Help — take place the month after you report your new circumstances.

Continuing to get Extra Help *next* year, starting January 1, depends on whether you've become financially better off this year. You can lose Extra Help (or receive less benefit) next year if

✔ Your income rises above the limits for Extra Help

✔ The value of your savings and other countable resources rises above the asset limits for Extra Help

✔ You cease to qualify for one of the programs that makes you *automatically* eligible for Extra Help — Medicaid, SSI, having your Medicare premium paid by your state, or being in a state Medicaid spend-down program

Finding out where you stand

What will happen next year, and how you'll find out, depends on how you qualified for Extra Help in the first place, as follows:

✔ **If you qualified for Extra Help automatically:** If nothing has changed — that is, if you continue to receive Medicaid or SSI benefits, or are still having your Medicare Part B premiums paid by your state — you don't need to do anything. You'll continue to receive Extra Help. If you no longer get help from any of these programs, Medicare will send you a notice (headed "Loss of Extra Help") saying that you no longer *automatically* qualify for Extra Help next year but that you can still *apply* for it. An Extra Help application should be enclosed with this notice.

✔ **If you qualified for Extra Help through a Medicaid medical spend-down program:** As long as you continue to qualify for Medicaid benefits, you'll still receive Extra Help. So if your medical expenses this year — for example, being in the hospital, going to the doctor, having lab tests, and so on — have been high enough to keep you on Medicaid at the end of the year, you'll still get Extra Help next year. But if those medical expenses are no longer high enough to qualify you for Medicaid, then you'll probably get a letter from Medicare saying you'll no longer receive Extra Help starting January 1. However, even if you lose your Medicaid spend-down, you may still receive Extra Help automatically next year, depending on the timing of when you met your spend-down this year. If your name is in the system in July, when Medicare compiles its list of people automatically eligible for Extra Help next year, you'll continue to receive Extra Help for all of next year.

✔ **If you qualified for Extra Help by applying:** In August or September, you may receive a letter and a form from Social Security asking whether your financial circumstances have changed. Not everybody receives this letter (which is headed "Review of Your Eligibility for Extra Help"), but if you do, you must fill out the form and return it to Social Security within 30 days. *If you don't return it, your Extra Help will end on December 31.* Social Security reviews your information and will notify you, saying whether you'll still qualify for Extra Help next year and, if so, whether your benefits will change. For example, if your income has gone down, you may get lower co-pays next year — or, if it has risen above a certain level, you may get "partial" instead of "full" Extra Help. Any changes will begin on January 1.

Taking Action if You're Denied or Lose Your Eligibility for Extra Help

Being told "No — you don't qualify" is a bummer. And it's even more of a blow to lose Extra Help at the end of the year after you've already been receiving it. But in either event, you may still want to persist in getting Extra Help or exploring other ways to ease your expenses. The following sections explain some options.

Appealing a "no" decision

You can always appeal Social Security's decision if you don't agree with it. Here's what to do, depending on whether you've been denied Extra Help or been told you'll no longer be eligible next year.

If you're denied Extra Help

You must appeal within 60 days of receiving a decision. (This deadline may be extended if you have good reason to miss it, such as being too sick to deal with it on time.) You can appeal in one of two ways:

- ✔ **Request a telephone hearing.** Call your local Social Security office or the SSA national help line (800-772-1213); or print an appeal request form from its Web site (www.ssa.gov), fill it out, and mail it in. You'll receive a letter confirming the date of your hearing and the number to call. (You can ask for a conference call if you want someone who's helping you to be on the phone at the same time.) The letter also explains how to send in documents showing evidence that supports your case.

- ✔ **Request a "case review."** This means having a Social Security agent review your application and any additional information or evidence you've sent in, but without being able to present your case in person.

After Social Security has reviewed your appeal, you'll receive a letter notifying you of the decision. If you win, you'll receive Extra Help backdated to the first day of the month in which you originally applied for the benefit. If you lose, but still disagree with the decision, you can file a further appeal in a federal district court within 60 days of receiving the decision.

If you're told that you'll lose eligibility

Mistakes are often made in vast bureaucracies. So if you think you've lost eligibility by error or an unfair judgment, don't hesitate to speak out. For example, if you've been told that you've lost your automatic right to Extra Help next year when you know you're still enrolled in one of the programs that give you that right (Medicaid, SSI, having your Medicare premiums paid by your state, or being in a Medicaid spend-down program), call Medicare at 800-633-4227 immediately. If you got Extra Help by applying and are now told — wrongly, in your view — that your income or assets are too high to continue receiving the benefit next year, you can appeal to Social Security by the procedures explained in the previous section. The notification letter you receive from Social Security should also explain the process.

In general, if you received Extra Help *automatically,* you should contact Medicare to resolve problems. If you *applied* for Extra Help, you should contact Social Security.

Getting Extra Help another way

Even if you're denied Extra Help or lose eligibility, you may still be able to get benefits in another way. Take a look at your options.

- ✔ **If you lose your *automatic* right to Extra Help:** You may still qualify by applying for it. The income and asset limits for Extra Help are higher than the qualification limits for Medicaid or SSI. You should apply as soon as possible after being notified that you won't qualify automatically next year, following the procedures explained in the earlier section "Applying for Extra Help."

- ✔ **If you applied for Extra Help but are denied or lose eligibility:** One of the ways to qualify for Extra Help automatically is by having your Medicare Part B premiums paid by your state under one of the Medicare savings programs. The income and asset limits for eligibility vary state by state. But some may be a little higher than the limits for Extra Help, and some states don't require an asset test at all. So if you're denied Extra Help (or lose eligibility) because your income or assets are a bit over the top, you might consider applying for this assistance. There's no guarantee that you'll get it, because enrollment for these programs is often limited to the funds a state has available. But it may be worth trying — and if you get this state assistance, you'll get full Extra Help automatically. Contact your State Health Insurance Assistance Program (SHIP) for information and help in applying.

- ✔ **If you lose Extra Help but qualify again in the future:** It may happen that you lose Extra Help on January 1, but become eligible again later in the year or in a future year. That's possible if your income or assets once again dip below the limits, or if the new limits (which Social Security announces in February or March of each year) make you eligible again. As soon as this situation happens, you can again apply for Extra Help. Or, if you're in a Medicaid medical spend-down program and lose both your Medicaid and Extra Help benefits on January 1, you may qualify for both programs again later in the year as soon as your expenses once again rise to the required level.

Seeking other help to pay for drugs

If none of the options in the preceding section work out, you may be able to get other kinds of help to pay for your medications.

- **A State Pharmacy Assistance Program (SPAP):** If your state has an SPAP, contacting it to find out whether you qualify is well worth it. These programs vary, but some of them give additional help to people of limited means who are enrolled in the Medicare Part D program — sometimes with income limits that are much higher than those required in Extra Help and with no asset tests. (For more details, see "An option to consider: Participating in a State Pharmacy Assistance Program" earlier in this chapter.)

- **Private and local pharmacy assistance programs:** Some companies that manufacture drugs, some national organizations for patients with certain medical conditions, some charities, and some local assistance groups offer help paying for drugs. For details on these, as well as other ways of reducing prescription costs, check out Chapter 16.

- **Falling back on the regular Part D program:** The costs are higher and the benefits aren't nearly as generous as under Extra Help, but you'll still have insurance and pay less for your drugs than being outside of Part D.

Looking for help to pay other expenses

If you can't obtain help paying for drugs, consider other federal, state, and local or private programs that might lower your other daily living expenses. Many people with low incomes are entitled to help in paying for food, housing, utility bills, and taxes, and they often don't even realize they're eligible.

The best and quickest way to figure out whether you qualify for any of these programs is to go to www.benefitscheckup.org. You don't have to give your name. Just enter your zip code and answer questions about your income and circumstances. Details of all programs that you may be eligible for, and how to contact them, appear on the screen. These may include the Medicare savings programs and State Pharmacy Assistance Programs mentioned earlier in this chapter, among many more. If you don't have computer access, you can get similar details from your State Health Insurance Assistance Program (SHIP; for contact info, see Appendix B).

Part II
Deciding Whether to Sign Up for Part D

The 5th Wave   By Rich Tennant

"You can stay with your current employer's health care plan, opt for Medicare Part D, or randomly pick 20 generic drugs from our Rotating Cage of Prescription Drug Coverage Plan."

In this part . . .

1 make it easier for you to make a critical decision — should you sign up for Medicare prescription drug coverage?

For many of you, the question is whether you even need to consider Part D. That'll be the case if you already have drug coverage from elsewhere, for example, from a current or former employer or union; from a federal program for veterans, the military, or Native Americans; or from state assistance programs. In these situations, you may not need Part D — but you always need to check to be sure. I show you how to do that, as well as suggest important factors to consider when deciding whether to switch to Part D or stay with the coverage you already have — and, in certain circumstances, how you can use Part D with your current coverage.

If you have no other coverage, you may be wondering whether you need Part D if you don't take any prescription drugs (or only the occasional one) right now. It's a reasonable question. I help you arrive at your own answer by inviting you to consider all the angles.

And finally, I explain what the Part D late penalty means and how it may be a weighty factor in deciding whether — and when — to sign up for Medicare drug coverage.

Chapter 6

Taking Other Drug Coverage and Sources into Account

*I*f you're one of the millions of Americans who already have insurance for prescription drugs, it's of utmost concern to know what will happen when you become eligible for Medicare. Will you lose your current drug coverage? Can you keep it? And if so, do you need to give Part D a second thought? This can be a head-scratching time, and maybe even a cause for real anxiety.

But don't reach for the Valium yet (regardless of whether your prescription plan covers it). In this chapter, I explain the importance of finding out where your current coverage stands in relation to Part D — a step that's essential in figuring out what to do next. Maybe you won't have to do anything and can forget about Part D for now — but you can't assume this without first finding out the facts of your own situation and how Part D rules apply to it. If you need to decide whether to stay with your present coverage or switch to Part D, I suggest some pros and cons to think about. I also explain the different kinds of drug coverage that can be used at the same time as Part D and how they fit together.

But first, you need to understand what counts as "other prescription drug coverage." I've heard people talk about "my coverage" or "my plan" when what they mean is some method of obtaining low-cost drugs that isn't actually coverage at all. *Coverage* equals *insurance* — in other words, a system that guarantees you protection from some of the costs of prescription drugs in the future as well as now. For quick reference, look at Table 6-1. It shows which methods of obtaining drugs count as coverage and which don't. I highlight those that are *not* coverage, and how they compare with Part D, in the last section of this chapter.

Table 6-1	Prescription Drug Coverage — What It Is and Isn't
These Count as Drug Coverage	*These Do Not Count as Drug Coverage*
Benefits from a current employer or union (including COBRA temporary insurance)	Low-cost drugs from Canada, Mexico, and other foreign countries
Retiree benefits from an employer or union	Drugs from pharmaceutical manufacturers
Veterans' or military retirees' benefits	Low-cost drugs from medical clinics
Medicaid benefits	Help from patient programs or charities
State Pharmacy Assistance Program (SPAP) benefits	AIDS drug assistance programs
Federal benefits for Native Americans	State drug discount programs
Medigap supplementary insurance	Pharmacy discount programs
Individual health insurance policies	Free samples from doctors

Finding Out Whether Your Current Drug Coverage Is Creditable

Creditable is another of those Part D–speak words that you've probably never come across before. *Creditable* — not to be confused with *credible* (meaning believable) — means something that can be credited or counted. Under Medicare rules, your current drug coverage is creditable if it counts as being at least as good as Part D coverage. This rule really matters. If the coverage you have now *is* creditable, you probably don't need Part D. If it's *not* creditable, you'll need to make some careful decisions.

Bear with me for a moment while I explain more accurately what creditable coverage actually means. The common definition I just used — "at least as good as Part D" — is a convenient shorthand, but it's also misleading. For example, I've heard people wonder why their employer drug coverage is regarded as "better than Medicare's" when it's actually costing them more — "If it's better, shouldn't I be paying less?" Or, conversely, wondering why their coverage isn't creditable when it seems a whole lot better than Part D — "Hey, mine has no doughnut hole!" The answer is that creditability has nothing to do with whether you, as an individual, get a better deal under your own plan than you would under Part D. Instead, it's a matter of accountancy. Your plan is considered creditable if whoever sponsors it pays at least as much money overall for everybody in the plan as Medicare would.

So in the following sections, I consider each kind of drug coverage listed in the first column of Table 6-1, how it fits in with Part D, and how to find out whether it's creditable. What you need to do as a result of this information is detailed in the later section "Deciding Whether to Stay with the Coverage You Have or Switch to Part D."

Drug coverage from a current or former (nonfederal) employer

I'm assuming in this section that you're an employee or retiree who has drug coverage based on employment in a private company, nonprofit organization, or state or local government. If you're a federal employee or retiree, whether military or civilian, you can go to the later section "Drug coverage for federal employees and retirees."

What happens to your drug coverage when you retire?

Ever since Part D began in 2006, employers or unions have had a choice of several different drug coverage options for their retirees.

- ✔ The great majority of employers have continued their own coverage, not least because, under Medicare law, the federal government pays them large subsidies to do so.

- ✔ Some employers have modified their coverage so it fits in with Part D. (See the later section "Having It Both Ways: Using Part D as Well as Your Own Drug Insurance" for more details.)

- ✔ Relatively few employers have dumped drug coverage entirely, obliging their retirees to fall back on Part D — though this may occur more in the future.

So what may happen when you retire? Possible options include

- ✔ Your current coverage remains available to you.

- ✔ Your current coverage ends, but your employer or union agrees to *wrap around* Medicare drug coverage by paying some or all of your out-of-pocket expenses in any Part D plan that you choose.

- ✔ You're required to join a specific Part D plan as a condition for continuing to receive healthcare benefits from your employer or union. These benefits may or may not cover some or all of your out-of-pocket expenses in Part D.

- ✔ Your current coverage ends, but your employer or union contributes a lump sum annually toward your Part D expenses. This amount is subject to tax.

- ✔ Your current coverage ends, and your employer or union makes no contribution to your out-of-pocket expenses in Part D.

As you approach Medicare age, the administrator of your health plan or your employer's human resources department should let you know your options for health and drug coverage in retirement.

What happens if you retire before age 65?

Remember that you can't join Medicare before turning 65 (unless you qualify at an earlier age because of disability), as explained in Chapter 1. So if you retire before you reach 65, you need to find out what health and drug coverage (if any) your employer or union will make available to you in the years or months that remain until you can join Medicare and enroll in a Part D plan.

If you won't be covered at all during this period, you may qualify for the *COBRA program,* which allows people to buy between 18 and 36 months of continuing coverage after they've left or lost jobs that provide health insurance. To find out more about COBRA, go to the U.S. Department of Labor's Web site at www.dol.gov or call the agency in your state that deals with labor and employment.

What happens if you work beyond age 65?

In many cases, employees with health and drug coverage who remain employed after they reach retirement age continue to receive their benefits until they retire, regardless of age. However, some employers require employees to switch to Medicare (and to Part D for drug coverage) as soon as they become eligible at age 65, even though they're still working. (If you work for a company or organization with 20 or fewer employees, you'll probably be required to enroll in Medicare when you reach 65, as explained in Chapter 1.) Sometimes employees' spouses who are younger than 65 continue to receive the plan's coverage until they, too, reach Medicare age. Your employer will notify you of any required changes before you turn 65.

How do you find out whether your drug coverage is creditable?

If you continue to receive full employer- or union-sponsored drug coverage in retirement or while working after age 65, you need to find out whether your coverage is creditable. You also need to know this information if you turn 65 when you're receiving COBRA temporary health insurance after losing or leaving a job. COBRA counts as employment-based coverage, so it comes under the same Part D rules.

The Medicare law requires your employer or union (or COBRA insurer) to inform you in writing whether your current drug coverage is creditable and, if so, whether it continues to be creditable from year to year. Your plan may provide this info in a letter, in its regular annual brochure, or in its Evidence of Coverage document that gives details of your coverage for the following year.

✔ If the notice says your coverage is creditable (or "at least as good as Medicare Part D coverage," which is intended to convey the same thing), you don't need to join Part D at this time.

✔ If the notice says your coverage is *not* creditable, it may or may not describe alternative options for you, but either way, you need to think carefully about what you do next. I cover points for you to consider in the later section "Deciding Whether to Stay with the Coverage You Have or Switch to Part D."

This notice about creditability is hugely important. If you don't receive it, call the plan administrators or your benefits department and insist that they provide this info in writing, as the law requires. (Most retiree plans can be relied on to send such notices, but employers sometimes forget to send them to employees who are still working.) If you're told your drug coverage is creditable, make sure you keep the written confirmation in a safe place — together with any follow-up mailings in subsequent years saying that your coverage continues to be creditable. Hanging on to these notices is a sensible precaution, because if you lose your creditable coverage, you may need to prove that you had it in order to join Part D without incurring a late penalty. (I explain the late penalty and its implications in Chapter 8.)

Drug coverage for federal employees and retirees

If you qualify for medical coverage through current or former employment with the federal government, you receive prescription drug coverage in one of two ways:

✔ **Federal Employees Health Benefits Program (FEHBP):** Drug coverage under this program for civilian federal workers, retirees, and their dependents is considered creditable. (For information or help on FEHBP benefits, go to www.opm.gov [or to www.opm.gov/retire if you're retired] or call toll-free 888-767-6738.)

✔ **TriCare for Life (TFL):** This Department of Defense healthcare program is for active duty and retired members of the military who are enrolled in Medicare, and for their dependents. Drug coverage under this program is considered creditable. (For information or help on TFL benefits, go to www.tricare.mil or call toll-free 800-538-9552.)

With drug benefits from either of these programs, you do *not* need to join a Medicare Part D plan. And if you lose this coverage, you can join a Part D plan without penalty as long as you begin Medicare coverage within 63 days of losing FEHBP or TFL benefits, as explained in Chapter 8.

You can be in either of these programs and have Part D at the same time (without losing FEHBP or TFL benefits) if there's any reason to do so. One reason may be if your income is low and you qualify for Extra Help under Part D. For more details on using both sets of drug coverage, see the later section "Having It Both Ways: Using Part D as Well as Your Own Drug Insurance."

Veterans drug benefits

If you're a veteran and enrolled in the healthcare system run by the U.S. Department of Veterans Affairs (VA), your prescription drug coverage is creditable. You do *not* need to join a Part D plan. This is also true of the CHAMPVA (Civilian Health and Medical Program of the Department of Veterans Affairs) program, which is available to a spouse, widow or widower, or child of certain veterans who were killed or disabled in the line of duty. In either program, if you lose this coverage, you won't pay a late penalty on joining Part D as long as your Medicare coverage starts within 63 days of losing VA coverage.

However, Medicare rules allow you to be enrolled in the VA system (including CHAMPVA) and in Part D at the same time. This can be an advantage, as I explain later in this chapter.

For more information or help on VA health and pharmacy benefits, go to www. va.gov/healtheligibility, visit a local VA medical facility, or call the VA Health Benefits Service Center toll-free at 877-222-8387. For CHAMPVA information, go to www.va.gov/hac or call 800-733-8387.

Medicaid drug coverage

If you've been getting drugs from your state under Medicaid (also known by other names in some states, such as MediCal in California, MassHealth in Massachusetts, and TennCare in Tennessee), you can't continue to do so after you become eligible for Medicare. Medicaid coverage is certainly creditable. But under the law, as soon as you turn 65 (or qualify for Medicare at an earlier age through disability), you must receive your drugs from Medicare Part D, not Medicaid.

You'll also automatically qualify for very low-cost coverage under Part D's Extra Help program. If some of the drugs you need aren't covered under your Part D plan, you may still be able to get them from Medicaid. Both of these scenarios are explained in detail in Chapter 5.

Drug coverage from a State Pharmacy Assistance Program

Many states have programs to help people pay for prescription drugs. But only some State Pharmacy Assistance Programs (SPAPs) offer drug coverage comprehensive enough to be regarded as *qualified* (which is different from creditable) under Part D rules. SPAPs become qualified if they meet Medicare requirements, the most important one being that they must coordinate with Part D by wrapping around it any extra benefits that they provide. (In 2008, 23 states have qualified SPAPs, according to Medicare: Colorado, Connecticut, Delaware, Florida, Illinois, Indiana, Maine, Maryland, Massachusetts, Missouri, Montana, Nevada, New Jersey, New York, North Carolina, Pennsylvania, Rhode Island, South Carolina, Texas, Vermont, Virginia, Washington, and Wisconsin, plus the U.S. Virgin Islands.)

Coverage from a qualified SPAP is definitely creditable. But this doesn't mean you can choose to get coverage from an SPAP instead of Part D. If you're already in a qualified SPAP, you'll be expected to join Part D — and, most likely, to apply for Extra Help — as soon as you become eligible for Medicare.

That's hardly a problem. Being enrolled in a qualified SPAP may greatly improve your Part D coverage in some or all of the following ways, depending on the specific program:

- ✔ **Lowering your out-of-pocket costs:** Some SPAPs pay some or all of Part D premiums, deductibles, and/or co-pays.

- ✔ **Offering low-cost coverage even if you don't qualify for Part D's Extra Help program:** SPAPs' income limits are generally higher than those required for Extra Help — and usually there are no asset tests — so you have a greater chance of qualifying, as explained in Chapter 5.

- ✔ **Providing coverage in the doughnut hole even if you don't qualify for Extra Help:** Any payments an SPAP makes for your drugs in the coverage gap count toward your Part D out-of-pocket limit, as explained in Chapter 15.

- ✔ **Covering needed drugs that aren't covered in your Part D plan:** Some SPAPs also cover drugs that Medicare excludes, such as barbituates and benzodiazepines, as explained in Chapter 4.

- ✔ **Coordinating coverage with Part D as seamlessly as possible:** I explain the ins and outs of this later in this chapter.

If you become eligible for Medicare while you're in an SPAP, the program will inform you of what you need to do about Part D, help you enroll in a plan, and, if appropriate, help you apply for Extra Help.

Drug coverage for Native Americans

If you're an American Indian or an Alaskan Native Elder who gets prescription drugs from the Indian Health Service, a Tribal Health Organization, or the Urban Indian Health program, your drug coverage is creditable. You'll be able to join a Medicare Part D plan down the road without paying a penalty. (But be sure to get a letter from your Indian healthcare provider saying that you have creditable coverage.)

Right now you may be getting your drugs free or at low cost from an Indian health pharmacy if you're enrolled in one of these programs, and this won't necessarily change when you become eligible for Medicare. You aren't required to join a Part D plan. However, it would be a big help to your community if you do. That's because the drug plan pays part of the cost of your prescriptions — and pays almost all of the costs, in fact, if you qualify for Part D's Extra Help program. This stretches the precious federal dollars that support your local clinic, allowing it to provide needed care for more people in your community.

As you approach age 65, visit your clinic or contact the benefits coordinator of your health program to talk over what it would mean for you to join a Medicare Part D plan and, if your income is limited, to apply for Extra Help.

Drug coverage from Medigap insurance

Medicare beneficiaries can buy private insurance policies to cover some out-of-pocket expenses of Medicare Part A and Part B and to fill in some gaps in Medicare coverage. These policies, known as Medicare supplementary insurance or Medigap, are explained in Chapter 1. Until Part D began on January 1, 2006, some of the policies included coverage for prescription drugs. But the Medicare law prohibited new policies with drug coverage from being sold after that date; it also barred people from having this kind of policy and being enrolled in a Part D plan at the same time. So if you still have a Medigap policy with drug coverage, it means you bought it before 2006 and haven't yet joined Part D.

Most Medigap policies aren't considered creditable compared with Part D. The standardized policies that include drug coverage — designated H, I, and J — are definitely not creditable. But some plans in Massachusetts, Minnesota, and Wisconsin (and some older policies dating from the 1980s and earlier in other states) may be creditable. You'll have received a notice from your insurer saying whether yours is creditable. If it isn't, you have the right to keep your policy — but you'd have to pay a late penalty (as explained in Chapter 8) if and when you decide to join a Part D plan for your drug coverage. I cover the implications of this in the later section "Understanding the Medigap dilemma."

Drug coverage from individual insurance

People who are self-employed or who receive no group health coverage from their employers sometimes purchase individual health insurance policies. Such policies are the most expensive kind of health coverage on the market, so even people who can afford them are often relieved to give them up when they become eligible for Medicare.

If your coverage includes prescription drugs and you want to continue it after joining Medicare, you need to contact your insurer to find out whether it's creditable under Part D rules. If it is creditable, you don't need to join Part D. If it's not creditable, joining a Medicare drug plan now would allow you to avoid a late penalty if you were to join one later on, as explained in Chapter 8. You can have individual insurance with drug coverage and be enrolled in Part D at the same time, as described later in this chapter.

Deciding Whether to Stay with the Coverage You Have or Switch to Part D

Stay or switch? Strangely enough, this decision doesn't only affect people whose coverage isn't creditable compared with Part D. As the costs of health insurance in general, and prescription drugs in particular, continue to climb, many retirees who are on fixed incomes but have employer or other coverage are beginning to find their health insurance less and less affordable. In some cases, Part D may offer a less expensive option. (See the nearby sidebar "What were they thinking . . . when they 'allowed' employers to dump drug coverage?" for more information.) But if you're in either of these groups, you need to be aware of all the consequences before deciding which way to go. Look before you leap — and look before you stay.

In the following sections — assuming that you already know whether your current drug coverage is creditable — I outline what you need to consider when deciding what to do next. For quick reference, Table 6-2 shows at a glance whether different types of drug coverage are creditable and what action you may need to take, if any.

Table 6-2   **What You Need to Do about Part D, Depending on Your Current Prescription Drug Coverage**

Type of Drug Coverage	Creditable or Not?	Action Required
Employer or union benefits for current employees or retirees	Depends on plan	1) None, if plan coverage is creditable. 2) If not creditable, must decide whether to keep it or switch to Part D, unless switching would affect medical benefits. 3) If required for people of Medicare age, must join Part D as condition of continuing to receive medical benefits.
COBRA temporary insurance	Depends on plan	None, if plan coverage is creditable, until COBRA insurance ends. If not creditable, must decide whether to add Part D.
Federal employees or retirees benefits (FEHBP)	Creditable	None. (Unless qualifying for Extra Help would provide greater benefits under Part D.)
Military active duty or retiree benefits (TFL)	Creditable	None. (Unless qualifying for Extra Help would provide greater benefits under Part D.)
Veterans health program drug benefits (VA or CHAMPVA)	Creditable	None. But can choose to have VA and Part D coverage at same time and use one to get drugs not covered (or costing more) in the other.
Medicaid	Not applicable	Must get drugs from a Part D plan after becoming eligible for Medicare.

Type of Drug Coverage	Creditable or Not?	Action Required
Federal health programs for Native Americans	Creditable	None. But joining a Part D plan and applying for Extra Help when appropriate would benefit funding for community healthcare.
State Pharmacy Assistance Program benefits (SPAP)	Creditable when "qualified" under Medicare rules	In most cases, must join a Part D plan when eligible for Medicare and, if appropriate, apply for Extra Help.
Medigap supplemental insurance that includes drug coverage	Not creditable in most cases	If not creditable, must choose whether to keep Medigap drug coverage or switch to Part D. Can't have both at same time.
Individual health insurance policy	Depends on plan	None, if plan coverage is creditable. If not, must decide whether to add Part D. Can choose to have both existing plan and Part D coverage.

What were they thinking . . . when they "allowed" employers to dump drug coverage?

Employers can generally do what they want about health and drug coverage, unless they're bound by a cast-iron union contract. Most employee health insurance comes with a caveat — the employer reserves the right to change the terms from year to year or end coverage completely. And as the cost of healthcare has risen inexorably, employers have been faced with three choices — eat the costs themselves, pass on more costs to employees and retirees, or terminate benefits. The result is that employer health insurance and retiree benefits, traditionally the cornerstone of the American health system, are steadily shrinking.

So what has been Part D's impact? Experts on health benefits are unanimous in saying that without it the situation would be far worse for retirees. That's because Congress didn't "allow" employers to dump drug coverage. Far from it. Congress actually gave a big incentive to employers to continue offering creditable retiree drug coverage after Part D went into effect — in the form of tax-free subsidies

(continued)

(continued)

amounting to an average of 28 percent of their retirees' drug costs. The result was that 82 percent of large employers took the subsidy and continued drug benefits.

After Part D began in 2006, I invited readers of the *AARP Bulletin* to recount what had happened that year to their own retiree drug coverage. Hundreds sent in their stories. At one end of the spectrum was a fortunate retiree in California who said he was still getting the same generous coverage he'd been promised on retirement in 1990 — zero premiums, deductibles, and co-pays. At the other end were people who'd lost drug coverage they'd had for years and understandably blamed Part D: "We were thrown to the wolves," said one. Between these two extremes were many experiences that threw light on some developments that retirees hadn't expected.

Although some reported their premiums had gone down, many others said they were paying more — and sometimes the premium hike had been so great that some suspected a deliberate attempt to force them out of the plan and into Part D. Naturally, they wondered why their insurance was costing more when their companies were now getting fat federal subsidies. One reason, benefits experts say, is

that the Medicare law didn't require the subsidy to be used to reduce retirees' share of the costs — or even specify how it should be used at all. Another reason is that in recent years many employers and unions have put caps on healthcare spending, so when it passes a certain point, the extra costs automatically trigger a rise in premiums for everybody in the plan.

Some of these retirees, even with creditable coverage, chose to drop their employer's plan and join a Medicare drug plan; and some reported saving enough money on premiums that they hoped would exceed any expenses they'd encounter in the doughnut hole, which hadn't existed in their company plans. Others found that they couldn't give up their drug coverage without also terminating their health coverage, not only for themselves but for spouses under age 65. And some found themselves in a single company-designated Part D plan that they were obliged to join as a condition for continuing to receive health insurance. "It's been a learning experience," one man said with feeling. Even so — at a time when benefits are shrinking and out-of-pocket costs are rising — Part D now provides a safety net for retirees that wasn't there before.

Considering the other factor: Medical benefits

If you're thinking about switching to Part D at all, your number-one priority is to find out *what will happen to your medical benefits* if you do so. Most employer or union health insurance combines medical and drug coverage into one package — for you alone, or comprehensively for you, your spouse, and any dependent children — with a single premium. Of course, there are many variations. But whatever kind of deal you have, these are the questions you should get answers to, depending on your circumstances, as soon as possible:

✔ If I drop just my drug coverage, will I also lose my (and my family's) medical benefits?

✔ If I drop my drug coverage, will my spouse (and/or dependent children) lose medical and/or drug benefits if he or she is under age 65?

✔ If I drop my drug and/or medical coverage, will I be able to get it back again if I want to return to my present plan?

✔ If I enroll in a Part D plan because my drug coverage isn't creditable, will I (and my family) automatically lose my/our medical benefits?

✔ If I'm expected to enroll in a specific Part D plan as a condition of continuing to receive drug coverage, will I lose my (and my family's) medical benefits if I choose to enroll in a different Part D plan?

These are critical questions. Chances are that your plan's benefits manager will send you a notice before you turn 65 and each year afterwards informing you of your options for the next year under the plan's rules. But if you haven't received such a notice, or remain unsure of the rules, contact the plan immediately to find out where you stand.

If this all sounds too gloomy, let me say that some employer and union plans are more flexible than these questions may suggest. Some do allow enrollees to continue receiving medical benefits even if they drop drug coverage. Some plans will continue benefits for a spouse under age 65 who isn't eligible for Medicare, even if the enrollee is no longer covered by the plan. And some plans allow enrollees who have dropped out to return at a later date. But, in general, these dispensations are more likely for Medicare-age people who are still working than for retirees.

If you have federal drug coverage under FEHBP, TFC, or the VA, you can choose to have Part D without risking any of your benefits. But be aware that if you're a retiree with FEHBP or TFC and you cancel it entirely, you can't get it back.

In the following sections, I delve into the details of two typical situations: when your drug coverage isn't creditable but switching to Part D is scary because you'll lose your medical benefits, and when your drug coverage is creditable but difficult to afford.

If your coverage isn't creditable but switching is risky

What if your employer or union drug coverage isn't creditable, but dropping it means losing your medical benefits as well? This is a real Catch-22 situation. Basically, you have three options:

▐ ✔ **Stay with your plan and hope that its drug coverage will continue for as long as you need it.** If drug benefits, or the plan itself, are terminated in future years, you'll face a late penalty upon joining Part D, as explained in Chapter 8.

✔ **Stay with your plan and also enroll in a Part D plan (which means paying an additional premium) to avoid a late penalty in the future if you lose or drop your current coverage.**

Check with your plan to be sure that enrolling in Part D doesn't automatically terminate your current drug and medical coverage. If it does, this isn't really an option.

✔ **Drop out of your plan and switch to Part D for your drug coverage and Medicare for your medical benefits.** Before doing this, look closely at your plan's medical coverage and compare it with your potential costs and benefits under the traditional Medicare program (on its own or with a Medigap supplementary policy) or a Medicare Advantage health plan, as explained in Chapter 9.

If your coverage is creditable but hard to afford

Before throwing out your creditable drug coverage, you'd be wise to carefully compare what you have now with what you'd get under Part D. Maybe your current benefits are difficult to afford because the premiums are much higher than they used to be — probably a lot higher than Part D premiums. But be cautious here and consider these points:

✔ If you're married and your spouse is covered under your plan, you're probably paying a single premium for both of you. In contrast, under Part D you'd each have to pay a separate premium.

✔ Part D has a gap in coverage (the so-called "doughnut hole," which I cover in detail in Chapter 15), and your present coverage almost certainly doesn't. If your costs are high enough to take you into the doughnut hole, this can greatly affect what you pay out of pocket for your drugs over a whole year. So you need to compare your likely *over-all* drug costs under your present plan with those in the Part D plans that are available to you. I explain how to do this in Chapter 10.

And what about your medical benefits? This question isn't as crucial for some people as others. Some retirees say that medical coverage under their union or employer plan isn't worth much anyway. But you still need to compare those benefits with traditional Medicare, with or without a Medigap policy, or a Medicare Advantage health plan, as described in Chapter 9 — especially if, under the rules of your current plan, you can't get it back after you've given it up.

Determining whether Extra Help can help

The Extra Help program provides comprehensive coverage that's less expensive than almost any drug benefits you could get elsewhere. (I say "almost" because a lucky few still pay absolutely nothing for their drug coverage under employer or union retirement plans.) So if your income is low, it's worth finding out whether you qualify for Extra Help, which I cover in detail in Chapter 5.

If you think you may qualify, don't do *anything* about your current coverage until you've applied for Extra Help and received a letter saying that you're eligible — because you don't want to jump out of the plane (or in this case the *plan*) without a parachute. Also, you need to know whether you qualify for full or partial Extra Help. Compared to your current drug coverage, full benefits may give you a better deal, but partial benefits may not.

What if you do qualify? Remember that you can get Extra Help only if you join a Part D plan. So all the questions I raised in the earlier section "Considering the other factor: Medical benefits" about how joining Part D may affect the medical side of your health coverage apply here too. If they do, you should ask your benefits administrator whether any exceptions are made for people who qualify for Extra Help.

But the most important factor in considering Extra Help is whether you'd have to drop your current coverage and, if so, whether you could get it back again if you needed to in the future. Some employer and union plans allow people to return. For example, the federal health plans (FEHBP, TFL, VA, and CHAMPVA) don't require enrollees to drop drug coverage if they join Part D, whether or not they receive Extra Help. Anyone else should check with their current plan, because Extra Help doesn't automatically continue year after year. If your circumstances change — for example, if your income rises above the limits — you could lose it.

Understanding the Medigap dilemma

If you still have Medigap supplementary insurance that includes coverage for prescription drugs, *and* you know that this coverage isn't creditable under Part D rules, you already face a late penalty if you switch to a Medicare drug plan now. (Ouch!) So should you stay with your Medigap policy or cut your losses and switch to Part D? Here are some points to consider:

✔ **The premium for your Medigap policy will probably increase a lot as the years go by.** This is because no new policies that include drug coverage have been sold since the end of 2005 and, by law, can't be sold in the future. Also, the majority of people who had these policies before 2006 switched to Part D then. So over time, fewer and fewer people will be enrolled in your plan. As the enrollment pool dwindles, premiums for those who remain in the plan are likely to increase.

✔ **The longer you postpone signing up for Part D, the more expensive it'll be when you do finally join the program.** The late penalty becomes larger each year that you delay, as explained in Chapter 8.

✔ **Medigap plans with drug coverage are expensive, and premiums may rise as you get older.** If you switch to a Medigap plan *without* drug coverage, your premium would be reduced substantially. You'd save more than you'd have to pay for Part D premiums, which don't vary according to age.

If you decide to switch to a Part D plan, remember that you can normally do so only during open enrollment from November 15 through December 31 each year. So if you miss this window one year, you'd accrue another 12 months of added late penalties before being able to sign up for Part D the next year. However, if you lose your Medigap coverage through no fault of your own — such as the plan ceasing business — you can sign up for a Part D plan at other times of the year.

What about the medical benefits of your Medigap policy? If you drop drug coverage from your current Medigap plan, you can choose to stay in it for your medical benefits on the same guaranteed terms. Alternatively, you can change to a different Medigap plan. Doing so may mean paying a higher premium, especially if you have a pre-existing health condition, though some insurers may voluntarily waive such requirements in these circumstances. (To find out more about the Medigap plans available to you, go to www. medicare.gov and click "Compare Medigap policies in your area.")

Having It Both Ways: Using Part D as Well as Your Own Drug Insurance

Having health insurance that wraps around Part D is useful because it fills in some or all of the gaps in Medicare drug coverage. Under current Medicare law, you can't buy specific wraparound coverage for Part D in the same way that you can buy Medigap insurance to use with Medicare Parts A and B. Getting such coverage depends entirely on the health benefits you already receive.

In the following sections, I explain how different types of insurance fit with Part D. In most cases, you enter a complex and sophisticated system known as *coordination of benefits.* This is intended to streamline the process so Part D enrollees with other drug coverage pay what they should for prescriptions at the pharmacy without having to file separate claims. Medicare's automated system records the details of each person's coverage under different insurers, and pharmacists can access this information instantly by computer. (To see what to do if this system doesn't work as intended, turn to Chapter 14.)

Medicare will send you a questionnaire, soon after you join the program and once a year afterwards, asking what other health and drug insurance you have, if any. You absolutely must fill out this form (legally, you're required to) and return it. Providing this info ensures that all the details of any extra coverage you have are entered into the system so your benefits and required payments can be coordinated properly. (This applies to medical coverage as well as drug benefits.) Medicare encourages plan sponsors (such as employers) to file this information too, but doesn't require it. So filling out the Medicare questionnaire is an important safeguard. It helps ensure that you won't pay more than you need to. If you don't receive this form, or if you lose it, call Medicare at 800-633-4227 to ask for one.

Employer or union coverage

If your employer or union plan no longer provides full drug coverage of its own, it may offer help by paying any (or all) of these expenses:

✔ All or some of your Part D premium

✔ All or some of your Part D deductible

✔ Your Part D co-pays (in total or up to a dollar limit)

✔ All or some of your out-of-pocket costs in the Part D coverage gap

Many employers or unions that provide wraparound coverage coordinate with Medicare. But some may require enrollees to pay out of pocket at the pharmacy and then claim reimbursement. Even if your plan coordinates with Medicare, keeping your pharmacy receipts is a good idea — at least until you know the coordination system is working smoothly, and especially after you've joined a Part D plan for the first time. The Explanation of Benefits statements that you receive from your employer/union plan and your Part D plan should reflect who has paid for what.

Federal drug benefits

Drug coverage from the Federal Employees Health Benefits Program (FEHBP) or from the military's TriCare for Life program (TFL) is much more generous than Part D. However, you and any covered dependents of Medicare age can be in a Part D plan at the same time if it would be an advantage — for example, if you qualify for Extra Help, because neither program offers additional benefits for enrollees with low incomes. If you do join Part D, your coverage will be coordinated with Medicare in the following ways:

✔ **FEHBP:** If you're retired, Medicare is the primary payer. This means that your Part D plan pays for covered costs first; your FEHBP plan pays whatever remaining costs it agrees to pay under its rules. If you (or your covered spouse) are still working, FEHBP is primary.

✔ **TFL:** Medicare is the primary payer, whether you're retired or still on active duty. TFL does *not* pay Part D premiums. But it does pay your out-of-pocket expenses for drugs that are covered under the TFL formulary. These include deductibles, co-pays, and the costs of drugs not covered by your Part D plan. If you should fall into the doughnut hole (as explained in Chapter 15), your TFL coverage becomes primary; you then pay the standard TFL co-pays for your prescriptions.

Veterans drug benefits

VA drug coverage, like the federal drug benefits in the preceding section, is also much more generous than Part D. The VA system covers more drugs than any Part D plan, has no premiums and much lower co-pays, provides coverage all year round (no doughnut hole), places an annual cap on co-pays for some veterans, and charges no co-pays for those with limited incomes who qualify. The only snag is that generally you must go to a VA facility to have a VA doctor write a prescription, and many vets live hundreds of miles from the nearest facility. Also, eligibility rules for getting VA healthcare (including prescription drugs) change from time to time.

The CHAMPVA program is somewhat different. You can fill prescriptions at retail pharmacies for 25 percent of the allowable cost, or get maintenance drugs free through the Meds by Mail program. No additional benefits are available for enrollees with low incomes.

Both programs allow you to enroll in Part D if you want to. Here's how each fits in with Part D:

- **VA:** You can choose whether to have Part D or the VA help pay for your drugs on a prescription-by-prescription basis. There is no coordination of benefits between the VA and Medicare, but all you need to do at the pharmacy is show either your Part D plan card or your VA health benefits card. Of course, you can't use both for the same prescription. The VA doesn't pay Part D plan premiums.

- **CHAMPVA:** Medicare is the primary payer, but CHAMPVA pays up to 75 percent of the cost of your Part D co-pays at retail pharmacies, or 100 percent after you've met an annual $3,000 out-of-pocket limit. You aren't eligible for the no-cost Meds by Mail program. CHAMPVA doesn't pay Part D plan premiums.

Coverage from State Pharmacy Assistance Programs

State Pharmacy Assistance Programs (SPAPs) that are qualified under Medicare rules (as explained earlier in this chapter) are required to coordinate benefits with Medicare. If you're in one of these programs, any extra benefits you receive are wrapped around Part D coverage, and SPAPs generally try to make the process as seamless as possible.

You should be able to get your prescriptions filled without having to bother about whether Part D, Extra Help, the SPAP itself, or, in some cases, Medicaid is actually helping to pay for them. If you have any reason to think you're being charged incorrectly, contact your SPAP for help.

Individual health insurance

Is there is any reason to stay with health insurance you buy yourself instead of switching wholesale to Medicare and Part D? There may be, if you have dependents not yet of Medicare age and if dropping coverage yourself may mean having to apply again for insurance for the rest of the family, maybe on less favorable terms. You need to check the consequences with your insurer.

If you decide to stay with your policy and enroll in a Medicare drug plan, you need to contact your insurer to see how it fits in with Part D — for example, whether your insurance is primary or secondary and whether your policy will cover some or all of your out-of-pocket Part D expenses. If the insurer doesn't coordinate benefits with Medicare, you may have to keep your pharmacy receipts and send them to your insurer for whatever reimbursement is allowed.

Factoring in Drugs from Other Sources

In the absence of insurance for prescription drugs, people turn to a variety of other sources to get them at less than retail cost. Often this happens in that twilight zone where uninsured folks in their late 50s and early 60s begin to develop health problems requiring medications but have not yet reached Medicare age. If you've been in this situation but are now approaching 65, you may be of two minds about what to do next. Perhaps you can't wait to leap into the Medicare prescription drug program and start getting some help with costs. Or you may be among those who are just plain suspicious of Part D, or concerned that it'll cost too much or be too much of a hassle to navigate — so why not stay with the system you've got?

I consider each of these alternative sources in some detail in Chapter 16 and cover how you might use them together with Part D, especially if you fall into the doughnut hole. But here I ponder a different question: Should you continue using them *instead* of joining Part D?

Certainly, doing nothing may seem easier than going to the trouble of choosing a Part D plan. But some other considerations may be more important: cost and certainty, for example. Here are some questions to ask yourself about your current method of obtaining prescription drugs:

- ✔ Will it provide the drugs I need reliably and indefinitely?
- ✔ Will it pay most of the costs if I suddenly need very expensive medications?
- ✔ Will it pay most of the costs if my income is very limited?

Most noninsurance sources aren't reliable in the long term. Low-cost drugs from medical clinics, patient programs, charities, and state drug discount programs may decline through lack of funding. Free samples from doctors depend on which drugs, and for how long, the drug manufacturers offer them. Free or low-cost drugs directly from the manufacturers often come with time limits — and there's no guarantee they'll supply another drug you may need in the future. Pharmacy discounts — even those $4-per-prescription offers from some supermarket pharmacies — cover only a limited selection of drugs. Even drugs from Canada or other countries may be disrupted if the drug manufacturers succeed in blockading the trade, or the source countries try to stop it, or U.S. Customs intercepts supplies to American customers — all of which has happened.

Nor do any of these methods provide catastrophic coverage against very high drug costs, or continuous help for people with low incomes in need of multiple drugs, as Part D does. Not that Part D is perfect — far from it. But on the whole, except for the doughnut hole, it provides the certainty of insurance coverage. Having Part D *and* using one or another of these alternative sources to supplement it if necessary, as explained in Chapter 16, may be a better way of covering all the bases long term.

Chapter 7

Considering Coverage if You Take Few or No Drugs Right Now

....

....

*H*ere you are in the pink of health and lucky enough not to be taking any prescription drugs — or perhaps only an antibiotic now and again. Maybe you've never needed anything beyond the occasional aspirin. And — even though you have no other drug coverage — you're asking yourself why on earth you should pay out good money every month to a Medicare drug plan when you'd be getting zip in return.

No doubt about it, this is a major dilemma for healthy people. Of course, you have every right not to join Part D. Maybe even the threat of a late penalty — the higher rate you'd pay for drug coverage if you delay enrolling in Part D, as explained in Chapter 8 — doesn't cut much ice with you. But I'm guessing that you also know, in your heart of hearts, that this isn't really the point.

The real question is whether you can afford to be without drug coverage when you also lack a crystal ball — or any way of peering into the future to see whether you'll fall prey to some unforeseen disease or injury that requires expensive meds to treat. That's the insurance factor, and although Part D provides less-than-comprehensive coverage (unless you qualify for Extra Help, described in Chapter 5), it does offer protection against cata-strophically high drug expenses that you may face if you're diagnosed with a serious illness. It covers you *if* you need it and *when* you need it.

In this chapter, I assume you're healthy, have no other drug coverage, and aren't inclined to enroll in Part D, or at least not for now. I highlight factors to think about when weighing the current state of your health against future risks. And I also suggest a compromise — how to find a Part D plan that will cost you the least money while still giving you an umbrella for insurance.

Balancing Today's Good Health against Tomorrow's Risks

On the whole, human beings are optimistic by nature, and it's often said that Americans are the most optimistic on earth. We don't expect bad things to happen to our bodies, and we're confident that, if ill health does hit us sometime in the far-off future, medical science will be able to fix it. Well, increasingly, medical research is finding answers — and very often they come in the form of prescription drugs.

In this section, I play devil's advocate. If you're on the fence about joining Part D, then you're figuring on being without any insurance against possible drug costs for months and perhaps years to come. So here I raise several "what ifs" about your chances of becoming ill and the potential costs of being without coverage.

The odds of getting sick

Around the time when the Part D drug benefit went into effect in 2006, I talked with a man in his 70s who passionately — and sincerely — argued against signing up. He described how healthily he'd lived, never smoking or drinking alcohol, always eating natural foods, and getting plenty of exercise and sound sleep. He believed that this long-held regimen would see him through, and he'd never need prescription drugs. I don't know what happened to this man, though I hope his excellent health continues. But a few months later, a good friend of mine who'd pursued an equally healthy lifestyle — to the extent of never letting red meat pass his lips — suddenly developed Parkinson's disease in his mid-60s. It seemed tragically unfair. But that's the point of this parable. Life can be unfair. Lightning strikes out of the blue. Stuff happens.

Living healthily is always the best way of preventing or postponing the common maladies that come with the aging process. And yes, it's also the best method of averting the need for many kinds of prescription drugs! Yet even the healthiest lifestyle can't completely protect you against all medical setbacks. These certainly include

✔ Genetic diseases that medications can help alleviate

✔ Physical injuries that are treated with painkillers, muscle relaxants, and other medications to help restore body parts to working order

✔ Surgeries that require medications for postoperative care and complications

But let's face it; most of us don't lead rigorously healthy lives. We smoke; we drink; we sit on our fannies all day; we choose a salad and pour bacon bits and fatty glop all over it. Along the way, our bodies are silently clocking the damage and doing their best to repair it — until one day, in our later years, the bill comes due. Warning signs appear. And then the doctor confirms we have some condition we need to do something about. Sometimes that just means changing our bad habits. Often it means taking prescription drugs to minimize the problem's effects or hold at bay a more serious medical event, such as a heart attack or stroke, that may otherwise occur.

I don't want to belabor this point unduly, but when you're figuring the odds against getting sick over the age of 65, it's useful to know what the odds are. Here are just a few facts, culled from statistics collected by the Alliance for Aging Research on its Web site, `www.silverbook.org`:

- ✔ At least 80 percent of Americans age 65 and over have at least one chronic condition (such as high blood pressure, heart disease, diabetes, arthritis, or vision disorders), and more than half have at least two.

- ✔ More than 1 in 5 Americans age 60 or older has diabetes.

- ✔ Among Americans age 65 to 74, 60 percent of men and 73 percent of women have high blood pressure.

- ✔ More than 37 million Americans 65 and older have one or more types of heart disease. The average age for a first heart attack is just under 66 for men and just over 70 for women.

- ✔ About 77 percent of all cancers are diagnosed in people age 55 and over, most often around age 70. More than two-thirds of prostate cancer cases occur in men age 65 and older. The greatest risk for ovarian cancer is to women in their late 70s.

- ✔ Alzheimer's disease affects 1 in every 10 Americans over 65 and nearly half of those over 85. Parkinson's disease affects 1 in every 100 Americans over age 60.

The cost of going without drug coverage

One of the costs of waiting to enroll in Part D until the time you think you need it is the late penalty, which increases the amount you'd pay for Part D coverage for every month that you delay. You may think that delaying offsets the penalty if you save money by not having to pay premiums in the meantime. I delve into this very point, along with everything else you need to know about the late penalty, in Chapter 8.

But you have to remember that — except for certain circumstances, also explained in Chapter 8 — after you've missed your deadline for enrolling in a Part D plan, you can sign up only once a year during the open enrollment period in November and December. Missing that window doesn't just mean another 12 months of added penalties. More importantly, it means another 12 months *without coverage.*

If you fall sick and need prescription drugs during that time, you'll pay the full cost out of your own pocket. That's obvious — duh! But do you have any idea how much you'd pay compared to the cost of being in a Part D plan? Of course not — it would depend on the drugs you had to take. (Where's that crystal ball when you need one?) But I can give you examples that illustrate the cost differences, and they may surprise you.

Retail drug costs versus out-of-pocket Part D costs

In Table 7-1, I show four brand-name drugs.

- ✔ I chose Fosamax because it's commonly used to prevent or treat osteoporosis, a condition that makes bones more fragile and likely to break. It affects 44 million Americans (1 in 2 women, 1 in 8 men), most often after the age of 60.

- ✔ I deliberately chose the other three drugs as examples of those used to treat "lightning-strike" medical problems — the serious kind that can creep up on you without warning, until you get the diagnosis. Gleevec, for example, is used mainly to treat chronic myelogenous leukemia (CML), a cancer that attacks bone marrow. Most of the 4,500 Americans who are diagnosed with CML each year are middle-aged or older, according to the National Cancer Institute. Gleevec is the most expensive drug on this list, but many anticancer meds cost a lot more, especially the new biologic ones that target cancers more specifically than older drugs.

Table 7-1	Out-of-Pocket Costs of Four Drugs Bought Retail or through a Part D Plan in 2008		
Brand-Name Drug and Dosage	**Drug Usage**	**Cost of One Year's Supply by Mail Order from Online Chain Pharmacy**	**Total Out-of-Pocket Cost for One Year in a Part D Plan, Including Premium, Co-Pays, Deductible, and Coverage Gap**
Fosamax, 70 mg, 4 tablets a month	Osteoporosis	$731.68	$556.00 (retail); $459.60 (mail order)
Prograf, 1 mg, 30 capsules a month	Antirejection after kidney or liver transplant	$1,389.01	$762.00 (retail); $658.00 (mail order)

Brand-Name Drug and Dosage	Drug Usage	Cost of One Year's Supply by Mail Order from Online Chain Pharmacy	Total Out-of-Pocket Cost for One Year in a Part D Plan, Including Premium, Co-Pays, Deductible, and Coverage Gap
Avastin, 4 ml vial, 1 vial a month	Colon and lung cancer	$7,425.00	$4,309.35 (retail); $3,779.03 (mail order)
Gleevec, 100 mg, 30 tablets a month	Leukemia	$10,788.88	$4,556.00 (retail); $4,415.39 (mail order)

Source: Part D costs from www.medicare.gov. Chain pharmacy prices from www.cvs.com, www.costco.com, and www.drugstore.com, June 2008.

I looked up the mail-order cost of each of these brand-name drugs at three online chain pharmacies, where you may well be buying your meds if you have no drug insurance. The results, in column three of Table 7-1, reflect the lowest cost for a full year's supply.

Then I ran the numbers to see what you'd pay for the same drugs (whether purchased from a retail pharmacy or by mail order) under the Part D plan that showed up as the least expensive in my own state of Maryland. (Costs vary among states because the same plan may charge a different premium in different states. Also, the plan that proved the least expensive turned out to be different for each drug.) And, believe me, I played fair! The results, shown in column four, reflect not only what you'd pay for just one of these drugs over a whole year (including co-pays, deductible, and full price in the coverage gap, which I cover in Chapter 15), but also the plan premiums. (And remember, the premium stays the same, no matter how many drugs you buy.)

In other words, Table 7-1 shows the difference between the price of each drug when purchased retail and what you'd pay for the whole insurance caboodle under Part D. The results speak for themselves. In each case, the Part D plan works out much cheaper — and for the most expensive medicine, you'd save more than half the cost.

I also took the comparison one step further, in a way not shown in Table 7-1. I wondered whether the price of these drugs would be lower at Canadian online pharmacies than the American ones shown in the table. So I checked out a reputable Canadian pharmacy that advertises itself as having the lowest mail-order prices (and often does). Here are its prices for four batches of 90-day supplies over a year (including $40 a year for shipping charges):

> ✓ Fosamax: $476
>
> ✓ Prograf: $1,480
>
> ✓ Avastin: Not available
>
> ✓ Gleevec: $13,027

As you can see, only Fosamax is less expensive at the Canadian mail-order price ($476) than under the Part D plan ($556). Yet this plan's overall cost would drop to $459 if the drug were bought in similar 90-day supplies by mail order instead of at a retail pharmacy. For the two other available drugs, Part D worked out far cheaper than Canada, even without mail order. And the price of Gleevec was nearly three times as much as the total out-of-pocket costs under the Part D plan. (If you're curious about buying prescription drugs abroad, flip to Appendix C for details on how to do it safely.)

The high cost of stopping maintenance drugs without coverage

Ignoring Part D brings another potential cost. Without coverage, people are less likely to take the drugs they may need to actually keep themselves healthy. These so-called *maintenance drugs* are taken regularly to keep certain conditions in check — for instance, high blood pressure, cholesterol, diabetes, osteoporosis, arthritis, and so on. Without those treatments, the risk of serious illness or injury rises hugely.

To take just one example: Untreated osteoporosis, which weakens bone tissue and greatly increases the risk of falling, is the most common cause of hip fractures. Such an injury can cause permanent disability or require hip replacement surgery that is extremely expensive. That too is a possible future cost — both physically and financially — of being without drug insurance. And ultimately a much higher one.

Compromising on Coverage at the Lowest Cost

If you read the earlier sections in this chapter, you know that turning your back on Part D is at best a gamble on your future good health. But, naturally enough, you still may be disgruntled when you think about forking over money each month — possibly out of a Social Security check that buys less and less each passing year — and not getting anything back.

Here's a possible compromise you can consider: Purchase coverage at the least possible cost by choosing a Part D plan that has the lowest premium in your area.

How low is low? That depends on where you live and the kind of Part D coverage you choose:

✔ **Part D stand-alone plans (PDPs)** — the kind that provide coverage *only* for drugs and are usually purchased as an add-on to traditional Medicare medical coverage — vary a lot in the monthly premiums they charge. The same plan can charge different premiums in different states, but each plan must offer the same premium to all enrollees within a state. In 2008, every state has at least one plan with a premium of under $20 a month, and 28 states have at least one under $15 a month. Only Arizona has a plan costing less than $10. (Puerto Rico has a PDP with a premium of $2.60, and the U.S. Virgin Islands has one costing $4.30.)

✔ **Medicare Advantage plans that include drug coverage (MAPDs)** — the kind that combine medical and drug coverage in a single package — also vary a lot in their premiums. Many MAPDs charge zero premiums for both medical and drug benefits. In 2008, all states, the District of Columbia, and Puerto Rico have at least one (and often many) MAPDs with zero premiums, though these plans aren't offered in all counties or zip codes. (None of the other U.S. territories have any Medicare Advantage plans.)

You can easily find out the lowest premiums of plans in your area for 2009 and subsequent years. This information is contained in the *Medicare & You* handbook that is sent to everybody on Medicare in October each year. You'll find the list of PDP and MAPD plans that will be available to you in the following year toward the end of the handbook. You can also find these details by going to the Medicare Web site at www.medicare.gov and clicking "Learn More About Plans in Your Area." See Chapters 9 and 10 for more details about deciding on an MAPD or a PDP.

To give you a general idea, Table 7-2 shows the lowest premiums for PDPs in several states and how many MAPDs offered zero premiums in 2008. (**Note:** The asterisks in the MAPD columns indicate that the plans weren't available in all counties.)

Table 7-2		Lowest Monthly Part D Premiums in Selected States in 2008			
State	*Number of PDPs*	*Lowest PDP Premium*	*Number of PDP Premiums under $20*	*Number of MAPDs**	*Number of MAPDs with $0 Premiums**
Arizona	51	$9.40	4	85	20
California	56	$14.30	10	181	69
Florida	58	$12.10	2	269	80
Louisiana	50	$14.30	2	82	19
Minnesota	52	$13.90	3	79	8

(continued)

Table 7-2 *(continued)*

State	Number of PDPs	Lowest PDP Premium	Number of PDP Premiums under $20	Number of MAPDs*	Number of MAPDs with $0 Premiums*
New Mexico	55	$10.40	15	45	15
New York	55	$16.70	4	213	66
Tennessee	53	$18.00	1	114	24
Virginia	52	$15.10	2	79	14

Source: Part D plan details by state, 2008, at www.medicare.gov.

Among PDPs in the states, the lowest premiums range from $9.40 a month in Arizona to $18.00 in Alaska and Tennessee in 2008. These minimums are likely to rise in future years. Gone are the days of the $1.87 premium, which one plan offered in seven states in 2006, the first year of the Part D program, as a come-on to people to enroll.

MAPDs are likely to continue offering zero premiums as long as they keep getting the extra federal subsidies that allow them to do so. Paying no premiums (except for the standard Part B premium) is attractive to people who can't (or don't want to) pay premiums for drug coverage, including those who don't use prescription drugs right now. If you consider joining an MAPD plan for this reason, remember that the way you receive medical benefits is different from traditional Medicare, usually with restrictions on the doctors and hospitals you can go to and sometimes higher costs for certain services, as explained in Chapter 9.

One more thing: If paying the kind of premiums listed among PDPs in Table 7-2 would be a hardship to you, you should look into whether you qualify for the Part D Extra Help program. If you qualify for full Extra Help benefits, you wouldn't pay a premium at all, and qualifying for even partial benefits would reduce the premium. I explain the Extra Help program in detail in Chapter 5. You can also check out whether you're eligible for help under a State Pharmacy Assistance Program (SPAP) if your state has one. These too provide prescription drug coverage at a low cost.

Chapter 8

Confronting the Late Penalty

The Part D late penalty basically sets a deadline. It's a device for persuading you to join a Medicare drug plan when you first become eligible — and not just when you happen to feel like it. If the date of your personal Part D enrollment deadline passes and you enroll in Part D months or years later, prepare to

- ✔ Pay a penalty in the form of a surcharge that's added to every monthly Part D premium for as long as you stay in the program.
- ✔ Face a higher penalty the longer you delay signing up for Part D.
- ✔ Experience a probable increase in your penalty cost each year.
- ✔ Pay a lot more for the same drug coverage over time than if you'd signed up for Part D as soon as you were able.

Heavy stuff, huh? People considering Part D often think the late penalty is unfair, though actually it exists for several reasons (see the later sidebar "What were they thinking . . . when they created the late penalty?"). Medicare strictly enforces the late penalty — and takes the view that being confused about Part D is no defense for signing up late. If you have no other prescription drug insurance that's at least of equal value to basic Medicare drug coverage (or *creditable;* see Chapter 6), or if you're not receiving Extra Help (see Chapter 5), every month that you delay enrolling in Part D makes the penalty bigger. That's why I'm sharing its implications in the context of deciding whether you need to sign up for Part D right now. Very often, the late penalty is an important part of that decision — or a consequence of it.

So in this chapter, I explain how to avoid the penalty by signing up at the right time — depending on your individual circumstances. Then I describe how the penalty is calculated, how it grows ever larger over time, and whether putting off joining Part D is worth risking it.

What were they thinking . . . when they created the late penalty?

If you're like many people, you probably feel indignant about the late penalty. How can joining the Medicare drug program be voluntary if you're going to be penalized for not signing up on time? Why can't you wait to join Part D until you need it, or when you choose to? Here are the arguments:

✔ Part D gives protection against future risks, just like any other form of insurance. You buy home insurance in case the basement catches fire; you buy car insurance in case you total the station wagon.

✔ If no one joined Part D until she needed prescription drugs, the system couldn't function. Here comes that insurance concept again: Healthy people must be in the system to spread the financial risk and hold down costs. If only sick people enrolled, drug coverage would be so expensive that most people wouldn't be able to afford it.

✔ Part D isn't the only Medicare program that has a late penalty. So does Part B, which imposes an extra 10 percent on the premiums for every year you delay signing up, for the same reasons given previously. But because almost everyone signs up for Part B as soon as they're eligible, the fact that a late penalty exists often goes unnoticed. (Part B helps you pay to see a doctor and use other outpatient services; see Chapter 1 for details.)

Of course, Part D isn't entirely insurance in the ordinary commercial sense. It's also a benefit, and that's why the late penalty seems a bit confusing. The federal government subsidizes your drug coverage in various ways — to a certain degree in the initial coverage period, and to a very large extent if your income is low enough to qualify you for Extra Help (which I explain in Chapter 5) or your drug costs are high enough to take you into the catastrophic phase of coverage. Nonetheless, Part D is built on insurance principles, with the late penalty as a cornerstone.

Avoiding a Late Penalty by Signing Up for Part D at the Right Time

The only way to avoid a late penalty is to meet your own particular deadline. Getting the timing right depends on your situation, which is probably one of the following:

✔ You're joining Medicare right now (or are about to do so) but don't have good drug coverage.

✔ You already have good drug coverage from another source (such as an employer health plan) but are about to lose it or drop it.

✔ You're just returning to live in the United States after living abroad.

✔ You've just been released from prison.

In the next few sections, I consider each of these circumstances and also provide a tip for sidestepping an obstacle hidden in the fine print that may trip you up if you don't know about it.

If you miss your personal deadline for joining a Part D plan, your next chance to join is the annual enrollment period between November 15 and December 31 (with coverage beginning January 1). See the later section "The Price of Missing Your Personal Enrollment Deadline" to find out about the costs you have to pay for letting your deadline slide.

When you join Medicare and don't have creditable drug coverage

You can get Part D as long as you're enrolled in Medicare Part A (hospital insurance) and/or Part B (doctor and outpatient services), as explained in Chapter 1. Whether you need to enroll in Part D at the same time as you sign up for Medicare depends on whether you have other drug coverage regarded as creditable under Part D rules. (Coverage is *creditable* when it provides at least as much value as minimum Medicare drug coverage. I explain this concept and how it affects decisions about joining Part D in detail in Chapter 6.) If you have creditable drug coverage when you sign up for Medicare, you don't have to sign up for Part D at the same time.

But what if you *don't* have such coverage?

- If you're turning 65 soon and *don't* have creditable drug coverage from another source, you need to enroll in a Part D drug plan at the same time as you enroll in Part A or Part B to avoid a late penalty. That means signing up within the span of your seven-month initial Medicare enrollment period, which starts three months before the month you turn 65 and ends three months after it. For example, if your birthday is in April, your enrollment period runs from the beginning of January to the end of July, and you need to enroll in a Part D plan in July at the latest (and start receiving Medicare drug coverage on August 1) to guarantee avoiding a late penalty.

- If you're joining Medicare at a younger age because of disability and *don't* have creditable drug coverage from elsewhere, the same rules apply. But in this case, your seven-month initial enrollment period begins three months before your 25th month of receiving disability payments and ends three months later. So, as in the preceding example, if your 25th month on disability falls in April, you need to sign up for a Part D plan in July at the latest to dodge a late penalty.

  If you join Medicare at a younger age due to a disability and incur a late penalty because you didn't sign up for Part D at the same time, you get another chance when you turn 65. You can use the regular seven-month Medicare enrollment period around your 65th birthday to re-enroll in Part D and get rid of the late penalty.

> ✔ If your income is limited and you qualify for Extra Help (as explained in Chapter 5), by law you *won't* be hit with a penalty if you sign up late.

When you lose or drop your current creditable drug coverage

If you have creditable drug coverage from another source, you *don't* need to enroll in Part D when you sign up for Medicare, as explained in Chapter 6. But what if you lose that coverage? Or your coverage suddenly ceases to be creditable? Or you decide to drop it?

> ✔ If you lose creditable coverage *involuntarily,* meaning that you lose it through no fault of your own — for example, if your employer's plan terminates or begins offering benefits that overall are of less value than Medicare drug coverage — you'll qualify for a special enrollment period in which you can sign up for Part D without incurring a late penalty. That period lasts for 63 days after you're notified that your creditable coverage will end *or* 63 days after the date it actually ends (whichever's later). See the later section "What the 63-day rule really means" for some crucial details if you're in this boat.
>
> ✔ If you deliberately drop your creditable coverage, perhaps if it becomes too expensive to maintain, you *won't* receive a special period to enroll in Part D. Instead, you must sign up during the annual enrollment, which runs from November 15 to December 31 each year. To avoid a late penalty, you can't go for more than 63 days without creditable coverage. So you'd have to keep your current coverage at least until the end of October, because your Part D coverage wouldn't begin until January 1. (Ideally, however, you'd keep your own coverage until the end of the year so you continue to be protected by insurance.)

You may find out that your previous sponsored coverage (which you've already lost or dropped) *wasn't* creditable only when you enroll in a Part D plan. Then, almost certainly, you'll be slapped with a late penalty. At that point, you'll need to ask the plan for a *reconsideration* — a review during which your claim of not realizing that your previous coverage wasn't creditable will be investigated. I cover this situation, as well as other circumstances in which people feel they've received a late penalty unfairly, in Chapter 13. That's where I also explain in detail how to go about asking for a reconsideration.

When you return to the United States after living abroad

You can't receive Part D coverage while living abroad, and you *aren't* expected to sign up for it until you return to live in the United States permanently. (This rule is different from the one for Part B enrollment when you've been living abroad, which I clarify in Chapter 1.) When you return to the U.S., you can join Part D without risking a penalty in one of two ways, depending on your circumstances:

- ✔ **If you turned 65 while living abroad:** You get a special initial enrollment period (IEP) to sign up with a Part D plan on your return. This period lasts seven months — three months before the month of your return to the U.S., the month of your return, and three months after your return. Enrolling in a plan no later than the end of the month before you return ensures you can use your Part D coverage as soon as you arrive back.

- ✔ **If you were eligible for Part D before moving abroad:** You get a special enrollment period (SEP) on your return. You can enroll in a plan without having to apply for an SEP (as I explain in Chapter 17). The SEP begins on the date of your return to the U.S. and ends 63 days later. (See the later section "What the 63-day rule really means" for details.)

When you're released from prison

You can't receive Part D coverage while incarcerated in a prison or any other correctional institution, and your stay doesn't count toward the Part D late penalty. In this situation, the rules are the same as for someone returning from abroad, as I explain in the previous section. If you turned 65 in prison, you get a seven-month initial enrollment period (IEP) to sign up for a Part D plan, lasting from three months before the month of your release to three months after. Otherwise, you get a special enrollment period (SEP) to sign up for a Part D plan, beginning on the day of your release and ending 63 days later. (See the following section for more on the 63-day rule.)

What the 63-day rule really means

The *63-day rule* is usually explained as the time you have during a special enrollment period to enroll in a Part D plan and avoid a late penalty. But this explanation isn't precisely accurate. Rather, you must be actually *receiving* Part D coverage within 63 days to avoid a penalty.

Say you lose your current creditable drug coverage on March 31. Counting 63 days from that date brings you to June 2. If you leave it to the last minute and sign up with a Part D plan on June 1 or 2, you're still within the 63-day time frame. But you're not avoiding the late penalty because, under Part D rules, your drug coverage actually begins on the first day of the month *after* you enroll — in this example, July 1. You're then penalized for one month without coverage, which may not amount to much money at first but can increase quite a lot with time, as I explain later in this chapter. So think in terms of 60 days instead (or 59 if the time frame includes February), and you'll be okay.

The Price of Missing Your Personal Enrollment Deadline

The purpose of this section isn't to scare you half to death, but to give you a practical awareness of what the late penalty means so that — if it figures at all in the decisions you make about joining Part D (and it may not) — you can make an informed choice. Here, I explain how the penalty is calculated and how it can grow over the years. In the end, only you can decide whether ignoring the late penalty is worth the risk.

Looking at how the late penalty is calculated

The basis of the late penalty is something called the *national average premium (NAP)*. Every fall, Medicare works out the average of all the premiums that Part D plans nationwide will charge during the following year. This dollar amount becomes the NAP for that next year. If you incur the late penalty, you'll pay 1 percent of the NAP for every month you were without creditable coverage and didn't sign up for Part D. This formula works out at 12 percent a year.

If you miss your personal deadline for joining a Part D plan, your next chance is the annual enrollment period that runs from November 15 to December 31 (with coverage beginning January 1). If you also miss that window, you have to wait another 12 months to sign up, increasing your penalty amount by another 12 percent. Every extra year of delay adds 12 percent to the penalty. Check out the following examples to see the math for yourself:

- ✔ Rebecca turned 65 and signed up for Medicare in March 2007. But by the time her personal enrollment period expired at the end of June, she hadn't signed up for Part D (and had no comparable drug coverage). Her next chance to join Part D was during the open enrollment period between November 15 and December 31, 2007. She decided to do it, and her drug coverage began January 1, 2008. By then she was six months over her deadline (July through December). So her late penalty in 2008 was 6 percent (1 percent × 6 months) of the 2008 NAP, which was $27.93. One percent of that amount is 28 cents. So Rebecca's monthly late penalty was calculated at 28 cents multiplied by 6 (her months without coverage), which came to $1.68. Medicare rounds the penalty to the nearest 10 cents, so Rebecca actually paid $1.70 a month in 2008, or $20.40 for the whole year, on top of her plan's premiums.

- ✔ Brad was 70 years old and already in Medicare when Part D drug coverage began in 2006. Because the program was just starting, the initial enrollment period for that year was extended into May. But Brad couldn't figure out what to do about Part D, and he let the deadline pass.

He had another chance to sign up during open enrollment at the end of 2006, but he let that go by, too. Finally, he enrolled in a Part D plan at the end of 2007. By then, he'd been without drug coverage for 19 months (June 2006 to December 2007). So in 2008, he paid a 19 percent penalty — 28 cents multiplied by 19, which came to $5.32. This amount was rounded to the nearest 10 cents, so Brad paid $5.30 a month, or $63.60 over the whole year, on top of his plan's premiums.

Understanding how the late penalty can add up over time

Maybe the amounts in the preceding section's examples don't sound like too big of a deal. But that isn't the end of it. Rebecca won't pay the same penalty amount she was first assessed — $1.70 a month in 2008 — for all the years to come. Nor will Brad pay his penalty — $5.30 a month in 2008 — for as long as he's in the Part D program. They'll both pay a new penalty amount each successive year, and so will anyone else who has a late penalty. That's because Medicare recalculates the NAP annually. If the NAP changes, the crucial 1 percent also changes — and so does everyone's penalty amount.

One part of the calculation doesn't change — the number of months anyone goes without drug coverage. For example, Brad will continue to pay a penalty of 19 percent of the NAP due to the 19 months he lacked drug coverage. But the dollar amount of that 19 percent will change each year as the dollar amount of the NAP changes. So in 2009, he'll pay 19 percent of the 2009 NAP, and the next year he'll pay 19 percent of the 2010 NAP, and so on every year.

I cover the NAP's yearly variation and provide some estimates of the effect of NAP changes over time in the following sections.

Wondering how much the NAP will change each year

If the NAP rises, everybody with a penalty pays more as time goes by. But the truth is, nobody knows how much the NAP will change annually. Even Medicare doesn't know until September of each year when it works out the average of all Part D plans' premiums for the following year. Whether the NAP rises or falls depends entirely on the plans.

Certainly you can find out what the NAP will be for *next* year. That information is included in the *Medicare & You* handbook that Medicare sends to all of its beneficiaries every October. The last section in the handbook explains Medicare costs for the following year, including the Part D national average premium (referred to more bureaucratically in the handbook as the *national base beneficiary premium*) and the 1 percent penalty amount. (You can also read the *Medicare & You* handbook online at www.medicare.gov.)

As this book goes to press, the 2009 NAP is unknown. So to date, only one NAP change, from 2007 — the first year the penalty was imposed — to 2008, has occurred. Between those two years, the NAP rose only 58 cents (from $27.35 in 2007 to $27.93 in 2008), which was far less than anyone expected. Will it always stay so low? Nobody knows. But it's worth remembering that in these days of Part D's infancy, the plans have tried to keep their premiums relatively low in order to attract customers. If the market shakes out in the future, with fewer plans competing, you can expect premiums to rise, taking the NAP upward as well.

Estimating how the late penalty may grow long-term

At this point, presenting a chart that shows exactly how much penalty amounts can grow over 5 years, 10 years, 20 years, or more would be useful. Of course, that's impossible due to the annual reassessment of the NAP. But, what the heck, I'm going to do some educated guesswork so you can at least get an idea of how those amounts can accumulate long-term.

The NAP may creep up very gradually by a dollar or less every year through-out the next decade or so. Or it may jump around all over the place — going up by $5 or $10 one year, or even going down by a few dollars or cents the next. But here I make very conservative assumptions. In fact, in Table 8-1, I make a totally unrealistic assumption — that the NAP doesn't rise *at all,* but remains basically the same ($28) as in 2008. Even so, you can see how the penalties mount up and become substantially higher with every year you delay joining Part D. (*Note:* These figures are raw calculations that haven't been rounded to the nearest 10 cents.)

Table 8-1		How Penalties Mount Up If the NAP Remains the Same as in 2008 ($28)			
Deadline for Joining Part D without Penalty	**Date Part D Coverage Began**	**Months without Drug Coverage**	**Months without Coverage × 1% of NAP = Monthly Penalty**	**Total Penalty Paid Each Year**	**Total Penalties Paid over 10 Years**
March 2008	March 2008	0 months	$0	$0	$0
June 2008	January 2009	6 months	6 × $0.28 = $1.68	$20.16	$201.60
December 2008	January 2010	12 months	12 × $0.28 = $3.36	$40.32	$403.20

Deadline for Joining Part D without Penalty	Date Part D Coverage Began	Months without Drug Coverage	Months without Coverage × 1% of NAP = Monthly Penalty	Total Penalty Paid Each Year	Total Penalties Paid over 10 Years
October 2008	January 2011	26 months	26 × $0.28 = $7.28	$87.36	$873.60
August 2008	January 2012	40 months	40 × $0.28 = $11.20	$134.40	$1,344

Now I'm going a bit further out on a limb, but still very conservatively. In Table 8-2, I assume the NAP will rise by $2 each year in the ten years from 2009 through 2018 — so it becomes $30 in 2009, $36 by 2012, and $48 by 2018. And since these numbers are just raw calculations, I haven't rounded to the nearest 10 cents.

Table 8-2		How Penalties Grow If the NAP Increases by $2 a Year from 2009 to 2018					
Deadline for Joining Part D without Penalty	Date Coverage Began	Months without Coverage	Penalty Paid in 2009	Penalty Paid in 2010	Penalty Paid in 2011	Penalty Paid in 2012	Total Paid in 2009–2018
March 2008	March 2008	0 months	$0	$0	$0	$0	$0
June 2008	January 2009	6 months	$21.60	$23.04	$24.48	$25.92	$280.80
December 2008	January 2010	12 months	Not enrolled	$46.08	$48.96	$51.84	$518.40
October 2008	January 2011	26 months	Not enrolled	Not enrolled	$106.08	$112.32	$1,023.36
August 2008	January 2012	40 months	Not enrolled	Not enrolled	Not enrolled	$172.80	$1,411.20

Deciding whether to risk ignoring the late penalty

I know what you're thinking. You're looking at that last figure in Table 8-2 — $1,411.20 as the possible accumulated ten-year penalty for someone who delayed signing up for more than three years — and wondering whether it's less than what you'd have paid in premiums for those 40 months. It may well be. But before deciding to ignore the late penalty and stay out of Part D for a few more years, consider the following:

✔ Table 8-2's numbers aren't real. They're purely a guesstimate. The actual penalty amounts may be higher.

✔ Table 8-2's numbers only account for the next 10 years. Penalties accumulated after 15 years or more — when you may be in your 80s and on a fixed income that doesn't go as far as it once did — are going to be a lot higher.

✔ At present the monthly late penalty is calculated on 1 percent of the NAP. But Medicare law allows for this amount to be increased to 2 percent at some unspecified future date. If that happens, the penalties would be doubled.

So delaying Part D enrollment is your choice — but recognize that it's a gamble. Remember the famous line from _Dirty Harry_ where Clint Eastwood is facing down a bad guy who doesn't know whether Clint still has a bullet left in his .44 Magnum? He says, "I know what you're thinking . . . [and] you've got to ask yourself a question: 'Do I feel lucky?' Well, do ya, punk?" Well, do you?

Part III
Choosing and Enrolling in the Right Part D Plan for You

The 5th Wave   By Rich Tennant

"Medicare's Part D drug policies are a little confusing. They'll cover my heart medications, but nothing for galvanizing, lubricants, or corrosion inhibitors."

In this part . . .

For many people, the most daunting part of Medicare prescription drug coverage is choosing a single Part D plan from among the scores that are available. But never fear. I walk you through the process with a focus on how to find the one that works best for you.

In Chapters 9 and 10, I help you whittle down all those plan choices to a manageable few so you can make an informed decision on the final one to pick. I explain why it's important to first decide how you want your Medicare medical benefits delivered — either through the traditional Medicare program or through one of Medicare's private health plans — and how this decision affects your choices for prescription drug coverage. Then I take you step by step through the process of comparing Part D plans — a strategy that focuses on your own individual needs and preferences and is less difficult than you may think, after you know how to do it.

Chapter 11 is something of a red alert. It warns you about scams and hard-sell marketing pressures to be on your guard against, and details how to avoid them. Finally, in Chapter 12, I explain how to enroll in a Part D plan if you're doing so for the first time.

Chapter 9

The First Cut: Deciding How You Want to Receive Your Medical Benefits

*C*hoices, choices, choices. Part D has an abundance of them, and for many people, selecting just one drug plan seems a daunting task. But before you begin comparing drug plans (which Chapter 10 delves into), you really need to be clear about how you want your Medicare *medical* benefits delivered. This is a critical first step in the Part D plan selection process — and one that affects and automatically narrows your drug coverage options.

Broadly, Medicare medical benefits are available through two very different delivery systems:

✔ **Traditional Medicare:** The original government system, in place since 1966, traditional Medicare works on a *fee for service* basis — Medicare directly pays a portion of the costs of any medical service it covers to any provider that accepts Medicare patients. You, the patient, pay a percentage of the cost, or in some cases a fixed amount, for each covered service you receive.

✔ **Private Medicare health plans:** Collectively known as the Medicare Advantage (MA) program, these plans provide alternatives to the traditional system and are run by private, Medicare-approved insurers. Medicare pays each plan a monthly amount for each enrollee's medical care. You receive your medical benefits through the plan of your choice and pay the charges required by the plan. Because plans vary greatly in their costs and benefits, you need to compare them carefully to pick the one that most suits your needs.

Whichever type of coverage you choose, you're still part of Medicare. But be aware that traditional Medicare and private Medicare health plans have big differences. Oh yeah, and then there are all the variations among the five types of Medicare Advantage plans — Health Maintenance Organizations (HMOs), Preferred Provider Organizations (PPOs), Private Fee-for-Service (PFFS) plans, Medicare Medical Savings Accounts (MSAs), and Special Needs Plans (SNPs). Not to mention yet another type of plan that isn't strictly part of the Medicare Advantage program — an HMO known as a Medicare Cost plan. Complicating matters further, Medicare even has rules about which kind of drug coverage you can choose depending on how you receive your Medicare medical benefits.

If you're already sure you want either traditional Medicare or a private Medicare health plan for your medical benefits — or are already in one or the other and want to remain in it — pass this chapter over and head straight to Chapter 10, which explains how to compare drug plans. But if you're undecided, read on.

In this chapter, I explain the differences between traditional Medicare and the various kinds of health plans that fall under the Medicare Advantage umbrella, as well as a few other individual programs. I also suggest items to consider when making a choice between traditional Medicare and a private Medicare health plan. And finally, if you opt for the Medicare Advantage system, I explain how to compare the MA plans available in your area to find the one that suits you best.

The Features of Traditional Medicare and Medicare's Private Health Plans

Your choice of medical care directly affects how you receive drug coverage:

- ✔ You can choose a stand-alone Part D plan — the kind that provides coverage only for prescription drugs — if you're enrolled in one of the following:

    - Traditional Medicare

    - A Private Fee-for-Service (PFFS) plan that doesn't offer drug coverage

    - A Medicare Savings Account (MSA) plan

    - A Medicare Cost plan that doesn't offer drug coverage

- ✔ You can choose a Medicare HMO, PPO, SNP, PFFS, or Cost plan that provides both medical care and prescription drug coverage in a single package.

- ✔ You can't have a stand-alone Part D plan while you're enrolled in a Medicare HMO or PPO plan, *even if it doesn't provide drug coverage.*

Your choice of medical care also reduces the quantity of your drug coverage choices. For example, if your area offers 50 stand-alone Part D plans and 50 Medicare Advantage (MA) plans that include drug coverage (by no means an uncommon scenario in urban areas), your options are instantly halved.

Good news: Nobody's going to ask you to take a quiz on all of this information! But you do need to do some homework to make an informed decision about getting your healthcare from either traditional Medicare or a private health plan — and, if you choose the latter, about the kind of Medicare Advantage plan you prefer. The more thoroughly you understand the differences among all of these choices, the more likely you'll be content with the one you pick.

Table 9-1 shows at a glance the main differences among traditional Medicare and the three types of private health plans most commonly chosen by Medicare beneficiaries. The following sections go further, with detailed information on all the plan choices available to you. In each case, I explain how each type of plan works with prescription drug coverage, to what extent you can choose the doctors and hospitals you go to, the eligibility rules, whether extra benefits (more than traditional Medicare covers) may be available, and what kind of out-of-pocket expenses to expect.

Table 9-1	Key Questions When Comparing Traditional Medicare and the Main Types of Private Medicare Advantage Health Plans			
Questions to Consider	*Traditional Medicare*	*Medicare HMOs*	*Medicare PPOs*	*Medicare PFFS Plans*
How do I get prescription drugs?	Only by joining a stand-alone Part D plan to add drug coverage for a separate premium.	Only by joining an HMO that offers drug coverage in its whole package of benefits. Not all do.	Only by joining a PPO that offers drug coverage in its whole package of benefits. Not all do.	By joining a PFFS that offers drug coverage. Or by adding a stand-alone Part D plan to a PFFS plan that doesn't offer drugs.

(continued)

Table 9-1 *(continued)*

Questions to Consider	Traditional Medicare	Medicare HMOs	Medicare PPOs	Medicare PFFS Plans
Can I get my medical care from any doctor or hospital?	Yes, anywhere in the country — as long as the provider takes Medicare patients (and accepts new ones).	No. You must go to in-network providers, except in an emergency. (But if it has a Point of Service option, you can go out-of-network for a higher co-pay.)	Yes. PPOs not only have networks of doctors and hospitals in their service area but also allow you to go out-of-network for a higher co-pay.	Yes, anywhere in the country — but only if the providers agree to the plan's conditions and payment terms. Not all do.
Must I have a primary care doctor?	No.	Yes.	No.	No.
Do I need a referral to see a specialist?	No.	Usually.	No.	No.
Can I get more benefits if I pay a higher premium?	No. But you can buy a private Medigap policy that pays most of your out-of-pocket costs and covers a few extra benefits.	Some plans offer some coverage for vision, dental, hearing, and/or other benefits.	Some plans offer some coverage for vision, dental, hearing, and/or other benefits.	Maybe, depending on the plan.

Questions to Consider	Traditional Medicare	Medicare HMOs	Medicare PPOs	Medicare PFFS Plans
How is my share of the costs decided?	You pay standard co-pays, which are the same for every-one in the traditional Medicare program.	You pay what the plan requires. Going out-of-network may mean paying full cost, except in emergencies.	You pay what the plan requires. Going out-of-network means paying more, except in emergencies.	You pay what the plan requires. Going to pro-viders who don't accept the terms, except in emergencies, means paying full cost.
Is there a limit on my out-of-pocket (OOP) costs?	No.	Maybe. Some plans set an annual OOP limit on some services.	Maybe. Some plans set an annual OOP limit on some services.	Maybe. Some plans set an annual OOP limit on some services.

Traditional Medicare

Also known as *original Medicare,* traditional Medicare is the program you're in, unless you opt for one of the private plans I describe later in this chapter.

- **Eligibility:** You must have Medicare Part A (hospital care) or Part B (outpatient care) or both, as explained in Chapter 1. To receive services, you can live anywhere in the United States or its territories.

- **Choice of doctors and hospitals:** You can go to any doctor or hospital that accepts Medicare patients (and is accepting new ones) anywhere in the country. You don't need a referral from a primary care doctor to see a specialist. (To find a doctor enrolled in Medicare, visit www. medicare.gov and click "Find a Doctor" on the home page. You can use this tool to search for a doctor by name, area, or specialty. Or you can always call Medicare at 800-633-4227 and ask for a list to be mailed to you.)

- **Out-of-pocket costs:** For outpatient care, you pay the standard Part B monthly premium ($96.40 in 2008 for most people; higher if your income is above $82,000 a year in 2008), annual deductible ($135 in 2008) and a percentage of the cost (20 percent in most cases, but possibly higher) of each Medicare-covered service. For hospital care, you pay a deductible ($1,024 in 2008) for each stay up to 60 days in a benefit period and co-pays for extra days, as explained in Chapter 1. There's no limit on out-of-pocket costs. You can buy private Medigap supplementary insurance for an extra premium to cover deductibles and co-pays in full or in part (see Chapter 1 for more about Medigap).

✔ **Extra benefits:** Traditional Medicare covers many kinds of healthcare, but by no means does it cover all the services you're likely to need. For example, it doesn't cover routine vision, hearing, and dental care. Medigap insurance may provide a few extra benefits, such as emergency care abroad and limited preventive care, depending on the policy you purchase.

✔ **Prescription drugs:** Traditional Medicare solely covers drugs used in hospitals or administered in doctors' offices and clinics. You need to join a private stand-alone Part D plan, for an additional premium, to get coverage for outpatient drugs.

Medicare Advantage plans

You can choose among several very different types of plans within the Medicare Advantage program. Some types, such as HMOs and PPOs, have been part of Medicare for many years. (You'll be familiar with the way these work if you've previously been in an HMO or PPO sponsored by an employer.) Other types of MA plans are much newer: Private Fee-for-Service (PFFS) plans, though available earlier, only became widespread from 2006 onward. Medicare Medical Savings Accounts (MSAs) and Special Needs Plans (SNPs) have been available in Medicare only since 2004. The following sections explain the key features of each type of MA plan.

Health Maintenance Organizations (HMOs)

Health Maintenance Organizations (HMOs) offer *managed care*. This is a healthcare delivery system designed to hold down costs, typically by requiring primary care doctors to act as gatekeepers in referring patients to specialists and other services. HMOs operate locally in limited geographical service areas — usually a county or even a zip code. The same HMO may offer costs and benefits different in one service area than in another that may be right next to it. Following are the main features of HMOs:

✔ **Eligibility:** You must have Medicare Part A and Part B and live within the service area of the plan you select. You can't join an HMO if you have end-stage renal disease (ESRD) — but if you develop it when already enrolled, you can remain in the plan.

✔ **Choice of doctors and hospitals:** You must be treated by doctors and hospitals within the plan's network of contracted providers in the service area, except in an emergency or if you urgently need care. You usually need a referral from your primary care doctor to see a specialist. (If the plan offers a *Point of Service* option, however, you can go out of network for a higher co-pay.) An HMO can supply you with its list of providers to help you find out in advance whether it covers your preferred hospitals and doctors.

✔ **Out-of-pocket costs:** Whether you pay a premium in addition to the Part B premium depends on the plan. Co-pays for specific services are often less, but sometimes higher, than those in traditional Medicare. Some plans set a limit on out-of-pocket spending in the year, usually on specified services. If you go outside of the plan's provider network (unless you have a Point of Service agreement), you're responsible for the full cost of treatment, except in emergencies.

✔ **Extra benefits:** Some plans offer vision, hearing, and/or dental services (though the extent of this coverage varies a great deal among plans); routine checkups; and other extras, like health club memberships. These bonuses are usually reflected in higher premiums.

✔ **Prescription drugs:** Not all HMOs offer prescription drug coverage. If you join a plan that doesn't, you can't get coverage from a stand-alone Part D plan.

Preferred Provider Organizations (PPOs)

MA plans that offer managed care with fewer restrictions than HMOs are known as Preferred Provider Organizations (PPOs). *Regional* PPOs cover large areas, maybe several states. *Local* PPOs operate within smaller areas, such as in one or several adjacent counties. Their features include the following:

✔ **Eligibility:** Like HMOs, you must have Medicare Parts A and B and live within the service area of your selected plan. You can't join a plan if you have end-stage renal disease (ESRD), but you can stay in a plan if you develop this illness after enrollment.

✔ **Choice of doctors and hospitals:** You can go to a doctor or hospital outside of the plan's provider network — but, if you do, it'll cost you more in co-pays. You don't need a referral to see a specialist. A PPO can give you its list of network providers so you can see in advance whether your preferred doctors and hospitals are covered.

✔ **Out-of-pocket costs:** The plan you select determines whether you pay a premium in addition to the Part B premium. Co-pays for specific services are different from those in traditional Medicare (often less, but sometimes higher). Some plans set a limit on out-of-pocket spending in the year, usually on specified services. Naturally, going to out-of-network providers (except in emergencies or for urgently needed care) costs more, often a lot more, though typically not the full cost.

✔ **Extra benefits:** Some plans offer vision, hearing, and/or dental services (though the extent of this coverage varies a great deal among plans); routine checkups; and other extras, like health club memberships. These are usually reflected in higher premiums.

✔ **Prescription drugs:** Not all PPOs offer prescription drug coverage. If you join a plan that doesn't, you can't purchase coverage from a stand-alone Part D plan.

Private Fee-for-Service (PFFS) plans

Private Fee-for-Service (PFFS) plans don't offer managed care. They directly pay providers for each covered service, similar to the way traditional Medicare works (which sometimes leads consumers to confuse the two). Here are the main features of PFFS plans:

- **Eligibility:** You must have Medicare Part A and Part B and live in the service area of the plan you select. You can't join a plan if you have end-stage renal disease (ESRD) — but if you develop it when already enrolled, you can remain in the plan.

- **Choice of doctors and hospitals:** You can go to any doctor or hospital that accepts the plan's conditions and payment rates, anywhere in the country, and you don't need a referral to see a specialist. But many providers don't accept PFFS plans, and it isn't easy to find out in advance which do, except by asking doctors and hospitals directly. (However, starting in 2011, PFFS plans must have written contracts with providers.) In addition, providers are allowed to accept or reject the plan for each service visit. So if the plan covers your care from a particular doctor or hospital once, there's no guarantee that you'll be covered next time.

- **Out-of-pocket costs:** Whether you pay a premium in addition to the Part B premium depends on the plan. Co-pays for specific services may be different from those in traditional Medicare — either lower or higher. Some plans set a limit on out-of-pocket costs in the year, usually on specified services. If you're treated by a provider who doesn't accept the PFFS plan's payment rates, you're responsible for the full cost of treatment, except in emergencies.

- **Extra benefits:** Some plans offer vision, hearing, and/or dental services (though the extent of this coverage varies a great deal among plans); routine checkups; and other extras, such as health club memberships. These add-ons are usually reflected in higher premiums.

- **Prescription drugs:** Not all PFFS plans offer prescription drug coverage. If you join a plan that doesn't, you can enroll in a stand-alone Part D plan to obtain coverage (unlike HMOs and PPOs).

Medicare Medical Savings Account (MSA) plans

Medicare Medical Savings Account (MSA) plans work very differently from other Medicare Advantage plans. Medicare gives an MSA plan a certain amount of money for each of its enrollees; the plan then deposits a portion of this money into a special health savings account for you. You draw on the money in the account to pay for medical care. If you use up the entire amount, you then pay 100 percent of your medical costs until you've reached the plan's deductible limit. Beyond that limit, the plan pays all of your costs for Medicare-covered services for the rest of the year.

MSAs offer the following features:

✔ **Eligibility:** You must have Medicare Part A and Part B. You can't enroll in an MSA if

- You have health coverage through Medicaid, the Department of Veterans Affairs (VA or CHAMPVA benefits), the Department of Defense (TRICARE military benefits), or the Federal Employees Health Benefits program

- You have other heath coverage (like a retiree plan) that would cover all or part of the MSA deductible

- You have end-stage renal disease (ESRD)

- You've already chosen to receive Medicare hospice care for a terminal illness (which is covered under Part A; see Chapter 1)

- You'll live in the U.S. for fewer than 183 days in the year

✔ **Choice of doctors and hospitals:** You can go to any doctor and hospital, but the cost may be lower if you choose a provider that has a contract with the MSA plan to treat its enrollees. If the MSA offers this option (and not all do), you can ask the plan for a list of providers.

✔ **Out-of-pocket costs:** This type of Medicare Advantage plan has no premium (aside from the Part B premium) and no co-pays. You pay the full cost of a medical service out of the money deposited in your health savings account. After this money is used up, you pay 100 percent out of pocket until you meet your deductible. The account deposit and deductible amounts vary from plan to plan. For example, if the deposit is $1,500 and the deductible is $4,000, your maximum out-of-pocket expenses in the year would be $2,500. (Some other examples for account deposits/deductibles in 2008 include: $1,000/$2,750; $1,250/$2,275; $1,300/$3,000; $1,575/$5,000.)

As long as you use the money in your account to pay for services that are covered by traditional Medicare, they count toward your deductible. After meeting the deductible, you pay no more for the rest of the year. If you don't use all the money in your account, the balance rolls over and is yours to use the following year — regardless of whether you enroll in the same plan or another plan.

✔ **Extra benefits:** You're free to use the money in your account for services not covered by Medicare (for example, routine eye and hearing exams), but these payments don't count toward your deductible.

✔ **Taxes:** MSA accounts aren't taxed, as long as they're used for what the IRS calls "qualified medical expenses." Each year you must report your account withdrawals to the IRS, using Forms 1040 and 8853, even if you aren't otherwise required to file an income tax return.

✔ **Prescription drugs:** MSA plans don't cover prescription drugs. You can enroll in a stand-alone Part D plan to receive drug coverage. You can use your MSA account to pay for your Part D premiums and co-pays, but these expenses don't count toward your MSA deductible.

Special Needs Plans (SNPs)

Special Needs Plans are relatively new additions to the Medicare Advantage program and aren't available in all areas. They're similar in structure to HMOs or PPOs (which I describe earlier in this chapter), but each individual SNP serves people in only one of the following specific categories:

✔ People who live in institutions (such as nursing homes)

✔ People who are eligible for both Medicare and Medicaid

✔ People who have at least one chronic or disabling condition (such as congestive heart failure, mental illness, diabetes, or HIV/AIDS)

I cover SNPs in more detail in Chapter 18. Here are their key features:

✔ **Eligibility:** You must have Medicare Parts A and B and live in the service area of your selected plan. To be accepted into an SNP, you must fall into the single category (one of the three previously described) that the plan serves. You can't join an SNP if you have end-stage renal disease (ESRD), unless the plan specifically offers care for this condition.

✔ **Choice of doctors and hospitals:** If the SNP works like an HMO, you must go to the doctors and hospitals within the plan's provider network, except in emergencies or for urgently needed care, and you need a primary care doctor to refer you to a specialist. If the SNP works like a PPO, you can go out-of-network for a higher cost and don't need a referral to see a specialist. The plan may assign a care manager to help coordinate your needs for healthcare and other services in the community.

✔ **Out-of-pocket costs:** The plan you select determines whether you pay a premium in addition to the Part B premium. Co-pays for specific services are often less, but sometimes higher, than those in traditional Medicare. Some plans set a limit on out-of-pocket spending in the year, usually on specified services. If your plan requires you to see only in-network providers, going outside of it would make you responsible for the full cost of treatment, except in emergencies or for urgently needed care. If you have Medicaid as well as Medicare, your Medicaid program may not pay the SNP's premium (if it has one), and you may pay different co-pays than those charged in traditional Medicare and Medicaid.

✔ **Extra benefits:** SNPs come with a built-in extra benefit in that they focus on your special circumstances or health condition and coordinate the services you need accordingly. Some plans offer vision, hearing, and/or dental services (though the extent of this coverage varies a great deal among plans); routine checkups; and other extras, like health club memberships or fitness classes. These bonuses are usually reflected in higher premiums.

✔ **Prescription drugs:** All SNPs must offer prescription drug coverage.

Three other types of Medicare health plans

Three types of plans don't fall within traditional Medicare or the Medicare Advantage program and aren't available in all parts of the country:

- ✔ **Medicare Cost plans:** These plans work like HMOs (which I describe earlier in this chapter), but, unlike MA plans, you can join a Medicare Cost plan if you have only Medicare Part B. If you go to doctors and hospitals outside of the plan's provider network for Medicare-covered services, traditional Medicare pays for your services, leaving you responsible for paying the usual costs and deductibles that apply in traditional Medicare. You can join a Medicare Cost plan at any time (if it's accepting new members), and you can also disenroll from it and return to traditional Medicare at any time. If the plan doesn't offer prescription drugs, you can enroll in a stand-alone Part D plan.

- ✔ **Programs of All-Inclusive Care for the Elderly (PACE):** These plans combine medical, social, and long-term care for frail people age 55 and older who are eligible for nursing home care but live in the community. All of them cover prescription drugs. PACE programs are covered in more detail in Chapter 18.

- ✔ **Medicare demonstration and pilot programs:** These are special projects that Medicare uses from time to time in specific parts of the country to test improvements in Medicare health coverage. If you want to know whether any demos or pilots are available in your area and how they work, call Medicare or your State Health Insurance Assistance Program (SHIP). See Appendix B for contact information.

Deciding between Traditional Medicare and a Private Medicare Health Plan

Knowing the key differences among Medicare's various health delivery systems — the traditional program and each type of private health plan, as described in the previous section — is essential in deciding which one to choose. Only you can make that decision. However, in the following sections, I highlight broader points to keep in mind when considering whether traditional Medicare or a private health plan is right for you. (I exclude PACE plans and demonstration or pilot programs here because their availability is limited.) I also touch on a situation that may not allow you a personal choice — being in a specific health plan chosen by an employer or union.

Weighing the systems

When you join Medicare and intend to rely on it for your medical needs (that is, if you aren't going to be receiving full benefits from elsewhere, such as an employer or union health plan), you automatically receive your care from the traditional Medicare program *unless* you specifically choose to switch to one of Medicare's private health plans. Similarly, if you're already in either traditional Medicare or one of the private health plans, you remain in that plan *unless* you take action to switch. In other words, you make the call.

Usually you can make this switch only during the annual open enrollment period from January 1 to March 31. (If you have Part D drug coverage, you also have from November 15 to December 31, as explained in Chapter 17.) Medicare allows some special circumstances for changing at other times of the year (see Chapter 17 for details). Also, you may have an opportunity to change your mind about the plan you join in certain situations, which I cover later in this chapter. Otherwise, you may find yourself locked into your choice, whether traditional Medicare or a private plan, for a whole year. So taking some time to consider which system you want is invaluable.

When making your decision, it may help to consider a wider perspective — how traditional Medicare and the Medicare Advantage program stack up generally in delivering healthcare. I take a big picture standpoint in the next several sections to touch on a range of issues: overall costs, premiums, co-pays, the long-term stability of costs and care, choice of providers and whether care is coordinated, extra benefits, and geographical service areas.

Thinking through these issues, and applying your personal preferences, enables you to settle on the Medicare system that works best for you. If you choose to go with a private health plan, see the later section "Comparing Medicare's Private Health Plans and Making Your Pick" for details on comparing individual plans in your area. You can also use the online search tool suggested in that section to compare the details of individual plans with traditional Medicare's standard offerings.

Overall costs

On the whole, most private plans offer lower costs to the consumer — sometimes charging no extra premiums — than traditional Medicare, for two reasons:

✔ Managed care plans (HMOs, PPOs, SNPs, and Medicare Cost plans) keep costs low by restricting care to their provider networks or by charging enrollees more to go out of those networks. They may also require enrollees to ask for prior authorization before covering certain kinds of treatment.

✔ Since a change in the law in 2003, Medicare has paid the private plans more on average for enrollees' care than it pays for people enrolled in the traditional system. The extra payments allow the plans to charge enrollees less and/or offer better benefits than traditional Medicare.

> (This fact accounts for most of the advantages in the Medicare Advantage system, but these extras could be much reduced if Congress acts to remove the extra payments, as some lawmakers and consumer groups are pushing for. I touch on this possibility in Chapter 21.)

However, Medicare's private plans may not be a less expensive option for everyone. The Government Accountability Office, which investigates public spending for Congress, recently reported that private plans generally charge enrollees more than traditional Medicare for services used by people with greater healthcare needs — those who require more (or longer) stays in hospitals and skilled nursing facilities or who use home healthcare services.

Premium costs

Many people in traditional Medicare pay three premiums: one for Part B, one for prescription drug coverage (Part D), and one for a Medigap supplemental insurance policy (see Chapter 1 for the basics of Medigap). Medigap insurance can't be used to cover out-of-pocket expenses in private plans, so dropping that premium to join one may save you money. But unless you have a private health plan that provides drug coverage and charges no premium of its own (as some do), you still pay three premiums — for Part B, for Part D, and for the health plan itself.

Co-pay costs

Private plans usually charge fixed dollar co-pays for doctor visits, which may be less expensive and more convenient than the percentage of the cost that traditional Medicare charges. But in comparing all plans, look carefully at the hospital co-pays. Traditional Medicare has a standard *deductible* ($1,024 in 2008), which is the limit you'd pay whether you're in the hospital for one day or up to 60 days in a benefit period. (I explain hospital benefit periods in Chapter 1.) The private plans usually charge a daily co-pay for a certain number of days in the hospital and often no co-pays between that number and up to 90 days or more. If you're in the hospital for five days and your plan charges a co-pay of $100 a day for the first six days, your bill would be $500 — or less than half what you'd pay under traditional Medicare at 2008 rates. But if the plan charges $250 a day, the bill for five days would be $1,250 — or $226 more than traditional Medicare.

Furthermore, if you need to go back into the hospital within 60 days of being discharged, you won't pay anything under traditional Medicare, because the deductible you've already paid for this benefit period covers your readmission stay. But under a private plan, you're charged new daily co-pays for the number of days specified by the plan.

You can purchase a Medigap supplementary policy that pays your hospital deductible, Part B deductible, and co-pays in traditional Medicare, making your costs more predictable. Under Medicare rules, you can't use Medigap to cover out-of-pocket expenses in a private health plan.

Cost and benefit stability

Private plans can change their costs and benefits each year — for better or for worse. Traditional Medicare is more stable, but it increases the Part B and hospital deductibles each year, and the 20 percent coinsurance it charges for most services also tends to rise as healthcare costs in general go up. Services that traditional Medicare covers generally don't change, although from time to time new ones are added.

Care stability

Traditional Medicare is there, year after year. Private health plans can choose annually whether to stay in Medicare or withdraw, or whether to enter or exit a particular service area. Occasionally Medicare doesn't renew a particular plan's contract. If any such changes occur, affected enrollees are notified in advance and can switch to another private plan or to traditional Medicare, but this change can be a disrupting experience.

Provider choice

The main reason people give for choosing traditional Medicare (or staying in it) is that they can go to any doctor or hospital they please. Or at least any that accept Medicare patients, and most providers still do. In contrast, the Medicare Advantage plans that offer managed care limit the choice of providers to those in their networks. However, this may be considered a benefit rather than a restriction if care is properly coordinated, as explained in the next section.

The growth of PFFS plans in recent years offers an alternative to managed care in that PFFS plans allow you to go to any doctors or hospitals that accept their payment terms. That's fine if all the providers you want in your area accept the terms. But not all do, and it's not easy to find out which ones accept a PFFS plan's terms in advance of joining it.

Care coordination

Managed care has generally gotten a bad rap, because many people see it as too restrictive, especially in terms of provider choice. But when care is coordinated properly, as it's supposed to be in HMOs, SNPs, and Medicare Cost plans, it can be of great benefit to the consumer. Because your care is handled and monitored by a single local system, you're more likely to be encouraged to get tests and screenings early enough to prevent serious health problems later on, and less likely to be prescribed drugs that may interact badly with each other, for example. PPOs may offer elements of coordinated care, but not if you exercise your right to go to out-of-network providers or see specialists without a referral. Traditional Medicare, PFFS, and MSA plans don't feature coordination of care.

Extra benefits

All private plans must provide the same medical services as traditional Medicare. But they can also include extra benefits in their packages that are well worth having. Some plans with these extras don't charge higher premiums, but most do — often quite a lot more. Look at any extra benefits carefully when comparing plans, because some provide significant coverage and others are very limited.

Geographical area

Considering your geographic location is important if you travel a lot or live in another state for part of the year. Traditional Medicare covers you anywhere in the U.S.; so do PFFS plans (at least in theory) and MSAs. However, HMOs, local PPOs, SNPs, and Medicare Cost plans require you to either go to providers within their local service areas or get preapproval to go outside the network. In a regional PPO, you can go to providers throughout the service region (sometimes several adjacent states) or get preapproval to go outside the network. Fortunately, all plans must cover emergency treatment or urgently needed care anywhere in the country. Some Medigap policies and health plans also cover emergency care abroad.

Recognizing when you may not have a choice

You may not be free to make a choice — either between traditional Medicare and the private plan system or among the private plans themselves — if you have health coverage from a current or former employer or union. Following are some of the ways this limitation can occur:

- ✔ Your current plan is a special one offered only to employees or retirees of the employer or union that sponsors it.

- ✔ Your current plan pays the premiums for a Medigap supplementary insurance policy. (This type of policy can be used only with traditional Medicare, not with a Medicare Advantage plan.)

- ✔ Your current plan gives you coverage under a specific Medicare Advantage plan — an HMO, PPO, PFFS, or an MSA plan — meaning you can't also be enrolled in the traditional Medicare program or any other MA plan.

Be aware that if you enroll in an alternative plan (unless it's an alternative specifically offered by your employer or union) you may automatically lose your current coverage for you and your dependents and may not be able to get it back. Always check with your current plan's benefits administrator before taking this step so you know the consequences.

Some people in this situation are faced with a real dilemma. For example, an increasing number of employers and unions are contracting with Medicare PFFS plans to cover their retirees. This move makes sense to sponsoring organizations with retirees all over the country, because in theory PFFS enrollees can go to doctors or hospitals anywhere. But some retirees have found that the only providers that accept their PFFS plan are far from their homes. If this Catch-22 happens to you, you can either put up with the plan or give up the retiree health benefit you've paid into for years. But first, why not holler loudly to the administrators of your employer or union plan to let them know what's going on and see whether they can fix it?

Comparing Medicare's Private Health Plans and Making Your Pick

The different types of Medicare private health plans (see the earlier section "Medicare Advantage plans" for details on each) aren't just single plans. Rather, each type is offered by a number of different insurers. And a single insurer may offer several plans in one or more of these categories. The result? A lot of different plans to choose from, each with its own mix of costs and benefits.

I'm not going to pretend that making this choice is necessarily easy. If you've had experience making two or three plan choices under employer coverage in the past, you know the score. Well, sort of — deciding between two or three plans pales before the choices in Medicare. And if you've never had to choose a plan before, the number and range of choices may come as a big shock. After all, you're not comparing apples to apples here. I mean, how do you compare one plan's flat dollar co-pay for visiting a doctor with another plan's percentage of the cost? How do you figure the trade-off between a relatively high co-pay for a hospital stay against a low premium?

Still, the difficulty of making that choice is no argument for not comparing plans. Whichever plan you choose may be a bit of a gamble, but insurance always is. And taking a hard look at the differences among the plans available to you makes your final decision an informed one. Regardless of the outcome, you can know you gave it your best shot.

In the following sections, I delve into how many private health plan choices you may face. Then I explain how to compare the details of the ones that interest you — either by making an online search that I walk you through, step by step, or by obtaining personal help. I also suggest ways of using this information to choose a final plan. Finally, I explain three circumstances in which you may be able to change your mind after enrollment and switch to traditional Medicare.

Determining how many plan choices you have

The number of Medicare private health plans for you to choose from depends very much on where you live. If you live in a heavily populated place, you probably have at least 50 plans available to you, including all the different types of Medicare plans. If you live in a very rural area, fewer than 15 plans may be available, and you may have far less choice among plan types. Rural areas often have no HMOs, local PPOs, or SNPs. They generally have one or two regional PPOs, one MSA plan, and a vast majority of PFFS plans.

Not all of these plans include drug coverage, so if you're looking for a plan that combines medical and drug benefits in one package, this preference reduces your number of plan choices.

You can get a very rough idea of how many Medicare health plans are available to you by looking at your *Medicare & You* handbook that Medicare sends out to all beneficiaries in October with information for the following year. Flip toward the back of the book to find a list of health plans in your state. (You can also read *Medicare & You* online at www.medicare.gov.)

However, you can't always tell from the handbook which plans are available in your neck of the woods. Plans' service areas may be described as being in select counties, or in a particular region of your state without specifying its borders. In other words, some of the plans listed may not operate in your zip code at all. What's more, the handbook's list gives only scant details about the plans — far too little info to make a reasoned choice among them. Fortunately, a better resource exists. Keep reading!

Finding a list of plans online

The fastest and most effective way of finding out your Medicare health plan options is to go to the Web site Medicare provides for this purpose. This useful tool allows to you compare plans head-to-head. (If you don't have access to the Internet, fast-forward to the section "Getting personal help to compare plans" later in this chapter.)

To navigate the Web site, follow these steps, which represent consecutive pages on-screen:

1. **On the www.medicare.gov home page, under Search Tools, click "Compare Health Plans and Medigap Policies in Your Area."**

2. **In the box on the left-hand side, click "Find & Compare Health Plans."**

3. **Click "Begin General Plan Search" on the right.**

4. **Enter your zip code, ignore the request for age and health status, answer the following questions, and click "Continue."**

5. **Read this page if you want to review the details you've provided or see the general information offered, then click "Continue."**

6. **Click "Continue to Plan List" to compare only the health plans' medical benefits at this stage. You can compare the plans' drug coverage later.**

7. **Examine the list of all the Medicare health plans available in your area by scrolling down the page.**

   The total number of available plans appears at the top. Table 9-2 gives a few examples of the kind of broad information, labeled Plan Summary, you'll encounter.

Table 9-2		Sample Plan Summary from Medicare's Plan Comparison Tool					
Plan Name	**Type**	**Monthly Premium**	**Covers Drugs?**	**Doctor Choice**	**Vision Services**	**Dental Services**	**Physical Exams**
Plan	HMO	$24.40	Yes	Plan doctors only	Covered	Covered (at extra cost)	Covered
Plan	PPO	$104.50	Yes	Any doctor	Covered	Covered	Covered
Plan	SNP	$0	Yes	Plan doctors only	Covered	Covered	Covered
Plan	PFFS	$43.40	No	Any willing doctor	Covered	Not covered	Covered
Plan	MSA	$0	No	Any doctor	Not covered	Not covered	Not covered
Plan	Cost	$0	No	Plan doctors only	Not covered	Not covered	Not covered
Original Medicare		$0	No	Any doctor	Not covered	Not covered	Not covered

As you can see in Table 9-2, the Plan Summary page gives a quick snapshot of each plan. The page shows at a glance the plan's name, its type, its premium (in addition to the Part B premium), and whether it includes drug coverage, restricts doctor choice, or covers vision/dental services and physical exams.

One column that appears in the Plan Summary on-screen, but is excluded in Table 9-2, is headed "Estimated Annual Cost for People Like You." This is a very rough estimate based on any information you give as to your age and health status in Step 4 of the previous list. A dollar amount is shown, even if you haven't provided this detail. This tool doesn't (and can't!) provide a reliable guide to your out-of-pocket medical expenses over the year in any plan.

The plan descriptions in Table 9-2 are only examples. Plenty of plans within each type charge premiums higher or lower than those shown, or vary in their inclusion of drug coverage and extra benefits. The only type that's always the same is the Original Medicare row, which shows details that are standard to the traditional Medicare program.

If you want, you can cut down the number of plans on-screen to show only the kind you're looking for. Go to the top of the page and click the "Show" button next to Select Criteria to Reduce Number of Plans Shown (optional). A menu of options will appear. Click the small box next to each kind of plan you want to see — for example, "Plans that include drug coverage." Then click "Apply Limits."

Be cautious of using this device to lessen the number of plans. For example, if you indicate that you want to see only plans that include drug coverage, you automatically exclude the traditional Medicare program from the list — yet it may be very useful to know what this program offers, as a kind of yardstick, when you're comparing specific medical benefits among plans. Similarly, if you specify a premium limit, you exclude all plans with premiums over that dollar amount. So you don't see plans that overall may give you a better deal — for example, somewhat higher premiums but lower co-pays. However, if you're looking specifically for an SNP or an MSA, checking those options reduces the number of plans that appear on-screen to those you wish to see.

Digging for plan details

After obtaining your Medicare plan options (see the preceding section for tips on doing so), you're now ready to look at the nitty-gritty details necessary to compare plans properly. These details include what the plan charges for visits to a primary care doctor or specialist, stays in a hospital, having an X-ray, or using an ambulance. Clicking any of the plan names in the left-hand column on the list brings up all of these details, and many more, for that plan.

Each details page provides a lot of information. Here are some guidelines to help you sort through it all:

✔ Comparing plans' benefits side by side is useful. Fortunately, you can do so for up to three plans at a time. On the main list page, click the little box that appears alongside the name of each plan you want to see, then click "Compare" at the top or bottom of the page.

The three-plan comparison device is also very useful for comparing details of the traditional Medicare program (always called Original Medicare on this site) with some of the private health plans you're considering. Scroll down the main plan list until you see Original Medicare and click the box beside it.

✔ The first chunk of information you see for any private plan is a quality assessment titled Plan Ratings. This section features stars, ranging from one (poor) to five (excellent), to grade how well the plan performs in categories like Getting Care from Your Doctors and Specialists and Managing Chronic Conditions. Select the "Click to view more details on Plan Ratings" link to see how Medicare arrived at these ratings.

This information can be useful in deciding which plans to avoid or in breaking a tie after whittling down your plan options to just two or three.

✔ In the next section, headed Important Information, you can see the plan's monthly premium, as well as if you have a choice of doctors and hospitals, need a referral to see a specialist, or must limit yourself to the plan's provider network. Look to see if the plan sets a cap on your out-of-pocket expenses — but be aware that this limit may apply only to certain services. You need to call the plan to find out which ones count.

✔ Pay special attention to the section headed Inpatient Care. Plans vary a great deal in the co-pays they charge for hospital stays — sometimes by hundreds of dollars. You should also compare these charges with the hospital deductible required under traditional Medicare. Look to see if you or your doctor must notify the plan before checking into the hospital for a nonemergency surgery or treatment.

✔ The Outpatient Care section gives details of costs to visit doctors and specialists, have outpatient surgery, or use an ambulance. It also states whether the payment method is a flat co-pay or a percentage of the cost. The following section gives similar details for outpatient tests, X-rays, lab services, and medical equipment (like wheelchairs). Look to see if you're required to ask the plan for prior authorization before receiving any of the services listed in this section.

✔ If the plan includes Part D prescription drug coverage in its package, details appear in the Additional Benefits section. You can see lots of stuff here about the plan's formulary, deductible, and co-pays for different kinds of drugs.

Here's a special tip: *Ignore these details!* It's impossible to tell what your drugs will cost under the plan from this information, or if they'll be covered. Instead, you need to do a different search according to the *specific* drugs you take. You can do this by going back and entering your drugs, their dosages, and frequency in Step 6, and then clicking on "View Drug Benefits" at the top of the main page. Or you can follow the more detailed instructions for comparing drug plans on Medicare's Part D plan finder tool that I walk you through in Chapter 10. Either way, you'll find out more precisely what your out-of-pocket drug expenses would be over the whole year in a plan.

> ✔ If the plan includes coverage for extra services — such as dental, hearing, and eye care — these details appear at the bottom of the Additional Benefits list. You may notice that some co-pays are given for Medicare-covered services. Traditional Medicare provides for a few medically justified services in these areas — for example, eye exams for people who have diabetes or are at high risk for glaucoma; eye glasses for people who've had cataract surgery; hearing tests for people who may need medical treatment as a result; and dental work required for a medical procedure, such as jaw surgery after an accident. But the private plan may offer checkups and procedures (like teeth cleaning) that aren't covered by traditional Medicare.

Getting personal help to compare plans

If you don't have access to the Internet, or just don't feel up to doing an online search yourself, you can still get the information you need to compare Medicare health plans properly. These alternatives include the following:

> ✔ Asking a family member or a friend to do an online search for you

> ✔ Calling the Medicare help line, your State Health Insurance Assistance Program (SHIP), or your Area Agency on Aging — which all give free help

> ✔ Talking to trained volunteers from a consumer group or senior center

These sources are the same as the ones I explain in Chapter 10's "Finding Personal Help to Compare Plans" section. So go there for details and contact information.

Watching out for hard-sell marketing pressures and scams

Of course, you can obtain details in ways other than the options I mention in the previous sections. For example,

> ✔ You may receive advertising materials from Medicare health plans through the mail.

> ✔ You may chat with a sales representative by phone or at a pharmacy, shopping mall, or senior center.

> ✔ You may consult an independent insurance agent or broker.

Just remember that fancy direct mail pieces and energetic sales reps are pitching the health plan they're supposed to sell. They're not going to compare their plan point by point with their competitors' plans! The same is true for some independent insurance agents, because they're paid higher commissions for some plans than others. So the plan they pitch may not be the right one for you.

Selling Medicare health plans is a ferociously competitive business — so stay on your guard against being pressured into buying a plan you don't want or don't understand fully. Yes, regrettably, you can be persuaded into buying a plan that's not right for you! That's why I urge you to read Chapter 11, in which I explain how to protect yourself against unethical hard-sell tactics, as well as downright illegal scams. There, I break down Medicare's marketing rules for plans, a list of matters to think about and check out before enrolling in a plan, and actions you can take if you're misled into joining a plan you don't want or understand.

Asking questions before you make your final choice

If you're here, I'm assuming you've now decided on a Medicare health plan for your medical care rather than traditional Medicare, and also that you've narrowed your plan choices to a manageable two, three, or four. Now all you need to do is get down to that final one.

Getting all of your information in order helps a great deal. If you research plans using Medicare's online comparison tool, you can print out the details of the few that interest you. If you call the Medicare help line at 800-633-4227 for the same information, you can ask the customer representative to mail you printouts for the plans you want to consider. You can also call the plans to ask for their info packets or visit their Web sites.

After you have this information, notice how the options can become tons clearer when you write down the key details alongside each other. The following questions are also reproduced in Worksheet 3 in Appendix A, along with spaces for writing out the answers for up to four plans. In the following list, I explain what action to take to find out specific answers to some of the questions. In all other cases, you can find the answers in your Medicare printouts, in the plan's info packet, or on its Web site.

Dive into the decision-making process by asking the following:

✔ **Will the providers (doctors and hospitals) that I prefer accept this plan?**

You can obtain provider network lists from HMOs, PPOs, SNPs, and Medicare Cost plans by mail on request or from their Web sites. In the case of PFFS plans, you need to ask your local doctors and hospitals.

✔ **Will this plan allow me to go to out-of-network providers for a higher co-pay?**

✔ **Will this plan cover my *nonemergency* healthcare needs outside of my home area?**

In the case of HMOs, PPOs, SNPs, and Medicare Cost plans, you have to ask the plan precisely what its service area is, and in what circumstances it may cover treatment outside that region. (Information on service area boundaries isn't given on the Medicare Web site or in the *Medicare & You* handbook.) PFFS and MSA plans don't have defined service areas.

✔ **What will my fixed costs (monthly premium on top of Part B premium; annual deductible in the case of an MSA) be in this plan?**

✔ **Does this plan put a limit on my out-of-pocket expenses in a year?**

You can get the cap amount from Medicare, the plan's Web site, or the plan's brochure. But you need to call the plan to find out which services count toward the cap.

✔ **What will I pay to visit my primary care doctor in this plan?**

✔ **What will I pay to visit a specialist in this plan?**

✔ **What will I pay to stay in a hospital in this plan?**

✔ **What are this plan's ratings for quality of care?**

You can only find this information on Medicare's online health plan finder or by calling the Medicare help line (800-633-4227).

✔ **Does this plan offer benefits for vision, hearing, or dental care?**

✔ **Does this plan offer preventive care (screenings, scans, tests) that meet my needs?**

✔ **Does this plan cover routine physical exams?**

Notice one question missing from this list: **Does this plan cover prescription drugs?** Yes, it's an important question. But, as I explain earlier in this chapter, the type of Medicare health plan you choose directly affects how you can get drug coverage. So remember that

✔ If one or more of the health plans on your shortlist includes prescription drugs in its benefit package, you need to compare the drug coverage details separately.

✔ If you're thinking about an HMO or PPO that doesn't include drug coverage, you can't add a stand-alone Part D plan to it. So if you want drug coverage, strike this health plan off your shortlist.

✔ If you're pondering a PFFS, MSA, or Medicare Cost plan that doesn't include drug coverage, you can enroll in a stand-alone Part D plan.

✔ If you're considering traditional Medicare, which doesn't include outpatient drugs, you can enroll in a stand-alone Part D plan.

Chapter 10 shows you how to compare drug plans effectively. Afterward, you can use Worksheet 2 in Appendix A to note the differences. Then, you can use this info together with Worksheet 3 to see which plan works best for you in terms of medical *and* drug coverage. When you reach that point, it's time to enroll, as explained in Chapter 12.

Knowing if you can make a change

What if you find, after you're in a Medicare private health plan, that you don't like it? Medicare allows you to switch plans outside of the regular open enrollment period only for several specific reasons, and unhappiness isn't one of them! However, here are some escape clauses (which are all explained in more detail in Chapter 17):

- ✔ **If your coverage in a Medicare health plan starts January 1:** You have the right to switch to traditional Medicare or to another health plan during the first three months of the year, through March 31. However, you can't use this opportunity to drop or add drug coverage.

- ✔ **If you receive Extra Help:** You can change to another Medicare health plan that offers drug coverage, or to traditional Medicare and a stand-alone drug plan, at any time during the year.

- ✔ **If you joined a Medicare health plan as soon as you enrolled in Medicare at age 65:** Medicare considers this first year in the program as a trial period. So you have the right to disenroll from the plan at any time within 12 months of first receiving coverage from it in order to switch to traditional Medicare and a stand-alone Part D plan. You also have a guaranteed right to buy a Medigap policy within 63 days of your plan coverage ending.

- ✔ **If this is your first time in a Medicare health plan and you dropped a Medigap policy to join it:** You have the right to return to traditional Medicare and be reinstated in Medigap at any time during your first 12 months in this plan.

- ✔ **If you joined a Medicare Cost plan:** You have the right to disenroll from it and switch to traditional Medicare at any time. If you received drug coverage from this plan, you can also switch to a stand-alone Part D plan at the same time.

Chapter 10

Making a Smart Choice among Medicare Prescription Drug Plans

Medicare advises people who are choosing a Medicare prescription drug plan to consider the three Cs — *cost, coverage, and convenience.* That's perfectly true. But I say add three more Cs — *compare, compare, compare!* And even a fourth: Do it *carefully!* I can't emphasize this point enough: Comparing plans carefully is the single most important step you can take in finding the Part D plan that's best for you. It may save you unexpected hassle. It'll certainly save you money.

"Well, yeah," you say. "But what about the fact that I'm faced with more than 80 drug plans in my area? And they're all different!" I know that the number of plans makes choosing just one — let alone the right one — seem a daunting prospect. But take heart, because you don't have to grope your way through the multitude of all of those plans. In this chapter, I demonstrate a strategy for navigating the Part D maze that focuses only on *your* needs.

First, I explain why comparing plans properly is better than the less-than-ideal alternatives you may be considering. I also share how to make two simple (yet essential!) lists of your needs and preferences to help you get the most out of an invaluable tool: the online Medicare Prescription Drug Plan Finder. I walk you through this tool step by step so you can whittle all those plans to a manageable few in the fastest and most effective way. I then show you how to drill down into a plan's details to help bring you to a final choice. Finally, I suggest ways of getting personal assistance comparing plans, if you need it. In essence, this chapter's purpose is to help you avoid that queasy feeling that often comes after making an important decision — did I do the right thing?

Understanding the Need to Compare Plans Carefully

There's a famous scene in *Indiana Jones and the Last Crusade* where Indy and his enemy choose what each thinks to be the Holy Grail from an array of goblets. The evil Nazi picks a gold one, and instantly dies a horrible death. "He chose . . . poorly," observes the ancient knight who's been on guard duty for about 700 years. Indy picks a simple wooden cup. "You," intones the knight, "have chosen . . . wisely."

Well, maybe the Part D plan that's best for you isn't the Holy Grail exactly. But you still need to choose wisely to get it. And there are so many poor ways of choosing. Like these:

- ✔ **Picking the same plan as your spouse, your best friend, your next-door neighbor, or your second cousin.** (Why? Because they're not you! They don't take the same prescription drugs as you.)

- ✔ **Choosing the plan with the lowest premium in your area.** (Why? Because, unless you don't take any drugs right now, premiums are far less important than co-pays in adding to your out-of-pocket expenses under any plan.)

- ✔ **Agreeing to enroll in a plan that a sales agent pitches to you at a shopping mall, local pharmacy, senior center, or anywhere else.** (Why? Because the agent's talking up the plan he's paid to sell, without a thought to your personal needs or preferences.)

- ✔ **Picking a plan from the marketing brochures that plans send to your home.** (Why? Because these are advertising materials designed to make a sale, again without regard to your own circumstances and needs.)

- ✔ **Deciding on the plan with the most familiar name.** (Why? Because it won't necessarily cover your drugs at the least cost.)

Using any of these methods to choose a plan isn't much better than closing your eyes and jabbing a pin in a list, because none of them account for the prescription drugs that *you* take. Your own set of drugs — down to the exact dosage of each and how often you take them — is the most important factor in picking the plan that's right for you. It's the essential key to choosing wisely.

In the next two sections, I explain how to recognize the best plan for your needs and why comparing plans carefully is worth the effort.

What's the best plan, anyway?

In theory, the best plan is the one that provides any prescription drug you may conceivably need, not just now but also in the unforeseeable future. But that's not how Part D works. No plan covers every drug, as I explain in Chapter 4. And unless you can find out the drugs that each plan covers and count them all up — a daunting task considering many plans have thousands of drugs on their formularies — it's impossible to know which plan covers the most.

I believe that the best plan has to be the one that covers all, or almost all, of the drugs you're taking *now* — meaning the time when you're deciding which plan to sign up for — at the lowest out-of-pocket cost and with the fewest hoops to jump through to get those drugs. If it turns out later on that you need a drug that's not on your plan's formulary, you can ask your doctor whether an alternative formulary drug may work as well for you (as explained in Chapter 16). Otherwise, you can try using the exceptions process to ask the plan to cover your prescribed drug (see Chapter 4) or, if you're turned down, you can appeal the decision (see Chapter 19).

You can also change to another Part D plan at the end of the year during open enrollment (or during the year in certain circumstances, as explained in Chapter 17). In fact, it's wise to compare plans annually, because they change their costs and benefits each year, so the plan that's best for you this year may not be as good for you next year.

Is comparing plans worth the effort?

Comparing plans carefully is definitely worthwhile! Doing so tells you

- ✔ Which are the three or four plans that cover all of your prescription drugs but cost you the least out of pocket over the whole year.

- ✔ Which of these plans has the fewest or no restrictions for your drugs. (Different kinds of *restrictions* — prior authorization, quantity limits, or step therapy — are described in Chapter 4.)

- ✔ Which of these plans gives you the best discounts if you choose generic drugs or want to receive your meds by mail order.

- ✔ Which of these plans has the most reasonable *co-pay structure* — that is, the different amounts you pay in each tier of charges — in case you need more meds later in the year. (For example, Plan X may charge a co-pay of $45 for all of its nonpreferred brands, whereas Plan Y may charge more than $100 for drugs in its own nonpreferred brand tier.)

- ✔ Whether you're going to fall into the *doughnut hole* (also known as the coverage gap; see Chapter 15 for full details) with the set of drugs you take now and, if so:

  - • At which point in the year that's going to happen.

  - • Whether that's going to occur later under one plan than another.

  - • Whether any of these plans cover *your* drugs in the doughnut hole.

✔ Which of these plans have network pharmacies convenient for you.

✔ Which of these plans have a mail-order option, if you want one.

✔ Which of these plans allow you to fill your prescriptions in any state if you travel or live away from home for part of the year.

Certainly, you can find the answers to a few of these questions just by reviewing the *Medicare & You* handbook, which gives some details of all Part D plans in your area. (Medicare mails this publication to you each October.) Or you can look at individual drug plans' marketing brochures and Web sites. But you won't find answers to all of your questions, or even to the most important one of all — which plans cover your drugs at the least cost.

The only really effective way of getting that critical information is to create the lists of your meds and plan preferences and use the online Medicare Prescription Drug Plan Finder, or get someone else to use it for you, as explained later in this chapter. This tool is also the *safest* way of choosing a plan. Why? Because when you do the comparison, you remain in control. You can't fall for a sweet sales pitch — or worse, fall prey to a scam or a hard sell from some unscrupulous person who exploits your uncertainty for personal gain. (See Chapter 11 for the scoop on marketing scams and hard sells.)

Will you avoid Part D buyer's remorse?

Most folks don't compare Part D plans before choosing one, period. Surveys show that most often they rely on word-of-mouth recommendations or choose a plan sponsored by an insurer with a familiar name. So I'm guessing millions of Part D enrollees out there are paying far more than they need to for their drugs. Here are a few examples of how comparing plans carefully can save you money — and how failing to do so can teach you a hard lesson.

Bill's story: Going by a well-known name

Back in November 2005, a few weeks before Part D started, I was having dinner at a friend's house when another guest, Bill, told me he'd signed up with a plan. I asked how he'd chosen it. Well, he'd picked an insurer whose name he knew and felt he could trust. Fine, I said, but let's do a comparison. We borrowed a laptop, and I ran the information for his six meds through the online Medicare Prescription Drug Plan Finder. It took about 15 minutes. The least expensive plan — also provided by a well-known insurer — turned out to cost about $1,000 a year less than the one he'd chosen. Because we were still within the open enrollment period, he was able to switch plans. Every year since then I've run the numbers for Bill. And every year the plan that worked out best for him was different than the plan he'd had the year before.

Joel's story: Choosing the same plan as your spouse

Before he retired, Joel had health insurance from his company that covered drugs for both himself and his wife, Mae. When they needed Part D, Joel left it to Mae to pick a plan for both of them, because she took a lot of drugs, and he rarely took any, and they felt more comfortable being in the same plan. So Mae chose Plan X, which covered all of her drugs for a monthly premium of $61, and signed them both up. Mae was okay, but Joel was actually wasting money. Because he almost never needed drugs, he'd have been better off on Plan Y, which had a premium of $12.10 (the lowest in his area) and would've saved him $48.90 a month, or $586.80 over the course of the year.

Joanne's story: Failing to research a sales pitch

Joanne was in the mall buying gifts for her grandkids when a sales rep invited her to sit down, have a cup of coffee, and talk about Part D. Joanne already had a plan and wasn't thinking of changing it, but she was happy to take a load off and listen for a few minutes. What the rep said about Plan X sounded like a better deal than her current plan, so Joanne signed up on the spot. What she didn't know was that for her set of drugs (two brand-names and two generics) Plan X ranked 27th in expense out of the 51 drug plans in her area. If she'd compared the plans according to the drugs she took, instead of listening to a sales pitch, she'd have found Plan Y. This plan had higher premiums than Plan X. But Plan Y charged lower co-pays for her generics ($4 per prescription rather than $8) and placed her brands in its preferred brand tier (with co-pays of $25), whereas Plan X placed them in its nonpreferred tier with co-pays of $55. So over the course of the year, Joanne paid $1,764 with Plan X, whereas she'd have paid $996 under Plan Y — a savings of $768.

Getting Organized with Two Crucial Lists

The information you must have at hand before comparing Part D plans properly — whether you hop online and use the Medicare Prescription Drug Plan Finder yourself or get someone else to do it for you — is very simple. All you need (besides your zip code, which you already know) is

- ✔ An accurate list of your prescription meds
- ✔ A list of personal preferences that may make you lean toward one plan rather than another

In the following sections, I explain how to make your drug list complete and accurate in all of its details and how to note the kinds of preferences that may be important to you.

Creating an accurate list of your meds

Take a sheet of paper or use the worksheet provided in Appendix A. Have in front of you all of those bottles that contain the prescription medications you're currently taking — tablets, capsules, liquid solutions, sprays, creams, or whatever form they come in. Then make a list of their exact names, their dosages, and how often you take them *(frequency),* using the information provided on the pharmacist's labels. Alternatively, you can ask your pharmacist for a printout of all of your prescription drugs.

Whichever method you choose, your list should look something like Table 10-1 — but with details for your own drugs, of course, in place of my examples.

Table 10-1	What a Detailed Drug List May Look Like	
Exact Medication Name	*Dosage*	*Frequency*
Verapamil HCL ER	120 mg	1 a day
Fosamax	70 mg	1 a week
Carbidopa/levodopa	25/100 mg	3 a day
Xalatan SOL 0.005%	2.50 ml bottle	1 bottle a month
Santyl OIN 250u/gm	30 gm tube	1 tube every two months

I'm not just being persnickety in saying you should note down these three items — name, dosage, and frequency — exactly as they're written on the container label. Following are some good reasons for being strictly accurate with each one:

✔ **Exact medication name:** Many prescription drugs have the same name but come in different forms, with their differences marked by a second word or combination of letters following the name.

For example, verapamil hydrochloride, a generic drug used to treat high blood pressure, irregular heartbeats, and chest pain, is shown in Table 10-1 as verapamil HCL ER. The *ER* stands for extended release, but this drug is also available in three other variations: a plain form (without additional letters); an *SR* form (sustained release); and a *CR* form (controlled release), meaning the drug is absorbed into the body at different rates. Because this drug is a generic, a plan's co-pays for any of these forms are likely the same — but the full price of the SR form is generally twice as much as the ER or CR forms, which makes a difference in the deductible or doughnut hole. So using the wrong initials in a plan search can distort your overall out-of-pocket cost results.

✔ **Dosage:** Using the wrong dosage in a plan search may also distort your cost results. Part D plans often charge the same co-pay for different strengths of the same drug — but not always. Even the full price may be the same for different dosages — but sometimes it isn't. In this case, you pay more for a higher dosage in the deductible period (if you have one) or in the doughnut hole (if you fall into it), and also if the plan you choose charges *coinsurance* (a percentage of the price) for your drugs in the initial coverage period rather than fixed co-pays. (I explain the difference between co-pays and coinsurance in Chapter 3.)

✔ **How often you take your drugs:** Of the three factors that can alter your out-of-pocket costs during a plan search, frequency is the most important. If, by mistake, you say you take a pill *once* a day when in fact you take it *twice* a day, the search results will show a cost that's half as much as you'll actually pay when filling your prescription at the pharmacy. That's one surprise you don't want! The converse is just as distorting. If, for example, you take a drug once a *week,* but by mistake say in a plan search that you take it once a *day,* the results will show an out-of-pocket cost seven times higher than what you'd actually pay.

The accuracy of the costs you're quoted in a plan search depends very much on the accuracy of the drug names, dosages, and frequencies you enter into the plan finder. These details are equally important if you ask someone else — such as a customer representative on the Medicare telephone help line, or a counselor at your State Health Insurance Assistance Program (SHIP) — because this person, too, is going to use Medicare's plan finder to assist you. (I explain how to find personal help with comparing plans later in this chapter.)

Drawing up a list of your plan preferences

Finding a plan that covers all of your drugs and costs you the least out of pocket may be top on your list of priorities. But chances are high that you're going to identify several Part D plans that cover your drugs and vary by only a few dollars in the overall amount they charge. So consider some other factors that may be important to you, like these:

✔ **Are the pharmacies in this plan's network convenient to where I live?** Each plan has its own network of pharmacies, and going to a pharmacy outside that network costs you a lot more (maybe even full price) for your drugs. (See Chapter 14 for more on this topic.) Before finally selecting a plan, you need to be sure it has network pharmacies within a reasonable distance of your home.

✔ **Does this plan have a mail-order option?** If you prefer to receive all or some of your prescriptions by mail order in 90-day supplies (which costs less in many plans), you need to be certain that the plan offers a mail-order service. Some plans don't. (I discuss mail order in more detail later in this chapter.)

✔ **Does this plan restrict any of my drugs?** Any plan may require you to ask permission before it'll cover certain drugs through restrictions known as prior authorization, quantity limits, or step therapy. (I explain these requirements and how to deal with them in Chapter 4.) Because plans impose restrictions on different drugs, you'll want to look for a plan that has the fewest restrictions on your drugs, or none at all.

✔ **Will this plan cover my prescriptions when I'm away from home?** If you expect to travel during the year or live in another state for part of the year, you want a plan that covers your prescriptions at network pharmacies throughout the United States. Some plans offer a national service and some don't. (None cover drugs purchased abroad.) See the later section "Searching for pharmacies if you travel or live away from home for part of the year" for more information.

✔ **Does this plan have a good customer service track record?** Plans that answer calls without keeping you on hold forever, respond to questions properly, pay their share of prescriptions correctly, and deal with complaints promptly are obviously preferable. Some plans provide more satisfactory customer service than others. See the later section "Assessing customer service" for details.

So how do you sort out the wheat from the chaff on all of these questions? The answers are available through Medicare's online plan finder, and I show you how to find them later in this chapter. If you'd rather not go online yourself, you can get a hand comparing plans as explained in the later section, "Finding Personal Help to Compare Plans."

Introducing the Medicare Prescription Drug Plan Finder

Medicare's online prescription drug plan finder is an interactive Web site that allows you to plug in details of your own prescription drugs to find out which plans cover them and approximately what each plan will charge you. In other words, this tool makes light work of an otherwise difficult calculation by doing the math for you automatically. I walk you through the process step by step later in this chapter.

You can use the plan finder to compare Part D coverage and costs within

✔ Stand-alone plans (PDPs), which provide *only* drugs and are the type of plan you need if you're enrolled in traditional Medicare for your medical coverage

✔ Medicare Advantage plans (MAPDs) that provide prescription drugs and medical coverage in one package

✔ Special Needs Plans (SNPs), which in some areas offer comprehensive care for people in certain situations, such as living in a nursing home, being chronically ill, or receiving Medicaid services

Using the plan finder to compare coverage and costs for your drugs is essentially the same process within all these groups. But if you're considering a Medicare Advantage or Special Needs plan, you need to compare details of the medical services they provide as well as drug coverage. I explain why in Chapter 9.

Everybody who wants impartial information about Part D plans uses the online plan finder. And I mean everybody! Not only people in Medicare but also doctors, pharmacists, social workers, counselors, advocates, and help groups. Gee, that sounds an awful lot like anybody who's assisting a Medicare beneficiary in finding a Part D plan! Clearly, everyone depends on the plan finder. So it's reasonable to ask: How reliable is it?

The plan finder is a complex and sophisticated computer program. And it's unique: No other insurance system offers consumers a way to compare plans head-to-head to find the best deal. But of course such comparisons are only as reliable as the pricing information fed into them — in this case, by the Part D plans themselves.

Medicare officials say they rigorously monitor the accuracy of plan prices and, when errors are detected, remove all information about that plan from the Web site until corrections are made. Medicare also includes pricing accuracy as one of the measures in its quality assessment system, which rates individual plans from one star (poor) to five stars (excellent). Officials say the ratings, displayed on the plan finder, are based on Medicare's own regular reviews and the number of complaints it receives from consumers.

Nonetheless, the plan finder isn't free from glitches and errors. Here are some tips for avoiding, or minimizing, your chances of choosing a plan based on misleading information, as well as how to deal with it if you accidentally do:

✔ **Know that Medicare posts new plan information for the following year in mid-October.** This is when the potential for pricing errors is most likely, because every plan changes its costs and benefits from year to year, and huge amounts of detail are being uploaded onto the system. If you do a plan search at this time, recheck the information after open enrollment starts on November 15.

✔ **After you've used the plan finder to choose the plan you like best, but *before* enrolling in it, it's sensible to**

   • **Double-check the accuracy of the drug information you entered into the plan finder — especially dosages and frequency.**

   • **Print out the plan's complete details for your set of drugs and keep this hard copy with your records.**

- **Call the plan to verify the full price it charges, or will charge for next year, for each of your drugs (at the dosages and quantities you specify) and your co-pay or coinsurance amounts during the initial coverage phase.** If you're considering getting your drugs by mail order, ask for those prices and co-pays too because they may be different. Keep notes of this conversation; the plan likely won't confirm the details in writing.

✔ **Bear in mind that although plans' fixed costs, such as premiums, deductibles, and co-pay tiers, are invariably accurate on the plan finder, the prices quoted for drugs are an estimate.** The exact prices can vary according to the pharmacy you go to and may fluctuate during the year.

✔ **If you discover errors, report them to Medicare.** Your information will be investigated and fed into its quality rating system. (See the later section "Discovering omissions or discrepancies on the plan finder" for some scenarios to watch out for and how to resolve them.)

✔ **If you believe you were misled into enrolling in a plan due to erroneous pricing information on the plan finder, you have the right to ask Medicare for a special enrollment period to switch to another plan.** This scenario is when keeping a printout of the details you got from the plan finder comes in handy, because you probably need to show evidence.

The plan finder is now vastly more user-friendly than when it first went live in October 2005, and every year Medicare introduces improvements. So it's possible that adjustments made for 2009 and beyond will slightly alter the navigation steps I explain in the rest of this chapter. I don't expect such alterations to be great enough to trip you up as you follow the steps, though some of the link details may change. However, if you get stuck, know that every fall I update my "Quick Route Through the Medicare Drug Plan Finder" guide on the *AARP Bulletin*'s Web site. You can find it at `bulletin.aarp.org/yourhealth/`.

Moving Step by Step through the Medicare Plan Finder — The Fast Way

The Medicare Prescription Drug Plan Finder is loaded with information and offers several different kinds of searches. But in this section, I focus on a quick way of getting to a plan comparison without you having to give out your Medicare ID number or any other personal details, except for your zip code and drug list. This procedure is a totally anonymous process.

On a technical note, it's also a process that's best tackled with high-speed Internet access. You can do it with a dial-up connection, but your search will be slower and, for that reason, more frustrating. Perhaps you can use high-speed access at a friend's house, a library, or a local senior center.

If you don't have access to the Internet or just don't feel up to doing an online search yourself, you can skip this section and go directly to the later section that suggests ways of getting personal help to find the same info.

If you have yet to create the all-important lists of your current prescriptions and your drug plan preferences, flip back to the earlier section "Getting Organized with Two Crucial Lists." Without this information at your fingertips, you can't use the plan finder to full effect and won't obtain accurate enough information to be able to compare plans properly.

The following 15 simple steps are designed so that you can sit at your computer and use them to navigate the plan finder, keystroke by keystroke. Sometimes I tell you to ignore certain questions or information. This is stuff you don't need right now, but that you can return to later when you begin to compare plans in detail, according to your circumstances and preferences. (I consider those details in the next section.)

1. **Go to www.medicare.gov and click "Compare Medicare Prescription Drug Plans" on the home page.**

   If you're doing this search anytime from mid-October through December 31, you'll see two links — one that leads you to plan information for this year and the other to plan information for next year. Just click the one you need.

2. **Click "Find & Compare Plans."**

3. **Click "Begin General Search" in the right-hand box.**

   Ignore "Begin Personalized Search" in the left-hand box.

4. **Enter your zip code.**

5. **Ignore the age and health status boxes.**

6. **Select the "No" buttons for the next three questions and click "Continue."**

   Note: If you qualify for Extra Help, you need to click the third button and answer the questions that appear in order to obtain accurate information about your costs as you progress through the plan finder. So look at the specific information about choosing a plan in Chapter 5 before going further.

   If you live in an area with a zip code that spans more than one county, you may now be directed to a page that asks you to select the county you live in.

7. **Ignore this page (Review Current Coverage and Consider Options) and click "Continue."**

8. **Click "Enter My Drugs."**

9. **Enter the name of your first drug in the box and click "Search for Drug."**

   Another box appears, showing several drug names. Click the one you take and then click "Add Selected to Your Drug List." (You can also use the alphabetical list to search for your drug.) The drug you've selected then appears in a list box. This box also tells you whether a generic version of each drug is available.

10. **Repeat this search for each drug you use and click "Continue."**

    When all of your drugs are on the list (but before clicking "Continue"), click the little box below the list to remove the check mark to ensure that lower-cost generics aren't automatically substituted for your specific meds. (I explain how you can use the plan finder to discover more about using generics or other alternatives to lower your drug costs later in this chapter.)

11. **Change the listed dosages and quantities to exactly match what you take.**

    This is the most critical step in the process in terms of finding out what you'll pay for your drugs in different plans, as explained in the earlier section "Creating an accurate list of your meds."

    - **Dosage:** If your exact dosage doesn't appear beside each drug name on the screen, use the dropdown menu to find it and click that dosage. For example, if Lipitor is one of your drugs, you'll see the default given as 10 mg, but you can change this dose to 20, 40, or 80 mg. (If no menu appears, only one dosage exists for that drug.)

    - **Exact form of drug:** If your drug comes in different forms (such as extended or controlled release), these variations are identified by their initials and appear together with dosages on the same dropdown menu. Click the exact form you take.

    - **Quantities:** Plug in how many doses you take each month. For example, if you take two pills a day, delete the default of 30 a month and type in 60. If you take a drug less frequently — say once every three months — use the dropdown menu to make that change. Click "Continue."

12. **Choose whether to save your drug list.**

    Saving your list is a good way to avoid having to enter your information all over again if you lose it through a computer crash, or if you want to resume your drug plan search later on.

    Select a password date that's easy to remember, such as your birthday, and click "Continue." You'll then receive a 10-digit ID number to use when retrieving your list. Make a note of the number and then click "Continue." (If you don't want to save the list, click "Skip this Step.")

13. **Ignore the invitation to select a pharmacy and click "Continue."**

    Selecting a pharmacy is unnecessary at this stage and may prevent you from finding plans that are the least expensive for your drugs. Searching for pharmacies separately, at a later stage, is a safer method. (I explain this search in the later section "Examining retail pharmacy choices.")

14. **Arrive at the page headed Your Personalized Plan List.**

    What you now see is a list of five stand-alone drug plans, which the plan finder has ranked as the five least expensive plans for *you* at pharmacies in your area. The ranking automatically takes into account the cost of premiums and the drugs you've entered under each plan. If you want to see drug information for Medicare Advantage or Special Needs plans in your zip code instead, click those links at the top of the page.

    To see more plans in your area, click the "10 per page," "20 per page," or "All one page" links at the bottom of the plan list. All the plans are ranked in *ascending* order of your likely total out-of-pocket costs for the year, so the plan shown first is the least expensive.

15. **Pat yourself on the back for getting to where you can start narrowing down your options.**

This page is actually the beginning, not the end, of your search, because it shows only the broadest information. But you can see — as the simplified version used as an example in Table 10-2 also shows — that it already gives you, in the second and third columns, an idea of what you can expect to pay out of pocket over the whole year in each plan, either at retail pharmacies or by mail order. (The dollar amount includes premiums, drug co-pays, and costs in the deductible and coverage gap phases, if applicable.)

The plan finder's rankings are based on the expense of drugs purchased at the various plans' in-network retail pharmacies, as you can see in the second column of Table 10-2. But the plan finder also shows likely costs for the same drugs when purchased through each plan's mail-order service. These amounts are often (though not always) lower than the retail pharmacy cost. As a result, the order of the plans in terms of overall expense changes. Plan X may be the least expensive under the retail pharmacy option, but Plan Y may be least expensive under mail order. *Note:* The "Lower this cost" link in these two columns refers to alternative drugs that you may be able to take to reduce your costs further, as I explain later in this chapter.

Table 10-2	Example of a Personalized Plan List from the Plan Finder Comparison Tool					
Plan Name and ID Number	Esti-mated Annual Cost, retail phar-macy	Esti-mated Annual Cost, mail order	Monthly Drug Prem-ium	Annual Deduct-ible	Cover-age in the Gap	Num-ber of Network Pharm-acies
Plan name (ID number)	$1,038 Lower this cost	$975 Lower this cost	$23.50	$0	No gap cover-age	5
Plan name (ID number)	$1,169 Lower this cost	$1,012 Lower this cost	$16.10	$175	No gap cover-age	4
Plan name (ID number)	$1,182 Lower this cost	$954 Lower this cost	$37.50	$0	All gener-ics	5
Plan name (ID number)	$1,211 Lower this cost	$1,211 Lower this cost	$26.30	$275	No gap cover-age	5
Plan name (ID number)	$1,226 Lower this cost	$984 Lower this cost	$38	$0	Pre-ferred gener-ics	3

Source: Medicare Prescription Drug Plan Finder, www.medicare.gov, *2008.*

Careful, though — this page doesn't give the whole picture. So don't stop now. To make an informed choice among your plan options, you need to get cozy with their details, as I explain in the next section.

Drilling Down to Drug Plan Details

The list of plans — which I call the *main plan list* — described in the preceding section's Step 14 gives only a general idea of coverage and costs. Now you need to look at the details of each plan — or at least of the four or five plans that head the list.

To start, click the name of the first plan at the top of the left-hand column. This action brings up a page headed Plan Drug Details, which gives a lot of information about your drugs and costs under the selected plan. When you're finished looking at this plan's details, click your browser's back button to return to the main plan list. You can then click the next plan's name to bring up its details.

You can also look at the details of up to three plans side by side at the same time. Click the little box to the left of each plan's name on the main list and then click the "Compare" button above.

Notice that this format is more compressed and doesn't display the particulars as clearly as the full plan details pages. It also omits two important bits of information — whether your drugs come with any restrictions (such as prior authorization, quantity limits, or step therapy) and bar graphs that show your monthly out-of-pocket expenses over the year. That's why I recommend looking at each details page in turn rather than taking the shortcut offered by this side-by-side comparison.

Here's an explanation of what's on each details page as you scroll down:

✔ **Plan quality ratings:** This rating system uses stars to indicate a plan's performance in certain areas — such as customer service, getting prescriptions filled, accuracy of quoted prices, responsiveness to complaints, and so on — based on Medicare reviews and consumer complaints. Stars range from one (poor) to five (excellent).

✔ **Fixed costs:** These expenses refer to the plan's monthly premium and annual deductible, if applicable.

✔ **Estimated out-of-pocket cost over the whole year (including premiums):** This info appears in two dollar amounts — one shows your total costs if you buy all of your drugs from preferred retail pharmacies in your plan's network (30-day supplies), and the other shows your total costs if you buy meds by mail order (90-day supplies). Mail order is usually (though not always) less expensive, but some plans don't offer this option. (If you're looking at this page partway through the year, the right-hand column shows total costs for the remainder of the year.)

✔ **Drug coverage information:** This breakdown shows the list of drugs you entered into Medicare's online plan finder and the *tier* (level of charges) that applies to each drug. Tiers typically range from 1 (least expensive) to 4 or 5 (most expensive), as explained in Chapter 3. (To find out the actual co-pays for these tiers, click "View Important Notes and Benefit Summary" on the menu at the top left of the page.)

If any of your drugs aren't covered under this plan, the phrase NOT ON FORMULARY appears in the Tier (Formulary Status) column.

The columns farther to the right are very important. They show whether the plan places restrictions on any of your drugs — that is, whether you need to obtain the plan's permission before they'll be covered. These restrictions are prior authorization, quantity limits, or step therapy (as explained in Chapter 4.) When you make a final choice among plans, you may want to choose one with few or no restrictions.

✔ **Monthly drug cost details at preferred network retail pharmacies:** This chart shows what each of your drugs, if purchased from a preferred retail pharmacy in your plan's network, will cost on a monthly basis at four different coverage levels:

- The period before you meet your annual deductible (if the plan has one)

- The initial coverage phase when you pay co-pays or coinsurance

- The coverage gap (doughnut hole) when you pay 100 percent of the cost of your drugs, unless this plan covers them in the gap or your costs aren't high enough to reach it

- The catastrophic phase of coverage when you pay low co-pays after reaching a certain out-of-pocket expense limit

The left-hand column on this chart shows the full price of each of your meds under this plan — that is, the price the plan has negotiated with the manufacturers. You pay this price before meeting your deductible or while you're in the coverage gap. If the full price also appears in the Initial Coverage Level column, it can mean one of two things — either the drug isn't covered on the plan's formulary or the full price is less than the co-pay would be, so the plan charges you the lower of the two. If you see a co-pay rather than the full price in the Gap column, it means the plan covers this drug in the gap.

✔ **Monthly drug cost details when purchasing drugs by mail order:** To see a similar chart showing mail-order costs, click the "Show" button on the right-hand side. (If the plan doesn't offer mail order, this option doesn't appear.) Although mail-order drugs are always bought in 90-day quantities, this chart shows costs by the month (30-day quantities) to make comparisons easier.

✔ **The local pharmacies within this plan's network:** Knowing which of your local pharmacies are in the plan's network is important, because going out of the network costs you a lot more, possibly even full price. If you follow the instructions in the previous section, you won't see any pharmacies listed. So how can you find out which of your local pharmacies participate in the plan? I explain how in the "Finding the pharmacies in a plan's network" section later in this chapter.

✔ **Out-of-pocket costs at a month-by-month glance:** The bar chart at the end of the details page is a useful way to see how your expenses may change from month to month under this plan and whether (or when) you're going to fall into the doughnut hole. (For examples, see Chapter 15.) If the plan has no deductible and your drug costs are too low to take you into the doughnut hole, the cost for each month is the same. Otherwise, different monthly amounts appear according to coverage level. For a detailed breakdown, click "Show explanation of these costs."

The bar chart you see on this page shows monthly costs if you buy your drugs at the plan's in-network retail pharmacies. To see a similar bar chart for mail-order costs (if the plan offers this option) click the "Show" button on the Cost Estimator for Mail Order Pharmacy panel.

I go into more detail on these bar charts as they relate to the doughnut hole in Chapter 15.

✔ **Filling prescriptions outside your home area:** If you travel or live in another state for part of the year, you need a plan that covers your prescriptions at its network pharmacies anywhere in the U.S. To find this information, click "View Important Notes and Benefit Summary" on the menu at the top left of the page. The summary indicates whether you can use this plan to get your prescription drugs outside its service area.

✔ **How this plan's costs next year compare to its costs this year:** When you're doing a plan search during open enrollment (November 15 through December 31), the plan finder shows the details of *next* year's costs and benefits by default. To see *this* year's information, click "Click here to display [year] plan data" at the top of the page. This option disappears on January 1.

If you click "View Important Notes and Benefit Summary" and nothing happens, your Web browser may be blocking pop-ups. Disable your pop-up blocker to access this information.

Making Additional Worthwhile Searches to Help Pick a Plan

If you've looked at the details of the first several plans on the main plan list, you may now have a rough idea of which ones seem the most promising. But, once again, don't stop here. You need more information before making a well-educated choice among the handful of plans you're now considering. In the following sections, I suggest other worthwhile searches, along with some relevant tips and warnings. These sections explain how you can use the online Medicare Prescription Drug Plan Finder to explore the following six topics in depth: examining drug coverage details, lowering your drug costs, determining mail-order prices, making pharmacy choices, assessing customer service, and filling prescriptions away from home.

When you've done these additional searches and are ready to make a final selection, print out the details of your top four plans and compare them, point by point. You can use the worksheet in Appendix A to make the comparison easier.

Looking at the nuances of drug coverage details

The plan finder shows a lot of information about drug coverage on each plan's details page. But as you dive in, consider the info in the following sections to help you understand some nuances that aren't immediately apparent or that may puzzle you.

Reviewing the pricing of covered drugs

When examining a plan's details page for the prices of your covered drugs, some items may strike you as odd. Here are the explanations:

✔ If a drug is covered but shown as full price in the initial coverage period, that's probably because the full price is lower than the co-pay, so the plan charges you the lesser of the two amounts. You can check this by looking at the plan's usual co-pay for the relevant tier of charges — click "View Important Notes and Benefit Summary" on the menu at the top of the page. For example, if the full price of your Tier 2 drug is $15.50, but the normal co-pay for Tier 2 drugs is $20, you're charged the lesser amount.

✔ If you see that Drug X is charged as a co-pay in the Gap column, whereas Drug Y is charged at full price, then Drug X is one of the drugs that this plan covers in the doughnut hole, but Drug Y isn't.

✔ If you see an odd-looking price in the initial coverage column — for example, $23.97, rather than a nicely rounded dollar amount like $24 — it means that this plan charges coinsurance, not a flat co-pay. (Flip to Chapter 3 for more on coinsurance and co-pays.) So the price shown is a percentage of the full price.

✔ If you see that the cost of a drug in the Catastrophic Coverage column is higher than the standard catastrophic co-pay — $2.25 per prescription for generics or $5.60 for brand-names in 2008 ($2.40 and $6.00 respectively in 2009) — it means that you're being charged 5 percent of the drug's cost instead of the co-pay. Under Part D law, you pay either a co-pay or a maximum 5 percent of the full price, whichever's the higher amount.

✔ If the full cost of your drugs is very high, you may see what seems to be a most peculiar profile for your monthly out-of-pocket expenses on the bar chart at the end of each plan's details page. The chart may show a very large amount in the first month's column (amounting to several thousand dollars) and very small amounts for the rest of the year. That's because your drug costs are so high that you go through the deductible (if any), the initial coverage period, and the doughnut hole in the very first month. The small amounts thereafter are low-cost catastrophic coverage.

✔ If you look at the bar charts for drugs purchased by mail order, you may notice a strangely uneven profile in your out-of-pocket expenses over the year — for example, $400 in months 1, 4, 7, and 10, and $25 in the other months. That's because you're buying your drugs in three-month supplies, in advance. During the second and third month of each quarter, you have no outlay, except for the plan's premium ($25 in this example).

Finding the pricing for drugs a plan doesn't cover

Be aware that you can't tell just by looking at the main plan list whether all of your drugs are covered by any particular plan — or whether a plan imposes restrictions on any of them. For that, you have to go to each plan's details list and look at the Drug Coverage Information section (see the earlier section "Drilling Down to Drug Plan Details"). Drugs that a plan doesn't cover have NOT ON FORMULARY next to their names. But wait, there's more!

The main plan list and each plan's details page show a dollar amount representing your estimated annual cost under each plan. But that amount *includes the full price of any drug that the plan doesn't cover.* The plan finder presents the information this way because, if it excludes the price for an uncovered drug completely, the overall cost of that plan appears lower than what you actually pay. Including the full price of an uncovered drug in the overall estimate gives you a better idea of what your out-of-pocket expenses are likely to be under that plan, especially when you're comparing it with the costs of a plan that covers this drug.

A plan may cover a specialty drug (usually Tier 4 or higher) if you purchase it from a network pharmacy — but may not if you get it from the plan's mail-order service. So when looking at mail-order prices, be sure to check out this info.

Discovering omissions or discrepancies on the plan finder

When you can't find something you're looking for, or the information seems wrong, there may be an explanation or it may be the result of a glitch or error on the plan finder. In the following scenarios, if you need to report the problem to Medicare, call the help line at 800-633-4227:

✔ **You enter the name of a drug, and the plan finder doesn't find it.** First, check that the name you're entering is spelled correctly or try to find it on the alphabetical list provided. Verify that the med in question is a prescription drug and not an over-the-counter drug or a vitamin — Part D doesn't cover these kinds of medication. If nothing checks out, call Medicare to report the error, or to see whether there's a reason this drug isn't on the list.

✔ **The plan finder doesn't allow you to enter the dosage of your drug.** First, check that the dosage you're trying to enter is correct, according to the medication label. If it's right, report the omission to Medicare immediately. In the meantime, enter the dosage that's nearest to yours — very often a plan's co-pays are the same for similar dosages.

✔ **The name of one of your drugs doesn't appear in the cost details of the plan you're looking at.** First, check in the Drug Coverage column that the drug is in fact on your list of selected drugs. If it's not, scroll down the page and add it to your list. If the drug is already on the list, but not showing up in the cost details, Medicare may have temporarily removed the information after discovering that this plan submitted incorrect pricing. Check back a day or two later. If it's still not there, call Medicare to report the omission.

✔ **The price given for a drug under one plan is very different from the price given under several other plans.** Prices vary a good deal among plans, but mistakes happen. For example, occasionally plans submit the generic price to the plan finder rather than the specified brand-name price. You can check this by entering the name of the generic version on your drug list and seeing whether its price is the same as the price given for the brand-name. If it is, report that to Medicare immediately.

Checking to see whether the numbers add up

Many people like to do their own math to see if the calculations made on the plan finder actually add up properly. In some cases, checking the math yourself is easy to do. For example, if a plan has no deductible and your drug costs aren't high enough to take you into the doughnut hole, your out-of-pocket costs will be the same each month. Just add the cost of the premium to your monthly co-pays — then look at the bar chart at the bottom of the plan's details page to see whether the monthly totals displayed there are the same. Multiply this monthly total by 12 to check the annual out-of-pocket cost shown at the top of the page.

Calculating costs on your own is much trickier if the plan has a deductible and/or your drug costs are high enough to take you into the coverage gap — or through the gap and into catastrophic coverage. In these situations, your monthly costs fluctuate according to the coverage level — and the change from one to another most often doesn't fall neatly at the end of any given month. The calculation is *possible*. But quite frankly — and I speak from experience — you can go nuts trying to figure it out with pen and paper, or even with a calculator. In these circumstances, you probably need to have faith that the figures on the plan finder are pretty much correct.

Lowering costs with alternative drugs

You can dramatically reduce your costs if any of the brand-name drugs you take now have a generic version or a similar, older alternative that your doctor thinks would work just as well for your medical condition. I discuss these kinds of medications and why they're less expensive than brand-name drugs in detail in Chapter 16. But in this section, I show you how to find lower-cost alternatives and their comparative prices on the plan finder.

In Step 10 of my navigation guide in the earlier section "Moving Step by Step through the Medicare Plan Finder — The Fast Way," I advise you to remove the check mark from the little box at the end of the list of drugs you've entered. That's because, if you leave the box checked, the plan finder automatically replaces the names of your drugs with generics, if any exist. It can be a shock to see a totally unfamiliar name appear in your drug list without realizing what's happened. And it seems to me that you'd prefer to find out the prices of your prescribed drugs *before* looking to see whether any lower-cost alternatives exist. That way, you know how much you'd save if you switch to the alternatives.

Here, I assume that you've searched plans on the basis of the drugs you're taking now and have a shortlist of the plans that work out least expensively. Now you can see whether those costs can be brought down further. Choose a plan on the main plan list and click "Lower this cost" in the second column. Or click the plan's name to get to the plan details page and click "Lower My Cost Share" on the menu at the top left. The page that appears on your screen will look like the example in Table 10-3.

Table 10-3	Sample of How to Lower Your Costs with Less Expensive Meds			
Drug	*Estimated Cost Share before Savings*	*Lower-Cost Drugs*	*Estimated Cost Share after Savings*	*Pharmaceutical Assistance Program*
Lipitor 20 mg	$20/month	Similar drug: 75%	$5/month	Yes
Plavix 75 mg	$20/month	N/A	$20/month	Yes
Zoloft 100 mg	$89.81/ month	Generic: 94.43%	$5/month	Yes
Total:	$129.81/ month		$30/month	

Source: Medicare Prescription Drug Plan Finder, www.medicare.gov, *2008.*

Do your drugs have any lower-cost alternatives?

As you can see in the example in Table 10-3, the plan finder shows you which brand-name medication has a similar drug that can be used instead, which has a generic version, or which has no alternative. (Not all brand-name drugs have alternatives to date, as I explain in Chapter 16.) The list shows the percentage and dollar differences in co-pays or coinsurance between the brand-name drugs and the suggested alternatives. And it shows the savings over a month — in this case, almost $100.

If these cost savings sound too good to be true, let me assure you that this example is the result of an actual search using this set of drugs. What's more, Zoloft isn't covered on the formulary of this particular plan — the odd figure in the second column shows the full price — but the generic *is* covered, at a fraction of the price. (Under a different plan, which covers Zoloft as a nonpreferred Tier 3 drug with a co-pay of $54 a month, using the Tier 1 generic version reduces the co-pay to $4.)

On-screen, this page shows drug costs at retail pharmacies. You can also see the mail-order costs by clicking "Show Mail Order (90-Day Supply) Prices" at the top of the list. Opting for mail order may bring down your costs even further. Under the plan used for the example in Table 10-3, the similar drug (for Lipitor) and the generic (for Zoloft) each cost nothing under the mail-order option, reducing the overall monthly cost by half, to $15 a month.

As usual in Part D, savings on lower-cost drugs vary a great deal among plans. So after examining these details under one plan, look at similar cost savings for other plans on your shortlist by using the same steps. As a result, a different plan may now work out as the least expensive for you.

And what about that fourth column on the right-hand side of Table 10-3? This column shows whether any of the drug manufacturers' patient assistance programs offer this drug for free or at low cost for eligible people with limited incomes. (I describe these programs as a possible way of lowering costs in the coverage gap in Chapter 16.) If a "No" appears in that column, it means the drug isn't available under an assistance program. If a "Yes" appears, you can click it for details about the program — including the income limits for qualifying and how to apply.

One more useful bit of information is on this page. Notice the State Programs heading above the chart. These are State Pharmacy Assistance Programs (SPAPs) that are offered in some states for people whose incomes are limited but who don't qualify for Medicaid. Clicking the link takes you to a page that provides details of the program in your state and how to contact it.

Which drugs would lower the cost?

If you find you can lower your costs with some alternative drugs, be sure to know their names and whether they require different dosages from the brand-name drugs you take now. You can locate this information on the plan finder by clicking the "Similar drug" or "Generic" link in the third column of the Lower My Drug Cost Share list. Doing so brings up a new list, which looks similar to the example in Table 10-4.

Table 10-4	Sample of How to Find Lower-Cost Drugs			
Your Prescription	*30-Day Quantity*	*Type*	*Cost Share*	*Pharmaceutical Assistance Program*
Lipitor 20 mg	30	Tier 2	$20/month	
Lower-Cost Options				
Pravastatin Sodium 40 mg	60	Tier 1	$5/month	No
Lovastatin 40 mg	60	Tier 1	$5/month	No
Simvastatin 40 mg	30	Tier 1	$5/month	No

Source: *Medicare Prescription Drug Plan Finder,* www.medicare.gov, *2008.*

This example shows Lipitor, one of a group of drugs called statins widely used to treat high cholesterol. Currently, it doesn't have a generic form. But some older statins, such as Crestor and Zocor, do have generic versions, and these generics are the lower-cost options shown in the left-hand column.

Generics and similar older drugs sometimes require different dosages and/or quantities to achieve the same clinical effect as the brand-name drugs they're copying. As you can see in Table 10-4, someone taking 20 mg of Lipitor once a day needs to take 40 mg of simvastatin once a day or 40 mg of pravastatin or lovastatin twice a day for these alternatives to work as effectively. Most plans charge the same co-pays for generics regardless of dosage or quantities (as this one does), but some may not. So be sure to check the co-pays when looking at your own drug list.

This chart also shows whether a drug manufacturer's patient assistance program will cover the drug in question. When the given alternatives to the brand-name drugs are generics, as in this example, the answer is "No." If a given alternative is an older brand-name drug, the answer may be "Yes."

How do you use the information you find?

If you discover an opportunity for lowering your costs through this kind of search and decide that you want to try any of the suggested alternative drugs, you need to talk to your doctor about whether the substitute may work well for you. Printing out the page that gives the names, dosages, and quantities for these alternatives and showing it to your doctor is a good idea.

Considering mail order

The third column of the main plan list shows at a glance an estimate of what each plan charges for your meds over the whole year if you buy all of them by mail order. If the plan offers a mail-order service — and if most of your drugs are *maintenance medications* you take regularly, which makes getting them in 90-day supplies worthwhile — you may find that this option lowers your costs. (You can find examples of mail-order savings in Chapter 16.)

The savings generated by using this option vary a great deal among plans. You may find that the whole ranking of least expensive plans changes. For example, a plan that's shown as the fifth least expensive under the retail pharmacy option may actually be number one under mail order. That's because one plan may charge exactly the same for your set of drugs, whether by retail or mail order; another may charge a lot less for mail order over the whole year. For this reason, having a quick look at the mail-order costs for more than five plans is worthwhile. Some plans charge lower co-pays (as well as a lower full price) for mail order — for example, nothing for Tier 1 generic drugs, compared with $5 for retail. To see specifics, go to the details page of each plan you're considering and click the "Show" button on Monthly Drug Cost Details at Mail Order Pharmacy.

If you're considering mail order, reviewing the detailed list of monthly costs in the mail-order list for each plan is sensible. Some plans charge *higher* co-pays for mail order — for example, $7 for mail-order generics compared with $4 for generics from a retail pharmacy.

And here's another important pitfall to watch out for: Some plans don't cover certain drugs under their mail-order option at all, even though the same drugs are covered at a retail pharmacy. These are often *specialty drugs* — the rarest and/or most expensive meds that are placed in a plan's highest tier of charges — which you must buy at a pharmacy that stocks them. For example, one plan charges a monthly co-pay of $270 for a cancer drug purchased at retail pharmacies, but it charges full price — $743 — when the same drug is bought by mail order. The plan finder (at least in 2008) doesn't highlight this fact. You have to look carefully at the mail-order cost list to find out. If the price of a drug shown in the Initial Coverage Level column on that list is the same as in the Full Cost of Drug column, the drug isn't covered by mail order.

Examining retail pharmacy choices

Being able to use your plan coverage at retail pharmacies within a convenient distance from your home is obviously an important consideration when choosing a plan. (Even if you prefer mail order for your regular meds, sooner or later you may need a short-term drug, such as an antibiotic, purchased locally so you can start taking it immediately.) Most Part D plans, especially those offered by big insurance companies, have a wide selection of network pharmacies, including large chains and smaller independent pharmacies. And many of the same pharmacies are within the networks of different plans.

When you're enrolled in a Part D plan, you must go to one of the pharmacies within its network to ensure paying the price you expect. Going out of the plan's network costs a lot more (unless you do so for an unavoidable, legitimate reason that your plan accepts, as explained in Chapter 14), and these payments don't count toward the out-of-pocket limit that lifts you out of the doughnut hole (see Chapter 15).

The plan finder provides tons of info on pharmacy choices, but you need to tread carefully in your search, as I explain in the following sections.

Identifying the pharmacies in a plan's network

In Step 10 of the earlier section "Moving Step by Step through the Medicare Plan Finder — The Fast Way," I advise you to ignore the invitation to select a pharmacy at that stage. Here's why:

- ✔ If you click "Yes" (when asked "Do you want to select a specific pharmacy or pharmacies from which you prefer to purchase your drugs?"), a list of pharmacies in your area appears on-screen. But you have no way of telling which of these pharmacies are in any plan's network.

- ✔ If you select a pharmacy on this list, the plan finder's search engine looks first for plans that include the pharmacy in its network; your out-of-pocket costs are a secondary consideration. In other words, you may not find the least expensive plan.

- ✔ This list may include names that aren't regular pharmacies, but may be doctors' offices or hospital departments that dispense specialty drugs (such as medications used to treat cancer). Most plans don't include these dispensers in their networks. If you select such pharmacies at this stage, the out-of-pocket costs that appear on the plan details page are going to be based on the full price of all of your drugs.

A better way to identify in-network pharmacies is to go to the individual plan details pages first, before searching for any pharmacy information, to get an idea of which plans are best for your set of drugs. Then you can find out which pharmacies are in the network of any plan you're considering.

Click "View Pharmacy Network" on the menu at the top left of the plan details page to reveal a list of pharmacies within a certain distance of your zip code. (If this link doesn't work, turn off your pop-up blocker.) In densely populated urban areas, this distance may be as little as half a mile. In rural areas, it may be seven miles or more. To widen the mileage radius, alter the distance shown in the box and click "Find Pharmacies."

The resulting list shows the pharmacies within the plan's network, meaning that the plan covers any of its formulary drugs that you purchase there. The Pharmacy Type column to the right indicates which pharmacies supply certain kinds of drugs — for example, those that are *home infusion* (self-injected) or *specialty* drugs (like some cancer medications). In the column at the far right, a Yes or No indicates whether pharmacies are preferred by the plan, meaning you may purchase your drugs at these locations at somewhat lower prices.

Comparing prices among in-network pharmacies

Even within the same plan's network, different pharmacies may offer varying prices for your drugs. The out-of-pocket annual totals shown on the main plan list or at the top of each plan's details page reflect the *average* of the prices offered by the plan's *preferred* pharmacies in your area — that is, all those pharmacies with which the plan has negotiated the best discounts.

To see price differences for your set of drugs among specific pharmacies in each plan, follow these steps:

1. **Go to the *main plan list,* scroll down to the My Pharmacies section, and click "Change Pharmacy Selection."**

   The result is a list of all the pharmacies within the smallest mileage distance of your zip code.

2. **Expand the mileage radius to see more pharmacies farther away by scrolling down the page until you see the Change Criteria to Revise List of Pharmacies section.**

   You can alter the distance shown in the box by using the dropdown menu and clicking the distance you want. Then click "Update List." If the new list of pharmacies is large, you must click the "All one page" link to see them all.

   Be aware that this list shows *all* the pharmacies in your area and doesn't specify which ones are in the network of any particular plan.

3. **Select your desired pharmacy by clicking the little box alongside its name and then click "Continue."**

   You can check up to two boxes, if you prefer. Either way, this step returns you to the main plan list.

4. **Choose one drug plan by clicking its name.**

   The details page of your selected plan now appears with the prices charged at your chosen pharmacy. Its name is shown in the Full Year Cost and Monthly Drug Cost Details sections. If you selected two pharmacies, both appear in the Full Year Cost section. To see monthly cost details of the second pharmacy, click the "Show" button on the panel displaying that pharmacy's name.

5. **Observe whether your selected pharmacy is in this plan's network.**

If it isn't, note the warning message (above the Monthly Drug Cost Details section) that states: "You'll pay 100% of the cost for drugs at this pharmacy because it is not in the plan's network." In this case, only the full price of your set of drugs is displayed.

6. **Return to the main plan list and repeat the process step by step to see prices at other pharmacies.**

Comparing pharmacy prices this way can be a laborious procedure. So I recommend that for each plan you're considering, check that a few familiar pharmacies are in the plan's network (by clicking "View Pharmacy Network," as explained in the previous section) before doing anything else. Then select those pharmacies, one by one, as explained in Step 3. Make a note of each pharmacy's annual overall costs for each plan you're considering so you can compare them more easily. Remember that the prices of most pharmacies within each plan's network vary only a little, but these prices can change during the year.

The most important step is to make sure that the Part D plan you choose has at least one pharmacy in its network within a convenient distance of your home. And no, after you're in a plan you *don't* have to stick with one pharmacy from which to buy all or any of your drugs. If you have plenty of network pharmacies to choose from, you can always shop around among them when filling your prescription.

Knowing what to do if you already have a favorite pharmacy

You may especially like a certain pharmacy and you'd prefer to continue using it. Chances are pretty high that this pharmacy is in the network of at least one of the Part D plans on your shortlist, or even in all of them.

But what if it's not? You can make a new search (using the pharmacy selection tool explained in the preceding section) to find another plan that has this pharmacy in its network. Then you need to compare this new plan's costs with the prices of your shortlist plans. The difference may amount to only a few dollars over the year. On the other hand, the difference may be quite large. In that case, you need to consider whether cost outweighs convenience, or vice versa.

Assessing customer service

Naturally, some plans are better than others when it comes to providing good customer service and other kinds of performance. Medicare's online plan finder helps you assess this, before you join a plan, by publishing quality ratings for each plan on its details page. This page includes an overall quality rating expressed in the form of stars and ranging from poor (one star), through fair (two stars), good (three stars), and very good (four stars), to excellent (five stars). This rating system gives a broad idea of how Medicare and plan enrollees have rated the plan overall.

But you can also drill down further to see how the plan rates on a range of specific performance measures — from how long it takes to get a live person on the phone to how well the plan handles appeals. To see this detailed breakdown, click the link labeled "Click to view more details on Plan Ratings" immediately above the stars. Doing so brings up a page showing three main areas of performance:

- ✔ **Drug plan customer service:** This category includes statistics on how long a plan keeps you or your pharmacist on hold during a call, how often such calls are disconnected in mid-conversation, how helpful the plan is in providing information, and how many complaints are filed about the plan.

- ✔ **Using your plan to get your prescriptions filled:** This category indicates how easily enrollees get their prescriptions filled, complaints about the plan's benefits and access to medications, complaints about problems met in joining or leaving the plan, and the frequency with which the plan delays making timely coverage determinations or appeals decisions.

- ✔ **Drug pricing information:** This category focuses on the accuracy of prices submitted to the plan finder, the frequency with which a plan changes prices, and complaints about out-of-pocket costs, for example being charged the wrong amount for a prescription or a premium.

To see all the details in these three categories, click "Show All Plan Ratings" at the top of this page. Click "View Numbers" at the top left to see the actual numbers on which a plan's stars are based (for example: time on hold — 25 seconds, or complaints about drug plan — 2.5 per 1,000 enrollees).

Medicare arrives at this information through regular monitoring of the plans, complaints from consumers enrolled in each plan, surveys among enrollees, and some independent assessments. You can see more details of how each point is measured by clicking "Click to view Data Sources" under each of the three category headings. If a plan is new to the Part D program, you may see the phrase "Insufficient data" next to some of the measures.

The more often enrollees let Medicare know how their plan is doing, the more useful these quality ratings become for people choosing a plan. So if you have a legitimate complaint about the plan you're enrolled in, tell Medicare! Just call the Medicare help line at 800-633-4227 (877-486-2048 for TDD users) and say you want to file a *grievance* — the Medicare term for a complaint. (I cover how to file a grievance in Chapter 19.)

Searching for pharmacies if you travel or live away from home for part of the year

If you travel a lot, you need a plan that allows you to fill prescriptions anywhere in the country. You can initially find out which plans do by clicking the "View Important Notes and Benefit Summary" link in the top-left menu on each plan details page. To confirm this information, check directly with the plan you select *before* enrolling in it, because some plans may allow this service for medical necessity only and not as a matter of convenience.

If you're a snowbird or have any other reason to spend a large chunk of the year away from home in a particular place, you certainly need a drug plan you can use in both regions. So you probably want to search for pharmacies in both zip codes. If so, spare yourself a deal of confusion by saving your list of drugs when doing an initial search to find plans in your home area. *Don't* use your retrieval ID number to look at plans in the other zip code. Instead, enter your list of drugs all over again and save it a second time to get a different ID number. When the plan finder saves your original search, it automatically embeds the first zip code, along with the pharmacies located in that area. So if you use the same ID retrieval number for the other zip code, where pharmacies are different, the information can be distorted. For example, you may see a message saying, "You'll pay 100% of the cost for drugs at this pharmacy because it is not in the plan's network" — even if you haven't selected a particular pharmacy. Creating a second search prevents this confusion from happening.

Finding Personal Help to Compare Plans

Not everyone has a computer or access to the Internet. Not everyone is familiar or comfortable with online searches. And you know what? That's a-okay. Don't feel badly if you've glanced at the previous sections on navigating the Medicare Prescription Drug Plan Finder and think "she may as well have written in hieroglyphics." You can find the same information by getting help from a live person.

Yes, at this point it may seem easier to choose a Part D plan by one of the unwise methods I mention earlier in this chapter — you know, signing up for the same plan as your spouse, opting for a plan with a well-known name, or listening to a sales pitch. But don't go wobbly on me now.

The whole point of this chapter is to help you find the plan that's best for *you* — the one that covers *your* drugs at the lowest cost. So don't be put off when I say the plan finder is the most efficient way of getting there. The following sections list people you can turn to for help.

Asking family or friends for assistance

You may not be into computers, but I'm willing to bet someone in your family or circle of friends is. And, no matter how antsy you feel about asking for help, finding the right Part D plan is an excellent reason to do just that.

Maybe you have teenage grandchildren who are whizzes at electronics — and wouldn't they be thrilled if you asked them to help! Never underestimate the ability of youngsters to pick their way through a complicated database without turning a hair. They've grown up with this stuff and know perfectly well that they're more expert than you. (Even folks nifty on computers dread the day when their last child leaves home, depriving them of on-the-spot tech support.) Some families now make the process of helping their older members pick a Medicare prescription drug plan for the following year into an annual event. Lucky coincidence that Thanksgiving falls slap in the middle of the Part D open enrollment period, eh?

Of course, you don't want to pitch even your favorite relative or best friend into the Medicare Prescription Drug Plan finder cold turkey — especially at Thanksgiving! Fortunately you can help her out. Give her your list of prescription drugs and the previous sections of this chapter to read and let her take it from there. After she finds a shortlist of two or three likely plans and prints them out, you can compare the options to make your final pick . . . for this year anyway.

Seeking help from professionals

By professionals I don't mean people who are necessarily making a whole career out of giving Part D advice. I mean people who are trained to help, whether they're being paid or they're volunteering. By contacting any of the following three services, you can talk to someone who can use the plan finder to identify a Part D plan that suits you — and, best of all, the services don't cost you a penny.

Calling the Medicare help line

You can call the official Medicare help line toll-free at 800-633-4227 (or 877-486-2048 for TDD users with impaired hearing) and ask a customer representative to find the two or three plans that best meet your needs and to mail printouts of their details to you. The rep just needs to know your Medicare ID number, your zip code, and the names of the prescription drugs you take, plus their dosages and how often you take them. Remember, making an accurate list of your drugs is essential. Flip to the section titled "Creating an accurate list of your meds" for help organizing this crucial information.

How helpful is the help line? Medicare uses contracted workers as customer representatives and gives them basic training, though their knowledge of Part D isn't extensive. Feedback from consumers (and others who call the number to test the quality of the service) is mixed, as you may expect. Some callers get through to a rep in a jiffy; others remain on hold for ten minutes, or much longer. Some are satisfied with the information they receive; others aren't.

So when you're looking to find a Part D plan, it helps to be as specific as possible. Use the following steps to explain what you want:

1. **Tell the rep whether you're looking for drug coverage through a stand-alone prescription drug plan (PDP), a Medicare Advantage plan (MAPD), or a Special Needs Plan (SNP), as explained in Chapter 9.**

2. **Ask the rep to run a plan search using the details of your prescribed drugs — without substituting generics for them at this stage.**

3. **Tell the rep whether you qualify for Extra Help.**

   If you're eligible for *full* Extra Help (as explained in Chapter 5), say whether you want a plan that doesn't charge a premium, or whether you're prepared to pay part of the premium for a plan that may suit you better.

4. **Ask the rep to do an initial search for the least expensive plans that cover your drugs *before* talking about pharmacy preferences or ways to lower your drug costs.**

5. **When the rep has completed this initial search and has a shortlist of possible plans, ask him to check whether each plan**

   a. Covers all your drugs

   b. Places any restrictions (prior authorization, quantity limits, or step therapy — see Chapter 4) on any of your drugs

   c. Has in-network pharmacies that are convenient to you

   d. Offers a mail-order service that covers 90-day supplies of your drugs (if this option is important to you)

   e. Covers your prescriptions at its network pharmacies in all 50 states and/or the territories (if this option is important to you)

6. **Ask the rep to check the mail-order prices of your drugs in several plans to see whether these prices generate more savings.**

7. **Ask the rep to check whether you can reduce your expenses by using lower-cost drugs in each plan on the shortlist and, if so, by how much.**

8. **Ask the rep to mail you printouts of the three plans that best meet your needs.**

   The printouts should include full details of mail-order service, a list of each plan's network pharmacies in your area, and details of the costs of lower-priced drugs in each plan. Ask the rep to confirm that these details are captured before mailing the printouts to you.

   If the customer service rep refuses to give you all the info you ask for, ask to speak to the rep's supervisor. You have a right to ask as many questions as you like to find a Part D plan that suits your needs. If the rep gives the impression that finding a plan for you is tedious or taking too much time, you also have the right to complain.

When you receive the printouts, you can compare each plan to make a final choice by using the worksheet in Appendix A, if desired.

Calling your State Health Insurance Assistance Program

State Health Insurance Assistance Programs, called SHIPs, provide expert free counseling services — specifically for people in Medicare — in all 50 states, the District of Columbia, Puerto Rico, Guam, and the U.S. Virgin Islands. Nationwide, more than 12,000 SHIP counselors (mainly trained volunteers) assist more than 2 million people every year with a wide range of Medicare problems, including how to choose a Part D plan. Go to Appendix B to find contact information for your local SHIP.

When you call your SHIP, you can schedule a face-to-face meeting with a local counselor or arrange to talk over a toll-free phone line. If English isn't your first language, you can ask to speak with someone who knows yours. A SHIP counseling session may resolve a comparatively simple situation quickly and can be especially valuable if your circumstances are complicated.

When helping you choose a Part D plan, the SHIP counselor needs to know

- The names of your drugs, their dosages, and how often you take them in order to search the plan finder
- Whether you're looking for drug coverage through a stand-alone prescription drug plan or a Medicare Advantage health plan
- Whether you're eligible for Extra Help

The counselor can also help you choose a Medicare Advantage plan or apply for Extra Help, if necessary.

Calling your Area Agency on Aging

Every state and U.S. territory has an Area Agency on Aging (AAA) that provides a multitude of local services for people age 60 and over, including assistance with Medicare issues. In many cases, local AAAs rely on the SHIPs, described in the preceding section, to provide counseling on Medicare and

Part D. But some have their own trained volunteers who can give personal help in finding a Part D plan.

Find the number of your local AAA by calling the national Eldercare Locator toll-free at 800-677-1116. Calls are accepted on weekdays from 9 a.m. to 8 p.m. Eastern time. You can speak with someone in one of 150 languages, including Spanish. For more information on local services, visit www.eldercare.gov.

Taking advice from other sources

You may well be able to get advice on picking a Part D plan from a variety of other sources. For example, many people report that they turn to their doctors, pharmacists, and insurance agents. Others receive help at senior centers, seminars, and info sessions of many kinds. Others are turning to new Part D plan-finding businesses that are popping up on the Internet.

Which of these info distributors can you trust to find a plan that meets your personal needs? Essentially, when can you believe what you hear — and when should you be skeptical? Following are some rules of thumb that may help:

✔ Just because someone is a professional doesn't necessarily mean he knows enough about Part D to be of use to you in picking a plan. Doctors and pharmacists are professionals in their own fields and may be absolutely terrific at their jobs. But unless they're able to run your particular set of drugs through the plan finder to search for the plan that covers your drugs and costs you least, they can't really help you.

✔ Insurance agents are also professionals, and many of them are very knowledgeable about Part D. Others aren't, and some are paid high commissions to sell a particular Part D plan (as explained in Chapter 11). If you have an agent who's handled other insurance for you in the past and whom you trust, you may naturally turn to him to find a Part D plan. However, you should ask whether he's able to use the plan finder to search for your best bet. If not, going to someone who can may be wiser.

✔ People on Medicare are often invited to info sessions at senior centers, retirement communities, hotels, or other venues and offered help in finding a Part D plan. Some of these sessions are an excellent value — for example, the ones run by volunteers from SHIP or other consumer groups. These trained people either show you how to use the plan finder yourself or run the numbers for you to help you pick a plan.

Other sessions are basically sales pitches for a single insurance company, promoting only the Part D plans it sells. If you hear information that dwells on a plan rather than your personal needs — or someone tries to sign you up for a plan on the spot — consider that an immediate red flag. And if whoever's sponsoring the session offers you dinner on the house or other freebies, get out of there fast! These sneaky hard-sell tactics are real, as are outright scams, but I give you the tools to avoid them in Chapter 11.

✔ Wherever an opportunity opens up, some entrepreneur steps in to fill it. So the number of enterprising businesses offering to find Part D plans for seniors, usually for a fee, really isn't surprising. If these operations are legitimate, whether offered through the Internet or by mail, they rely on the Medicare plan finder for their results. And if the results are good, you may consider your money well spent. But as of this writing, these plan-finding businesses are too new to assess whether they're all legitimate or whether at least some may involve a new type of scam. In any case, why pay for a service you can get for free from someone you know you can trust, such as a family member, friend, or SHIP counselor?

What were they thinking . . . when they created so many Part D plans?

Strangely enough, nobody expected there'd be so many Part D plans. In fact, members of Congress were uncertain whether enough private insurers would offer enough Part D plans to provide competition, especially in rural areas. Some insurance honchos even predicted that the industry wouldn't be interested in offering *stand-alone plans* — the kind that provide only drugs and no other healthcare — because such plans had never existed before and were regarded as unprofitable. (The chief executive officer of one leading insurance company went so far as to call stand-alones "a harebrained idea" that just wouldn't fly.) So when the law was written in 2003, it included a clause allowing the federal government to provide its own fallback drug plan in any area where fewer than two private plans entered the market. In other words, Congress guaranteed that at least two drug plans would be available to everyone on Medicare.

At least two! How quaint that seems today, with at least 50 stand-alone plans and dozens of Medicare Advantage plans plying their wares in every locality. What happened? As it turned out, the insurance industry — drawn by large federal subsidies — saw Medicare prescription drug coverage as a money-making bonanza.

The result was much like the California Gold Rush of the mid-1800s, with scores of insurers scrambling to carve out their share of a huge new market. That's how Medicare beneficiaries came to be confronted with a bewildering number of choices.

So will there always be so many plans? Some experts anticipate that over time the market will shake out, with only a few of the largest plans — those that have attracted the greatest number of enrollees — remaining in business. This scenario would reduce the choices but, with less competition, probably also increase enrollees' costs. Another potential turnaround is if Congress reduces or eliminates federal subsidies to plans, causing many of them to pull out of Part D. And yet another possibility, favored by some members of Congress and health policy experts, is to simplify plan choices by standardizing their designs — limiting them to maybe ten different options, each provided by a number of insurers at varying costs — in the way that Medigap supplementary insurance works today. Meanwhile, until any of those scenarios happen (or some entirely different development occurs), it's safe to say the days of a Part D plan plethora won't be over anytime soon.

Chapter 11

Buyer Beware: Avoiding Scams and Hard-Sell Marketing

In This Chapter

▶ Protecting yourself against outright scams

▶ Resisting aggressive and unethical sales tactics

Medicare Parts C and D are commercial marketplaces where products (in this case, Medicare health plans and prescription drug plans) are sold to consumers (Medicare beneficiaries). And like every other marketplace, they attract their share of swindlers and rip-off artists whose sad aim in life is to separate unsuspecting customers from their money.

But you aren't going to be easy meat! You aren't going to give those creeps any chance to exploit your uncertainties and trust! You may not come up against any of them at all, but if you do, you'll be prepared. Why? Because I'm going to show you how to see through their deceptions and sweet talk so you know when to show them the door, hang up the phone, or walk away.

In this chapter, I explain how to be on your guard against two quite different types of deceptive practices: the outright scam and the hard sell. I also suggest what you can do — maybe even to reverse the situation — if you do get ripped off.

Steering Clear of Outright Scams

An *outright scam* is when some thief pretends to be from Medicare, Social Security, or a Part D plan and asks for sensitive information — such as your Social Security, credit card, or bank account number — in an attempt to steal your identity or money.

Outright scammers have nothing to do with Medicare. They're just using Medicare (and most often Part D) as a pretext to cheat you of your hard-earned cash. The scam may be relatively simple — like trying to con you into paying a nonexistent enrollment fee for a false Part D plan. Or it may be a much more serious attempt to commit identity theft.

Identity thieves hunt for key pieces of personal information — Social Security numbers (or Medicare IDs, which are the same thing), credit card or bank account numbers, and even dates of birth and mothers' maiden names if they can get them. Whatever personal data they pull about you, identity thieves use it to buy merchandise, apply for new credit cards in your name, or make a profit by selling it to other identity thieves. Many of them have managed to buy big-ticket items, like houses, cars, and even expensive medical care, by successfully pretending to be someone else.

This crime not only robs people of money but also of their good credit rating, which is a much more worrying loss. Restoring your credit rating can take months or years of effort. Clearly, identity theft is a nightmare you want to avoid at all costs. That's why I explain what you need to know in the following sections.

Red flags to watch out for

Scams happen unexpectedly. You answer the phone or the doorbell and find someone who sounds or looks perfectly respectable offering to help you. How can you tell whether to trust this person? Here are some pointers you should recognize as instant red flags:

- ✔ **A person at your door saying he's from Medicare or Social Security:** The real agencies never send anyone to your home on official business without an appointment.

- ✔ **A person claiming he represents a particular Part D plan:** No one can come to your home uninvited to sell any kind of Medicare insurance. Doing so is illegal. Also, Medicare prohibits plans from cold-calling you on the phone. They can call only at your request. So if someone calls without your permission, it's probably a scam.

- ✔ **A person asking for an enrollment fee or an advance premium payment:** You should never have to pay for someone to enroll you in a Medicare health or drug plan. Nor should you pay any one-time payment that supposedly takes care of your premiums for months, years, or forever. Neither the enrollment fee nor the advance premium payment exists, so asking for either is illegal.

- ✔ **A person requesting your personal financial or identification information:** Never ever give out your Social Security or Medicare ID number, or any details about your credit cards, bank accounts, or other financial information — especially on the phone. Legitimate callers don't ask for this info.

A few lies already reported to Medicare

Con artists dream up new and creative ideas all the time for ways to target older Americans and steal their money and/or identities. Following are some typical scams involving Medicare and Part D that seniors have reported:

- ✓ **The loss of Medicare coverage threat:** The caller claims to be a government official needing to check your Social Security (or Medicare ID) number — and threatens or implies that if you don't provide it, you'll lose your Medicare coverage. Medicare already has these numbers. You can't lose Medicare benefits by refusing to give them out.

- ✓ **The Medicare refund tactic:** The caller claims to be from Medicare, says you're due for a refund, and asks for your bank account number in order to deposit your money. This refund doesn't exist; if it did, Medicare wouldn't contact you this way.

- ✓ **The "no more cash" routine:** The caller claims to be from Medicare or another agency that sounds official and says that under a new Medicare rule you'll no longer be able to pay cash for your Part D co-pays at the pharmacy. Instead, you must pay by credit or debit card, so of course the caller needs your card number on file, for security purposes. No such Medicare rule exists. You can pay for your drugs any way you please.

- ✓ **The bogus Part D enrollment fee:** The caller claims to be from a Part D plan, offers to enroll you for a fee, and asks you to pay by credit card. No plan or fee exists. Asking for a Part D enrollment fee is illegal.

- ✓ **The automatic premium deduction trick:** The caller claims to be from a Part D plan, supposedly enrolls you on the phone, and asks for your credit card or checking account number so the premiums can be automatically deducted every month. This plan doesn't exist. No real Part D plan can enroll you on the phone — unless you make the call — or ask for payments or financial information over the phone.

- ✓ **The ol' "Medicare's going out of business" line:** The caller claims to be a federal official, tells you that Medicare is discontinuing its services, and says that you can buy a plan that provides a similar service. This scam's a real whopper! Medicare isn't going away.

You're probably not going to encounter any of these scenarios. But it's wise to be alert to the possibilities, because being forewarned is good protection. And what if one of these situations does happen? You can hang up the phone or shut the door. You can say firmly that you're not interested. Yes, you can, even if you feel doing so is impolite! Don't be deceived by a friendly voice, a charming smile, a willingness to chat, or an apparent interest in your health and lifestyle. Con artists are experts at controlling the conversation to win your confidence and keep you on the phone or get invited inside. These people don't care about you. They're criminals who see you as a potential sucker. So show them you're not.

Who to contact to report a scam

The scams in the previous section are known only because seniors on the receiving end took the trouble to report them. Authorities who hear such reports send out alerts so the scams become widely known and more consumers are put on their guard. So if someone tries to scam you, do everyone a favor by reporting the incident to any of these offices:

- ✔ Your state's attorney general or insurance commissioner. (Their phone numbers are in the state pages of your phone book.)

- ✔ Federal Trade Commission — the official consumer protection agency.

  - • Call its toll-free help line at 877-382-4357 (TDD: 866-653-4261).

  - • Write to FTC, Consumer Response Center, 600 Pennsylvania Ave. NW, Washington, DC 20580.

  - • File a complaint online at www.ftc.gov.

- ✔ Inspector General of the Department of Health and Human Services.

  - • Call 800-447-8477 (TDD: 800-337-4950).

  - • Write to the Inspector General, HHS, Attention: Hotline, 330 Independence Ave. SW, Washington, DC 20201.

  - • Send an e-mail to HHSTips@oig.hhs.gov.

Actions you can take if you're ripped off

Suppose you fall for a scam, despite your best intentions. You may be able to stop a payment by contacting your bank or credit card company immediately, before the transaction clears. Similarly, if you give your credit card or checking account number to someone who uses it to buy items without your consent, the credit card company or bank usually refunds the money — even if it has already been taken out of your account — after you report the theft and the company investigates it.

If you give out any personal information — such as your Social Security or Medicare ID number, or your credit card or bank numbers — you should seriously assume that you may be a victim of identity theft, even if you don't immediately see any evidence of it. The following can give you excellent advice on what to do next:

- ✔ **The Privacy Rights Clearinghouse:** This California-based, nonprofit consumer organization provides assistance and information to likely or actual victims of identity theft. For fact sheets on identity theft, call 619-298-3396 (or write to Privacy Rights Clearinghouse, 3100 Fifth Ave., Suite B, San Diego, CA 92103). You can also read the fact sheets online at www.privacyrights.org/identity.htm.

⮑ **The Federal Trade Commission:** This agency provides an Identity Theft Hotline for consumers (877-438-4338) and a guide, *Take Charge: Fighting Back Against Identity Theft.* You can call the hotline for a free copy (in English or Spanish) or find it at www.ftc.gov/idtheft. Go to the same Web site to obtain more information and a complaint form.

Stories from the front lines

Soon after the hard-sell tactics used by some sales agents became publicly known, I invited readers of the *AARP Bulletin* to let us know if they'd encountered any. Here are a few of their stories:

⮑ Bobby, a 75-year-old retired construction worker living in Oklahoma, was happy with his coverage from traditional Medicare and veterans benefits. "I'd been in Medicare since 1985," he said. "I wasn't going to do anything to jeopardize that." But he listened when the saleswoman came to his home and sold him what he thought was a Medigap policy. "She said it was supplementary insurance that paid what Medicare didn't," he recalled. "She lied to me." Soon afterwards, he was rushed to his local hospital in a coma and spent ten days there. It was only then that he discovered she'd actually signed him up for a Medicare HMO. Bobby's hospital wasn't in the HMO's provider network, and the plan refused to pay his $45,000 bill. It did pay finally, because plans must cover emergency care. But Bobby — while still believing he was in traditional Medicare and able to go to any hospital — had already started a course of radiation treatment costing $16,000, which the plan also refused to pay. Eventually, after disenrolling from the HMO and enduring months of hassle, Bobby was able to get Medicare to pay for his treatment retroactively.

⮑ Elinor, a 79-year-old retired nurse living in Florida, had recently been widowed and was stressed out after caring for her husband through a long, difficult battle against cancer. She knew she didn't want the Medicare HMO plan the saleswoman was pitching. "But she kept pushing," Elinor said. "And because I wasn't in the best frame of mind at that time, in order to get her the heck out of the house, I signed the paper." Soon after checking with her doctors and finding they didn't accept the plan, Elinor wrote canceling the enrollment (as the agent had told her she could) and thought that was that. But the first time Elinor tried to fill a prescription, using her old stand-alone Part D plan card, the pharmacist told her she wasn't covered by it any more — she was in an HMO. It took six months of constant calls before Elinor was finally able to disenroll from the HMO and return to her original coverage from traditional Medicare, the Part D plan, and Medigap insurance. "I should never have had to go through this nightmare, all because of that insensitive, fraudulent agent," she said. "Normally, I never sign things. But I got caught at a bad time when I was vulnerable, and she used it."

⮑ Eva and her husband, who live in North Carolina, had a Medigap supplementary policy that was becoming increasingly expensive. It had reached almost $300 a month for both of them by the time she got a call from someone asking about supplementary insurance. So she agreed for a salesman to come to their home to talk about it. "This man came and said he

(continued)

(continued)

could offer insurance for $98 a month," she said. "It was the $98 that sold me, I guess. But never once did he say it was a Medicare Advantage plan." In fact, it was a Private Fee-for-Service type of MA plan. And although the salesman told her it was "good anywhere," Eva quickly found that none of her local doctors or hospitals would accept it. Getting disenrolled from the plan was "the worst rigmarole I've ever seen." And she met others who'd had the same experience. Like them, she said, "I just thought I was buying a cheaper supplementary policy."

Reprinted from the October 2007 issue of the *AARP Bulletin,* a publication of AARP. Copyright 2007 AARP. All rights reserved.

Resisting Hard-Sell Marketing Tactics

The *hard sell* is when a plan's salesperson or an independent insurance agent uses aggressive or unethical tactics — such as bait-and-switch — to try to push you into signing up for a plan you don't want or whose consequences you don't understand.

Part D plans and Medicare health plans aren't supposed to pressure or mislead you into buying one plan versus another. Medicare has rules to prevent such practices — though arguably not enough — and some of the plans themselves have voluntarily agreed to a code of conduct designed to stop what they call "rogue" salespeople from making hard sells. Still, hard sells can (and do!) happen.

You may never meet the kind of hard-sell tactics I warn about in the following pages. But whether you're a Medicare beneficiary or someone looking out for an older relative, being alert to the possibilities and knowing how to protect yourself (or your loved one) against such pressures is wise.

In the next several sections, I describe types of salesmanship to be aware of and suggest three lines of defense for resisting marketing pressure. The most important of which is understanding at least the main differences among kinds of Medicare insurance and the consequences of changing from one type to another. I also share the rules on what plans can and can't do when trying to make a sale — and checks you can make before signing on the dotted line. Finally, I explain what you can do to reverse the situation if you're tricked or misled into joining a plan you don't want or understand.

Assessing different kinds of salesmanship

REMEMBER

You need to be able to distinguish among three kinds of salesmanship, ranging from the acceptable through the unethical to the downright illegal:

✔ **Straightforward salesmanship:** Agents accurately describe the plan they're paid to pitch (whether a stand-alone Part D plan, Medicare Advantage health plan, or Medigap policy) and clearly explain how it'll add to, or change, the consumer's existing insurance. This plan may not be the best one for the consumer — only an impartial comparison of several plans can determine that, as explained in Chapters 9 and 10 — but the agents are doing their job fairly.

✔ **Unethical bait-and-switch:** The consumer is interested in a stand-alone Part D plan or Medigap insurance. But the agent is trying to sell a Medicare Advantage plan without being honest about the consequences of making that change. The consumer may be persuaded to sign up for the MA plan, not understanding that it can mean losing her current doctors and hospitals in traditional Medicare, her existing drug plan, her Medigap insurance, or in some cases, her retiree health coverage.

✔ **Illegal enrollment:** In the worst cases — not common, but known — agents say or do anything to get a signature, usually for enrollment in a Medicare Advantage plan. This sales approach includes the following:

- Saying consumers will lose Medicare or Medicaid benefits if they don't sign or saying that Medicare's ending

- Entering nursing home rooms uninvited

- Signing up very frail or mentally ill people who can't properly make a decision

- Telling people their signatures are needed only to confirm that they've met with the agent

- Forging signatures on the enrollment form

All of these tactics are exploitative and prohibited by law. Selling Medigap insurance to anyone already enrolled in an MA plan is also illegal.

How can such scenarios happen? After these sorts of tactics first became publicly known in 2007, Medicare announced a crackdown on abuses and set tougher rules for the hiring and training of sales agents. In 2008 Congress prohibited certain practices. Perhaps these regulations (described later in this chapter) are now curbing the most disgraceful kinds of exploitation. But one underlying problem hasn't changed, at least at the time I'm writing this book.

Plans are still allowed to pay agents higher commissions for selling Medicare Advantage plans than stand-alone drug plans. For example, agents may be paid $40 to $80 for each stand-alone Part D plan they sell, but up to $500 for each Medicare Advantage plan. (That's because MA plans are far more profitable for the insurers.) So it doesn't take a rocket scientist to see that the system encourages abuse. Unless Medicare requires individual insurers to offer the same commission for every type of plan they sell, it's difficult to see how hard-sell tactics can be outlawed completely. Unscrupulous agents will always be attracted by bigger bucks.

Understanding the various types of Medicare insurance

How is it possible for sales agents to persuade people to sign up for Medicare Advantage plans they don't want? Are these folks dumb, or what? Absolutely not! Sometimes their signing can be the result of bullying tactics that take advantage of a senior's vulnerability, as in some of the experiences described in the nearby sidebar "Stories from the front lines." But often it happens because people simply aren't armed with their first line of defense: They don't understand the differences among varying types of Medicare insurance. And who can blame them?

Just think how many types are out there, all with Medicare in their names. Traditional Medicare. Medicare Advantage. Medicare Medical Savings Accounts. Medicare (Medigap) supplementary insurance. Medicare drug coverage. And those types are just the broad divisions. You can't even rely on the names of the insurers to tell them apart. Many large insurers sell Medicare Advantage plans, Medigap policies, and stand-alone Part D plans.

Now's a good time to take another look at Table 1-1 in Chapter 1, where you can see at a glance the broad differences between each type of Medicare insurance. I explain in more detail how the different types of Medicare Advantage plans vary from each other, and from traditional Medicare, in Chapter 9.

Here, I focus on what you need to know to avoid being *misled* by a sales agent. I emphasize *misled* because there's nothing wrong with choosing a Medicare Advantage plan when you know what you're buying. Millions of people enrolled in them are satisfied with their coverage. But if you're in traditional Medicare now and someone actively tries to enroll you in an MA plan, be aware of the following consequences of switching:

- ✔ You'll receive your Medicare benefits through the MA plan — not through traditional Medicare — and must accept the plan's conditions.

- ✔ You may not be able to go to the same doctors and hospitals that treat you now in the traditional Medicare program.

- ✔ If you enroll in a Medicare HMO or Special Needs Plan that restricts your choice of doctors and hospitals to those in its network, and you go outside of that network, you'll be responsible for the full cost of the treatment — except in an emergency. (In an emergency, the plan must cover your treatment anywhere.)

- ✔ If you enroll in a Private Fee-for-Service plan and are treated by a doctor or hospital that doesn't accept the plan's terms and conditions, you'll be responsible for the full cost of the treatment — except in an emergency. Also, a provider can decide whether or not to accept the plan's coverage on each visit a patient makes.

✔ If you enroll in a Medicare Medical Savings Account Plan (MSA), be aware that after you use up the money deposited into your account, you'll be responsible for the full cost of any medical services until you meet your deductible. One or two days in the hospital can completely gobble up the typical deposit amount. (The structure of an MSA is similar to a Part D plan in that they both have a gap in coverage in the middle. In a drug plan, it's the doughnut hole; in an MSA, it's the deductible.)

✔ If you have standard Medigap supplementary insurance, you can't use it to cover your out-of-pocket expenses in an MA plan. Medigap policies can be used only with traditional Medicare.

✔ If you're enrolled in a stand-alone Part D plan, this coverage is automatically canceled as soon as you're enrolled in an MA plan — even if the MA plan doesn't provide drug coverage.

✔ If you have retiree health insurance from an employer or union, you may lose this coverage by being enrolled in an MA plan. (For more about this possibility, see Chapter 6.)

In addition, here are a couple of tidbits to be aware of when listening to pitches for Medigap supplementary policies or stand-alone Part D plans:

✔ Medigap policies typically cover out-of-pocket expenses in traditional Medicare no matter which hospital or doctor you choose, anywhere in the country. Medigap SELECT policies are the exception. They have lower premiums but require you to use specific hospitals, clinics, and doctors within a geographical area (except in an emergency) in order to receive the insurance benefits.

✔ Individual insurers typically offer two or three different stand-alone Part D plans. The one with the highest premium is usually an enhanced plan with extra benefits (for example, some coverage in the doughnut hole, also known as the coverage gap; see Chapter 15 for an introduction). If you don't need these extras, the higher premium may not be worthwhile. The only way to decide — and avoid undue pressure to buy the most expensive plan — is to compare plans properly according to the drugs you take, as explained in Chapter 10, instead of relying on a sales pitch.

Getting familiar with Medicare marketing rules

Knowing the can's and can'ts of what plan sponsors or their sales agents are allowed to do when selling their products is your second line of defense in spotting whether a sales pitch is out of line and should be mistrusted. Medicare has had most of the following regulations in place for several years, but some are tougher rules put into effect after the marketing abuse scandal erupted. All refer to both Medicare Advantage health plans and stand-alone Part D plans, unless otherwise stated.

Medicare allows plan sponsors to

- ✔ Send promotional materials to you through the mail — but not enrollment forms.

- ✔ Send sales reps to your home — but only with your prior permission and only to discuss the single type of coverage (for example, stand-alone drug plan, Medicare Advantage plan, or Medigap insurance) that you specify when making the appointment.

- ✔ Give sales presentations in public places like shopping malls or hotels.

Medicare doesn't allow plan sponsors to

- ✔ Send salespeople to your home uninvited.

- ✔ Telephone you directly to make a sales pitch — *unless* you invited the call or already have a relationship with the plan.

- ✔ Tell you that a home visit is required for the purpose of explaining details of the plan or for you to enroll in it.

- ✔ Ask for personal information on the phone, including your address, prescription meds, Social Security number, credit card or bank account numbers, or any other financial information.

- ✔ Enroll you in a plan on the phone — unless you call the plan.

- ✔ Give sales presentations or distribute enrollment forms in doctors' offices, hospitals, pharmacies, long-term care facilities, or anywhere patients go to receive healthcare-related services (except in common areas such as public lounges at such facilities).

- ✔ Give sales presentations at educational events such as health information fairs and community meetings.

- ✔ Offer free gifts, cash, meals, or other giveaways to encourage you to enroll in a plan

Medicare requires plan sponsors to

- ✔ Explain clearly in their marketing materials and verbal sales pitches that not all doctors and hospitals accept their Medicare Advantage plans.

- ✔ Ensure that any independent sales agents they hire are licensed by the state in which they work.

- ✔ Guarantee that sales agents are paid the same commission for each MA plan the sponsor sells in any given year. Also, that agents are paid the same commission for each stand-alone Part D plan the sponsor sells. (But a sponsor can pay commissions for MA plans that are different from stand-alone drug plans.)

✔ Train sales reps, independent insurance agents, and brokers who sell their products, and hire only those candidates who score at least 80 percent on a written test of their knowledge of the Medicare program, its rules, and the details of the plan(s) they'll sell.

✔ Ensure that sales agents who meet with consumers to discuss a particular type of plan (such as Medigap insurance) can't also, at the same meeting, discuss other types of plans (such as MA health plans or stand-alone Part D plans) but must instead schedule a separate appointment, at least 48 hours after the first, to discuss another.

✔ Call consumers who sign up for any MA plan to check that they understand its conditions and consequences, and allow them the opportunity to withdraw from the enrollment if they want to.

Thinking and checking before you sign

Taking the time to think and verify information is most certainly your third line of defense against signing up for the wrong plan. Never let anyone rush you into enrolling in a plan. If a sales agent tries to push you into signing on the dotted line before leaving (or before you leave a sales presentation) — well, that's a red flag right there. If the agent asks for your signature just to confirm that he has met with you, that red flag's on fire. A legitimate agent doesn't ask. A legitimate agent respects your desire to think it over.

Ask for the agent's name and contact information. Then take your time, preferably several days, to consider the plan carefully. You can also use this time to do some checking so you can make an informed decision:

✔ Read any sales material carefully, especially the fine print.

✔ Check that the plan is the kind you want — a Medicare Advantage health plan, a stand-alone Part D plan, or Medigap insurance. If it's a Medicare Advantage health plan, check what type. (I explain each type of Medicare health plan in Chapter 9.) The sales material should say clearly what kind of plan it is. (Starting in 2010, the type of plan must be incorporated in each plan name.) You can also

   • Look up its name and ID number in the back pages of your *Medicare & You* handbook.

   • Call the Medicare help line at 800-633-4227.

   • Go online to `www.medicare.gov` and click "Learn More About Plans in Your Area."

✔ If you're considering a Medicare HMO, PPO, or Special Needs plan, but want to continue going to your preferred doctors and hospitals, verify that the plan covers them. You can call the plan and ask for its provider directory, or you can look at the directory on the plan's Web site. You can also ask your doctors and hospitals whether they accept the plan.

✔ If you're considering a Private Fee-for-Service plan, check with your local doctors and hospitals to find out whether they accept the plan. (PFFS plans currently aren't required to have a provider network. Starting in 2011, they must have written contracts with providers so that consumers will then be able to find out more easily which providers accept specific PFFS plans.)

✔ If you're considering any kind of Medicare health plan, and want prescription drug coverage as well, confirm that it covers drugs. Many MA plans don't.

Knowing what to do if you're misled into joining a plan you don't want

Medicare has some consumer protections for people who believe they were tricked or misled into enrolling in a Medicare Advantage health plan they don't want, or joined without understanding the consequences. Here's what you can do:

✔ Call the Medicare helpline at 800-633-4227 (TDD: 877-486-2048), explain the circumstances, and say you want a special enrollment period to disenroll from the plan and either switch to another MA plan or be reinstated in traditional Medicare. Your case will probably be investigated.

✔ If you have medical bills that the plan refuses to pay — for example, if you were treated by doctors and/or a hospital outside of the plan's provider network when you thought you were still covered by traditional Medicare — call the Medicare help line and ask to be reenrolled into traditional Medicare *retroactively* — that is, dating back to the time you joined the plan. Medicare will then pay any outstanding bills at its usual rate, and you'll pay the usual share of the cost.

✔ If calling the Medicare help line doesn't bring results, call again and ask to be put in touch with a caseworker at your regional Medicare office. Or ask the help line for the phone number of the regional office that serves your state. Then call that office to explain what happened.

In certain situations, you have the right to disenroll from your present MA plan and either join another one or switch to traditional Medicare, even if you can't show that you were misled by a plan. I explain these circumstances in Chapters 9 and 17.

You can also get in touch with your State Health Insurance Assistance Program (SHIP — check out Appendix B for contact info) for help if you need to. And you can report sales agents who use unethical tactics to the offices of your state's insurance commissioner or attorney general (these phone numbers are in the state pages of your telephone directory).

Chapter 12

Signing Up for a Part D Plan for the First Time

. . . .

In This Chapter

▶ Recognizing when you can enroll in Part D without incurring a late penalty

▶ Confirming some last-minute items before signing up

▶ Understanding the process of enrolling in a Medicare drug plan

▶ Figuring out why your enrollment may be held up or rejected

. . . .

*P*hew! The hard part's over. You've chosen a Part D plan — either a stand-alone drug plan or a Medicare health plan that comes with drug coverage. In contrast, signing up for that plan's usually a cakewalk.

In this chapter, I assume you're joining Medicare Part D for the first time. Even so, people may be plunging into the Part D pool from a number of points, so I consider these different circumstances in explaining when to enroll in a plan. Then I suggest some last-minute checks you can — and should — make *before* signing up. After that (at last!), I show you how to enroll and give you some tips on the process. Finally, I explain how an enrollment application may occasionally be delayed or denied.

Stay Informed: Knowing the Right Time to Enroll

The right time to enroll in Part D is when you can sign up without incurring a *late penalty* — extra payments that add to your premiums for as long as you stay in the program. In Table 12-1, the white area shows when you can enroll in Part D for the first time to avoid a late penalty. The shaded area shows when you can sign up if you delay and miss these deadlines, or deliberately drop your current drug coverage — in which case you should probably prepare to face a late penalty.

Table 12-1		When to Enroll in Part D for the First Time
Circumstance	*Enrollment Period*	*When You Can Enroll (To Get Coverage and Avoid a Late Penalty)*
First joining Medicare at age 65 (with no other creditable drug coverage)	Initial enrollment period (IEP)	Any time in the seven-month period that begins three months before the month you turn 65 and ends three months after it. Sooner rather than later — preferably no later than halfway through the final month of your IEP.
First joining Medicare because of disability (with no other creditable drug coverage)	Initial enrollment period (IEP)	Any time in the seven-month period that begins three months before the month you receive your 25th disability check and ends three months after it. Sooner rather than later — preferably no later than halfway through the final month of your IEP.
After losing creditable drug coverage (through no fault of your own)	Special enrollment period (SEP)	Any time within the 63-day SEP that begins when you receive notice that your current drug coverage will end *or* when it actually ends (whichever is later). Make sure Part D coverage starts *before* the 63 days are up.
Returning to the U.S. after living abroad	Initial enrollment period (IEP) or special enrollment period (SEP)	If you turned 65 while abroad, any time in your seven-month IEP — from three months before the month of your return to three months after it. Otherwise, any time within the 63-day SEP that begins on the day of your return to the U.S. Make sure Part D coverage starts *before* the 63 days are up.
After being released from prison	Initial enrollment period (IEP) or special enrollment period (SEP)	If you turned 65 while incarcerated, any time in your seven-month IEP — from three months before the month of your release to three months after it. Otherwise, any time within the 63-day SEP that begins on the day of your release. Make sure Part D coverage starts *before* the 63 days are up.
After missing any of these deadlines	Annual enrollment period (AEP)	Only during the AEP from November 15 to December 31 each year. (You'll pay a late penalty based on any months without coverage.)

Circumstance	Enrollment Period	When You Can Enroll (To Get Coverage and Avoid a Late Penalty)
After deliberately dropping creditable drug coverage	Annual enrollment period (AEP)	Only during the AEP from November 15 to December 31 each year. (You'll pay a late penalty based on any months without coverage.)

In the following sections, I describe the three kinds of enrollment periods in Table 12-1 in more detail and explain why you shouldn't wait until the last minute to enroll in a Part D plan. For the full scoop on how you can avoid the late penalty, head to Chapter 8.

Distinguishing among different enrollment periods

Medicare permits three types of enrollment periods:

- **Initial enrollment period (IEP):** Medicare assigns you a seven-month IEP around the time of your 65th birthday or, if you're younger and have a disability, around the time you receive your 25th Supplemental Security Income (SSI) check. You can use this time frame to sign up for Medicare Parts A and B, according to your circumstances, as explained in Chapter 1. You can also sign up at this time for a Part D plan if you don't have *creditable drug coverage.* Basically, this term means drug coverage from elsewhere (like an employer or union) that's considered at least as good as Part D. (Still baffled? Take a look at Chapter 6, which covers creditable drug coverage in detail.) If you lived abroad or were in prison at the time of your 65th birthday, you get a special IEP, also lasting seven months, to sign up for Part D upon your return to the U.S. or upon your release, as explained in Chapter 8.

- **Special enrollment period (SEP):** Medicare allows you an SEP to join Part D in certain circumstances — if you lose creditable drug coverage through no fault of your own or have an unavoidable break in coverage. You get an SEP if your employer terminates your drug benefits or reduces coverage so it's no longer creditable. You also receive an SEP if you turned 65 before moving abroad or going to prison and want Part D coverage after your return or release.

  If you're eligible for an SEP, all you have to do is sign up with your chosen Part D plan and make sure that your coverage starts within the allotted time. You *don't* have to apply for an SEP in any of the circumstances shown in Table 12-1.

✔ **Annual enrollment period (AEP):** If you don't have creditable coverage and fail to sign up for a Part D plan before your IEP or SEP expires, you can't sign up for a plan until the next AEP that starts November 15 and ends December 31. As a result, you'll be without drug coverage until January 1 and will face a late penalty. Also, if you deliberately dropped creditable drug coverage (instead of losing it involuntarily), you can sign up for Part D only during an AEP.

If you qualify for low-cost drug coverage under Part D's Extra Help program (see Chapter 5), you can enroll in a Part D plan any time you want during the year. Your coverage starts on the first day of the month after you enroll. You won't incur a late penalty, even if you sign up late.

Recognizing why you shouldn't sign up at the last minute

Your Medicare prescription drug coverage begins on the first day of the month after you enroll in a plan. Technically, you can sign up on the very last day of an initial or annual enrollment period (for example, December 31) and still be covered the next day (in this case, January 1).

But — and this is an alert for the chronic procrastinators — putting off enrolling until the last minute isn't the best idea. In fact, Medicare recommends signing up at least two weeks before your deadline. Here's why:

✔ The plan needs time to verify the information you provide on the enrollment form (such as your eligibility to receive drug coverage) or to get back to you if the information is incomplete (see the later section "If your enrollment is delayed" for more).

✔ You want to be able to mosey over to the pharmacy and pick up your meds without hassle after your Medicare drug coverage begins. Giving your Part D plan enough time to upload your data into the computer system increases the odds of this process going smoothly. (Flip to Chapter 14 for the basics on filling your prescriptions.)

✔ If you have a special enrollment period, you must receive Part D coverage before the 63 days are up to avoid a late penalty. If you wait longer than 60 days to enroll, you can incur a penalty, depending on where your SEP falls in the calendar, as explained in more detail in Chapter 8.

✔ Here is a different reason for signing up as early as you can: If you have a seven-month IEP and enroll in a Part D plan during the *first three months* of that period, your coverage starts on the first day of the month in which you turn 65 or in which you become eligible through disability — even if those dates fall at the end of the month.

Play It Safe: Making a Few Final Checks before You Sign Up

Yes, I know — you've had enough of all this rigmarole by now and just want to join the darned plan! I sympathize. But remember that after you're enrolled, you'll probably be locked into the plan for the whole year. So I don't feel comfortable saying, "Okay, go ahead," without suggesting a few practical, final precautions. Following them is entirely up to you, of course, but playing it safe never hurts, and sometimes it pays off big-time.

- ✔ **Make sure you live in the plan's service area.** If you live outside this area, your enrollment won't be accepted.

- ✔ **Keep the plan details as a record of why you chose the plan.** If you chose it from the online Medicare Prescription Drug Plan Finder, print out all the details that show your likely costs and keep them safe. If you called the Medicare help line for the same information, keep the printout the customer rep sent you. You need this record if, after enrollment, you believe the plan's charging more for your drugs than it quoted on the plan finder and you want to change to another plan as a result, as explained in Chapter 17.

- ✔ **Double-check the details of your costs under the plan.** Make sure the drug information you entered into the plan finder is correct, as I describe in Chapter 10. If the details you entered — especially each drug's dosage and how often you take it — aren't accurate, the quoted costs aren't going to be accurate either. Verify your likely costs by looking at your printout and/or calling the plan.

- ✔ **Make sure that this plan is the one you want and that you understand its conditions.** This check is especially important if you chose this plan on the advice of a salesperson or insurance agent, or from marketing materials sent through the mail. If you're not sure this plan is "the one," call it — not the salesperson — to confirm you understand exactly what you're buying. When people are misled into joining an inappropriate plan, it's often because they didn't fully understand the plan's conditions and consequences, as explained in Chapter 11.

- ✔ **If the plan is a Medicare HMO or PPO, make sure it includes drug coverage.** If you join an HMO or PPO that doesn't cover drugs, you won't be able to get drug coverage any other way for the rest of the year, as I describe in Chapter 9.

- ✔ **If the plan is a Private Fee-for-Service plan or a Medicare Cost plan, confirm that it includes drug coverage.** If it doesn't, and you want drug coverage, you should choose and enroll in a stand-alone Part D plan before your enrollment period expires. The same is true of Medicare Medical Savings Account plans, which don't cover drugs.

If you chose your plan through a search of Medicare's online plan finder, you won't have to verify whether the plan is in your service area or includes drug coverage. Because you must enter your zip code at the beginning of this search, all the plans that appear on-screen are available in your area, and all of them cover prescription drugs. Otherwise, you can call Medicare at 800-633-4227 to check these details.

Take the Plunge: Enrolling in a Plan

Actually enrolling in a plan is the easy bit. You still have choices on how to do it, but they're simple ones. The process is the same whether you're enrolling in a stand-alone prescription drug plan (PDP) or a Medicare health plan that includes drug coverage (MAPD). All you need are your Medicare ID number and the name of the plan you want to join. Then you can sign up, or a legal representative can do so on your behalf, in any of the following ways:

- **Calling Medicare's help line toll-free at 800-633-4227:** Tell the customer representative you want to enroll in a Part D plan. Have at hand your Medicare ID number and the name of the plan.

- **Visiting Medicare's Web site at www.medicare.gov:** On the home page, look for a menu headed Prescription Drug Plans in the top right-hand corner and click "Enroll." Doing so takes you to the Medicare Part D enrollment center. Most plans allow enrollment through the center, but a few may not. If your chosen plan doesn't, the customer representative at the center can give you that plan's phone number.

- **Calling the plan directly:** You can find the plan's customer service number in its marketing materials, on its Web site, or on the top right of its plan details page (if you chose the plan on Medicare's plan finder or asked Medicare to mail you details of the plan).

- **Visiting the plan's Web site:** If the plan offers online enrollment (not all do), you can find its Web site address in its marketing materials and on the top right of its plan details page on Medicare's online plan finder. Or you can do an Internet search for the plan's name.

- **Completing a paper application:** Call the plan and ask it to send you an application. Fill out this paperwork, sign it, then mail or fax it to the address or number provided.

And that's it! Well, almost. Whichever way you choose to sign up, you'll be asked a number of questions you must answer before your enrollment can be completed. Be prepared by having this info ready:

- Your name, address, and phone number
- Details of your Medicare coverage, as shown on your Medicare ID card

✔ Details of any other drug coverage you may have

✔ Circumstances indicating that you may qualify for Extra Help

✔ How you want to pay your premiums

✔ If you live in a long-term care facility, such as a nursing home

A Part D plan can't ask you for your bank account or credit card information during the enrollment process, regardless of whether you enroll on a paper form, by phone, or online.

Enrollment is a legal contract between you and the plan. So if you can't manage the enrollment process yourself, either through incapacity or illiteracy, the person who enrolls you must be someone who has the authority to do so under your state law. This person can be a legal representative, a court-appointed guardian, or a family member or caregiver who has *durable power of attorney* — that is, someone authorized to make medical decisions on your behalf. When making the enrollment request — whether on paper, online, or on the phone — your representative must attest that she has the appropriate legal authority and can show documentary proof if the plan requests it. She must also provide her contact information.

In the following sections, I tackle in detail three important issues that may arise during the enrollment process.

Grasping the importance of your address

No, your Medicare prescription drug plan doesn't care a scrap whether you live in a mansion or a minivan. But the address you provide determines

✔ **If you live in the plan's service area:** No plan will accept your enrollment if you don't live in its service area. For stand-alone drug plans, that means living in the state the plan serves. For Medicare health plans, this area is defined as the region (a state, county, or zip code) that the plan serves. Even for plans that don't have defined service areas, you must sign up for the one that's offered in the area where you live.

✔ **Where your permanent residence is:** You can't be enrolled in two plans at the same time, so if you live in different states during the year, you can't have one plan per address. When enrolling in a plan, you must give the address of your *permanent* or *primary residence* — the place considered to be your normal home (for example, the one used on tax forms). If you provide a post office (PO) box number as your address, the plan must contact you to confirm that you live in its service area.

If you're homeless or don't have a fixed address, the Part D plan you want may accept the address of a shelter or clinic, a PO box number, or anywhere else that you receive mail.

Deciding how to pay the premiums

When enrolling, you'll be asked how you want to pay your monthly premiums to the plan. Here are your options:

- ✔ Ask the plan to bill you directly and pay the premiums every month by check, money order, or credit card.

- ✔ Have the premiums deducted automatically from your monthly Social Security checks. (The plan arranges this deduction for you.)

- ✔ Agree for the premiums to be automatically sent to the plan each month by Electronic Funds Transfer from your bank, or charged to your credit card. (The plan will ask you to fill out and return a form, along with a voided check from your bank account or your credit card details.)

Many people choose to have their plan premiums taken out of their Social Security checks, in the same way that Medicare Part B premiums are deducted. But this payment method can cause difficulties. There have been many instances of Social Security failing to make plan premium deductions for the first two or three months, and then taking them all out of a single check. Or, in the case of people who've switched from one plan to another, deducting two premiums rather than one for several months. Similar errors can occur in automatic payments from a bank account or credit card.

Disclosing other drug coverage you have

During the enrollment process, you'll be asked whether you have any other drug coverage — for example, coverage from an employer or union, veterans or military benefits, private individual insurance, or a State Pharmacy Assistance Program (SPAP). The Part D plan needs this info for two main reasons:

- ✔ **To protect you:** In some cases, joining a Part D plan can automatically cancel your other medical and drug coverage, as explained in Chapter 6. If you have creditable drug coverage from elsewhere, the plan may contact you to confirm that you understand the consequences of joining Part D. You'll have 30 days to respond. If you don't respond within this time frame, your enrollment will be denied, as I explain later in this chapter.

- ✔ **To coordinate your benefits properly:** Listing any other benefits you're entitled to means that the plan can log them into its computer system so that when you go to fill your prescriptions, the pharmacist knows what to charge you and whom to bill. Otherwise, you may pay more than you should. I explain more about how this coordination of benefits works (and how it sometimes doesn't) in Chapter 14.

Don't Give Up: Understanding Why Your Enrollment May Be Delayed or Denied

Your enrollment isn't complete until your chosen plan accepts it. Within ten calendar days of receiving your enrollment request, the plan must send you one of these items:

- ✔ A notice acknowledging your completed application, together with a copy of it, and details about the plan's costs, benefits, and conditions
- ✔ A request asking for more information to complete the application
- ✔ A notice saying your application has been denied

If you receive only the acknowledgment, your enrollment probably will be confirmed very soon, and you'll receive your membership card and Evidence of Coverage, as explained in Chapter 13. Read the following sections if your plan sends you either a request for more information or a denial notice.

If your enrollment is delayed

Enrollment can be delayed if

- ✔ You haven't completed all the information required on the enrollment form, and the plan needs to get back to you
- ✔ You don't submit additional information as soon as you're asked
- ✔ Medicare doesn't immediately confirm that you're eligible
- ✔ The plan discovers you have coverage from elsewhere (such as employer or union health benefits) and contacts you to be sure you understand the consequences of joining the plan

In all of these cases, the plan will contact you either by mail or phone. So it's important to look out for a letter from your plan, or to return messages it has left on your answering machine. If you're asked for more information and don't provide it within 30 days, the plan has no choice but to consider your application incomplete and reject it.

What if your enrollment's delayed past the date when your coverage should begin? In this situation, the plan covers you until the matter is resolved. (During this time, you can use a copy of your enrollment form or the plan's acknowledgment as proof of coverage at the pharmacy until your plan membership card arrives, as explained in Chapter 13.) But if your enrollment is ultimately denied for any of the reasons in the next section, you'd have to repay the plan for any services used.

If your enrollment is denied

If you're in Medicare, you have an absolute right to Part D coverage. So if a plan turns you down, you need to know why. Here are the possibilities:

- ✔ Your eligibility for Medicare can't be found in the official records.

- ✔ You didn't answer all the questions on your enrollment application, didn't complete it within the required time, or failed to respond to the plan's request for additional information.

- ✔ You don't live within the plan's service area.

- ✔ Your enrollment period has expired.

- ✔ You applied outside the time frames for initial or annual enrollment, and you don't qualify for a special enrollment period.

- ✔ You have creditable drug coverage from an employer or union, and you didn't respond within 30 days to the plan's request for confirmation that you understand how joining Part D can affect this coverage.

- ✔ You've applied to a Medicare Advantage plan but don't have Medicare Part A and Part B. (Both are required for MA plans. To join a stand-alone Part D plan, you need only one or the other. To join a Medicare Cost plan, you need only Part B.)

- ✔ You've applied to a Medicare Advantage plan but already have end-stage renal disease. (ESRD patients can't join an MA plan.)

- ✔ You've applied to a Medicare Advantage plan that isn't currently accepting new enrollees.

- ✔ You've applied to a Special Needs Plan but don't fall within the category of people it serves, as explained in Chapter 9.

- ✔ You've applied for a Medicare Medical Savings Account plan but don't meet its eligibility requirements, as explained in Chapter 9.

If your enrollment's denied, the Part D plan or Medicare must send you a letter explaining why. You don't have the right to appeal against an enrollment denial. But if you think the given reasons are incorrect, call the number on your denial notice as soon as possible. Provide information showing why you think the denial is incorrect. If that doesn't work, contact your regional Medicare office to explain the problem. (For the office number, call Medicare at 800-633-4227.) You can also get expert advice and help from your State Health Insurance Assistance Program (SHIP) or the Medicare Rights Center; see Appendix B for contact info.

Part IV
You're In!
Navigating Part D
from the Inside

The 5th Wave   By Rich Tennant

"We'll whisper your name when your
migraine medication is ready."

In this part . . .

Now that you're in a Part D plan, I help you deal with many situations that can arise. For those of you who've joined a plan for the first time, I begin by explaining what happens immediately after enrolling. Then I consider in detail many aspects of receiving Medicare drug coverage — things you need to know about filling your prescriptions, falling into or avoiding the coverage gap (the infamous "doughnut hole"), lowering your drug costs, switching from one Part D plan to another or being dropped from a plan, using your Part D coverage in a long-term care facility, filing complaints against your plan, and appealing against decisions your plan makes that you don't agree with.

Whether you're new to Part D or already a veteran of the program, you'll find a lot of useful information and tips here to help you. This part is your go-to reference section for navigating Part D from the inside in all sorts of circumstances.

Chapter 13

You've Just Signed Up — What Happens Now?

In This Chapter

▶ Checking out your membership card and other important info from your plan

▶ Determining when your coverage begins

▶ Getting organized — why keeping records pays off

You're in. Medicare has confirmed your enrollment, and you're going to get drug coverage under Part D. Whether that makes you feel elated, relieved, or wary, you've overcome the hurdle of making several important, and perhaps difficult, decisions. Congratulate yourself!

So what happens next? This chapter explains what to expect from your drug plan the first time out. I begin with the question of when your drug coverage actually starts, according to your circumstances. Then I describe what you'll receive from your plan — namely, your membership card and a lot of important documents to read. I also explain what to do if you're told you need to pay a late penalty. Finally, I clue you in on why keeping good records pays off in tracking your coverage and expenses, and in protecting yourself in case of disputes. Even if this isn't your first time in a Medicare prescription drug plan, you may find some of this information helpful.

Knowing When Your Coverage Will Start

Can't wait to get that drug coverage? It's what you've signed up for, after all. You won't have to wait long — less than one month in most cases. But your coverage doesn't start until the date it becomes *effective,* meaning the very first day you can fill a prescription under your Part D plan, even if you receive your membership card in the mail before then.

When you're joining a Part D plan for the first time, the date your coverage begins depends on the following circumstances:

- ✔ You're just coming into the Medicare program because you're turning 65 or qualifying through disability.

- ✔ You're just coming into the Medicare program after a delay due to turning 65 while living abroad or in prison

- ✔ You've received a special enrollment period because you lost your creditable drug coverage from an employer or some other plan, or because you recently came out of prison or have returned to the U.S. after a period living abroad.

- ✔ You failed to join Part D when you were first eligible and now need to enroll in a drug plan during the annual enrollment period at the end of the year.

- ✔ You qualify for Part D's Extra Help because your income is limited.

Table 13-1 shows when your coverage begins in all of these situations.

Table 13-1	When Your Drug Coverage Starts
Your Situation	*When Your Coverage Begins*
If you sign up for a plan during your initial Medicare enrollment period upon turning 65	On the first day of the month in which you turn 65, if you enrolled in the plan during the previous three months. Or on the first day of the month after enrollment if you signed up in the month of your birthday, or during the following three months.
If you sign up for a plan because of disability during your initial Medicare enrollment period	On the first day of the month in which you receive your 25th disability payment, if you enrolled in the plan during the previous three months. Or on the first day of the month after enrollment if you signed up in the month you received your 25th check, or during the following three months.
If you sign up for a plan during a special initial enrollment period due to turning 65 while abroad or in prison	Immediately after your return to the U.S. or your release from prison, if you enrolled in the plan during the previous three months. Or on the first day of the month after enrollment if you signed up in the month of your return or release, or during the following three months.

Your Situation	When Your Coverage Begins
If you sign up for a plan during a special enrollment period	The first day of the month after you enrolled in the plan.
If you sign up for a plan during annual enrollment from Nov. 15 to Dec. 31	January 1.
If you qualify for Extra Help under Part D	The first day of the month after you enrolled in the plan. You can sign up for or change Part D plans in any month of the year when you receive Extra Help.

As you can see in Table 13-1, the longest you can wait to start coverage after enrollment is six weeks. And that's only in one particular situation: if you delay joining Part D beyond when you were first eligible and need to wait for open enrollment at the end of the year. If you sign up on the first day of that period, November 15, your coverage starts six weeks later on January 1.

The shortest wait can be as little as one day. If you enroll in a plan on the last day of a month, your coverage becomes effective the first day of the following month — in other words, the next day. (However, I don't advise cutting it that fine. Loading your coverage info into Medicare's computer system takes a while, so enrolling at the last minute can cause delays when filling your first prescriptions, as explained in Chapter 14.)

Of course, if you're already in Part D, your current coverage lasts until the end of the calendar year — midnight on December 31. If you decide to switch plans and sign up for another during open enrollment (November 15 through December 31), coverage in your new plan starts January 1. (See Chapter 17 for details about switching plans.) If you stay in the same plan, your coverage just rolls on through the following year.

Receiving Your Plan's Card and Other Important Stuff You Need to Read

Soon after you enroll, your plan will send you a bunch of stuff through the mail. So watch for its arrival and get out your glasses! This is important information you must read — even if you've been in a Medicare drug or private health plan before. In the next several sections, I show you what to expect and check up on when you receive your plan's membership card, its Evidence of Coverage document, and other information. I also touch on the form you should send back to the plan showing what other types of coverage you may have for prescription drugs or medical care. And I explain what to do if you're told you need to pay a late penalty on your Medicare prescription drug coverage.

You receive a membership card and information about coverage regardless of whether you're joining Part D for the first time, have just switched from one drug plan to another, or are remaining in the same plan you had last year. In this last situation, even though you don't need to re-enroll, you still get a new card and Evidence of Coverage (EOC) document for the new year. That's because some details of your coverage have likely changed since the previous year. (Your plan sends advance warning of any changes in its Annual Notice of Change [ANOC], mailed in the fall, and incorporates them in your new EOC document. So if you didn't read the ANOC, be sure to read the EOC.)

The membership ID card: Your key to coverage

The very first mailing you receive from your new Part D plan is an acknowledgment of your enrollment request, which the plan must send you within ten calendar days of receiving it. This mailing also tells you when you can expect your coverage to become effective, as explained in the previous section. The plan sends your membership ID card either with this mailing or soon afterward, and you can start using it at the pharmacy as soon as your coverage begins.

If you don't receive your card by the time your coverage starts, you can use what your plan calls its *proof of coverage* to fill your prescriptions until your card arrives. This proof may be a copy of your enrollment form, the plan's acknowledgment of your enrollment request, or a letter from the plan stating that you're entitled to coverage, starting on the effective date. (See Chapter 14 on what to do if you encounter problems obtaining your prescriptions the first time out.) Note that *proof of coverage* isn't the same as the Evidence of Coverage document, which may arrive either with your membership card or several weeks later.

When you receive your plan's membership card, keep it safe. The card is your key to getting prescription drugs and letting your pharmacist know what you should pay, as I explain in Chapter 14. You need to present it at the pharmacy each time you fill a prescription. So keep it in your wallet. (If you were in a different Part D plan previously, destroy your old card — but be sure to do so only after your new coverage begins.)

In the following sections, I explain the details you need to check when you receive your card and give you pointers on how to keep track of different Medicare cards you may have.

Double-checking the details

Verify that the information on your card is correct. It should include

- ✔ The plan's name
- ✔ Your name and membership ID number
- ✔ The plan's customer service phone number(s)
- ✔ The plan's mailing address

Make sure this plan is the one you signed up for. If you're not certain, take a look at your plan's info packet (which it must send you soon after it receives your enrollment request, ideally before your coverage begins). You can also check the plan's name and identification number that appears on your membership card against information in your *Medicare & You* handbook or on Medicare's online plan finder tool. Or you can call Medicare's help line to check what kind of plan it is. If it turns out you're enrolled in the wrong plan — for example, this plan's a private Medicare health plan rather than the drugs-only plan you wanted — flip to Chapter 17 to find out what to do.

Playing your cards right

You may find yourself with several cards entitling you to different Medicare services. And sometimes it isn't easy to see at a glance which card is which, or to remember what each is used for. It can be especially confusing if, for example, you have a prescription plan and a Medigap policy that are provided by the same insurance company, and its name appears on both cards.

Presenting the correct card when you show up at a doctor's office or hospital, or use any other medical service, is critically important. That's because the card tells your provider whom to bill. For example, if you're in a Medicare private health plan, you must show the plan's card and not your Medicare ID card. If by mistake you show your Medicare card instead, the provider will bill Medicare and not the plan. Medicare will then deny your claim, and you or the provider will have a lot of hassle sorting it all out. So it pays to know your cards and use them appropriately.

Here's how to identify and use each of the Medicare cards you may have:

- ✔ **Your red-white-and-blue Medicare ID card:** Use this card to obtain medical services if you receive your health benefits through traditional Medicare. The card shows your name and Medicare ID number. It says whether you're entitled to Medicare Part A, (hospital services) or Part B (doctor visits and other outpatient care), or both, as well as the date(s) on which your coverage became effective. The card also provides the phone number of the Medicare help line.

✔ **Your Medicare private health plan card:** Use this card (*not* your Medicare ID card) to get medical services if you're enrolled in a Medicare private health plan (such as an HMO, PPO, Special Needs Plan, Private Fee-for-Service plan, a Medicare Cost plan, or a Medicare Medical Savings Account; see Chapter 9 for details on these plans). If your plan includes drug coverage, you may be able to use the same card at the pharmacy when filling your prescriptions, or you may be given a separate card to use at the pharmacy, depending on the plan. Either way, the plan's name, its identification number, and contact information appears on the card. So does your name and membership number.

✔ **Your Medicare stand-alone prescription drug plan card:** Use this card to get your prescriptions filled under Part D if you receive your medical benefits from traditional Medicare or a Medicare private health plan that doesn't cover drugs (Medicare Medical Savings Accounts, as well as some Private Fee-for-Service plans and Medicare Cost plans). The card shows your name, your plan membership number, the plan's name, its identification number, and its contact information. Your card likely has wording that indicates you're entitled to Medicare prescription drug coverage. It may simply say PDP — initials that stand for Prescription Drug Plan, the phrase Medicare uses for stand-alone Part D plans.

✔ **Your Medigap supplementary insurance card:** Use this card to prove that you have separate insurance to help cover your co-pays for medical services when you're enrolled in traditional Medicare. Show it every time you receive services from a doctor, hospital, or other provider. (Medigap insurance can't be used to cover out-of-pocket costs in Medicare private health plans, as explained in Chapter 9. Nor can it be used for prescription drug expenses, as explained in Chapter 15.) The card shows your name and membership number, the name of the insurance company, its contact information, and the type of Medigap plan you have (marked with a letter of the alphabet, *A* through *L*) — for example, MEDIGAP F.

Information about your plan: Your new bedtime reading material

Sooner or later (either together with your plan's membership ID card or separately) you'll receive a sizeable information packet that should include the following documents about your new plan:

✔ **Evidence of Coverage:** This booklet is your legal contract with the plan, so be sure to keep it in a safe place. It contains masses of stuff you can use for reference when you first join the plan and throughout the year. Here are some examples:

• **Phone numbers:** Call if you have any questions or problems.

- **An explanation of how the plan works, its conditions, and its rules:** This part lays out the plan's responsibilities in giving you coverage and the rules you must accept. It shows the plan's costs and benefits for this year, which may be different from those the same plan provided last year.

- **Details of the plan's benefits and costs:** If this is a drugs-only plan, the Evidence of Coverage explains what the plan charges for different kinds of covered drugs. If it's a Medicare private health plan, you'll find this info, plus details of how much you'll pay for every covered medical service, like doctor visits, hospital stays, and many more.

- **An explanation of your legal rights if you have a complaint against the plan or disagree with a decision it makes:** This section includes detailed instructions on how to file a complaint or make an appeal. (I cover the general process of doing both in Chapter 19.)

✔ **The plan's drug formulary:** The *formulary* is a list of all the medications the plan covers. It shows which drugs come with restrictions such as prior authorization, quantity limits, and step therapy. (I explain what these restrictions mean, and what you can do about them, in Chapter 4.)

✔ **The plan's pharmacy network:** The *pharmacy network* is a list of all the pharmacies in your area that accept your plan's card. This list shows which ones are *preferred* pharmacies (where your drugs may cost less) or *specialist* pharmacies (which stock special drugs, like those that are injected or require careful handling), as explained in Chapter 14.

✔ **The plan's provider directory:** If your plan is a Medicare managed care plan (HMO, PPO, Special Needs Plan, or Medicare Cost plan), this *provider directory* is a list of doctors, hospitals, and other facilities in your area that are in the plan's network and have agreed to treat its members.

✔ **The plan's service area:** The service area is a list of all the zip codes that your plan (if it's a Medicare managed care plan) covers.

Everything in your plan's info packet is critical. If any of the items listed here are missing, call the plan and ask for them, according to your type of plan:

✔ If you're in a Medicare managed care plan that covers prescription drugs, you need all these items. (Private Fee-for-Service plans and Medicare Medical Savings Accounts don't have limited service areas or provider directories.)

✔ If you're in a stand-alone plan that covers only prescription drugs, you just need the first three items on the preceding list.

A form for disclosing other coverage: Your chance to put it all out there

Your plan's packet includes a form asking whether you have other coverage for prescription drugs and/or medical care. The plan may have already requested this information on your enrollment form, as explained in Chapter 12, but the separate form in your info packet probably requires more details. Filling out this form and returning it to the plan as instructed are in your best interests.

The plan needs to know of other coverage so all of your benefits can be coordinated properly. This *coordination of benefits* means you don't pay more than you should, and, in most cases, you don't have to make separate claims, as explained in Chapter 14. So if you're entitled to drug and/or medical coverage from any of the following, enter that on the form:

- ✔ A current or former employer or union (or COBRA insurance)
- ✔ The Veterans Affairs (VA or CHAMPVA) health program
- ✔ The Department of Defense (TRICARE)
- ✔ The Federal Employees Health Benefits program (FEHB)
- ✔ The Indian Health Service, a Tribal Health organization, or the Urban Indian Health Program
- ✔ A qualified State Pharmacy Assistance Program (SPAP)
- ✔ An individual health insurance policy

I explain each of these programs, and how they fit in with Medicare prescription drug coverage, in Chapter 6.

A late penalty assessment: Your price for missing your enrollment deadline

Not long after you enroll in Part D for the first time, you may receive a letter from your plan saying you need to pay a late penalty. This scenario should happen *only* if you miss your deadline for joining Part D and go for more than 63 days without *creditable coverage* — drug coverage that's at least as good as Part D, such as you may have had from an employer or union. (If you haven't the faintest idea what I'm talking about here, you need to read Chapter 6 to get familiar with creditable coverage and Chapter 8 to find out about the late penalty — and fast!)

How your plan decides whether you should be penalized

Every plan is responsible for finding out whether any new enrollees should have a late penalty. Plans can do so by obtaining the information from Medicare, making their own inquiries, or sending an *attestation form* to new enrollees. If you receive this form, you have up to 30 days to respond and indicate whether you've had creditable coverage for drugs and, if so, where you got it from.

This is the time when any notices you've kept about former creditable coverage come in very handy, as covered in Chapter 6. However, if you've lost this proof, be aware that Medicare requires your plan to accept letters from any former employer or union confirming the creditable coverage you once had. So when you return your attestation form, be sure to add the name of and contact info for your former employer or union and, if possible, the dates when your creditable coverage began and ended so your plan can verify them. Or, if you prefer, you can ask the benefits department of your former employer or union to send you a similar letter, and you can attach a copy to your attestation form. (But be careful not to miss that important 30-day deadline for returning the form. Send it in on time, even if the requested letter hasn't arrived.)

If the plan decides you have an unexplained gap in your drug coverage, it informs Medicare, and someone there does the math to work out the amount of your late penalty. The plan then notifies you of this amount and tells you how it was calculated (according to a formula I explain in Chapter 8).

How your plan may be wrong

What if your plan slaps you with a late penalty you don't think you deserve? That's a real curve ball. But your plan may have gotten it wrong. Here are some of the ways mistakes can happen:

- ✔ Your record of coverage hasn't been verified due to computer glitches or other screw-ups in the system. People have occasionally received these letters after being in Part D ever since it began — and therefore couldn't possibly deserve a late penalty! Gotta love technology.

- ✔ You had drug coverage but didn't know it wasn't creditable because the plan that provided it didn't clearly inform you of this fact.

- ✔ During the time in question, you were living abroad or in prison and therefore couldn't sign up for Part D. Provided you started receiving Part D coverage within one of the special enrollment periods granted after your return or release, as explained in Chapter 12, you shouldn't face a late penalty.

- ✔ You went without creditable coverage for a certain length of time, but not for as many months as the letter claims. The length of time without coverage determines the amount of your late penalty, as explained in Chapter 8.

- ✔ You qualified for Extra Help (see Chapter 5) and joined a Part D plan between May 15, 2006, and December 31, 2008. The late penalty was waived during this period for people eligible for Extra Help and without creditable coverage. Congress has now made this waiver permanent, so starting on January 1, 2009, nobody eligible for Extra Help faces a late penalty.

- ✔ During the time in question, you were living in an area affected by Hurricane Katrina. Medicare allowed a special enrollment period extending from May 15 to December 31, 2006, and waived the late penalty for this six-month period for people living in certain parishes on the Gulf Coast when the hurricane hit in August 2005.

What your rights are if you think your plan is wrong

When your plan sends you a letter regarding your late penalty amount, it encloses a notice headed "Your Right to Ask Medicare to Review Your Part D Late Enrollment Penalty," which explains your right to challenge the ruling. It also encloses a form you can use to request a *reconsideration* — in other words, an independent review of the decision. You have 60 days from the date on the letter to complete and return the form to the address provided. (You can authorize someone else to fill out the form on your behalf if you want; follow the instructions on the form.) If you choose to request a reconsideration, you must still pay the late penalty throughout the process until a decision is made.

On the form, check off any circumstances that apply to you or write other reasons on a separate sheet. Add copies (*not* the originals) of any documents that support your case, which may include proof of creditable coverage from a former employer or union, or a previous plan's benefits summary that didn't explain whether the plan's drug coverage was creditable, for example.

Be sure to meet all deadlines or, if you have a good reason why you can't, request an extension by following the instructions on the form. Otherwise, your case will be dismissed, and you'll have no further opportunity to argue it.

You should receive a decision from the Independent Review Entity (IRE), the official panel that conducts the reconsideration, within 90 days of the IRE receiving your request. (The decision may come a lot sooner, but it depends on how many similar cases the IRE is dealing with.) The IRE can extend the reconsideration process for up to 14 days for good reason, such as to examine more evidence. Here's what happens next, based on the IRE's decision:

- ✔ **If the decision goes in your favor:** You no longer face a late penalty. Your plan must then refund any late penalty fees you've already paid during the reconsideration process. Or, if the penalty is reduced, the plan must refund any overpayments you've made.

- ✔ **If the decision goes against you:** You're stuck with the late penalty amount. You can't appeal against a negative decision.

How to pay the late penalty

If your plan premiums are deducted from your monthly Social Security check, then the late penalty is automatically taken out of it, too. If the plan sends you a monthly bill for premiums, the late penalty is added to the bill. If you prefer, you can choose to pay the penalty on a quarterly or annual basis.

Nice 'n' Neat: Starting and Keeping Careful Records

People tend to be pretty slapdash about keeping records. Overwhelmed by junk mail, sometimes you toss the lot and lose something important. You put a vital document in a folder and then forget where you put the folder. Or you start off with the best intentions to sort and keep records in a file cabinet or computer file, and then — just like New Year resolutions that evaporate come February — you somehow fail to update them.

But if there's one set of records you should keep safe, accessible, complete, and up-to-date, it's all the accumulated bits of paper relating to your medical and prescription drug insurance. Doing so helps you keep track of your expenses and see how your drug coverage is panning out through the year (how close you're coming to the doughnut hole, for example; see Chapter 15 for more on this topic). It also serves as a protection in case you get into any disputes with your plan and need hard facts to argue your case. In the following sections, I share how to tidy up your medical and drug insurance records, including how to store them online (if you're so inclined).

Keeping hard-copy records you can rely on

If you hit a pothole while cruising down the Part D highway, you don't want to have to scramble for your paperwork only to find it's missing or unreadable because Fido used it as a new chew toy. In the next several sections, I present some suggestions for keeping records in such a way that you can actually find them when you need them.

Filing each type of insurance separately

Depending on how many different kinds of insurance you have — traditional Medicare, a stand-alone Part D plan, a Medigap supplemental insurance policy, a Medicare private health plan that includes drug coverage, or any other insurance (such as retiree or veterans health benefits) — keep records for each one in a separate file. Even if you have only one plan, creating one file for its medical benefits and another for its drug coverage is practical. Label each folder with the name of the plan and the type of insurance.

Keeping your Evidence of Coverage and other plan information

Your Evidence of Coverage booklet is a legal document that contains details of your legal rights and how to exercise them if you need to, as explained in the earlier section, "Information about your plan: Your new bedtime reading material." If you have more than one plan, file each EOC and other documents in the appropriate folder for each plan so you can access them easily.

Tracking your expenses and level of coverage

Your plan must send a regular statement, called the *Explanation of Benefits,* about the treatment you've received and what you've paid. In the case of Part D, every EOB is worth keeping because together they show you

✔ How much you and your plan are paying for your drugs as the months go by. (The total amount paid by you and your plan affects your coverage level.)

✔ How close you are to the doughnut hole and, if your costs are high enough to land you in it, how much more you need to spend out of pocket before you qualify for the low costs of catastrophic coverage. (I explain the doughnut hole, catastrophic coverage, and other coverage levels in Chapter 15.)

✔ How much you've spent out of pocket on drugs during the year to date in this plan — in case you need to switch to another plan partway through the year (as explained in Chapter 17) and want to ensure that all of your payments under the old plan will count toward your out-of-pocket limit in the new one.

Hanging on to documents that may help you resolve problems

Medicare has a system consumers can use to resolve disputes with their plans — whether they involve complaints against traditional Medicare, private Medicare health plans, or Part D plans — at several levels of appeal. (I explain the procedures for filing grievances and appeals in Chapter 19.) In Part D, you may need to ask the plan to cover a nonformulary drug or waive a restriction.

Keeping records of any interaction with your plan — including notes from phone conversations — helps your case if you need to file an appeal.

Opening and reading your mail

When an envelope marked with your plan's name shows up in your mail box, open it! This advice may sound obvious, but plans too often send unwanted marketing materials to their members (sometimes unrelated to the health or prescription drug plan they're on), and it's easy to get into the habit of disregarding everything. But some plan mailings are important and may require timely action on your part. Here are some examples:

✔ The plan notifies you that it's going to stop covering one of the drugs you're taking and gives you 60 days' warning. Or it informs you that one of your drugs has been taken off the market for safety reasons, and the plan will no longer cover it.

✔ The plan alerts you that it's disenrolling you and terminating your coverage for some reason (as explained in Chapter 17) and gives you a certain amount of time to respond.

✔ The plan has decided you should pay a late penalty (as explained earlier in this chapter) and gives you 60 days to respond.

✔ The plan sends you its Annual Notice of Change (ANOC) — as all plans must do in October — which shows how its costs and benefits, and maybe its whole design, will change for the following year. (I explain more in Chapter 17 about the critical importance of reading the ANOC *every year.*)

✔ The plan informs you that it's withdrawing service from your area, not renewing its contract with Medicare, or going out of business entirely. (See Chapter 17 for more on these possibilities.)

Tracking information online

Everything's going electronic, and Medicare's no exception. Following are two ways you may be able to keep track of your medical information online, up to a point, if that's your preference:

✔ **On Medicare's Web site:** Medicare offers a free way of accessing some of your personal medical information through its MyMedicare Web portal. Among other tasks, you can use this tool to

- Track your health claims in traditional Medicare

- See which preventive tests and screenings you're entitled to

- Order a replacement for a lost Medicare card

- Keep a list of your medications

To create a personal account, go to www.MyMedicare.gov, click "Need to Register?," and enter your Medicare ID number. About two weeks later, Medicare will send you the password you need to access your account. Oddly, the password is sent via regular mail!

✔ **In a personal health record:** An increasing number of Medicare drug and private health plans are offering personal health records (PHRs) to their members for free. A *PHR* is an online tool that allows you to enter and keep any information you choose about

- Your medical history

- The visits you make to doctors and other medical services

- The dates of tests and screenings you need for your health condition

Call your plan or visit its Web site to see whether it offers a PHR. You can also download a PHR that's not connected to any health plan for free from the Internet.

These personal accounts may be a convenient way of storing files that are of interest to you — information downloaded from the Internet about your health condition, for example — or keeping a record of your treatments and setting up a calendar for your medical appointments. In some cases, you may be able to arrange for e-mails alerting you to tests, screenings, and checkups that are due. As more doctors transfer to electronic recordkeeping, you may be able to arrange to have their records of your visits, diagnoses, and tests transferred to your account. In this way, you choose what information you want to put into your account.

On the flip side, neither the MyMedicare site nor PHRs provide a way of tracking all your medical records and expenses as comprehensively as you can do the old-fashioned way — by filing paper. At least not yet. Also, many people remain uncomfortable with committing sensitive health information to a Web site. Both the operators of the MyMedicare portal and the suppliers of PHRs (including some of those private Medicare health plans) maintain that the accounts are secure and can be accessed only with your permission. But look carefully at the contract agreement (which you must sign) to see whether they retain the right to share your information with other parties.

Chapter 14

Filling Your Prescriptions

I bet you've never compared your pharmacist to a pilot in the cockpit of a fighter jet! Yet both pros have something in common: They rely on warp-speed electronic calculations to do their jobs. The pilot, facing enemy action, uses those calculations to fend off a missile attack. The pharmacist, facing Part D, uses them to tell you how much to pay for your Lipitor this month. *Top Gun* in a white coat!

This comparison may seem far-fetched, but it really isn't. Just think how many calculations are necessary to arrive at that single payment. What you pay for each prescription depends on which Part D plan you're in, where you're at in the coverage cycle, whether you're receiving Extra Help or additional coverage from outside of Part D, and even the pharmacy you go to. That's complex math!

But all of these factors are chewed up somewhere in the ether and instantly spat out onto your pharmacist's computer screen. If all goes smoothly, the result is the correct amount you should pay. If not, your pharmacist often can help you sort matters out. So the pharmacy is the front line in Part D, because your pharmacist is the go-between in your dealings with a drug plan. He's the channel for your drug coverage and a useful person to answer questions.

This chapter has answers to issues that can arise when filling your prescriptions. I explain the various ways you can get your meds through Part D, the importance of going to pharmacies in your plan's network whenever possible, and how your plan's card is the key to coordinating all your benefits. I also cover what may happen the first time you have your prescriptions filled under a new Part D plan — because that's when you're most likely to hit any bumps in the road.

Choosing How to Fill Your Prescriptions

As ever in Part D, there are choices, rules, and pitfalls you need to know about when it comes to filling your prescriptions. The following sections explain the choices you have — between getting your drugs at a retail pharmacy or by mail order, if your plan offers that option — and the times when you may need to have a prescription filled at a specialty pharmacy that stocks and handles certain kinds of drugs. (Another option, long-term care pharmacies for people living in nursing homes, is covered in Chapter 18.)

Of course, you don't have to choose just one pharmacy and stick with it. You can obtain your drugs from any pharmacy that accepts your plan's card (and any others in an emergency; see the later section "Going to the Right Pharmacies and Avoiding the Wrong Ones"). And if you want to use mail order for some prescriptions and a retail pharmacy for others, that's your call.

Retail pharmacies

By *retail pharmacy* I mean the bricks-and-mortar kind on Main Street that you walk into (as opposed to the mail-order pharmacies that you visit only on the end of a phone or online). Part D plans use a variety of retail pharmacies — large chains, supermarket pharmacies, and small independent locations.

You may choose to fill your prescriptions at a retail pharmacy (instead of going through mail order) for very personal reasons. You know the pharmacist, you like the staff, and it's a good place to stop by for a chat with neighbors. Retail pharmacies have more general advantages, too, if you have one in your immediate area. When you need a medication for some acute condition that comes on fast, you can get it quickly. And your pharmacist is an expert source of help if you have questions about your health condition or the drugs you're taking. If you're housebound, a local pharmacy can often deliver meds to your home. However, if you live in a very rural area, with a retail pharmacy a long distance away, it may make more sense to choose mail order. (I go into the pros and cons of mail order later in this chapter.)

Every Part D plan has its own *network* of retail pharmacies — those pharmacies that accept the plan's card. And every plan must ensure that at least one in-network pharmacy is within a reasonable distance of enrollees' homes. What's a reasonable distance? That depends on where you live:

✔ In an urban area, you're likely to have dozens of in-network retail pharmacies to choose from — many within half a mile or so, and some even within walking distance.

✔ In a very rural area, getting to the nearest in-network retail pharmacy may mean driving ten miles or more. If only one such pharmacy is within that sort of distance, all the Part D plans in the area are likely to include it in their networks. (Head to Chapter 10 for suggestions on how to check up on convenient pharmacies when choosing a plan.)

Part D plans label some retail pharmacies in their networks as *preferred*. Generally, this means that the plan has a business relationship with these pharmacies, having negotiated lower dispensing fees or other special arrangements with them. Going to one of your plan's preferred pharmacies

✔ Costs you somewhat less for your prescriptions than if you were to visit a nonpreferred pharmacy (as explained in Chapter 16).

✔ Possibly allows you to get your meds in 90-day supplies in one of the following ways:

- By paying the same amount or co-pay for 90-day supplies as you'd pay for three separate 30-day prescriptions.

- By paying the same discounted price or co-pay for a 90-day supply as you'd pay if you got the drugs from your plan's mail-order service.

- By paying the discounted mail-order price or co-pay for a 90-day supply, plus an extra amount for dispensing fees.

- By paying the same co-pay for a 90-day supply as for a 30-day supply. (This option applies *only* if you're receiving Extra Help.)

To find out which retail pharmacies are preferred, look at your plan's pharmacy network list in your information packet (see Chapter 13), call the plan, or go to its Web site.

Mail-order pharmacies

Most plans offer a mail-order service for filling prescriptions, though not all do. Using this option can be convenient and save you money. But when deciding about mail order, consider the following:

✔ You can only purchase 90-day supplies, so mail order is best used for medicines you take regularly over a long period of time.

✔ Most plans (though not all) offer discounts for mail order — sometimes substantial ones. You may have lower co-pays and pay less in the deductible period and in the doughnut hole (formally known as the coverage gap; see Chapter 15) than at a retail pharmacy. (I explain more about possible savings and give examples in Chapter 16.)

✔ Because you pay for a three-month supply in advance, you pay more upfront than if you buy a 30-day supply each month. And in certain circumstances, you may fall into the doughnut hole earlier as a result.

✔ Your drugs are mailed directly to your home, which may be convenient, especially if you're homebound or live miles from the nearest retail pharmacy in your plan's network. Shipping is free.

✔ You have to remember to phone in your next prescription or reorder online and allow time for delivery (usually seven to ten days) to ensure you don't run out of your meds before the new ones arrive.

To find out how to use your plan's mail-order service, check out the plan's info packet, go to its Web site, or call its customer service number. Regardless, you'll probably need to fill out a form to request this service.

Specialty pharmacies

Certain drugs must be handled extra carefully when they're being dispensed — such as some drugs used for cancer, transplant rejection, multiple sclerosis, and other treatments. If you take one of these types of drugs, you need to purchase it at a specialty pharmacy that's equipped to handle it. (The Food and Drug Administration allows some of these drugs to be distributed *only* to specialty pharmacies.)

The *specialty* label may be applied to a regular pharmacy that meets the conditions for dispensing these drugs, to a hospital pharmacy department, or to a doctor's office. Your plan's pharmacy list should indicate which specialty pharmacies are in-network.

If no in-network specialty pharmacy is in your area, you can go out of network, but call your plan first for guidance. Due to the circumstances, some Part D plans don't offer mail-order service for these kinds of drugs.

Going to the Right Pharmacies and Avoiding the Wrong Ones

A pharmacy is a pharmacy is a pharmacy, isn't it? How can there be right ones and wrong ones? This classification has nothing to do with quality. It's just that going to a pharmacy outside your plan's network, except in special circumstances, has consequences — consequences that cost you money. By staying in your plan's network, you get your meds at the plan's regular charges and ensure the costs count toward your out-of-pocket limit. I explain what you need to know in the following sections.

Using in-network pharmacies

Your Part D plan gives you access to a large number of retail pharmacies, either within its service area or all across the country. All of these pharmacies accept your plan's card. That means you pay whatever the plan requires for your drugs and no more. Preferred pharmacies within the network may charge you less, as I touch on in the earlier section "Retail pharmacies."

You can identify the retail pharmacies (including specialty ones) in your plan's network by looking at the list in the plan's information packet, going to its Web site, or using the Medicare Prescription Drug Plan Finder at www. medicare.gov (as explained in Chapter 10). If your plan allows you to fill prescriptions anywhere in the U.S. and you need to do so while traveling, you can call its customer service number (shown on your card) to check on network pharmacies where you are. Or you can show your card at any pharmacy and ask whether it's in your plan's network.

If you move away from where you live now and need to switch to a different Part D plan in your new area, the new plan sends you details about its in-network pharmacies there as part of its enrollment package. If you remain in the same plan — for example, if you're in a statewide stand-alone drug plan and you move to a new home within the same state — you can find a list of local in-network pharmacies by calling the plan, visiting its Web site, or going to the Medicare Prescription Drug Plan Finder at www.medicare.gov.

Most plans, though not all, offer a mail-order service. If you prefer to obtain your meds this way, you must use the in-network mail-order service specified by your plan. (The plan won't cover your drugs if you use any other mail-order pharmacy, even if the plan doesn't provide one of its own.) You can request mail-order service on a form your plan sends you if you check this option on your plan enrollment form or if you call the plan and ask for it.

Avoiding out-of-network pharmacies

Except in certain circumstances that I describe in the next section, these are the consequences of filling prescriptions at an out-of-network pharmacy:

- ✔ **You pay a lot more for your drugs.** In most cases, you pay the full price. Sending the receipts to your plan doesn't do a scrap of good. The plan isn't going to pay for them, period.

- ✔ **These payments don't count toward your out-of-pocket limit.** If you fall into the doughnut hole, your plan disregards these payments when calculating your *true out-of-pocket costs (TrOOP)* — your expenses that count toward the limit that ends the coverage gap and triggers the beginning of catastrophic coverage, as explained in Chapter 15.

Knowing when going out of network may be okay

Obviously, situations may arise when you need to have a prescription filled outside of your plan's pharmacy network. These times include

✔ When you're traveling outside your plan's service area within the U.S. (and maybe abroad, if your plan allows this exception for emergencies), and you run out of your meds, lose them, or become ill and need drugs for treatment.

✔ If you need to fill a prescription quickly outside business hours, but can't find a 24/7 network pharmacy within a reasonable driving distance.

✔ If you need to start taking a specialty drug quickly and don't have access to in-network pharmacies that stock this type of drug.

✔ When undergoing emergency or urgent treatment in a hospital, clinic, or outpatient facility and you receive Part D–covered drugs from the facility's pharmacy, but it's not in your plan's network.

✔ If you have to leave your home area after a local calamity that's been declared a state or federal disaster or a public health emergency.

Medicare expects all Part D plans to guarantee coverage at out-of-network pharmacies in any of the preceding circumstances — providing the plan covers the drugs in question and the request is reasonable. But if you regularly go to a 24/7 pharmacy that's outside your plan's network because you find it more convenient to shop late at night, expect the plan to quibble.

If you need to go out of network for any other reason than those I provide here, call your plan in advance and ask whether it's okay to do so. A quick phone call may save you time, money and frustration in the long run.

When filling prescriptions out of network, you normally pay the full cost and later send the receipts to your plan, asking for the appropriate refund. If you can't afford the full cost, call the plan and request assistance. (If you're receiving Extra Help, which I describe in Chapter 5, ask the pharmacist for aid.) What if the plan rejects your claim for a refund? You can file a complaint and appeal against the decision, as explained in Chapter 19.

Your plan *is* allowed to charge you more for going out of network, even in these special circumstances. Whether it does depends on its policy. If you do have to pay more, though, the extra cost counts toward your out-of-pocket limit (as explained in Chapter 15). However, if you receive Extra Help, you can't be charged any more than you would be at an in-network pharmacy. Also, you can't be charged more if you're enrolled in a Private Fee-for-Service plan that provides drug coverage (see Chapter 9), even if it has a pharmacy network.

Unlocking the Information in Your Membership Card

It's all in the cards! No, your Part D plan membership card doesn't magically foretell the future — except maybe to show how close you are to the dough-nut hole. Yet it has a lot of detail locked inside that you can't see on the sur-face. This information is all about you. I tell you how to decipher these facts and make sure they're right in the next couple of sections.

Understanding what your membership card says about you

So what deep secrets does your card reveal about you? Nothing sexy, that's for sure — no exciting dark strangers in your past or future. But it does say a lot about your personal coverage for prescription drugs and what you should pay for them. Following is what your card reveals when the phar-macist scans it through the computer system, depending on your plan and individual circumstances:

- **Which Part D plan you belong to:** Zillions of Part D plans are out there, so your pharmacist needs to know whom to bill and where to send the purchase details.

- **Which phase of coverage you're in:** You may be in one of four phases, and in order for your pharmacist to bill you properly, he has to know which one applies to you at which time. I cover the various coverage levels in detail in Chapter 15, but here's a quick breakdown:

  - The deductible (when you pay the full price, if your plan has one)

  - The initial coverage phase (when the plan pays a share of the cost of your drugs)

  - The doughnut hole (when you pay the full price, if your costs are high enough to land you in it)

  - The catastrophic coverage phase (when you pay very little, if your overall costs run that high in a year)

- **Whether you receive Extra Help:** This program for eligible people with limited incomes, which I explain in Chapter 5, reduces your payments a great deal and provides continuous coverage throughout the year (meaning no doughnut hole).

- **Whether you receive other drug coverage from elsewhere:** Your phar-macist needs to know whether to bill your former employer or union plan, a State Pharmacy Assistance Program (SPAP), or another source, in addi-tion to or in place of your Part D coverage. See Chapter 6 for more details.

 ✔ **What you should pay for each prescription:** All of these factors play into what you actually pay at the pharmacy:

   • The phase of coverage you're in

   • Whether you have extra benefits

   • What your plan charges as co-pays or coinsurance

   • Whether your plan has negotiated any discounts from this particular pharmacy

Making sure your benefits are correct and coordinated

The electronic wizardry that records all of your information saves a lot of hassle. Otherwise — just imagine! — you'd have to file a refund claim for every single prescription. But like any other automated system that relies on human input, it isn't free from error.

Here's what you can do to help ensure you receive all the benefits you're entitled to and pay the correct amounts:

 ✔ **Tell your plan what other coverage you have.** If you have any other coverage at all, letting your plan know these details is crucial. The best way to guarantee that your plan coordinates all of your benefits is to fill out the form it sends you upon enrollment asking for these details. Medicare also sends you a similar form when you first come into the program. See Chapter 13 for more about disclosing other coverage.

 ✔ **Know how other coverage fits in with Part D.** If you receive insurance coverage from outside of Medicare — such as an employer or union plan, federal health benefits, or a State Pharmacy Assistance Program (SPAP) — your plan can give you specific details about how its coverage coordinates with Medicare prescription drug coverage. Or you can flip to Chapter 6 for the details of how Part D coordinates with each type of alternative coverage.

 ✔ **Show your Part D plan card at the pharmacy.** Presenting your card every time you fill a prescription — even during the deductible phase or the doughnut hole when you're paying the full costs — ensures that your pharmacist charges you the correct amount according to your level of coverage. It also guarantees that the payments will count toward your out-of-pocket limit (as explained in Chapter 15).

✔ **Check your statements.** The *Explanation of Benefits (EOB) statement* that you receive regularly from your Part D plan, and any type of health insurance coverage, shows which of your payments the plan has covered. Reviewing the EOB is your best way of checking the accuracy of your payments and tracking your expenses and progress through different coverage levels.

✔ **Tell your plan if your benefits situation changes.** If you get a new job that affects your drug coverage — for example, your new employer pays your Part D premiums, whereas your previous one didn't — or your current employer alters your benefits, write or fax your plan with this updated coverage information. (If new employment now gives you creditable coverage that you didn't have before, you can disenroll from your Part D plan, as explained in Chapter 17.)

✔ **Take action if you think something's incorrect:** Contact your Part D plan if you think you're paying more than you should — the wrong amount for any of your drugs or for the coverage level you're on, for example. (If this approach doesn't resolve the issue, see Chapter 19 for how to file a complaint or an appeal.) If the issue involves another plan that provides additional drug coverage and coordinates with Part D, contact that plan for help.

Putting Your Plan to the Test: Filling Your Prescriptions on Day One

Day One is when you go to a retail pharmacy to fill a prescription for the first time under your new Part D plan. Whether you're a newbie to Part D or you've switched to a new plan, I bet you're wondering: How easily will I get my drugs under this new coverage? Will I hit any snags?

In the following sections, I suggest what you can do to make the process go as smoothly as possible. And, in case you do encounter problems, I explain what to do so you don't leave the pharmacy without your medicine.

Dodging possible snags and delays by verifying your coverage

Normally, the procedure you follow to have your prescriptions filled under a Part D plan is simple; you just go to the pharmacy with your prescription (or have your doctor call it in), show your plan membership card, and pay whatever's due. But when you go to a pharmacy for the first time under a new Part D plan, your pharmacist needs to verify your coverage, especially if you haven't yet received your card or your enrollment information isn't yet in the pharmacy's computer system.

You can help speed up the process and avoid or minimize delays by following these tips:

✔ **Pick the right pharmacy.** Make sure the pharmacy you go to is in your plan's network. (I explain why doing so is important earlier in this chapter.) You can find a list of in-network pharmacies in your plan's information packet (see Chapter 13 for details on this packet). If you haven't yet received one, call the plan and ask which of your nearest pharmacies are on the list. Or you can call ahead to a pharmacy to check if it's in your plan's network.

✔ **Take proof of your Part D coverage with you.** These items include

- Your plan membership card (see Chapter 13 for more about this and other cards)

- Your red-white-and-blue Medicare card

- A photo ID (if you have one)

✔ **Have the pharmacist call the plan to confirm that you're enrolled if you haven't yet received your membership card.** To smooth this process, provide your pharmacist with as many of the following as possible:

- The plan's name

- The plan's Medicare identification number (which you can find on the enrollment form you filled out, if you kept a copy)

- A letter from the plan acknowledging your enrollment request (if you've received it already)

- A letter from the plan confirming your enrollment (if you've gotten one)

- A copy of your enrollment request (if you haven't yet received the plan's acknowledgment or confirmation)

✔ **Bring your Extra Help documentation, if you qualify due to limited income.** Your plan's membership card should be enough to confirm your eligibility, but if you haven't yet received it, bring one of these items with you:

- Your Extra Help confirmation letter from Social Security or Medicare, or any recent letter you've received from either agency

- A copy of your Extra Help application, if you filled one out

- Your Medicaid card, if you're receiving benefits from your state medical assistance program

- Any recent letters confirming that you receive Supplementary Security Income (SSI) or have your Medicare premiums paid by your state

Ensuring you don't leave without your meds

What if your pharmacist can't confirm your plan membership? Or says that your plan doesn't cover one of your drugs, or that you need to get permission from the plan before it will cover a drug? What if she asks you to pay more for your drugs than you think you should? Any of these what-ifs can happen.

But let me give you a direct quote from Medicare. On December 28, 2007, in a statement that offered tips to consumers when filling prescriptions for the first time under a new Part D plan, the agency said: "Don't leave the pharmacy counter without your medicines." There — that's straight from the horse's mouth. But of course the circumstances may be different from person to person. I tackle what to do in certain situations in the next few sections.

If your pharmacist can't confirm your enrollment in a plan

It takes time for plans to get details of new enrollees into the computer system, especially in early January when many people have just switched plans. If you have no proof of coverage (as explained in Chapter 12) or your pharmacist can't verify your enrollment on the phone, here are your options:

- ✔ Pay for your drugs (at full price), keep the receipts, and send copies to the plan. Doing so is important, even if your plan has a deductible, because the payments count toward your out-of-pocket limit (as explained in Chapter 15) as long as the plan has a record of them. The plan then refunds you any money that's due. However, if your enrollment is denied (see Chapter 12 for how this situation can occur), the plan doesn't cover these bills.

- ✔ Ask your pharmacist to call Medicare's dedicated pharmacy hot line, which is used for this purpose if you can't afford the prescriptions.

If your pharmacist says the plan won't pay for one of your meds

Your pharmacist will probably tell you if your plan doesn't cover a drug you've been prescribed, or if the med comes with restrictions requiring the plan's consent before you can get it. (I explain these restrictions — prior authorization, quantity limits, and step therapy — and what to do about them in Chapter 4.) Whether she gives you this information or not, call your plan to find out why your coverage is being denied and what you should do about it.

If you're newly enrolled in the plan and you've already been taking this drug, you have the legal right to a 30-day supply so your treatment isn't interrupted. Ask your pharmacist to fill the prescription under your plan's *transition* or *first-fill policy*. If she's reluctant to do so, ask her to call your plan for approval. If you haven't previously filled a prescription for the drug in question at this pharmacy, the pharmacist can call your doctor to verify that you're currently taking it. Bringing in a current bottle containing this medication may also help. But note that this is only a temporary solution. You must take immediate steps to change to a drug your plan does cover or work with your doctor to get the restriction lifted, as covered in Chapter 4.

If your pharmacist asks you to pay more than you think you should

One common explanation for your pharmacist asking you to pay more than you think you should for drugs is this: You qualify for Extra Help, but your pharmacist can't get immediate confirmation through the system. If you have Medicaid, show your card. If you're receiving Supplementary Security Income (SSI) payments or your state pays your Medicare premium, tell the pharmacist. In all of these situations, you automatically qualify for Extra Help. If you applied for Extra Help, bring the letter from Social Security that says you qualify. Either way, you should be charged only small co-pays for your drugs (as explained in Chapter 5).

If you've applied for Extra Help but haven't yet heard whether you qualify, you have two options:

✔ You can pay the plan's normal co-pays for your drugs and keep your receipts. After you receive a letter from Social Security confirming that you're eligible for Extra Help, the plan must refund you the difference between what you paid and what you would've paid under Extra Help — dating back to the time you applied for it.

✔ If you can't afford to pay the usual co-pays upfront, tell the pharmacist, who has the discretion to help you under Medicare rules. (At the very least, if you have less than a three-day supply of your meds left, the pharmacist must allow you an emergency supply.) Don't be too shy or proud to ask and, just like the Medicare honchos say, don't leave the pharmacy without your meds.

The following situations may also result in you paying more at the pharmacy than expected, but they're easy to check before you leave home:

✔ **Your plan has a deductible.** In this scenario, you pay the full cost of your drugs until you've met the amount of the deductible and your coverage begins. If you're not sure whether your plan has a deductible, you can find out by looking in your plan's Evidence of Coverage document or, if you haven't received it yet, call the plan.

✔ **The pharmacy isn't in your plan's network.** In this case, you're asked to pay the full price of your drugs. Fortunately, this situation is easy to avoid — just go to another pharmacy that *is* in the plan's network. Again, you can find this information in your Evidence of Coverage or by calling the plan. However, if this is an emergency or another situation that allows you to go out of network (as explained earlier in this chapter), be sure to keep receipts for anything you pay.

Chapter 15

In and Out of the Coverage Gap

*J*ust imagine. For months you've been filling a prescription for $30 a month. Then one day, you go for a refill and the pharmacist says, "That'll be $185, please." You shriek, you're outraged, you think it's a mistake. But no — you just fell into the doughnut hole. Suddenly, you're paying full price.

It's no wonder that this *doughnut hole* — the universal nickname for what is officially called the *coverage gap* — is the most criticized and unpopular part of the Medicare drug benefit. Unlike almost any other kind of insurance, Part D gives some coverage for your first slice of drug costs and, if your out-of-pocket expenses for drugs are high enough, another chunk of coverage later in the year. But in the middle, there's this gap, and falling into it means having to pay every cent of drug costs out of your own pocket, unless you have other insurance that picks up any of it.

The doughnut hole doesn't affect everybody. You won't fall into it if

   ✔ Your total drug costs (what you and your plan pay) aren't high enough to reach the limit of initial coverage over the whole year

   ✔ You receive Extra Help, which has no gap, as explained in Chapter 5

   ✔ You have additional benefits that cover your expenses through the gap

   ✔ You're enrolled in a Medicare drug plan that covers all of your drugs in the gap

Even if none of these apply to you, you may still be able to avoid the gap or lessen its impact. But the gap exists, and it's wise not to ignore it. This chapter explains how the doughnut hole works, how to tell whether you'll fall into it, and how you may be able to cover some of your costs in the gap with additional benefits. Chapter 16 describes additional methods of bringing down your drug costs.

I use "doughnut hole" or "coverage gap" or just "the gap" interchangeably in this chapter — they all mean the same thing.

Understanding the Basics of the Coverage Gap

It may be hard to get your head around an insurance concept you've never met before. After all, car insurance doesn't suddenly stop sometime through the year after you've clocked a certain number of miles. And home insurance doesn't come with a clause saying you'll be covered all year except, say, for July and August. But it's amazing how quickly folks catch on to the idea of the Part D doughnut hole when their pocketbooks are at stake. You will too — I guarantee it!

In the following sections, I walk you through the mechanics of the doughnut hole in some detail so you can grasp exactly how it works. I also explain what drops you into the gap, what gets you out of it, and certain Medicare rules about the gap that you need to know.

The yawning gap in the middle of coverage

As I explain in Chapter 2, Medicare drug coverage has four phases over the course of a calendar year. The doughnut hole is the third phase. But whether you go through only one phase, two, three, or all four depends mainly on the overall cost of the drugs you take during the year.

- **Phase 1, the deductible:** In this phase, you may pay full price for your drugs until the cost reaches a limit set by law ($275 in 2008, $295 in 2009) and drug coverage actually begins. If your plan has a deductible (many plans don't), this period begins on January 1, or whenever you start using Medicare drug coverage.

- **Phase 2, the initial coverage period:** This phase begins when you've met the deductible, if there is one. Otherwise, it begins on January 1, or whenever you start using Medicare drug coverage. In this phase, you pay the co-pays required by your plan for each prescription; the plan takes care of the rest of each drug's price. Phase 2 ends when the total cost of your drugs — what you've paid *plus* what your plan has paid — reaches a certain amount set each year by law ($2,510 in 2008, $2,700 in 2009).

✔ **Phase 3, the coverage gap:** This phase begins if and when you reach the dollar limit of Phase 2. Unless you have other insurance that helps fill in the gap (see the later section "Avoiding or Narrowing the Coverage Gap with Other Benefits" for more information), you pay 100 percent of your drug costs until your total out-of-pocket expenses (except for premiums) reach another dollar amount set by law ($4,050 in 2008, $4,350 in 2009).

✔ **Phase 4, catastrophic coverage:** If your drug costs are high enough to take you through the gap, coverage begins again at a greatly reduced cost. In this period, you pay the standard catastrophic co-pay ($2.25 per prescription for generics or $5.60 for brand-names in 2008; $2.40 and $6.00 respectively in 2009) or 5 percent of the cost of your drugs, whichever is higher. Medicare picks up the remaining cost. Catastrophic coverage ends on December 31. The following day, January 1, you return to Phase 1 (or Phase 2 if your plan has no deductible), and the whole cycle starts over again.

Look again at the last sentence in the preceding paragraph — *on January 1, the whole cycle begins all over again.* In other words, the four phases repeat every calendar year. I want to be sure you understand this, because some folks think that after they've struggled through the doughnut hole and emerged into the rarified air of catastrophic coverage, this last phase goes on forever. Sorry — it doesn't. But then, the doughnut hole doesn't go on forever, either. Even if you ended the year paying full price in the gap, you'll get back to Phase 2 coverage again next year as soon as you've met the deductible, or as early as January 1 if your plan has no deductible.

To make more sense of this annual progression, take a look at Table 15-1. It shows how one Medicare beneficiary (Anna) with high drug costs — $800 a month for several prescriptions — went through all four phases and what she and her plan paid each month in 2008.

This example is based on the standard benefit for minimum drug coverage that Congress designed and that many plans stick to (as I explain in Chapters 2 and 3). In other words, Anna is in a plan that charges her a full deductible and 25 percent of the cost of her drugs in the initial coverage period, and offers no coverage in the gap. If she were in a plan that varied the standard design, her costs would be different. *Note:* The calculations are based on the deductible and dollar limits for the initial coverage period and coverage gap that applied in 2008. These amounts are raised each year.

Table 15-1	One Woman's Dollar Journey In and Out of the Doughnut Hole in 2008		
Month	**Anna Pays**	**Anna's Plan Pays**	**Total Cost of Her Drugs**
January (*before* meeting deductible)	$275	$0	$275
January (*after* meeting deductible)	$131.25	$393.75	$525
February	$200	$600	$800
March	$200	$600	$800
April (*before* reaching coverage gap)	$27.50	$82.50	$110
April (*after* reaching coverage gap)	$690	$0	$690
May	$800	$0	$800
June	$800	$0	$800
July	$800	$0	$800
August (*before* reaching catastrophic coverage)	$126.25	$0	$126.25
August (*after* reaching catastrophic coverage)	$33.70	$640.05	$673.75
September	$40	$760	$800
October	$40	$760	$800
November	$40	$760	$800
December	$40	$760	$800
Total costs in 2008	**$4,243.70**	**$5,356.30**	**$9,600**

In Table 15-1, you can see that Anna paid the deductible (Phase 1) and then 25 percent of her costs in the initial coverage period (Phase 2). She hit the doughnut hole (Phase 3) in the first few days of April, as soon as her total drug costs reached $2,510. She then paid full price until early August, when her out-of-pocket spending since the beginning of the year reached the $4,050 limit. (The shaded rows in the table indicate her total time in the doughnut hole.) Then she came out of the gap and started receiving coverage again at the catastrophic level (Phase 4), paying only 5 percent of the cost of her drugs until the end of December.

Over the entire year, Anna paid less than half (44 percent) of what her drugs actually cost. But a full three-quarters (75 percent) of her expenses came right in the middle, in the doughnut hole. Note that this example focuses on Anna's payments and savings in buying her drugs under Part D. But, in addition, Anna must pay her plan a monthly premium to receive Part D coverage. A premium of $26 a month, for example, would add $312 to her annual expenses.

What drops you into the doughnut hole

You reach the limit of the initial coverage period (Phase 2 in the previous section's list) when the money *both you and your plan* pay for your drugs reaches the dollar amount set by law ($2,510 in 2008, $2,700 in 2009). It isn't just what *you* have paid. This point is often overlooked, or misunderstood, with the result that folks fall into the gap a lot sooner than they expect to. I don't want this to happen to you.

So say, for example, that your co-pay for one of your prescriptions is $25. During the initial coverage period (Phase 2), your plan pays the rest of the price it has negotiated for the drug — say $75. The full price of the drug is $25 + $75 = $100. The $100, not the $25, counts toward the limit. And what you've paid to the plan each month in premiums just to receive drug coverage doesn't count at all.

What lifts you out of the doughnut hole

You get out of the gap as soon as your *own* out-of-pocket spending on drugs since the beginning of the year reaches the limit set by law ($4,050 in 2008, $4,350 in 2009). In this case, what your *plan* has paid doesn't count. And other rules (no surprise here) outline what counts as "out-of-pocket" spending and what doesn't.

These payments count toward the coverage gap limit:

- ✔ Your initial deductible (if your plan has one) during Phase 1.

- ✔ Your co-pays (or coinsurance) in the initial coverage period (Phase 2) or in the doughnut hole if your plan covers any of your drugs in the gap.

- ✔ Out-of-pocket payments that you've made in the doughnut hole for drugs bought through your plan at a pharmacy in your plan's network (Phase 3).

✔ Payments for your drugs bought through your plan and made by a family member, a friend, a charitable group, or a State Pharmacy Assistance Program (any phase). (I cover State Pharmacy Assistance Programs later in this chapter and charities in Chapter 16.)

✔ Any payment you make toward the cost of your drugs in the coverage gap when a third party (such as an employer or union plan or a pharmaceutical company's assistance program) picks up the rest of the tab. (I describe these types of extra coverage in the later section "Avoiding or Narrowing the Coverage Gap with Other Benefits.")

These payments do *not* count toward the limit:

✔ The monthly premiums you pay to the plan.

✔ Payments made by your plan for your drugs during the initial coverage period or in the doughnut hole. (Some plans, as you see later in this chapter, cover some drugs in the gap.)

✔ Payments you make for any drugs not covered by your plan (unless, for medical reasons, the plan has agreed to pay for a drug that it doesn't normally cover; see Chapter 4 for more on this).

✔ Payments you make for drugs at pharmacies outside your plan's network of pharmacies.

✔ Payments made for your drugs by a current or former employer or union, a government program (such as Veterans Affairs, TriCare, Indian Health Services, or Black Lung), or any other group insurer.

✔ Payments for drugs made under workers' compensation or automobile or liability insurance.

✔ Payments made by AIDS drug assistance programs.

✔ Payments for drugs bought from Canada or other foreign countries.

✔ Payments for low-cost drugs (or the value of free ones) received from a drug manufacturer's patient assistance program.

✔ The value of free samples your doctor has given you.

Rules for buying your drugs in the doughnut hole

As you may notice from the lists in the previous section, Medicare has some strict rules to persuade you to continue buying your drugs through your plan in the gap. Part D allows *only* payments for drugs covered by your plan *and* purchased from a pharmacy within your plan's network to count toward the out-of-pocket limit that gets you out of the doughnut hole. The following sections detail what these mean and factors to keep in mind.

Using drugs covered by your plan

Drugs covered by your plan generally are the ones that are on your plan's *formulary* (the list of drugs the plan helps pay for). The full cost of these drugs counts toward your out-of-pocket limit in getting out of the coverage gap. So does the cost of any nonformulary drugs that your plan agrees to cover if you've won an exception to its policy (as explained in Chapter 4). Any other drugs *don't* count toward your out-of-pocket limit.

For example, say that you're taking four meds — W, X, Y, and Z — but your plan covers only the first three. In the coverage gap, when you're paying full price, these three drugs cost a total of $200 a month, every cent of which counts toward your out-of-pocket limit. So do your co-pays for them in the initial coverage period (Phase 2) that precedes the gap. In contrast, you pay the full price (say $100 a month) of the fourth drug, Z, throughout the year because your plan doesn't cover it. For the same reason, none of your payments for Drug Z count toward your out-of-pocket limit.

If you start using a new medication when you're in the gap, check to see whether the new drug — or a similar one that would work just as well for you — is on your plan's formulary. If it is, the money you spend on it will count toward getting you out of the doughnut hole. (To find out, call your plan or look at the formulary on its Web site.) Also, remember that if the new drug isn't on the formulary, you can still ask for an exception to get it covered, even while you're in the doughnut hole.

Buying drugs from pharmacies in your plan's network

Pharmacies in your plan's network are those that accept your plan's membership card. If you buy your drugs from any of these pharmacies (or from your plan's mail-order service) during the gap, your payments *will* count toward your out-of-pocket limit. Otherwise, they won't. So if you find a lower price outside the network, you have to decide whether the savings are worth not having the payments counted.

Deciding whether you should stick to the rules

If your overall drug costs are high, you need all your payments in the gap to count in order to reach catastrophic coverage as quickly as possible. But if your costs are in the medium range, and you're pretty sure you won't get out of the gap before the end of the year — or you can't afford the money it takes to get out of the gap — you may feel you have nothing to lose by getting lower-cost drugs elsewhere. (You can find ways to do this in Chapter 16.)

Keep in mind, though, that this choice can be a bit of a gamble. You can't be entirely sure that you won't develop a new medical condition that requires more drugs, and maybe expensive ones, later in the year — all of which, if bought through your plan, will move you faster through the doughnut hole.

Making sure your gap purchases count

If you continue to get your drugs at any of your plan's in-network pharmacies during the gap, be sure to show your plan's card to the pharmacist. Even though the plan doesn't pay anything toward your drugs during this phase, your payment is logged into the computer system and counts toward your out-of-pocket limit. You may also want to keep the pharmacy receipts as a record of these payments, just in case you and your plan later disagree about the date when you emerge from the gap and become entitled to catastrophic coverage.

The consequences of stopping premium payments in the doughnut hole

You're expected to pay monthly premiums through the gap. This rule bugs many people, which isn't surprising. In the doughnut hole, you're basically paying good money for no coverage. Medicare officials argue that your premiums cover the cost of coverage over the whole year, including the generous catastrophic period. But what if your drug costs are enough to land you in the gap but nowhere near high enough to get you to the catastrophic level before the end of the year? Or what if you simply can't afford the amount it takes to get out of the gap? Why continue paying premiums?

If you stop paying premiums, you'll likely be thrown out of your plan and lose coverage. Here's why that may not be a good idea:

- ✔ If you want to go back into Part D at a later date, you'll pay a late penalty — an amount that adds to your premiums and increases over time, as explained in Chapter 8.

- ✔ You may be required to repay the premiums you owed before enrolling in a Part D plan again.

- ✔ The plan you dropped out of may go after you for the premiums you didn't pay, arguing that you broke your contract.

- ✔ And — you never know — you may need coverage later in the year if you come down with some unforeseen health problem that requires treatment with expensive drugs.

What were they thinking . . . when they created the doughnut hole?

In designing the Medicare drug benefit in 2003, Congress decided to give comprehensive coverage to people with low incomes (Extra Help) or high drug expenses (catastrophic coverage). But to sell the program politically — as well as to attract wealthier and healthier enrollees to spread the cost burden — Congress had to give coverage to everybody else too. It was impossible to cover everyone comprehensively within the $400 billion originally budgeted for the program, so something had to give. Inventing the doughnut hole solved the problem for the government's purse strings, but created one for many enrollees' pocketbooks.

Determining Whether You'll Fall into the Coverage Gap

Nobody likes nasty surprises — and, as many folks have found out, falling into the doughnut hole unexpectedly can be a real shock. So it's worth finding out in advance if and when you'll face the coverage gap. Calculating this isn't easy to do on your own, but the following sections explain ways to find out how close you are.

Reviewing statements from your plan

Your Medicare drug plan is required to send you regular statements showing

- ✔ How much you and the plan have spent to date for your drugs
- ✔ How close (or not) you are to the end of the initial coverage period and the beginning of the doughnut hole

If you go into the gap, the statements also show how much more you have to spend to get out of it before you can start receiving catastrophic coverage. Statements are normally sent monthly, unless you haven't filled any prescriptions in a particular month. You can also request a statement at any time by calling your plan. Some plans offer personalized access to their Web sites so enrollees can keep track of their status online.

Using charts on the Medicare Web site

The Web site for comparing Medicare drug plans at www.medicare.gov has a convenient tool you can use to see at a glance whether the doughnut hole will affect you and, if so, when it will hit. This is a very cool tool that creates personalized bar charts showing your likely out-of-pocket costs under different plans, according to the drugs you take, month by month through the year.

The charts on the Medicare Web site are so useful in estimating how your expenses may rise and fall during the year that going to some trouble to look at them is well worth it. (If you don't have access to the Internet, you can ask someone else to do it for you.)

To have a personalized chart created for you, you must first enter the names of each of your drugs (plus their dosages and how often you take them) on Medicare's online Prescription Drug Plan Finder. (For a step-by-step guide on how to do this quickly, go to Chapter 10.) Your costs under different plans are then automatically calculated. Ideally, you'd do this search when you're comparing Medicare drug plans to decide which one to pick. You can then look at the charts included with each plan's details. Or, if you're already in a plan, you can go directly to that plan's details to see your chart.

You'll find your personalized chart at the bottom of the plan details page — so be sure to scroll down so you don't miss it. The chart displayed there calculates your out-of-pocket costs (including premiums) on the basis of drugs bought from a retail pharmacy in the plan's network. To see a chart showing your costs if you buy your drugs from the plan's mail-order pharmacy (if the plan offers this option), click the "Show" button next to the heading Total Monthly Cost Estimator for Mail Order Pharmacy. To see details of how each month's costs are calculated, click "Show Explanation of These Costs" alongside either chart.

Every chart varies according to the drugs you take and the plan's overall design. Figures 15-1 and 15-2 are two examples of what the charts look like.

- ✔ Figure 15-1 shows the monthly out-of-pocket profile of a person in a plan with a deductible and no coverage in the gap, but this person's costs aren't high enough to take her through the doughnut hole to the catastrophic coverage level.

- ✔ Figure 15-2 shows the monthly out-of-pocket profile of a person in a plan with no deductible and no coverage in the gap, but this person's costs are high enough to move him through the doughnut hole so he receives catastrophic coverage until the end of the year.

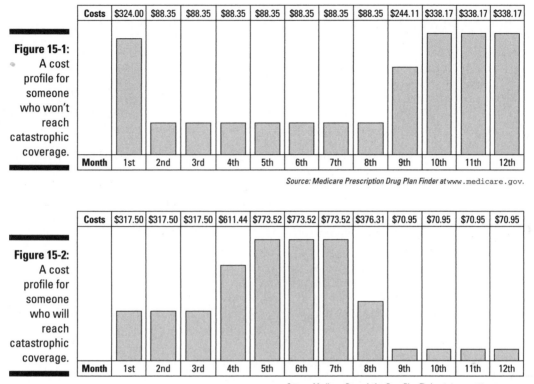

Costs	$324.00	$88.35	$88.35	$88.35	$88.35	$88.35	$88.35	$88.35	$244.11	$338.17	$338.17	$338.17
Month	1st	2nd	3rd	4th	5th	6th	7th	8th	9th	10th	11th	12th

Figure 15-1: A cost profile for someone who won't reach catastrophic coverage.

Source: Medicare Prescription Drug Plan Finder at www.medicare.gov.

Costs	$317.50	$317.50	$317.50	$611.44	$773.52	$773.52	$773.52	$376.31	$70.95	$70.95	$70.95	$70.95
Month	1st	2nd	3rd	4th	5th	6th	7th	8th	9th	10th	11th	12th

Figure 15-2: A cost profile for someone who will reach catastrophic coverage.

Source: Medicare Prescription Drug Plan Finder at www.medicare.gov.

Each chart shows a profile of the user's out-of-pocket costs under that particular plan — one with a deductible and one without — month by month throughout the year. The dollar amounts at the top of each bar are the total of what the user pays each month, including premiums.

The bar charts in Figures 15-1 and 15-2 come in many variations, according to each plan's charges and benefit design. For example, if you're in a plan with no deductible and your drug costs aren't high enough to reach the doughnut hole, the payments for each month, January through December, will be the same. If you're in a plan with no deductible that covers all of your drugs through the doughnut hole, that too will show the same flat payments each month.

The examples in Figures 15-1 and 15-2 show cost profiles over the whole year — typically the kind of bar chart you'd see during the annual open enrollment period (November 15 to December 31) when you're comparing plans to pick one for next year. But what if you come into Part D partway through the year? Or change your medications during the year — dropping some or adding some? Here's how the charts work in those circumstances:

- ✔ **If you join Medicare Part D partway through the year:** You'll still see a profile of your projected costs over the whole year, but the *dark shaded* bars will show your actual monthly costs for the rest of the year. Say that you turn 65 and enroll in the program in November. Your cycle of coverage then begins in December, starting with the deductible (if any) and the initial coverage period. You'll see a dark shaded bar in Month 1 that shows your costs in December. The other months (2 through 12) are shown in light shading, but are irrelevant because, in this example, after December you'll be into a new cycle of coverage. If you start coverage in June, say, the dark bars also begin in Month 1 (representing June), and continue through Month 7 (representing December). Again, the light-shaded bars in Months 8 through 12 are irrelevant because after December you'll be in next year's cycle of coverage.

- ✔ **If your drugs change during the year:** In this case, you can update your drug list on the plan finder to see how your cost profile will change. You must revise your list of drugs (omitting any you've stopped taking and adding any new ones) and then click the plan you're *currently* enrolled in to see your new cost profile on the bar chart. Again, as explained in the preceding bullet, the dark bars on the chart indicate what you'll pay for the rest of the year.

Avoiding or Narrowing the Coverage Gap with Other Benefits

In Medicare as a whole, you've always had the right to purchase extra insurance that's specifically designed to pay for out-of-pocket expenses, like Part A and Part B deductibles and co-pays. (This is known as Medigap supplementary insurance, which I explain in Chapter 1.) You'd expect this type of insurance to also cover out-of-pocket expenses in Part D — especially those in the doughnut hole. But no, it doesn't. The law specifically forbids it. (See the nearby sidebar "What were they thinking . . . when they didn't allow Medigap to cover prescription drugs?" for more information.)

However, you may be able to get other benefits that help fill in the doughnut hole, either completely or partially. In the following sections, I consider help given through employer or union health plans, State Pharmacy Assistance Programs, and the few Medicare drug plans that offer some coverage in the gap. (I outline other ways of reducing your drug costs, which may also help you avoid the doughnut hole or lessen its impact, in Chapter 16.)

What were they thinking . . . when they didn't allow Medigap to cover prescription drugs?

In designing Part D, Congress specifically prohibited Medigap insurance from covering prescription drugs in all policies sold after Part D began. The law allowed people who already had such policies to continue using them — but barred those folks from having Medicare drug coverage at the same time. The law also decreed that those folks would be hit with a late penalty if they were to drop drug coverage from Medigap and join Part D in the future.

Consumer advocates vigorously opposed this clause in the law, arguing that buying additional benefits should be a personal decision, as it is in other forms of insurance. Lawmakers who supported the clause argued that Medicare beneficiaries needed to remain "aware" of the real cost of prescription drugs (as in, presumably, "feeling the pain").

But there was also strong political pressure to get as many people as possible into Part D and to keep the program firmly within the control of Medicare's private health and drug plans.

Leaning on employer benefits

Some employer or union health benefits provide drug coverage that *wraps around* Part D — in other words, it pays for some or all of enrollees' out-of-pocket costs in a Medicare drug plan. Sometimes this wrap-around drug coverage includes paying for drugs in the doughnut hole, either wholly or in part. (You can find more information in Chapter 6 on how employer and union drug benefits fit in with Part D.)

Any money your employer or union pays toward your drugs during the gap does *not* count toward your out-of-pocket limit, and therefore delays or eliminates your chances of qualifying for catastrophic coverage later on. (Not that this matters, because you're saving money anyway.) But anything *you* pay does count. Employers are expected to coordinate benefits with Medicare drug plans. Still, keeping the receipts for your share of these payments in the gap is a good idea, just in case you need to give proof to your drug plan.

Filling in with veterans benefits

If you're enrolled in the healthcare program run by the Department of Veterans Affairs, *and* you're in a Part D plan, you have the right to use either the VA or your drug plan to obtain medications, on a prescription-by-prescription basis, as explained in Chapter 6. So you can use your VA benefits to cover prescriptions in the Part D coverage gap. These payments don't count toward the out-of-pocket limit to get out of the gap, but your co-pays count.

For more information or help on VA health and pharmacy benefits, go to www.va.gov/healtheligibility, visit a local VA medical facility, or call the VA Health Benefits Service Center toll-free at 877-222-8387. For CHAMPVA info, go to www.va.gov/hac or call 800-733-8387.

Seeking additional coverage from a State Pharmacy Assistance Program

In 2008, ten State Pharmacy Assistant Programs (SPAPs) provide some coverage in the doughnut hole for residents with incomes under a certain level who are enrolled in Medicare drug plans. They are Connecticut, Delaware, Illinois, Maine, Massachusetts, Nevada, New Jersey, New York, Pennsylvania, and South Carolina. Help in the gap varies a great deal among these programs, from quite limited assistance to full coverage. (For more on how SPAPs fit together with Part D, see Chapter 6.)

Any payments an SPAP makes for your drugs in the gap *do* count toward your out-of-pocket limit — as long as the program is "qualified" under Medicare Part D rules (as those listed previously are; see Chapter 6 for an explanation of "qualified"). So these payments do *not* delay or erase your chances of qualifying for catastrophic coverage later on if your drug costs go that high.

Getting lucky with a Medicare drug plan that covers your drugs in the gap

Most Part D plans stick to the basic plan designed by Congress — that is, they don't give any coverage in the doughnut hole. But some do, in one of two ways:

- ✔ **Plans that cover only generic drugs in the gap:** Generics have the same active ingredients as the brand-name drugs they are copying but cost far less, as explained in Chapter 16. In 2008, every beneficiary in every state has access to at least 14 plans that offer generic coverage in the gap. Most of these plans have higher-than-average premiums.

- ✔ **Plans that cover generics *and* brand-name drugs in the gap:** These plans have become much scarcer since Part D began in 2006. In that year, people in 46 states had access to at least one stand-alone prescription drug plan (the kind that most people in Medicare have, to complement the traditional Medicare health program), which offered full coverage of generics and brand-name drugs in the gap. In 2007, such plans were available in 39 states. In 2008, only one stand-alone plan in one state gave any brand-name coverage in the gap, covering only about 30 drugs.

Among Medicare Advantage plans that provide both healthcare and drugs (see Chapter 9), gap coverage for brand-name drugs has also gotten scarcer. MA plans that covered all the drugs on their formularies in the gap were available only in a few counties across the nation in 2008, mainly in large urban areas in California and Florida.

REMEMBER

If you have one of these *fill-in plans,* the money your plan pays toward your drugs during the gap does *not* count toward your out-of-pocket limit, but your co-pays *do* count.

REMEMBER

How do you know whether a fill-in plan is worth it?

If you're considering a plan that offers any coverage in the gap, think about these points before signing up for one:

- ✓ **Will the plan give you any benefit in the gap?** If you use a lot of generic drugs, you may assume that a plan offering gap coverage for generics is your best bet. Well, it might be — but not necessarily. Most generics are so inexpensive that you'd need to use a very large number of them to rack up enough costs to even reach the gap. So why pay a higher premium for one of these fill-in plans if you'll never hit the gap anyway? A plan that covers all your brand-name drugs as well as generics may well be a good deal if the drugs are costly enough to take you into the gap. But you generally can find such plans only in a few Medicare Advantage plans in local areas — which means considering their health benefits as well as their drug coverage before you sign up, as explained in Chapter 9.

- ✓ **Will the plan cover all of your drugs in the gap?** In the first two years of Part D, the fill-in plans usually offered full coverage in the gap for all drugs on their formularies. By 2008, only a very few Medicare Advantage plans did. The rest use much vaguer terms to describe their gap coverage: for example, "some generics and some brands" or "some generics" or "all preferred generics." These terms often conceal a very limited range of drugs, often the least pricey ones on a plan's formulary.

- ✓ **What will you be charged for your drugs in the gap?** Most fill-in plans charge the same co-pays for drugs in the gap as they charge during the initial coverage period. But some charge more. One plan in 2008 charged a $15 co-pay in the gap for the same generic drug that cost $2 in the initial coverage period — in other words, more than seven times as much. Some other plans charge three or five times as much. At the other end of the generosity spectrum, some plans don't charge anything for generics, either in the initial coverage period or in the gap.

So how do you avoid these traps? In every case, you need to compare plans to find out whether a fill-in plan is actually worth it, according to the drugs you take. The only effective way to do this is to run the names of your drugs (plus their dosages and how often you take them) through Medicare's online plan finder. Doing so automatically shows you the plans that cover your drugs at the least expense — including whether the plans offer any coverage in the gap. (I explain how to use the plan finder, or get someone else to use it for you, in detail in Chapter 10.)

Will there be more gap coverage in the future?

It's always possible that more plans will offer full coverage in the gap in future years. You'd expect them to, because there's obviously a demand. But don't hold your breath. Private insurers are in this business to turn a profit, and they're leery of offering full-coverage plans that attract people who need the most drugs and make the most claims — and therefore cost insurers the most money. In 2006 and 2007, full gap coverage was offered consecutively by two insurers, and each eliminated it at the end of one year, citing financial problems. Many people saved a lot of money when enrolled in these plans — while they lasted. Their disappearance was bad news for people with high drug costs who most need coverage in the gap, especially those taking brand-name drugs that don't have a comparable generic yet.

When open enrollment (November 15 to December 31) comes round each year, check to see whether any new plans are offering gap coverage for the following year. To find out, look in the plan listings at the end of your *Medicare & You* handbook, which Medicare mails to you in mid-October, or go to www. medicare.gov and click "Learn more about plans in your area." Still, as I suggested earlier in this section, the only way to find out whether any fill-in plan would benefit you is to use Medicare's online plan finder, either yourself or by getting someone else to do it for you, as suggested in Chapter 10.

Chapter 16

Bringing Down Your Drug Costs

In This Chapter

▶ Lowering your costs to stretch your coverage

▶ Decreasing your expenses in the coverage gap

*T*he difference between a co-pay and the full price of a prescription drug can bring on serious sticker shock. And the increase in your out-of-pocket cost happens very suddenly if you cross the line into the doughnut hole, which I explain in detail in Chapter 15. So doing everything you can to stay clear of the gap makes sense. That means making the coverage you have at the beginning of the year last as long as possible. In this chapter, I suggest several ways to do that. Of course, these suggestions can help lower your expenses even if you're unlikely to hit the doughnut hole.

And what if you fall into the gap despite your best efforts? Not everyone sees the gap in the same way:

✔ Some folks with very high drug costs want to race through the gap to get to those generous catastrophic benefits as quickly as they can.

✔ Others, also with very high costs, would like to do the same, but they simply don't have the money it takes to get there. (***Remember:*** You have to pay a large chunk on your own to get out of the gap.)

✔ The majority of people have costs in the medium to high range and expect to fall into the gap but not get out of it before the end of the year.

If you're in the second or third group, you'll want to lessen the impact of the doughnut hole while you're in it. In this chapter, I suggest ways to do that, too.

Stretching Your Coverage

That first slice of coverage in Part D, the phase known as the "initial coverage period," really isn't very large. It *sounds* pretty good — coverage for up to $2,510 of drug costs in 2008 ($2,700 in 2009). But this amount isn't just what *you* pay (read Chapters 2 and 15 for more about costs during the initial coverage period). It means the full cost of your prescriptions (what you pay *and* what your plan pays). And with drug prices as high as they are, it doesn't necessarily take many meds for you to see your initial coverage swallowed up before half the year has passed.

I guess you'd prefer this not to happen to you. So somehow you need to s-t-r-e-t-c-h that coverage, which may turn out to be as healthy for your wallet as physical stretching is for your body — yoga for the pocketbook, perhaps. Even if you can save only a few dollars here and there, they all add up and stave off the sorry day when you may hit the doughnut hole. In the following sections, I highlight practical ways to do this, starting with one that may surprise you.

Taking a hard look at your meds

Think about all of the medications you take. Do you really need them all? This may sound like an impertinent question, but I don't mean it that way. Many people are being over-prescribed without realizing it. In a health system where you can see many different doctors, and there's little or no coordination among them, taking more meds than you really need is quite easy. Your primary care physician may prescribe two or three drugs, and various specialists may prescribe more.

This isn't just a matter of cost. Some drug combinations can work against each other in subtle and complex ways that harm your health. And the more meds you take, the greater the possibility that this can happen. Researchers have also found plenty of examples of people developing new symptoms — for example, depression, headaches, or constipation — which are actually side effects of one of the drugs they're already taking. But without realizing this, they go back to their primary care doctors who often . . . yes, prescribe yet more pills.

Now don't take this the wrong way. I'm not suggesting that you suddenly stop taking any of your drugs or lose faith in your doctor. Far from it. But make sure that all the medications you're taking are necessary and safe when used together. If some aren't, then cutting back will save you money *and* protect your health.

The American Society of Consultant Pharmacists (ASCP), whose members are pharmacists specializing in medication management for older people, recommend that seniors review their prescriptions if they currently

✔ Take five or more medications

✔ Take more than 12 medication doses a day

✔ Take medications for three or more medical problems

✔ See more than one physician who prescribes drugs on a regular basis

The following sections explain how you can get your meds reviewed.

Consulting your primary care doctor

Some physicians encourage patients to bring all of their medications into the office, and they're often amazed to see the variety of pills that are poured onto their desks. So your primary care doctor may — and certainly should — welcome a request to review yours. You can either take in the containers or make a list of all the drugs you're currently taking — not just prescription drugs, but also over-the-counter medicines, herbal remedies, and vitamins. If you make a list, make sure to include

✔ The full name of each of your drugs

✔ Their dosages

✔ How often you take them

✔ How long you've been taking them

✔ The name of the physician(s) who prescribed them

It's a good idea to keep this list in your wallet and show it to any physician who prescribes a new medicine for you. Then the doctor can decide on the spot whether the new drug is really necessary or how it may interact with others you're already taking. If you're newly enrolled in Medicare Part B and go for your "Welcome to Medicare" exam — the only routine checkup that Medicare covers — this would be another opportunity to produce the list and ask the doctor to review it.

During this review, ask your doctor these specific questions:

✔ Do I still need this drug? If so, why?

✔ Is this drug safe to take with all the others I'm taking?

✔ Is this drug appropriate for people of my age?

✔ Does this drug perform essentially the same function as another drug I'm taking? If so, do I need both?

✔ Is there a medicine I'm not taking that I should be taking?

✔ Are there any changes I can make in my daily life that will make taking this drug unnecessary?

Turning to a pharmacist

Pharmacists are experts on the active ingredients in medicines, how they work in your body, and how different drugs may interact. In fact, pharmacists are more expert on this topic than doctors, and they're often willing to spend more time answering patients' questions, such as those I suggest in the previous section. You can ask for an appointment to see a pharmacist face to face to review your drugs, or you can drop off your list of meds and arrange to call later for the pharmacist's opinion. ***Note:*** You may be charged a fee for the review.

If you live in an area that has a School of Pharmacy, you can inquire whether any of its advanced students are interested in performing a review. Many schools offer this service as part of students' clinical training, under faculty supervision, at the school or in local clinics at little or no charge. To see whether there's a school near you, go to the American Association of Colleges of Pharmacy's Web site at www.aacp.org and click "Pharmacy Schools." Or call the AACP at 703-739-2330.

A relatively small but growing number of pharmacists have been trained in pharmacology as it relates to seniors. They know the drugs that older people shouldn't be taking, how some drugs cause additional symptoms that don't affect younger people, and which meds are risky when used in combination with others. These pharmacists have *CGP* after their names, which stands for *Certified Geriatric Pharmacist,* a professional credential.

Many CGPs make regular visits to nursing homes and senior centers. If a CGP works in your community, you can make a private appointment for her to come to your home, review your meds, and, if necessary, discuss the results with your physician. CGPs typically charge a fee for this service — about $100 an hour — but if you take multiple meds, you may find it money well spent. To find a CGP, go to www.ccgp.org/consumer/locate.htm and click your state, or go to www.seniorcarepharmacist.com and click "Find a Senior Care Pharmacist in Your Area."

Qualifying for Medication Therapy Management programs

Part D plans are ideally placed to monitor the drugs their enrollees are taking because each plan has all (or most) of those drugs already logged into its computer system. Under the 2003 Medicare Modernization Act, Part D plans are required to offer what is known as *Medication Therapy Management (MTM)* for a certain group of enrollees. These are people who have several chronic diseases *and* take multiple drugs that cost at least $4,000 a year.

You can't choose to join an MTM program, but if your plan says you qualify and invites you to take part in one, consider doing so. The benefit doesn't cost you anything — by law, you can't be charged a fee. But know that what the program actually does depends on the plan. At best, your plan may provide a face-to-face meeting or a telephone conversation with a pharmacist who can review your meds and suggest ways you can manage your health conditions more effectively. These may include recommendations for different or fewer medications, other drugs that may suit you better, or lifestyle changes that can improve your health and make you less dependent on pills. Some plans' MTM programs fall short of this kind of service. You may only get an automated phone call reminding you to fill a prescription, or printed materials that give only general advice about your medical condition. If your plan invites you to join an MTM program, it sends details of the services it provides.

MTM programs in Part D are still relatively new. Over time, however, many of them may become more comprehensive, offering a valuable service to enrollees who take multiple drugs.

Switching to less expensive drugs

The most dramatic way you can lower expenses is to switch to less expensive drugs that work equally well for your medical condition. If you're like many people, you may hesitate to mention cost as a problem when the doctor is writing out a prescription. And you probably think that if it's what the doctor ordered, then that drug must be the best one for you. Well, maybe it is. Or maybe another one is far less pricey but just as good.

The fact is that the newest brand-name drugs — often the ones that doctors prefer to prescribe — are almost always the most expensive. Sometimes hugely expensive. (The nearby sidebar "What were they thinking . . . when they made prescription drugs so expensive?" explains some of those reasons behind the costs.) But often you have two other options: generic drugs and older brand-name medicines.

Checking out generic drugs

A *generic* is an inexpensive copy of a brand-name drug. It can be sold only after the original brand has been on the market for a number of years and its patent — which grants exclusive marketing rights — has expired. Generics may look different; they may taste different. But before they can be sold, the U.S. Food and Drug Administration (FDA) must certify that generics contain the same *active ingredients* (the chemicals that work in your body to counteract disease or improve your health) as the brand-name drugs that they're copying — and that they're as safe. They should work exactly the same way.

What were they thinking . . . when they made prescription drugs so expensive?

When a pharmaceutical manufacturer brings out a new drug, it has exclusive rights under the patent laws to sell that drug without competition for a lengthy period, about 10 to 17 years. These laws allow the manufacturer to recoup the millions of dollars it has taken to research and develop the drug. While the patent protection lasts, the manufacturer tries to make as much money as possible from that drug — selling it at a high price, advertising it to consumers extensively on television, and sending legions of salesmen along to doctors to persuade them to prescribe it. The largest-selling (and most heavily promoted) medicines earn billions of dollars.

In recent years, drug companies have been heavily criticized for the tactics they use to keep profits high — sweetening sales pitches to physicians with gifts and free lunches, spending millions of dollars lobbying Congress and state legislatures to pass bills that are favorable to the industry and ditch bills that aren't, and doing everything they can to extend patent protections and keep generic copies off the market as long as possible. When the first generic version does eventually go on sale, its manufacturer also gets six months of exclusive sales, so the drug costs only a little less than the brand's price. But after that, more manufacturers produce generic versions and prices drop dramatically, often to less than 20 percent of the original brand price.

This market-based approach is unique to the United States, which has by far the highest drug prices in the world. Other Western governments regulate or negotiate drug prices in various ways to keep them affordable for consumers and taxpayers while allowing manufacturers a reasonable profit. In 2003, the American drug industry was successful in getting a clause written into the Medicare drug benefit law that specifically prohibits Medicare from negotiating Part D prices directly with the drug companies. (Instead, prices are negotiated by individual Part D insurers, who have far less bargaining power than Medicare.) Consumer advocates strongly opposed this ban, arguing that the Department of Veterans Affairs, also a federal agency, has long negotiated drug prices directly on behalf of the veterans heath service. Although Congress has passed several bills allowing direct negotiation for Part D, none (at least at the time I'm writing this) have yet become law.

Do they? Millions of people take generics and experience no differences between them and the original brands. Some people, though, are convinced that generics don't work so well for them. It's hard to say whether this is a psychological reaction or a real physical effect. But human bodies are both complex and highly individual. If an identical drug can affect two people differently, then so can a brand-name drug and its generic version — even if the only actual distinctions between them are the *non*-active ingredients that provide a different color, texture, or taste. (And if these ingredients may affect your condition, your doctor will tell you.) The only way to find out whether a generic works for you is to try one — and to do so, perhaps, with the expectation that it will work as well for you.

Of course, not all of today's brand-name drugs have generic equivalents. But over the last few years, a great many best-selling brands have lost their patent protection, and generics have surged onto the market. Generic versions of Tamoxifen (to treat breast cancer), Prozac (depression), Zocor (high cholesterol), and Norvasc (high blood pressure) — to name only a famous few — are available for a fraction of the cost of the originals. Many more will be developed in coming years.

Understanding what an "older" brand-name drug is

The newest and most heavily promoted drugs aren't always brilliant innovations that are unique in treating a particular medical condition. Most of them aren't very different from brands that have been around for a number of years. Often, their only claim to "newness" is offering more convenience — a pill you can take once a day rather than three times a day, for example — or even slighter variations. In 2002, the FDA approved 78 new drugs for market but classified only 7 of them as improvements over older drugs.

So why do consumers spend so much on these "new" drugs that are no better than old ones? The answer, largely, is television. Drug companies spend millions of dollars advertising their latest product to persuade folks that this is the drug of choice. "Ask your doctor . . .," they say. And if enough of us do, the drug becomes a blockbuster. A well-known example is Prilosec — remember "the purple pill" for heartburn? — which earned up to $6 billion a year until its patent expired in 2001. Its manufacturer then poured many more millions into advertising Nexium, a pill almost identical to Prilosec, except that it had a new patent and no generic competition. And many people bought Nexium, even after the FDA decided that Prilosec was safe enough to be sold without a prescription. Checking retail prices at a leading chain-store pharmacy, I found that a 30-day supply of 20 mg Nexium costs $168; generic Prilosec (omeprazole) costs $63; and over-the-counter Prilosec is just $20.

There's another reason, besides cost, why older drugs may be a better bet than the latest ones out of the lab. They've been on the market for more years, and millions more people have used them. That means they have a longer track record showing how safe they are.

Determining how much you can save by switching

Just by using lower-price drugs, you stretch your Part D initial coverage, because the overall total cost of your drugs adds up to bring you closer to the doughnut hole. But you also reduce your co-pays. Generic medicines are almost always placed in the lowest tier of charges, often with co-pays under $10 for each prescription. A few plans charge nothing for generics. Older brand-name drugs often have lower co-pays too.

To see how this works, take a look at Table 16-1. It shows how one man (Jim) lowered his costs by well over a third and stayed out of the doughnut hole.

Table 16-1	How Jim Cut His Costs and Steered Clear of the Doughnut Hole		
Jim's Combination of Medications	Monthly Costs in the Initial Coverage Period	Monthly Costs in the Coverage Gap	Total Annual Out- of- Pocket Costs
4 brand names + 1 generic	$174	$337	$2,740
4 generics + 1 brand name	$64.50	$0	$774

Source: Dollar amounts derived from the 2008 Medicare Prescription Drug Plan Finder at www.medicare.gov.

Here's how Jim achieved these savings. The least expensive Part D plan that covers all of his usual medicines — four brand-names and one generic — in 2008 was going to cost him $2,740 (including premiums totaling $282) over the whole year. It would also put him in the doughnut hole for the last four months — so in early September his out-of-pocket costs would jump from $174 a month to $337. But then Jim found generic versions for three out of four of his brand-name drugs. Under the same Part D plan, two generics would cost him $4 per prescription, rather than the $54 he'd pay for each brand, and the third would reduce the brand-name price by about 66 percent. Over the year, he'd pay $774 and cut his monthly costs to $64.50. So Jim talked to his doctor, changed to the generics, avoided the gap, and saved nearly $2,000.

If Jim had been in a plan that charged coinsurance rather than co-pays, he'd still have saved money. In one such plan, the total cost of his generics and single brand-name drug comes to less than $1,900, well short of the $2,510 that would put him in the gap. After a deductible of $275, his 25 percent coinsurance plus premiums would come to $66.10 each month from March through December, making his out-of-pocket cost $936 for the whole year.

When you're considering generics, you can play savvy in another way too. Consider, for example, Prilosec, which is used to treat heartburn. Generic Prilosec (omeprazole), while costing far less than its brand-name version, still costs $63 a month at full price, three times as much as over-the-counter Prilosec ($20). However, if you're in a Part D plan that charges, say, a $5 or $10 co-pay, or even no co-pay at all for generics, you'd be better off paying for the generic through your plan, at least in the initial coverage period, than buying the OTC version at full price. On the other hand, if you fall into the doughnut hole and have to pay the full price of generic Prilosec through your plan, the OTC version may then be a better bet.

Finding out more about lower-cost drugs

Your doctor is the best person to ask about whether a generic or older drug is available because ultimately, if there is, she's going to be the one who decides whether it would work well for you. You'll also want to discuss whether an older drug may have other side effects or require a different dosage than the brand you're taking now. (You'll also want to make sure the generic or older drug is on your plan's formulary. If it's not, the plan will charge you full price.)

Your pharmacist, too, can be a good source of information on which lower-cost drugs are available. Or you can identify them by using the online Medicare Prescription Drug Plan Finder at www.medicare.gov, as explained in Chapter 10.

You can also do a bit of homework yourself by exploring the value of different kinds of medicines that are used to treat your health problem. By "value" I mean which drugs are considered to provide the best clinical benefits in their class, according to head-to-head comparisons based on the best available scientific evidence. This kind of comparison is known as *evidence-based research* and was pioneered by the Drug Effectiveness Review Project at the Health and Sciences University in Portland, Oregon. Each review investigates the safety, side effects, and effectiveness of all drugs used for a single specific medical condition — such as high cholesterol, diabetes, heart disease, allergies, depression, and many more. The resulting reports are increasingly used by doctors and big drug payers, such as state Medicaid agencies, to determine which drugs are most worth the money. After all, if five drugs are equally effective, why choose the priciest?

The scientific reports are difficult for most folks to read — they're long and technical — but the Consumers Union has translated its results into free, easy-to-read summaries that consumers can use to help them discuss medications with their doctors. You can find these summaries at www.crbestbuydrugs.org.

Buying drugs by mail order

Most Part D plans offer a mail-order service and charge less for drugs purchased this way. This option means ordering 90-day supplies at a time, so it works best for *maintenance drugs* — those that need to be taken regularly throughout the year. Part D plans don't charge extra for postage and packing in delivering orders to your door.

Be careful, though, to check that your plan's mail-order service will actually save you money. Some plans charge exactly the same for mail-order drugs as they do for drugs bought at pharmacies. And a few plans don't cover certain drugs on their formularies under the mail-order option — which means the ones omitted cost far more, maybe even full price. You can call your plan to check price differences for your drugs under the two options. Or, if you use Medicare's online plan finder at www.medicare.gov to see which plan will charge you the least for your drugs (as explained in Chapter 10), you can see this info at a glance.

But checking is worth it, because you may get lucky. Remember Jim, who I mention earlier in this chapter, saving a bundle by choosing more generic drugs and keeping himself out of the doughnut hole? He took it a step further and saved even more money, as you can see in Table 16-2. The plan he's enrolled in charges nothing for generics bought from its mail-order service, so he pays only for his single brand-name drug plus the monthly premium, reducing his annual expenses by another $242. Lucky Jim indeed.

Table 16-2	How Jim Used Mail Order and Cut His Costs Further		
Jim's 4 Generics and 1 Brand-Name Drug	**Monthly Costs in Initial Coverage Period**	**Monthly Costs in Coverage Gap**	**Total Annual Out-of-Pocket Costs**
Drugs bought at pharmacy	$64.50	$0	$774
Drugs bought by mail order	$44.33	$0	$531.96

Shopping around for the best prices at local pharmacies

Prices for the same prescription drugs at local pharmacies can vary quite a lot, even within a plan's network of pharmacies. That's because the plan negotiates dispensing fees and other costs with each of these pharmacies and makes better deals with some than with others. (See Chapter 14 for the scoop.) This negotiating won't affect you if you're in the initial coverage period and paying flat co-pays for your prescriptions. But if you pay *coinsurance* — a percentage of the cost of your drugs — or are paying full price in the deductible phase or the coverage gap, then you can probably shave a few dollars here and there off your prescriptions by shopping around.

Your plan includes a list of its pharmacies in your area in the information packet it sends you upon enrollment (or it can supply another on request), or you can view it on the plan's Web site. You can also check out price differences among local pharmacies on Medicare's online plan finder at www.medicare.gov, as explained in Chapter 10.

What about those pharmacies that sell selected generic drugs at low cost, sometimes for as little as $4 for a 30-day supply? These pharmacies — Wal-Mart, Target, Safeway, and Kroger, among others — offer these prices year-round to all of their customers. (In other words, they're not temporary discounts.) If any of these pharmacies is in your plan's network, you have the right under Medicare rules to buy a covered drug at the pharmacy's asking price through your plan when you fill the prescription. The payments count toward your out-of-pocket limit, and you don't have to send the receipts to your plan.

For example, say that your generic medicine costs $4 at the supermarket. If your plan's co-pay for this drug is $6, you'd save $2 by paying the supermarket price. Similarly, if your plan's full price for the drug is $10, and your usual share is 25 percent of the cost ($2.50), you'd pay 25 percent of the supermarket price ($1) instead of $2.50. And if you're paying full cost in the deductible phase or the coverage gap, you pay $4 rather than $10. (Of course, if your plan normally charges nothing for generics, the supermarket price isn't a deal.)

Lowering Drug Costs in the Coverage Gap

I'm going to assume you've done everything you can to stay out of the coverage gap by following the advice earlier in this chapter and in Chapter 15 — but here you are still, pitched right into it. Of course, any of the suggestions earlier in this chapter can also help lower your expenses in the gap. Even at full price, a generic drug, for example, is likely to ease the sucker punch to your wallet more than a brand-name one will. But for many people, generics aren't yet an option. According to one government report, 37 percent of Part D prescriptions dispensed in the first half of 2006 had no generic versions. So the following sections offer some alternative ideas.

Low-cost drugs from manufacturers

Many drug-making companies run patient assistance programs that offer their own brands for free or at very low cost to people with incomes under a certain level and no prescription coverage. When Medicare Part D began, these companies stopped assistance to people enrolled in the programs. Later, however, a few large companies changed course and now offer the same help to folks with Medicare drug coverage under certain conditions. Here are the pros and cons of patient assistance programs:

✔ **Pros:** This is a good way of lowering costs dramatically in the gap if you don't qualify for Extra Help under Part D or for your state's pharmacy assistance program — provided that one or more of your drugs is made by a company that gives this help and you meet its eligibility conditions.

✔ **Cons:** The value of these drugs doesn't count toward the out-of-pocket limit that gets you out of the gap. The application process can be a hassle, and if each of your drugs is made by a different company, you may have to apply several times over. In some cases, this assistance is only temporary — maybe three months or so — or must be renewed through another application every year.

Each company has its own rules on eligibility for its program and how to apply. You'll probably need your doctor's recommendation. Your doctor or pharmacist may be able to tell you which of your drugs are covered by a manufacturer's assistance program and may even have application forms handy. State Health Insurance Assistance Programs (SHIPs) offer help with applying (see Appendix B for contact info). So do some national associations and patient support groups that specialize in a particular health condition. The Web site www.pparx.org lists company assistance programs, the drugs they cover, their eligibility rules, and how to apply.

Low-cost drugs from abroad

Prescription drugs are often much less expensive abroad because, unlike the U.S., most other governments regulate prices. Millions of Americans have saved money this way by filling prescriptions by mail order through the Internet, especially from Canada, or by hopping across the border. Here are the pros and cons of buying low-cost drugs from abroad:

✔ **Pros:** When you're paying full price in the gap (and you don't expect to get out of it), this option is worth considering. Brand-name drugs from abroad can cost half as much as the same ones here. Generics are usually not less expensive, but in some cases, you can buy new generics that are approved for sale in their own countries but not yet available on the American market.

✔ **Cons:** The cost of drugs from abroad doesn't count toward the out-of-pocket limit that gets you out of the gap. Unless you take sensible precautions, you may fall victim to scams and counterfeits. It's still illegal under American law to fill prescriptions this way. Nobody, however, has been prosecuted for importing drugs for their own personal use. Also, the recent falling value of the American dollar has made buying drugs from abroad less of a good deal than it has been in the past.

The first rule of obtaining drugs from abroad is to *be careful.* The Internet is Wild West territory, full of scams for the unwary, and this is especially true of the trade in prescription drugs. So you'll need to pick a licensed pharmacy that has a reputation for good, ethical service. To find out how to buy drugs from abroad safely, go to Appendix C.

Other options

When you're in the doughnut hole and trying to make your expenses more manageable, every avenue is worth exploring. Depending on your circumstances, you may be able to get help to lower your costs in some of the following ways:

- **State Pharmacy Assistance Programs (SPAPs):** I cover the big SPAPs that provide coverage to wrap around the Part D drug benefit, depending on your income, in Chapter 15. But many other state programs provide help with prescription drugs — for example, discount programs or low-cost drugs for specific medical conditions. To find out whether your state has a program, and its details, go to www.medicarerights. org/rxframeset.html. Or call your State Health Insurance Assistance Program (SHIP; see Appendix B for contact info).

- **Free or low-cost clinics:** Each state has clinics or health centers that provide health services, including prescription drugs in many cases, for which patients pay what they can afford. These services are supported by the U.S. Health Resources and Services Administration. For contact information in your state, go to ask.hrsa.gov/pc. Or call your state Department of Health or Area Agency on Aging. Look in the state pages of your phone book for contact info.

- **AIDS Drug Assistance Programs (ADAPs):** These programs help people with HIV-AIDS pay for HIV-related medications. They operate in all 50 states, the District of Columbia, and the U.S. territories. To qualify, your income must be below a certain level, which varies from state to state. If you're in one of these programs as well as a Medicare drug plan, you can use ADAP assistance to pay for HIV drugs in the coverage gap, though the payments don't count toward the out-of-pocket limit. You can find details of each program at www.atdn.org/access/states. Or call the AIDS Treatment Data Network at 800-734-7104 for help and information.

- **Certified charities and patient organizations:** If your income is low but a bit too high to qualify for Extra Help (which I cover in Chapter 5), you may be able to get help paying for drugs in the gap through a charity or a patient support association that specializes in a specific medical condition. These payments *do* count toward your out-of-pocket limit. To find such assistance, go to www.benefitscheckuprx.org or call your State Health Insurance Assistance Program (SHIP) — see Appendix B for contact info.

✔ **Pharmacy discounts:** Many pharmacies offer discounts on drugs, either temporarily or through discount cards. If you happen to see that a discounted price is less than the price you're paying under your Part D plan in the deductible phase or in the coverage gap (in other words, when you're paying full price), you have the right to buy the drug at the pharmacy's cash price instead of using your plan's card. Provided that you send the receipt to your plan, this payment counts toward your out-of-pocket limit. (It's only counted, though, if the drug is covered by your plan and the pharmacy is in the plan's network of pharmacies, as explained in Chapter 15.)

✔ **Free samples from your doctor:** If you have trouble paying for drugs in the gap, don't be shy about asking your doctor for free samples, which most doctors receive from drug manufacturers. It's one way the companies persuade doctors to prescribe their products — most often the newest and most expensive ones. For this reason, the drug you need may not be in your doctor's sample cupboard, but it's worth asking.

Chapter 17

Switching to Another Plan

· ·

· ·

*A*fter you're in a Part D plan, and all the hard work of choosing one and signing up for it is behind you, probably the last thing on your mind is changing to another plan. But it makes sense to know *when* you can switch plans if you want to or need to, *when* you can drop out of a plan (yeah, there are rules about this too), and *whether* you should compare plans all over again at the end of the year to see if you'd get a better deal with a different one.

You can switch plans during three time frames, depending on the plan you're now in and your reasons for switching:

- ✔ **November 15 to December 31 each year:** This is when anybody in a Part D plan (a stand-alone drug plan or a Medicare health plan that includes drug coverage) can change plans for the following year.

- ✔ **January 1 to March 31 each year:** This is when you can change from traditional Medicare to a Medicare health plan, or the other way around; or you can change from one Medicare health plan to another — whether it provides drug coverage or not. However, you can't change from one stand-alone drug plan to another. Also, you can't use this period to *drop* or *add* drug coverage (if you haven't already got it).

- ✔ **Special enrollment periods:** These are allowed at any time of the year, but only in certain circumstances. They come with time limits.

This chapter focuses mainly on *switching* Part D plans at certain times, according to the preceding situations. (For details about enrolling in a plan for the first time, go to Chapter 12.) I also explain the circumstances in which you can drop out of a plan — or be dropped by a plan. Finally, I cover the big end-of-year question — stay with the plan you have or switch to another? — and suggest points to keep in mind when you make that decision.

Switching Part D Plans at Standard Enrollment Times

You can understand why Medicare doesn't allow everybody to switch Part D plans any time they feel like it — that would be chaos. And you can understand why Medicare allows special enrollment periods for special circumstances at any time of the year (I describe these special periods in detail later in this chapter). But why, oh why, does it have *two* open enrollment periods at different times? Wouldn't it be simpler to have just one free-for-all once a year? Of course. But you're stuck with two.

Table 17-1 lays out the possibilities for switching plans during the two standard time frames — eight possible combinations, depending on the health and drug coverage you have. (The shaded rows show options for people *without* drug coverage.) But it isn't as complicated as it looks. Find your situation — the kind of plan you have now — in the left column, and then look across to see which type of plan you can switch to and at what time. In each situation, you have no more than two choices of plan types to switch to.

Table 17-1	Switching Plans: From Which, To What, When	
If You're in This Plan Now:	*You Can Switch to:*	*And Enroll at This Time:*
A stand-alone drug plan *with* traditional Medicare *or with* a Medicare health plan without drug coverage	Another stand-alone drug plan to use with the same type of health coverage	*Only* from November 15 to December 31
Traditional Medicare *and* a stand-alone drug plan	A Medicare health plan *with* drug coverage	November 15 to December 31 *or* January 1 to March 31
A Medicare health plan *with* drug coverage	Another Medicare health plan *with* drug coverage	November 15 to December 31 *or* January 1 to March 31
A Medicare health plan *with* drug coverage	Traditional Medicare *and* a stand-alone drug plan	November 15 to December 31 *or* January 1 to March 31

If You're in This Plan Now:	You Can Switch to:	And Enroll at This Time:
A Medicare health plan *without* drug coverage	A Medicare health plan *with* drug coverage	*Only* from November 15 to December 31
A Medicare health plan *without* drug coverage	Traditional Medicare *and* a stand-alone drug plan	*Only* from November 15 to December 31
A Medicare health plan *without* drug coverage	Traditional Medicare *alone* (no stand-alone drug plan)	November 15 to December 31 *or* January 1 to March 31
Traditional Medicare *alone* (no stand-alone drug plan)	A Medicare health plan *without* drug coverage	November 15 to December 31 *or* January 1 to March 31

If you *haven't* already signed up for Medicare prescription drug coverage, you can use the January 1 to March 31 enrollment period only to switch to another health plan that *doesn't* cover prescription drugs. I mention this as a warning because I've heard of some people (who'd missed their previous deadlines for getting drug coverage) joining a Medicare Advantage health plan during this period without realizing it wouldn't cover their drugs. So if you want drug coverage, be sure to sign up at the right times — and if you join a Medicare health plan, always check that it actually covers prescription drugs.

After you figure out when you can switch to a new plan and what kind of plan you can switch to, all that's left to do is enroll. In the following sections, I explain what you need to do to switch plans and the actions you can take if you change your mind about your newly chosen plan.

Enrolling in a new plan

When switching to a new Part D plan in either of the standard enrollment periods, all you have to do is enroll in it, following the process I describe in Chapter 12. You don't have to disenroll from your present plan or even notify it. Your new enrollment is logged into Medicare's computer system, and you're automatically disenrolled from your previous plan as soon as your new coverage starts. If you enroll

✓ **November 15 through December 31:** Your old drug coverage finishes at midnight on December 31. Your new coverage starts January 1.

✓ **January 1 through March 31:** Your new drug coverage starts the first day of the month after you enroll — February 1 if you enroll in January; March 1 if you enroll in February; or April 1 if you enroll in March.

Figuring out how many times you can change your mind

What if you switch to another plan during one of the standard periods and then change your mind, either because you've found yet another plan you prefer, or because you decide you want to return to the plan you just switched out of? If the enrollment period hasn't yet expired, these are your options:

- ✔ **November 15 through December 31:** Within this period, you can technically change Part D plans as often as you want. The last plan you enroll in by December 31 is the one you'll have the following year. But be cautious of changing more than once — it can cause problems getting your information into the system, as described in Chapter 12.

- ✔ **January 1 through March 31:** You're allowed to switch plans only once during this period, so you can't change your mind, unless you qualify for a special enrollment period, as explained later in this chapter.

One exception is worth keeping in mind. Suppose you were in traditional Medicare and switched to a Medicare Advantage health plan in the January to March period and then regretted the change. You've already used up your single chance to switch. *But* if this is your first time ever in a Medicare health plan *and* you dropped a Medigap supplementary insurance policy when you joined the plan, you have the right to return to traditional Medicare and get back your Medigap policy at any time within 12 months of joining the plan, as explained in more detail later in this chapter.

Switching Plans during a Special Enrollment Period

Some people need to switch plans outside of the standard enrollment periods. So Medicare allows *special enrollment periods* (SEPs) in certain circumstances. You can use these at any time in the year, but most have specific time limits. You have to switch plans within this allotted time — otherwise, you lose your chance and must wait until the next standard enrollment period to change plans. In some situations, this lag can leave you without coverage for several months.

In the following sections, I explain a number of circumstances in which you can obtain an SEP to change plans. I also tell you how to apply for an SEP (if you need to apply) and how to ensure your records are transferred safely. But I don't include SEPs granted for situations that are covered in other chapters. Flip to the appropriate chapter if you're

✔ Enrolling in a Part D plan when first joining Medicare (see Chapter 12)

✔ Receiving Extra Help (see Chapter 5)

✔ Entering, leaving, or living in a nursing home (see Chapter 18)

✔ Joining or leaving a Special Needs Plan or a Program for All-Inclusive Care of the Elderly (see Chapter 18)

✔ Enrolling in Part D after returning from living abroad or being in prison (see Chapter 12)

✔ Joining or leaving Part D because of employment-related issues (see Chapter 6)

Knowing when you can use SEPs to change plans

Special enrollment periods cover a wide range of circumstances. The ones listed in the following sections are those you can use to switch plans. In each case, I explain the conditions for getting it, how long the SEP lasts, and when coverage in the new plan begins.

If you move permanently out of your plan's service area

The time frame of your SEP for switching to another plan depends on when (and if) you notify your current plan of your move.

✔ If you tell your plan in advance, your SEP begins the month before your move and ends two months after the month of your move.

✔ If you tell your plan *after* you move, your SEP begins on the date you notify the plan and lasts for two months.

✔ If you don't notify your plan of the move, your plan will disenroll you after six months. You then get an SEP that lasts two months.

In all of these cases, after switching to another plan, you can choose when your new coverage will begin — either on the first day of the month after enrolling in the new plan or up to three months afterward.

Even if the company that sponsors your old plan (whether a Medicare health plan or a stand-alone drug plan) offers the same or other plans in your new home area, you have the right to switch to a different one if new plans are available to you there. (But if you're in a stand-alone drug plan that serves an entire state, and you move to a new house within the state, your coverage will continue and you won't be entitled to an SEP.)

If you're in a Medicare private health plan and want to change to traditional Medicare

This SEP is available *only* if both of the following conditions are met:

✔ You joined this Medicare health plan during your initial enrollment period when you first became eligible for Medicare at age 65.

✔ This is your first year in the same plan.

If these two conditions apply to you, you have the right to switch to traditional Medicare (and a stand-alone drug plan) at any time within 12 months from the time your coverage in the plan started. You also have a guaranteed right to buy Medigap supplementary insurance, but you must apply for it no later than 63 days after your coverage in the health plan ends.

If you dropped a Medigap policy to enroll in a Medicare private health plan for the first time

This SEP gives you a one-time guaranteed right to buy another Medigap supplementary insurance policy and switch back to traditional Medicare if

✔ You've been enrolled in this health plan for less than a year; *and*

✔ This is the first Medicare health plan that you've *ever* been in

You *can't* obtain this SEP if you were enrolled in a Medicare health plan before, no matter how many years ago; see the later section "If you're considering a switch to a Medicare private health plan."

If these two conditions apply to you, you have the right to be reinstated in the same Medigap policy you had before joining the Medicare health plan (or, if it's no longer being sold, a policy from another insurer) at any time during your 12-month "trial period" with the health plan. You can use this SEP to disenroll from the plan and re-enroll in traditional Medicare, and you can also use it to enroll in a stand-alone drug plan. Your new coverage begins the first day of the month after you enroll. You can apply for the Medigap policy up to 60 days before, and no later than 63 days after, your plan coverage ends.

If your plan violates its contract with you

This SEP allows you to disenroll from your plan if it has broken its contract in some way — for example, it failed to provide promised benefits in a timely manner or in keeping with Medicare's quality requirements, or it gave you erroneous information that led you to enroll in the plan.

You must apply to Medicare for this kind of SEP, as I explain later in this chapter. If Medicare determines that a violation has occurred, the SEP will begin when Medicare notifies you. You can then disenroll from the plan and enroll in another or switch to traditional Medicare. If you don't immediately choose a new plan, your SEP lasts for 90 days after you disenrolled from your present plan. Your new coverage starts the first day of the month after you enrolled.

If you were tricked or misled into joining a Medicare private health plan

This SEP allows you to switch out of a plan that you joined based on misleading or incomplete information of the kind covered in Chapter 11. You must apply to Medicare for this SEP, as I explain later in this chapter, and your case will be investigated. If Medicare determines that your claim is valid, you can immediately disenroll from the plan. You can choose to join another Medicare health plan or to switch to traditional Medicare and join a stand-alone drug plan. (In this case you also have a guaranteed right to buy a Medigap supplementary policy, regardless of when you joined the plan that misled you, as long as you apply for a policy no later than 63 days after your plan coverage ends.)

Your new coverage begins the first of the month after you enroll. But in certain circumstances — for example, if you incurred costs that your old plan wouldn't pay for — you can ask for *retroactive* (backdated) enrollment so that Medicare can cover those bills (see Chapter 11).

If a federal employee made a mistake when processing your enrollment or disenrollment in a plan

This SEP allows you to join or switch out of a Part D plan after an error has been made. It begins the month Medicare approves the SEP and continues for two more months.

If your plan withdraws from your service area, doesn't renew its contract with Medicare, or is closed down

An SEP is given in each case, but the allowed periods for switching to another plan vary according to the situation. Medicare, your plan, or both will send you a letter that explains the circumstances, tells you how long your coverage will continue, and details when you can switch to another plan.

If you're enrolled in a qualified State Pharmacy Assistance Program

This SEP allows you to change from one Part D plan to another at any time of the year but only *once* a year. Your coverage begins the first day after the month you enroll in a new plan.

Before making a switch, contact your State Pharmacy Assistance Program (SPAP) for information because you'd need a plan that works with your SPAP coverage. If your SPAP automatically enrolled you in your current plan, you can't get an SEP to change plans. (I cover SPAPs and which ones are "qualified" in Chapter 6.)

You also get an SEP if you lose your eligibility to be in an SPAP. This SEP begins the month you lose eligibility and lasts for two months afterward.

If you have any other exceptional circumstances

If none of the situations listed previously apply to you, you have the right to ask Medicare to allow an SEP based on your own "exceptional" situation. From time to time, Medicare introduces new SEPs, sometimes because a consumer draws its attention to an exception circumstance for which an SEP hadn't existed before.

Applying for an SEP

You don't need to apply for most SEPs. Just go ahead and enroll in a new plan of your choice. It's the new plan's responsibility to confirm that you're entitled to an SEP. You'll receive an enrollment form asking for information, just the same as for any enrollment (see Chapter 12). If your enrollment is accepted, it means the SEP has been granted. If the enrollment is denied, you'll get a notice explaining why, as explained in Chapter 13.

You need to apply for an SEP if the reason for wanting one is that your plan violated your contract or you believe you were misled into joining the plan, as explained earlier in this chapter. Call Medicare at 800-633-4227, explain the situation, and say you want to apply for a special enrollment period to change to a new plan. Medicare will investigate and decide whether to allow an SEP.

Making sure your records are transferred

When you use an SEP to change plans during the year, the record of your drug usage and payments to date (from the beginning of the year) should be automatically transferred from your old plan to the new one.

It's very important that this is done, because your records show

- ✔ The total cost of the drugs you've used since the beginning of the year, which determines your coverage level
- ✔ Your total out-of-pocket expenses since the beginning of the year, which count toward the limit that ends the doughnut hole (if you fall into it)
- ✔ How much of the deductible you've paid (if there's a deductible)

How the deductible is transferred depends on whether the old and new plans have deductibles and the costs of the drugs you've used since the beginning of the year. These are possibilities:

- **If your old plan had a deductible and you've already met it, you can't be asked to pay a deductible under your new plan.** For example, Plan X has a deductible of $295, and your total drug costs so far this year come to $350, so you've met your deductible and started receiving coverage. When you join Plan Y, which also has a $295 deductible, you don't pay this amount but receive coverage at once.

- **If your old plan had no deductible, but your new one does, you must meet this deductible before receiving coverage.** For example, Plan X has no deductible, and you've received coverage for $250 worth of drugs (what you *and* your plan have paid) so far this year. But Plan Y has a deductible of $295. So you must pay a balance of $45 ($295 – $250) in Plan Y before coverage begins.

- **If your old plan had a deductible and you haven't yet met it, it depends on whether the new plan has a deductible.** For example, Plan X has a deductible of $295, but your total drug costs so far this year come to $100. Plan Y has a lower deductible of $200. Because you haven't met your deductible in Plan X, you must pay the difference in Plan Y ($200 – $100 = $100). But if Plan Y has no deductible, you pay no more and your coverage starts immediately.

Medicare requires the old plan to transfer your payments record to the new plan within seven days of your coverage ending in the old plan. Still, checking is wise. When you receive the first Explanation of Benefits statement from your new plan, compare it with the last EOB from your old plan to ensure that your record has been transferred and that it correctly reflects the phase of coverage you're in — the deductible, initial coverage period, coverage gap, or catastrophic coverage. If you've mislaid your last EOB, ask the old plan for a copy. If you think that the info hasn't been transferred correctly, call Medicare at 800-633-4227 and file a complaint.

Dropping a Plan without Joining Another (Or Being Dropped)

Most people are allowed to drop out of a Part D plan voluntarily *only* during the standard enrollment periods or during some of the special enrollment periods specified earlier in this chapter. Clearly, if you switch plans, then technically you're disenrolling from the old one and enrolling in the new one — even if disenrollment is automatic as soon as you join another plan — and that's why the two actions are usually bundled together in Medicare's eyes.

But there may be circumstances in which you need to drop out of a Part D plan *without* joining another. And in a few situations, your plan can drop *you*. This section considers both scenarios. I also cover a special situation in which you may or may not be dropped — being late with your premium payments — and explain what to do if you've been disenrolled from your plan unfairly.

Being a plan dropout

You can get a special enrollment period to drop out of a Part D plan without joining another in the following circumstances.

If you move to a new job that has health benefits

You may need to drop out of a Part D plan if you take a new job that comes with health benefits and drug coverage. Here's what to do:

- ✔ Find out from your new employer's benefits office whether your new drug coverage is creditable. (*Creditable* means at least of equal value to Medicare drug coverage, as explained in Chapter 6.) If it's not, you need to ask whether keeping your present Part D plan could disqualify you from receiving health coverage from your employer. (I cover this possibility in detail, too, in Chapter 6.)

- ✔ Call or write to your current Part D plan, explain the situation, and ask to be disenrolled. You'll need to coordinate the date when your Part D coverage ends with the date when your new coverage begins.

  Your new employer's benefits office may make these arrangements for you — if so, it'll tell you.

If you become eligible for TriCare or VA drug coverage

You can get an SEP to drop out of your current plan if you start qualifying for military or veterans' benefits under the TriCare or Veterans Affairs programs. I describe benefits under these programs in Chapter 6.

If you move out of the United States

From your plan's point of view, going to live abroad just means that you're moving out of its service area. So the SEP is the same as if you were just moving somewhere else within the U.S., as explained in the earlier section "If you move permanently out of your plan's service area." But in this case, you won't be joining a new plan because Part D won't cover you when abroad. When you return to live permanently in the U.S., you can apply for another SEP to enroll in a Part D plan again, as explained in Chapter 8.

If you decide you just want out of Part D

You do *not* get a special enrollment period for this purpose. You're expected to wait until the November 15 to December 31 open enrollment period to do that. However, if you get an SEP to disenroll from a plan — for example, if you're moving out of its service area — there's no obligation to sign up for another plan. Similarly, there's no obligation to sign up for another plan if you come to the end of the year and decide not to re-enroll. In this case, you need to deliberately request disenrollment from the plan — otherwise, your enrollment automatically continues the following year. And, of course, there's no obligation to re-enroll if you stop paying premiums and get disenrolled by your plan.

If you drop out of a plan and don't enroll in another, Medicare will probably send a letter warning that going without drug coverage would mean incurring a late penalty if you decide to enroll again in Part D in the future. But what you really need to think about — beyond the threat of a late penalty — is what it could mean to be without coverage for even a few months. Regardless of your reasons for dropping out of Part D, you may want to take a look at Chapter 7, which explains the implications of going without drug coverage.

Being dropped by your plan

A plan *must* disenroll you in any of these circumstances:

- **You move permanently out of its service area.** If you don't let the plan know you've moved, it will eventually find out from Medicare or from returned mail. The plan must try to confirm that the move is permanent, but if it can't contact you within six months, or receives no response, it must then disenroll you. (But if it confirms that your move is only temporary, it must continue your coverage.)

- **You are imprisoned.** The plan must disenroll you (because you can't be enrolled in Part D when incarcerated) after confirming the situation from public records.

- **You lose your eligibility for Medicare.** This can happen in these specific circumstances:

  - Your eligibility for Medicare is based on disability (including blindness or end-stage renal disease), but your disability ceases.

  - You have Part A (hospital insurance) only because you're buying it (as explained in Chapter 1). But you must also be enrolled in Part B (doctors' and outpatient services) to qualify. So if you stop paying either Part A or Part B premiums (or notify Social Security that you no longer want this coverage) your eligibility for Medicare (and Part D) ends.

✔ **You misrepresented other coverage you have.** If the plan receives evidence that you intentionally withheld or falsified information about coverage you have from elsewhere (such as an employer) — in other words, double-dipping — it must disenroll you, but *only* with Medicare's approval. Your coverage stops on the first day of the month after you're notified of the disenrollment.

✔ **You die.** At this point, you're done worrying about Part D! But for the benefit of family members: They can inform the plan, but it won't act until it's received an official death notification from the Social Security Administration via Medicare. Disenrollment takes effect on the last day of the month of the death. The plan must refund any premiums paid beyond that date.

A plan *can* (at its discretion) drop you in these circumstances:

✔ **You don't pay your premiums in a timely manner.** Because so many circumstances affect whether you're dropped from a plan when you're late with premium payments, I cover this possibility in more detail in the next section.

✔ **You "engage in disruptive behavior."** Medicare doesn't define exactly what this phrase means, except to describe it as behavior that "substantially impairs" the plan's ability to provide services to you or any other of its members. The plan can't drop you for this reason without first trying to resolve the problem, submitting thorough documentation to Medicare, and receiving Medicare's approval to disenroll you. The plan must also notify you of your right to appeal the decision (see Chapter 19 for details on appeals). Depending on the situation, Medicare may also grant a special enrollment period for you to switch to another plan without loss of coverage.

✔ **You allow someone else to use your plan card to obtain services or prescription drugs, or the information on your enrollment form was fraudulent.** The plan can terminate your coverage the first day of the month after it notifies you of disenrollment. The plan must inform Medicare, which will investigate the fraud.

A special case: Knowing what can happen when you don't pay your premiums

If you stop paying your premiums, or get behind with them, what happens next depends on your plan's policy. Under Medicare rules, your plan can choose to do any of the following:

✔ Nothing — in other words, allow your coverage to continue

✔ Disenroll you after giving you a grace period and notice

✔ Send you a letter inviting you to contact the plan if you receive Medicaid and/or Extra Help and are having difficulty paying the premium

Understanding when a plan can't disenroll you

There are two situations in which you *can't* be disenrolled from your plan for not paying premiums, regardless of its policy:

✔ **If you've asked for premiums to be paid out of your Social Security check:** The plan must work with Medicare to investigate why Social Security hasn't deducted the premiums or, if it has, why the plan hasn't received them. Whatever the reason, the plan can't disenroll you while you're considered to be in a state of *premium withhold* — that is, your premiums are being taken out of your Social Security check *or* you've asked for them to be deducted automatically in this way. Only if you change to being billed directly for your premiums can the plan ask you to pay the premiums and, if necessary, disenroll you if you don't pay.

✔ **If your full premium is paid by a State Pharmacy Assistance Program (SPAP) or another sponsor:** The plan must work with the SPAP or the sponsor (such as an employer or union that pays Part D premiums) to receive the premiums.

Receiving a warning of disenrollment and a grace period

Part D plans can't stop anybody's coverage without warning. A plan must first send proper notice of its intent to disenroll you and inform you of its *grace period* — a length of time that gives you the opportunity to pay the overdue premium(s).

The grace period must be at least one calendar month — though plans may choose to give longer periods, such as two or three months. The grace period begins on the first day of the month for which a premium is unpaid. Plans also have two options on how to deal with disenrollment after a grace period ends:

✔ **Single grace periods:** If one or more overdue premiums haven't been paid in full during the grace period, the plan can terminate coverage at the end of that period.

For example, Harry is in a plan with a two-month grace period. He fails to pay a premium due June 1, ignores the warning notice from the plan, and fails to pay the next premium too. His grace period is June and July. Because he doesn't pay the two premiums he owes by July 31, his coverage stops on August 1. (If he pays only one of the premiums by July 31, his coverage still stops on August 1. If he pays both premiums by that date, his coverage continues.)

✔ **"Rollover" grace periods:** These are more flexible arrangements that a plan can choose to provide. If more than one premium is owed, but you pay one premium during the grace period, this grace period stops, and the plan sends notice of a new grace period. This process continues until *either* you pay off all the owed premiums in full *or* you fail to make any payment during a grace period, at which time the plan can dis-enroll you.

For example, Maureen is in a plan with a two-month rollover grace period. She fails to pay a premium due June 1 and ignores the warning notice from her plan. Her grace period is June and July. In July she pays the June premium, but not the one for July. She gets another warning notice and another grace period for July and August. In August, she pays the July premium, but not the one for August. Her next grace period is August and September. Despite warning notices, she doesn't make a payment during this time, so her coverage stops on October 1. (If she pays for one premium during this time, her coverage and the rollover grace periods continue. If she pays both overdue premiums during this time, she's no longer in default and her coverage continues intact.)

Your plan's policy on disenrollment for not paying premiums and on grace periods must be clearly set out in your Evidence of Coverage. The plan is also required to inform you of these policies in its warning letters. If your grace period expires, the plan must send you a letter saying it's disenrolling you and giving the date when your coverage will end. The plan has the right to take action to recover the premiums you haven't paid — and/or the right not to re-enroll you until you've paid all premiums that you owe.

If you're disenrolled from a Part D plan because you haven't paid your premiums, you can re-enroll (or enroll in another plan) *only* during the November 15 to December 31 enrollment period. So you may go without drug coverage for several months, which may incur a late penalty (as explained in Chapter 8) when you sign up again.

If you and your spouse are enrolled in the same plan and pay your premiums by check, it's best to send separate checks for each monthly premium or, if you send a single check, clearly indicate on it that the payment covers both premiums. Otherwise, one of you may be mistakenly disenrolled.

Taking action if you've been disenrolled unfairly

Mistakes happen. Here are some examples:

✔ **They thought you were dead, and you're not!** This happens a bit more often than you'd think. It's most often due to an error in the Social Security files — in which case, your Social Security check has likely stopped arriving, too. Sometimes it's an error in Medicare's records.

✔ **They thought you lost your entitlement to Medicare, and you haven't.** Again, this can be due to an error in the official files.

✔ **They thought you'd moved away from your home area, and you haven't.** This may happen if you spend part of the year away from home, even if you're enrolled in a Part D plan at your permanent address and have a plan that allows you to fill prescriptions at in-network pharmacies anywhere in the country. This is a mistake made by your plan.

✔ **They disenrolled you by mistake.** Computer systems can throw up wrong information in a number of situations, due to entry errors or time lags. For example, if you enroll in another plan during the November–December open enrollment period, and then change your mind and re-enroll in your old plan — and you do so, as allowed, before the end of that period — you shouldn't be dropped from the old plan. If you are dropped, it's a mistake.

If you think you've been dropped from your plan unfairly, call Medicare at 800-633-4227 and say that you want to challenge the disenrollment. Medicare will investigate the situation. You should also call the plan and say that you want to remain enrolled. The plan must then tell you in writing that you should *continue to use its services* while your case is being investigated. If Medicare approves your challenge, your enrollment will be reinstated and backdated to the time you were dropped, so your coverage is unbroken. If you had to pay out of pocket for any services (such as filling prescriptions) in the meantime, the plan must reimburse you.

Conducting a Yearly Plan Review to Decide Whether to Stay or Switch

November. Time for raking leaves, travel plans, and turkey. It's a busy month as America prepares the pumpkin pies and gets ready for other holidays looming beyond the bustle of Thanksgiving. As if you didn't have enough to do, November is also the time when another pressing question arises: Should you stay with your current Part D plan next year, or should you switch?

Open enrollment from November 15 to December 31 allows everybody in Part D the opportunity to switch plans for the following year. But most people, in fact, don't even consider it. Well, I'm going to push against that trend — not to persuade you to switch, but to recommend that you look carefully at the changes your plan will make in its costs and benefits for next year and then compare them with what other plans are offering. Why do I want you to go to this trouble? Because *the plan that works best for you this year won't necessarily be your best deal next year.*

If you decide not to change plans, you don't have to do anything — you'll simply be re-enrolled automatically in your current plan for next year. But it's in your interests to arrive at that decision *after* you've considered the alternatives and not just because doing nothing seems the easiest option.

In the following sections, I explain how your plan can change and how you'll know about those changes, why it's worth shopping around to see what other plans are offering next year, and factors to bear in mind if you consider making a switch.

Reading your Annual Notice of Change to understand plan alterations

Almost every plan makes some changes for the new year. So the costs and benefits in place on December 31 may well be different on January 1. Here are the changes that *could*, though not necessarily *will*, occur:

- ✔ The plan may not be there next year. Plans sometimes withdraw from certain service areas, don't renew their contracts with Medicare, or, occasionally, go out of business or are terminated by Medicare.

- ✔ The insurance company that sponsors the plan may not offer this particular plan next year, but offers one or more different plans instead.

- ✔ The plan may alter its benefit design next year. For example, it may cease or start offering coverage in the doughnut hole (see Chapter 15), or it may change the structure of its tiers of charges for different drugs.

- ✔ The plan may change the amount it charges for premiums, deductibles, and co-pays — or switch drugs to different tiers so the co-pays change.

- ✔ The plan may alter its *formulary* (the list of drugs it covers) by dropping some drugs or adding others.

- ✔ The plan may change the restrictions it places on some drugs (prior authorization, quantity limits, and step therapy; see Chapter 4) by lifting them from some drugs and imposing them on others.

How will you know if any of these changes will affect you? In the case of the first possibility — that your plan won't exist next year — the plan (or maybe Medicare) will notify you in good time. And in that case, you'll have to enroll in another plan to continue coverage. For other changes, the plan must send you details in a document called the *Annual Notice of Change* (ANOC). It's arguably the most important mailing you'll receive from your Part D plan each year, and you should definitely read it. (See the nearby sidebar to find out what happened to someone who *didn't* read it.)

The plan must ensure that you get your ANOC no later than October 31. If you're new to Medicare and, for that reason, enroll in a Part D plan for the first time between October 31 and November 30 during your initial enrollment period, the plan must send the ANOC together with its Explanation of Benefits in its enrollment packet. If you don't receive an ANOC by the right date, call your plan and ask for it.

Beware of ignoring your Annual Notice of Change

It's really important to read the ANOC! Here are two examples of what happened to someone who didn't and someone who did:

✔ Suzie didn't read her ANOC and stayed with the same plan. The full impact didn't sink in until the following summer, and then she e-mailed me, very steamed. "I deliberately chose this plan because it covered me in the doughnut hole," she wrote. "Now I'm in it, and they won't pay. I feel I've been tricked!" When I explained that her plan's benefit design had changed at the beginning of the year — no longer giving gap coverage — and that the ANOC she'd received the previous October warned her of the changes, Suzie fessed up that she hadn't read it. "I won't make that mistake again," she said.

✔ Thomas began flipping through his ANOC without much interest, but then did a double-take when he saw that his plan's premium would be raised by $15 a month the following year. That made him look more closely at the whole document. He found the co-pays for two of his brand-name drugs would also go up, from $52 to $60 a month. So Thomas used Medicare's online plan finder to find out what he'd pay out of pocket for other Part D plans in the coming year, and switched to the one he felt would give him the best deal.

Comparing plans — yes, all over again!

I can hear the groans. No, no, not again! Of course, it's your choice to go to the trouble of comparing Part D plans this year and every year. But in my opinion — and, actually, all consumer advocates agree on this — shopping around is well worth it. Here's why:

✔ It's not just *your* plan that may change its costs and benefits — so will all the others. A plan you decided against last year may offer a better deal next year — for example, a reduced premium, lower co-pays, fewer restrictions, or even better coverage in the doughnut hole.

✔ If most plans in your area change their costs, this may alter the equation of which plan will charge you least overall. As I emphasize in Chapter 10, the specific drugs you use determine your out-of-pocket expenses in any plan. Only running the numbers again will show which plan offers you the best deal *next* year.

✔ Your personal set of drugs may have changed during the past year. That too alters the equation of which plan offers the best deal next year.

✔ If you don't take any drugs and have opted for the plan with the lowest premium (as suggested in Chapter 7), check whether your current plan or another will have the lowest premium next year.

✔ If you compare plans and decide to stay with the one you have, you'll have the reassurance of *knowing* that it's still the best one for you.

I'll throw in another reason why comparing plans every year is worthwhile if you use the online Medicare Prescription Drug Plan Finder. The more often you do it, the easier it gets. After you have the routine down, it may take only a few minutes to decide that your current plan is still the one for you or that another is better.

Convinced? If so, turn to Chapter 10 for a step-by-step guide to comparing Part D plans online, or for other ways of getting the same information.

Making your decision

If you're reading this section, I'm assuming that you've compared plan offerings for next year and are considering one or two alternatives to your current drug plan. Chapter 10 offers several suggestions for making a final choice among a shortlist of options — for example, checking convenient pharmacies, evaluating customer service, and being able to get prescriptions filled when you're away from home — which all apply here, too. But when you're deciding whether to switch plans, rather than choosing one for the first time, you need to consider a couple other points.

If you've won exceptions from your current plan

Did your current plan grant you an exception by covering a drug that isn't on its formulary? Or waive a restriction for any of your drugs because your doctor convinced the plan that it was necessary for your health, without the need for prior authorization quantity limits, or step therapy? If so, you need to find out whether your plan will allow these same exceptions to carry over into next year. Some plans do. Others may require you to apply for them again in the new year. The plan's ANOC should clearly say what its policy is on this point. If it doesn't, call the plan and ask for it in writing.

Of course, if your plan allows your exceptions to be carried over, that would save you hassle and be a big factor in deciding to stay with this plan next year. If it doesn't, you have nothing to lose by changing to another plan. But in considering another plan, be sure to check its restrictions. They may be imposed on the same drugs — or on different ones you take.

If you're considering a switch to a Medicare private health plan

If you're thinking of switching from traditional Medicare and a stand-alone drug plan to a Medicare Advantage plan, you need to compare its medical costs and benefits as well as its drug coverage (see Chapter 9).

What about your Medigap supplementary insurance policy, if you have one? When you've dropped Medigap insurance to join a Medicare heath plan for the *first time,* your first 12 months in the plan is regarded as a trial period. During this time, you can get a special enrollment period to switch back to traditional Medicare and buy a Medigap policy with the same company, on the same terms you had before. Otherwise, you can still buy a new policy, but it will likely cost more than your previous one. Here are some examples:

- ✔ Erica turned 65 in 2005, enrolled in traditional Medicare, and bought a Medigap policy. But in 2007, she joined a Medicare private health plan and gave up her Medigap insurance. After several months, she decided this was a mistake. Because she'd been in the health plan only a year — and because this was the only one she'd ever been enrolled in — she got back her Medigap insurance with the same company, on the same terms she had before.

- ✔ When he turned 65 in 1996, Enrico signed up for traditional Medicare and bought a Medigap policy. In 1999, he joined a Medicare health plan and gave up his Medigap. But at the end of the year, the plan stopped doing business in his area and he had to return to traditional Medicare. Because he'd been in the plan only a year, he was able to get back his Medigap policy on the same terms. In 2006, Enrico decided to try a health plan again. But this time he wasn't happy with it and returned to traditional Medicare for 2007. Because he'd been enrolled in a Medicare health plan back in 1999, he wasn't able to get back his old Medigap policy on the same terms. He took out a new policy, but because he was older now with more health problems, it cost him more.

Chapter 18

Staying in Long-Term Care (Or Helping Someone Who Is)

*T*he phrase *long-term care* covers several different living situations. It includes everything from staying in a nursing home through being in various kinds of assisted living facilities (where people can live independently but with access to support services) to living at home with support from personal caregivers and community services.

In most of these situations, the rules for Medicare Part D drug coverage are no different than those described in the rest of this book. But this chapter focuses on some special protections and rights — and things to consider — in regard to Part D for people in two types of long-term care. If one of the following situations applies to you, then you can't afford to skip this chapter:

✔ You're living temporarily or permanently in a nursing home or another institutional setting (such as a rehabilitation hospital or unit, long-term care hospital, or psychiatric hospital or unit) that offers round-the-clock nursing care and help with daily activities.

✔ You're staying in a skilled nursing facility (which may be located in a nursing home or a hospital) for needed care after an illness or injury.

For all these situations, I use the term *nursing home* throughout this chapter. And I need to define another term here, too. That term is *you.* In this chapter I address "you" (the patient), while understanding that many people going into nursing homes are too frail or sick to be able to cope with Part D issues. So when I say "you," I expect that, in many cases, you (the reader) will actually be a family member, friend, or other personal caregiver helping a patient who's in a nursing home.

In this chapter, I explain special Part D rules and rights that apply to people in nursing homes when paying for prescriptions or changing plans. I describe a special kind of Medicare health plan that focuses on the needs of people in nursing homes, and another Medicare program that provides comprehensive care designed to keep people out of nursing homes for as long as possible. Finally, I suggest sources of help.

Reviewing Your Drug Coverage When You Enter a Nursing Home

When you first go into a nursing home, it's likely that the last thing on your mind (or your caregiver's) is whether you need to do anything about your Part D plan. You have too many other practical and perhaps emotional issues to think about. And if you're already in a plan, why worry?

Well, you need to consider a few points about Part D, even at this difficult time. In the following sections, I explain why you need to find out how your meds are covered in the nursing home and why, in some circumstances, it may be wise or even necessary to change from your current Part D plan to another.

Understanding how your drugs will be covered

In most cases, while you're in a nursing home, your meds are covered under the usual conditions of your Medicare Part D plan (or under any alternative drug coverage you have, such as an employer or union health insurance plan; see Chapter 6 for details about different types of drug coverage). The following sections note three exceptions.

If you receive the Medicare skilled nursing facility benefit

If you're receiving the Medicare skilled nursing facility benefit, your prescription drugs are covered under Medicare Part A (hospital insurance) for a certain amount of time, and *your Part D plan isn't involved.*

Many people don't realize that Medicare does *not* usually cover what the agency calls *custodial care* in a nursing home. That means room and board, nursing care, and help with daily living activities. But the Medicare skilled nursing facility (SNF) benefit is an exception. To qualify, you need to be enrolled in Medicare Part A. You must also have spent at least three days as an inpatient in a hospital *and* need skilled care for nursing and rehabilitation services related to the illness or injury that put you into the hospital. A physician must refer you for SNF care under this benefit and certify that you need it as a matter of medical necessity. For example, a need for intravenous injections and physical therapy are reasons for this kind of continuing care.

If you qualify for this benefit, Medicare Part A covers all of your care in a Medicare-certified skilled nursing facility (either in a nursing home or hospital) for up to 100 days.

- For the first 20 days, Medicare Part A pays for all of your care needs — including the cost of your room and board, help with daily living activities, and prescription drugs — and you pay nothing.

- From 21 to 100 days in the facility, you're responsible for a co-pay (up to $128 a day in 2008).

If you're still in the SNF after the 100 days are up, you'll be responsible for all costs, and Medicare pays nothing. (However, a *different* illness or injury that requires skilled care after another three-day stay in the hospital would qualify you for another 100-day benefit period.) So from day 101, if you have Part D drug coverage, you must then get your prescription drugs through your Part D plan. Make sure, well before the SNF benefit runs out, that the plan covers your prescriptions (as explained in the later section "Asking important coverage questions on Day One") to prevent any interruption of treatment.

Just because the SNF benefit lasts for up to 100 days doesn't mean you can choose to stay in the facility that long. Your continuing eligibility to stay there is reviewed regularly and depends on whether your physician and/or other medical professionals (such as physical therapists) consider that further days or weeks at the facility will result in an improvement of your condition. So if your condition reaches a *plateau* — a point when the illness or injury isn't expected to get any better — you lose your eligibility for the SNF benefit and must leave the facility, even if you don't feel better and actually need continuing care.

If you receive full Medicaid benefits

If your state pays for your medical benefits under the Medicaid program and you're enrolled in Medicare Part D for your prescription drug coverage, you're probably already receiving Part D's Extra Help benefit (as explained in Chapter 5) and paying small co-pays for your meds. After a month in the nursing home, though, you should no longer pay *anything* for your meds for the rest of your stay. (In the event that you continue to be charged co-pays, call Medicare at 800-633-4227 or call your plan to get it to correct the mistake. Any undue payments you've made must be refunded to you.)

Medicaid also pays most of the costs of Medicaid-certified nursing homes for people with low incomes and few resources. Eligibility varies from state to state. Many patients who enter nursing homes pay the costs themselves or through long-term care insurance, but they become eligible for Medicaid when their savings are used up (or their insurance runs out and they have no savings to fall back on). In this situation, you receive a small allowance for personal needs. You're not expected to pay for prescription drugs out of this allowance — again, your Part D plan must not charge you anything for the drugs it covers. If the plan doesn't cover all the drugs you need, Medicaid may cover them instead (as explained in Chapter 5).

Ensuring all of your meds are covered when you enter a nursing home

Very often, people go into nursing homes after being in the hospital, where they're prescribed more or different drugs than they were taking before being hospitalized. For this reason, and so that your treatment isn't interrupted, your Part D plan must cover all the meds that you're taking when you first enter the nursing home for at least 90 days — even if the plan normally doesn't cover some of these drugs or restricts access to them. Some plans extend this transitional period for up to 180 days after their enrollees go into nursing homes. Your plan can tell you how long the transitional period lasts.

Asking important coverage questions on Day One

Physicians who care for people in nursing homes say there are good reasons for patients (or their caregivers) to consider their Part D plan carefully and find out whether it'll continue to work for them in these changed circumstances *as soon as possible after admission, or even before.* "Ideally," one physician told me, "they should do this on Day One." These are the questions to ask and why you should ask them:

- **Are any of the pharmacies that the nursing home uses also in my Part D plan's pharmacy network?** Nursing homes use special long-term care (LTC) pharmacies that dispense prescriptions in special packages — the drugs come in single doses, individually sealed, instead of the usual containers. This is for hygiene and safety reasons in a setting where nurses administer a great many different drugs to many patients. LTC pharmacies may be large companies that supply only nursing homes and other LTC facilities or, in rural areas, local retail pharmacies that can supply properly sealed medicines. All Part D plans must include LTC pharmacies in their networks. But if the ones your nursing home uses are *not* in your plan's network, the plan most likely won't cover your drugs. The nursing home won't pay for your meds if your plan doesn't cover them, even if you can't afford them.

- **Does my Part D plan cover the medicines that I'm taking *now?*** As explained earlier in this chapter, your Part D plan must cover all the drugs you're taking when you first enter the nursing home for at least 90 days. But it's wise to check whether the plan will continue to cover your prescriptions (especially if they're new ones) after this transitional supply has run out — and, if necessary, take steps to avoid having to pay full price for them at that time.

You can ask the nursing home administrator or social worker for the names of the long-term care pharmacies it uses; then call your plan and ask whether those pharmacies are in your plan's network. If you're not sure, the administrator or social worker can also tell you whether Medicare Part A is covering your stay (and your drugs) under the skilled nursing facility benefit. (I explain this benefit earlier in this chapter.) To find out whether your Part D plan covers your new prescriptions or imposes any conditions restricting your access to them (as explained in Chapter 4) — you should call the plan.

If you're *not* covered by the Part A skilled nursing benefit (or if it's run out), you may be facing at least one situation that requires action:

- ✔ **The LTC pharmacy isn't in your Part D plan's network.** You need to change your plan, as explained in the next section.

- ✔ **Your plan doesn't cover some or all of the drugs you now need or restricts immediate access to them.** You can ask your attending doctor whether any alternative drugs your plan does cover would work as well for you (as explained in Chapters 4 and 16). Or you can ask your attending doctor to request an exception to the plan's policy (see Chapter 4). In this case, it's important for the doctor to explain to the plan representative that you're in a nursing home and to fully describe why this particular drug is medically necessary for you and why an alternative covered by your plan wouldn't work as well or could cause additional medical problems. Other ways of dealing with this situation may be

   - Finding out whether Medicaid (if you're enrolled in the program) will pay for drugs your plan doesn't cover. Ask the nursing home social worker or a counselor at your State Health Insurance Assistance Program (SHIP) to help you. (For your local SHIP's contact information, see Appendix B.)

   - Switching to a Part D plan that covers your drugs or imposes no, or fewer, restrictions, as explained in the next section.

Switching to Another Plan

In general, the process of switching plans when you're in a nursing home is the same as it is for anybody in Part D (see Chapter 17). But when you enter a nursing home, you immediately have rights that most other folks don't have. In this section, I explain those rights and some additional tips. I also describe two special types of Medicare health plans that are available in some areas: Special Needs Plans and PACE plans.

Knowing your rights for changing plans

You have an absolute right to change your Part D plan, if you wish, when you enter or leave a nursing home, and at any time during your stay there. In other words, you don't have to wait until the general enrollment period at the end of the year. Instead, you automatically receive a special enrollment period (SEP) to make the change. You don't have to apply for this SEP or disenroll from your current plan — just enroll in a new plan, explaining the situation.

Recognize, too, that this right to switch plans applies if you're in any Medicare- or Medicaid-certified *institutional facility* — an umbrella term that sounds grim but actually comprises nursing homes, skilled nursing facilities, rehabilitation hospitals or units, long-term care hospitals, psychiatric hospitals or units, or intermediate care facilities for the mentally retarded.

Table 18-1 shows how often you can change Part D plans when you enter, live in, or leave any of the preceding facilities and when your new coverage starts.

Table 18-1	Switching Part D Plans in Long-Term Care Facilities	
Your Situation	**When You Can Change Plans**	**Your New Coverage Begins**
When you move into a facility and while you're living in one	Once a month	The first day of the month after you submit your completed application
When you move out of the facility	Within two months of leaving the facility	The first day of the month after you submit your completed application

Choosing and enrolling in a new Part D plan

Having the right to switch to a different plan doesn't overcome the fact that it's a hassle if you need to do so — especially when you, the patient, are too frail or sick to go through the process. In such circumstances, you'd think that the simplest way would be to ask the nursing home staff or your attending physician to point you to the plan they think would suit you best. But Medicare *prohibits* these professionals from doing so. This rule is intended to protect patients and prevent the possibility of doctors and nursing facilities receiving financial kickbacks for steering patients to a particular Part D plan.

But consumer and patient groups, long-term care physicians, and pharmacists point out that the rule lays a burden on many patients at a time when they are at their most vulnerable and unable to cope with it.

So if you're a family member, friend, or personal caregiver of the patient, you're likely to be the one helping to choose his new Part D plan. You may be able to choose a new plan by using Medicare's online Prescription Drug Plan Finder, following the guidance I give in Chapter 10. If you don't want to go online to compare drug plans, you can call Medicare or any of the other sources of help listed in Chapter 10.

Although nursing home staff, physicians, and pharmacists are banned from steering anybody to any one plan, they may be willing to do an objective search on the Medicare plan finder to identify the three or four plans that would suit the patient's needs best (according to the drugs needed), and then you can make a final choice from that shortlist.

After you've found a suitable plan, the patient needs to be enrolled in it, and he must sign the enrollment application. Or, if the patient is incapable of signing, you (as caregiver) may be able to do so. If you already have *durable power of attorney* — the right to make medical and financial decisions on the patient's behalf, according to the laws of your state — you can sign the enrollment form as explained in Chapter 12.

Checking out two alternative plan options

Two types of Medicare health plans are specially designed for people who are either in nursing homes or are eligible for nursing home care. These plans may be worth considering, according to your circumstances and preferences, if the plans are available in your area.

Special Needs Plans

Special Needs Plans (SNPs) are Medicare private health plans (usually HMOs or PPOs). Each one serves the specific needs of one group of people in three categories (see Chapter 9). One of these categories is for people who have been (or expect to be) in long-term care facilities, such as nursing homes or other institutions, for 90 days or longer.

SNPs, which came into existence in 2004, are still somewhat experimental. In 2008, Congress authorized them to continue through 2010, but also barred any new ones from setting up in 2009 and 2010 until Congress has again reviewed the program and decided whether to continue it. Meanwhile, existing SNPs may accept more enrollees. Only about half of Medicare beneficiaries have access to SNPs that serve nursing home residents.

SNPs for people in nursing homes and other types of long-term care (which include assisted living facilities) are supposed to offer ways to coordinate care and services. For example, an SNP may provide a case worker or care manager who helps patients coordinate Medicare and Medicaid benefits, links patients with needed community services, advises on managing health conditions, and maybe helps solve problems with drug coverage. These services, and their quality, vary a great deal among different plans. By 2010 all SNPs must provide a care management plan for each enrollee.

If you're considering joining an SNP for nursing home patients, find out not only its costs and benefits, but whether it covers the providers that you prefer — all the factors relating to Medicare health plans that I cover in Chapter 9. The SNP should cover most of the meds commonly used by nursing home patients. But it'll still have a formulary, so check that it covers the drugs you need.

You can enroll in this type of SNP (if one is available to you) when you enter a nursing home, regardless of the time of year. Your coverage starts on the first day of the month after you enroll. But if your special needs status changes so that you're no longer eligible for this kind of plan, you can switch to another Medicare health plan with drug coverage or to traditional Medicare and a stand-alone drug plan. This SEP begins in the month your special needs status changes and ends up to three months after you're disenrolled from the SNP.

You can find out whether there's an SNP for nursing homes in your area by calling Medicare (800-633-4227) or by going to its online plan finder at www. medicare.gov. You may also want to take advice from your State Health Insurance Assistance Program (SHIP), as explained in the later section "Getting Help for Yourself or Your Loved One."

Programs of All-Inclusive Care for the Elderly

Programs of All-Inclusive Care for the Elderly (PACE) is a Medicare program that helps people who'd otherwise need nursing home care to continue living in their own homes or with their families in the community for as long as possible. It provides comprehensive medical and social services — including home care, day care, physical therapy, dentistry, meals, social work counseling, transportation, and many other services. It also provides hospital and nursing home care should you need it. You can't choose your own doctors in a PACE plan. Instead, you're assigned a primary care physician who is one of a team of healthcare professionals working with you and your family to help maintain your overall health. The team also provides support to your caregivers. PACE programs include Medicare Part D drug coverage, so you don't have to join a separate drug plan.

You can join a PACE program if

- ✔ You're 55 or older

- ✔ You're certified by your state as being eligible for a nursing home level of care, after an assessment by the PACE plan's care team

- ✔ A program serves the area where you live and is accepting new enrollees

✔ You're enrolled in Medicare *or* Medicaid

✔ You're able to live safely in the community with the help of PACE

PACE has no deductibles or co-payments for any service, care, or prescription drug approved by your care team. Other costs depend on your situation:

✔ If you qualify for Medicaid, you pay a small monthly payment — and nothing for long-term care if you need it. The PACE plan determines the amount of the payment.

✔ If you don't qualify for Medicaid, you pay a monthly premium to cover the long-term care part of the PACE benefit and also a monthly premium for Medicare Part D drugs, in each case paying what the plan requires.

If you're eligible for an available PACE, you can join it at any time. If you're enrolled in Medicare, you get a special enrollment period to leave traditional Medicare or a Medicare private health plan to join the program. (You can't be in either of these programs at the same time as being enrolled in a PACE.) Also, you can leave a PACE any time you want to switch to traditional Medicare or a Medicare health plan.

To find out whether a PACE exists in your area, call Medicare (800-633-4227) or go to www.cms.hhs.gov/PACE/LPPO/list.asp. If you're interested in joining it, contact the plan to arrange a home visit with you or your caregiver, or a visit to the PACE center. The plan will schedule a meeting between you and its care team for a medical and social assessment that determines your eligibility for the program. For more on how PACE works, go to the National PACE Association's Web site at www.npaonline.org.

Getting Help for Yourself or Your Loved One

Don't hesitate to get help for yourself or your loved one; some problems you just can't cope with on your own. Here are some resources:

✔ **Your State Health Insurance Assistance Program (SHIP):** Whenever you need information or help with a problem with Medicare or Medicaid, including Part D and long-term care issues, your best bet by far is to phone your local SHIP immediately. This way, you get free, personal counseling from experts familiar with your area. For the phone number of your state SHIP, go to Appendix B.

✔ **Medicare long-term care information:** Medicare's Web site (www.medicare.gov) provides detailed information on different types of long-term care. On the home page, click "Long Term Care." The site also has useful info on all nursing homes in the country that are certified by Medicare or Medicaid, including details of how well (or not) they perform. Click "Nursing Home Compare." You can get the same info by calling the Medicare help line at 800-633-4227 and asking the customer service rep to search for details of the nursing homes you're interested in and send you printouts.

✔ **Your state long-term care ombudsman:** This is the person to contact if you have complaints or concerns about the care you receive in an LTC facility or are trying to find a facility. The ombudsman is trained to troubleshoot problems on behalf of people in nursing homes, board-and-care homes, and assisted living, and acts as their advocate. Every state, plus the District of Columbia, Puerto Rico, and Guam, has an LTC ombudsman. To find the name and phone number of the ombudsman for your area, go to the National Long-Term Care Ombudsman Resource Center's Web site at www.ltcombudsman.org. Or call your state Office of Aging (in the state pages of the telephone directory) for the number.

✔ **Your Area Agency on Aging:** These public services are provided by the federal Administration on Aging to help older people maintain their independence and remain in their community. Each agency acts as a resource center for linking seniors and caregivers with local services and support groups. Visit the national Web site at www.aoa.gov/eldfam/eldfam.aspx or call your local Agency on Aging at the number in the state pages of your phone book.

✔ **Family Caregiver Alliance:** This long-established organization offers programs at the national, state, and local levels to support families who provide long-term care at home for relatives or friends. Among FCA's numerous services, check out its Family Caregiver Locator to find many resources for caregivers in every state and its Caregiver Toolkit, a large resource of practical information. Visit its Web site at www.caregiver.org or call 800-445-8106.

✔ **National Family Caregivers Association:** This group supports, educates, and acts as a national advocate for more than 50 million Americans who care for sick or disabled elderly relatives. It also offers local training for improving at-home caregiving skills. Visit its Web site at www.nfcacares.org or call 800-896-3650.

✔ **AARP's Caregiver Web site:** The world's largest nonprofit organization for people age 50 and over, AARP maintains a Web site that provides practical information for caregivers of all kinds. Go here for an estimate of costs for nursing homes, assisted living facilities, home health aides, and adult day care in your state. Among many articles and tools, check out "Prepare to Care," a planning guide for new caregivers, and "Long-Distance Care-Giving," on what to do if a loved one far away needs help. Visit the Web site at www.aarp.org/families/caregiving.

Chapter 19

You Have Rights: How to Holler and (If Necessary) Holler Louder

. . . .

In This Chapter

▶ Starting with a game plan

▶ Knowing how to file a grievance or coverage determination request

▶ Appealing an unfavorable decision

▶ Getting help to make an appeal

. . . .

Sooner or later, you may have some sort of issue with your Part D plan. Note that I'm saying *may,* not *will.* But you should know that you have every right to challenge your plan's decisions — or even its ways of doing business — if you don't agree with them. You can try to resolve a variety of problems through different procedures, such as filing a formal complaint about your plan, requesting a coverage determination to get the prescription meds you need, or appealing a decision you disagree with. In this chapter, I walk you through these procedures and suggest ways to seek free professional help in making appeals.

Having a Game Plan in Mind

Before you embark on filing a grievance, a coverage request, or an appeal, I want to suggest a general game plan to make the process easier:

✔ **Have a rough idea of the kind of complaint you want to make.** The plan may categorize your complaint as an inquiry, a grievance, or a coverage determination, depending on whether you complain about

  • **One of the plan's policies in general terms:** In this case, the plan can treat your complaint as an inquiry and respond with a simple explanation of the policy.

- **How a policy affects you personally:** In this case, the plan must treat your complaint as a grievance or (if it concerns coverage or payment for a drug you need) as a coverage determination and take the appropriate action.

✔ **Put your problem in writing.** You can file a grievance or request a coverage determination just by calling your plan. However, if possible, put your complaint or request in writing so you have a record. If the matter is urgent, fax your complaint to the plan instead of mailing it. Be sure to date all communications.

✔ **Gather any documents that support your case.** Such documents include statements from your doctor, pharmacy receipts for drugs you think the plan should pay for, and so on, depending on the situation.

✔ **Keep all paperwork.** Retain copies of all letters or forms you send to the plan, letters you receive from the plan or a higher appeal body, transmission records of any faxes, and receipts and tracking numbers of any correspondence you send by registered mail. This way you have a paper trail if the plan tries to dodge your filing.

✔ **Make notes of conversations:** Keep track of all the people you talk to at your plan or at Medicare. Write down their names, the date and time you spoke to them, and their phone numbers. Having notes of your conversation gives you evidence that may prove valuable.

✔ **Try to use the right terminology.** Consumer advocates who help people with Part D appeals find that sometimes decisions are delayed or derailed simply because the consumer doesn't talk (or write) the same jargon that a plan uses. In this chapter, I tell you the correct terms for different situations. You don't have to commit them to memory — just know what they mean and have them handy when you need 'em.

✔ **Stick to the deadlines.** At every level of appeal, you have a certain length of time (usually 60 days) to file for a review of the previous decision. If it looks like you'll miss a deadline for good reason — such as sickness or a family crisis — you have the right to ask for an extension.

✔ **Don't give up.** If you think you're right and the plan is wrong, don't be put off by a "no" decision or feel intimidated by grand-sounding titles at higher appeal levels. The title "administrative law judge" may sound imposing, but ALJs more often decide in favor of consumers than plans. Therefore, if you have a reasonable case, you may just win it!

✔ **Get help if you need it.** You can designate anyone of your choice to help you, or to act on your behalf, in pursuing a complaint or an appeal. This person can be a relative, friend, consumer advocate, lawyer, physician, or anyone else willing to assist you. At higher levels of appeal or in tricky situations, it's best to seek help from someone experienced in dealing with Part D appeals on behalf of consumers, such as the advocates I suggest later in this chapter.

Filing a Grievance

A grievance covers many types of complaints — but *not* those that have anything to do with your plan covering your drugs or paying for them, which fall into the coverage determination category that I explain later in this chapter. Understanding the difference between the two is important, because a grievance is *not* open to further appeals.

What is a grievance?

A *grievance* is a complaint about any aspect of a plan's service or quality of care that requires some action from the plan to resolve. You can also file a grievance if the plan doesn't respond within a proper time frame to your request for any kind of coverage determination. Here are examples of situations when you may want to file a grievance:

- ✔ **Poor or unsatisfactory customer service:** You find it hard to get through to the plan on the phone, hang on hold for ages, or get disconnected. Plan representatives don't respond to questions satisfactorily, give wrong or inadequate answers, or are rude.

- ✔ **Misleading information:** You choose a plan on the basis of information — such as coverage or charges for your drugs — that turns out, after enrollment, to be untrue.

- ✔ **Absence of required notifications:** The plan doesn't send you required notices — such as its Annual Notice of Change (see Chapter 17), Explanation of Benefits statements (see Chapter 13), or warnings about formulary changes (see Chapter 4) — within the required time frames. Or you find the wording of notices or other written materials difficult to understand.

- ✔ **Problems at the pharmacy:** A pharmacy in your plan's network gives you the wrong medication, the wrong number of pills, or makes other mistakes in dispensing your drugs. You have to wait a long time to have your prescriptions filled, or a pharmacy staff member treats you rudely.

- ✔ **Poor quality of care for medical services:** You can't easily get appointments or have to wait too long for them. You have a problem with your care from doctors, nurses, hospitals, or other providers in the plan's network — including rude behavior and facility cleanliness.

- ✔ **Failure to transfer records:** You switch Part D plans during the year, and your old plan fails to send your coverage record to the new plan in good time.

- ✔ **Discrimination:** You feel that the plan treats you differently from its other enrollees or seems to be encouraging you to disenroll.

✔ **Receipt of unwanted marketing materials:** The company offering your plan sends you mailings that you didn't ask for and that are unrelated to the plan.

✔ **Tardy responses or decisions:** The plan fails to respond to your request for a coverage determination or an appeal, or it doesn't give you its decision within the required time frames. Or perhaps the plan denies your request for a fast coverage determination — in which case, the plan must make a decision within 24 hours.

How do you file a grievance?

To file a grievance, you can call the plan or write to it about your complaint. Look at the informational materials your plan sent you when you enrolled (I describe these materials in detail in Chapter 13). These documents give the appropriate phone numbers and address for filing a grievance, as well as an explanation of how to do so. You can also find this info on your plan's Web site.

You must file a grievance within 60 days of the incident that prompts it. You can file yourself or have someone else act on your behalf (as explained in the last section of this chapter). You may receive extra time, up to 14 days, for filing if you ask the plan for an extension of the 60-day time frame, for example if you're sick or have a family crisis during this period.

If you call about your complaint, the plan may be able to resolve it over the phone. Otherwise, the plan must tell you how to file a written grievance. In any event, the plan must give you a written response if you request it, if you complain in writing, or if the complaint involves a quality-of-care issue. The plan must respond no later than 30 days after receiving your complaint, or a lot sooner if the state of your health requires a fast decision. However, the plan may extend the 30-day period by up to 14 days if it needs more time to investigate your complaint — in which case, it must notify you.

A *Quality Improvement Organization* (QIO) is a panel of doctors and other health-care experts contracted by the federal government to monitor and improve care given to people receiving Medicare services. If you're complaining specifically about the quality of care you've received (whether under traditional Medicare, a Medicare private health plan, or a Part D plan), you have the right to file a griev-ance directly with a QIO, your plan, or both. The advantage of involving the QIO in your complaint is that the plan must then work with the QIO to resolve the problem. (But note that QIO complaints almost always involve *medical* services rather than problems with drug coverage.) Your plan must include the phone number and address of your state QIO in the enrollment materials it sends you. You can also call Medicare at 800-633-4227 (or 877-486-2048 for TDD users) for the number.

After the plan looks into your complaint, it should tell you what has been done to resolve it. If the plan decides that no action is needed — in other words, it doesn't think your complaint is justified — you can't appeal further. (However, if your complaint is a quality-of-care issue, the plan must inform you of your right to take it up with a QIO if you haven't already done so.) Alternatively, if the plan decides your complaint should be handled as a coverage determination request rather than a grievance, it must tell you how to go about doing that.

Requesting a Coverage Determination

Unlike a grievance (which I describe in the previous section), a *coverage determination* always relates to drug coverage or payment issues. You can ask for a coverage determination for both nonpayment-related issues (like requesting a nonformulary drug be covered) and payment-related issues (like asking to be reimbursed for going to an out-of-network pharmacy), as the following sections explain. (Should your Part D plan deny your request, you can appeal against the decision, as explained later in this chapter.)

Filing for a coverage determination when it comes to your meds

You may be standing at the pharmacy checkout before you discover that your Part D plan doesn't cover all of your drugs, or that it requires you to ask its permission before it'll cover certain ones. Your pharmacist may or may not give you a computer printout from the plan that states the reasons for this denial. Either way, you should contact the plan (using the phone number on your membership card) to make sure you understand why it isn't covering your drug(s). Alternatively, you may want your plan to charge a lower co-pay for a drug that's medically necessary for you.

You have the right to ask your plan to do the following (but be sure to always do so with your doctor's help, as I explain in Chapter 4):

- **Cover a drug not on its formulary:** You're asking for an exception to the plan's general policy and require a statement from your doctor explaining the medical reasons why you need the plan to cover this drug.

- **Waive a restriction:** You want the plan to put aside a restriction it has placed on one or more of your drugs — such as prior authorization, quantity limits, or step therapy.

✔ **Cover an excluded drug:** In most cases, plans have the right to refuse to cover any drugs that Medicare excludes from Part D. But sometimes Medicare pays for these drugs if they're prescribed for a specific medical reason that Medicare approves. If you're in this situation, you can ask the plan to cover the drug as an exception, with your doctor's support. (Chapter 4 lists excluded drugs and examples of times when Medicare is willing to pay for them.)

✔ **Charge you for a drug at a lower tier level:** If your doctor thinks that a nonpreferred, brand-name drug on your plan's formulary is the only one that will work effectively for you, you can ask for it to be covered at the plan's preferred-tier charge (see Chapter 3).

When you're filing for an exception, you need to ask your doctor (or another provider who can prescribe drugs) to support your case by sending a written statement to the plan. Your plan provides a form for this purpose. Under Medicare rules, the plan can't insist that your doctor use this form. Instead, it must accept any statement written on his letterhead. But using the form ensures that your doctor provides all the information that the plan requires. The address or fax number to which the statement should be sent is in your plan enrollment documents. Or you can call the plan for this information.

If your doctor thinks you need a decision immediately because your health may otherwise be at risk, he can ask for a fast decision, otherwise known as an *expedited* decision. Your plan must respond within 24 hours of receiving your doctor's request for an expedited decision — that's 24 hours by the clock, not business hours. Otherwise, the plan must respond within 72 hours (by the clock) of receiving the request.

Filing for a coverage determination when it comes to your hard-earned cash

You can ask your plan for a coverage determination in matters related to your pocketbook, as well as to your health. You don't need your doctor's support if

✔ **You think the plan is charging you at a higher tier level than it should:** Sometimes a plan moves a drug into a higher tier of charges. If this situation happens when you're already taking the drug, you have the right to continue paying the lower-cost tier rate for the rest of the year (see Chapter 3). If, instead, the plan charges you the new, higher rate, you can file for a coverage determination.

✔ **You want to be reimbursed for going to an out-of-network pharmacy:** Occasionally, you may have no choice but to go to a pharmacy outside your plan's network, as explained in Chapter 14. If you've done so for good reason and the plan doesn't reimburse the extra charges you've paid, you can file for a coverage determination. Be sure to send copies of the pharmacy receipts when making this request.

✔ **You want the plan to reimburse you for the cost of drugs you've already paid for:** This scenario may crop up in a number of situations. Perhaps confirmation of your enrollment in the plan was delayed, and in the meantime you paid for drugs out of pocket (as explained in Chapter 12), but your plan hasn't paid you back for its share of the cost. Or maybe you became eligible for Extra Help (or Medicaid, SSI, or a Medicare Savings Program) and should've been reimbursed for excess payments dating back to the time you applied, as explained in Chapter 5.

✔ **You don't think you've reached the doughnut hole, but your plan is charging you full price:** Look carefully at the Explanation of Benefits notices your plan has sent you and at your pharmacy receipts. Both show the plan's full price for the drugs, as well as your co-pay. The full price — that is, the combined amount that both you *and* your plan have paid from the beginning of the year — determines when you hit the doughnut hole, formally known as the coverage gap (see Chapter 15). If you think your plan's calculations are wrong, you can file for a coverage determination.

✔ **You believe you're through the doughnut hole and should be getting catastrophic coverage, but your plan is still charging you full price:** This situation is a dispute over your *TrOOP* — your true out-of-pocket expenses since the beginning of the year that determine when you get out of the doughnut hole. (Premiums and some other payments, including those for drugs purchased outside of your plan's pharmacy network, don't count toward TrOOP; see Chapters 3 and 15.) If you think your plan has calculated your TrOOP incorrectly, you can file for a coverage determination. Make sure to include copies of pharmacy receipts for all prescriptions you filled while in the doughnut hole.

If you're filing for a determination about any of these payment-related issues, then you don't need your doctor's help. You can file on the phone or (preferably) in writing either by submitting a letter or by using the plan's form. You can also download and print a Medicare form from www.cms.hhs.gov/MedPrescriptDrugApplGriev/Downloads/ModelCoverageDeterminationRequestForm.pdf.

The advantage of using a form is that it tells you what information is required. You can check off the box that applies to your situation. But if you call or write a letter instead, be sure to use the correct terminology. Say: "I want to request a coverage determination because . . ." Again, the plan should respond within 72 hours.

Anyone (a relative, friend, counselor, social worker, lawyer — basically whomever you appoint as your representative) can help you file for a payment-related coverage determination or make the request on your behalf. Be sure to call your plan to find out its requirements for appointing a representative. If you need free advice or help from a professional counselor, contact one of the organizations listed at the end of this chapter.

Dealing with your plan's response

After you've filed a coverage determination request, you should receive a decision quickly, within the time frames Medicare requires. But sometimes plans don't comply like they're supposed to. In the following sections, I explain what you can do if your plan doesn't respond promptly, and what to expect if your plan grants or denies your request.

If your plan doesn't respond within the required time frame

If your plan doesn't decide a coverage determination request within the required 24 hours (expedited) or 72 hours (standard), Medicare rules say that

✔ You can file a grievance with the plan (see "Filing a Grievance" earlier in this chapter).

✔ You can file a grievance with Medicare by calling its help line at 800-633-4227 (TTD: 877-486-2048).

✔ The plan should automatically refer your request to an Independent Review Entity (IRE) within 24 hours of failing to meet the required deadline. The IRE is normally the second level of appeal (as explained in the later section, "Level 2: Reconsideration by an Independent Review Entity"). But when a plan fails to decide a coverage determination in the first place, the usual next level of appeal (asking the plan to reconsider an unfavorable decision) is automatically skipped.

The Medicare Rights Center, which helps people file Part D appeals, suggests that in these circumstances, it's worth writing directly to the IRE yourself. Simply say:

> I assume that my Part D plan, [plan name], has forwarded to you my request for a coverage determination, because it has not responded to my request within the required time frame. I am asking for a coverage determination because [state reason]. I have enclosed documents to support my request.

Depending on the situation, these documents may include a copy of your doctor's statement requesting an exception, receipts from a pharmacy showing what you paid out of pocket, evidence that your plan has miscalculated your correct level of coverage, and the like. Advocates say that writing such a letter ensures that the IRE knows your plan hasn't acted on your request and may bring a faster decision. They also recommend filing a grievance either with Medicare or with the plan itself so the plan's delay is on record. (These complaints count when Medicare compiles its plan quality ratings, which are displayed in Medicare's online Prescription Drug Plan Finder.)

If your plan makes a decision in your favor

When a plan responds within the required time frame and grants your request, it has to make good on its favorable decision within a certain time:

✔ If the plan agrees to waive a restriction or cover a nonformulary or excluded drug, it must allow your prescription to be filled within 72 hours (standard) or 24 hours (expedited) of receiving your doctor's written statement.

✔ If the plan agrees to pay you back for a drug you've already paid for and received, it must send a payment to reimburse you no later than 30 days after receiving your request. (See the later section "Taking action if your plan has been told to pay up — but doesn't" on what to do if your plan doesn't send the payment within this time frame.)

If your plan refuses your request

Should your plan decide not to grant your request for a coverage determination, it must send you a letter explaining why. This letter also details the steps you can take to appeal the decision and gives you addresses for contacting the appropriate appeal bodies at each level of appeal, as explained in the next section.

Filing an Appeal against a Decision You Disagree With

The appeals process begins when your plan either turns down your request for a coverage determination or doesn't give you a decision within the required time frame (72 hours for a standard request, 24 hours for an expedited request). At that point, you have the right to take your complaint to the next level of appeal. If that level also gives you an unfavorable decision, you can take your complaint to the next highest appeal level, and so on. In the next several sections, I guide you through the five levels of appeal, explain how to handle delays you may encounter, and give you tips on obtaining help.

The appeals process is the same whether you're enrolled in a stand-alone Part D plan or in a Medicare health plan that covers prescription drugs.

Understanding the five levels of appeal

You have up to five opportunities to argue your case through the appeals process. Table 19-1 shows the five levels of appeal, together with the time frames for appealing at each level and the time it takes for a decision to be made. The table is useful for seeing the basic process at a glance, but there are many more details to be aware of. The following sections walk you through the procedures at each level of appeal.

Table 19-1	The Five Levels of Appealing Your Part D Plan's Decision		
Level	*What It Means*	*Time Limit for You to Request This Level*	*When Decision Must Be Made*
1. Redetermination by your plan	Asking your plan to reconsider its denial of your request	In writing within 60 days of the date of the notice from your plan denying the request	*Standard:* Within 7 days *Expedited:* Within 72 hours If plan fails to meet these deadlines, it has 24 hours to send the appeal to the IRE
2. Reconsideration by an Independent Review Entity (IRE)	Asking for a review of your plan's unfavorable redetermination decision	In writing within 60 days of the date of notice of your plan's unfavorable redetermination decision	*Standard:* Within 7 days *Expedited:* Within 72 hours
3. Administrative law judge (ALJ) hearing	Asking an ALJ in an independent, informal setting to review the IRE's unfavorable decision	In writing within 60 days of the date of notice of the IRE's unfavorable decision	Usually within 90 days but may be longer
4. Medicare Appeals Council (MAC) review	Asking the MAC to review an unfavorable decision by an ALJ	In writing within 60 days of receiving notice of the ALJ's unfavorable decision	Usually within 90 days but may be longer

Level	What It Means	Time Limit for You to Request This Level	When Decision Must Be Made
5. Federal court hearing	Asking a court to review an unfavorable decision by the MAC	In writing within 60 days of the date of notice of the MAC's unfavorable decision	Depends on court procedure

Source: Centers for Medicare & Medicaid Services.

Level 1: Redetermination by your plan

Redetermination, the first level of appeal, gives you the opportunity to challenge your plan's denial of your initial coverage determination request if you don't agree with this decision. You're asking the plan to reconsider its decision and, in effect, signaling your intent not to take no for an answer.

Your plan must send you detailed instructions on how to ask for a redetermination in the same mailing as its initial denial. You probably want to make this appeal as soon as possible after receiving the denial. However, you have up to 60 days after the date of the denial notice to make this appeal. If you need more time (due to sickness or some other good reason), you can ask for an extension. If you're asking for a drug to be covered, you can request a standard decision within 7 days or a fast (expedited) decision within 72 hours if your doctor thinks that further delay would put your health at risk.

Make sure to have supporting paperwork to back up your appeal. If you have documents supporting your request (such as your doctor's statement), or if you have new supporting evidence that you didn't send with your original coverage determination request, be sure to send all of this info now.

You have the right to ask your plan to give you any information or evidence it has regarding your request. Just be aware that the plan may charge you a fee for copying and sending these documents.

After you've submitted your request and supporting paperwork, the plan should send a coverage decision within the 7 calendar days or 72 hours requested. If the plan doesn't respond within these time frames, it should automatically forward your case file to the second level of appeal, the Independent Review Entity. (But, as I point out in the earlier section "If your plan doesn't respond within the required time frame," you can also file a grievance or write to the IRE yourself.)

If the plan decides

- ✔ **In your favor:** It must cover the drug you requested no later than 7 days after you filed for a redetermination, or sooner if your health requires the med. If your issue is related to payment, the plan should pay you the amount owed within 30 days of your filing.

- ✔ **Against you:** You have the right to appeal to the next level, the IRE. This is also the case if the plan only partially gives you what you've requested.

Level 2: Reconsideration by an Independent Review Entity

Reconsideration by an Independent Review Entity (IRE) is the second level of appeal, but the first level outside the plan to review your case. The *IRE* is an independent body, under contract with Medicare, and has no connection with your plan. (Medicare currently uses an organization called Maximus as its IRE. For more information on Maximus, go to www.medicareappeal. com.) At this level, you're asking the IRE to reconsider your case in the hope that it will reverse your plan's decision.

You can make this appeal yourself or have someone else act for you (as explained in the later section "Getting Help in Making an Appeal"). *Note:* You can't make this appeal through your doctor unless you've appointed your doctor as your chosen representative.

You must request a reconsideration in writing to the IRE, either in a letter or (preferably) on the standard form that your plan must send you when it denies your redetermination request. This form asks for contact info for you, your appointed representative (if you're using one), and your prescribing doctor. It also requires a copy of your plan's redetermination denial notice. If your doctor thinks you need a fast (expedited) decision from the IRE for the sake of your health, you can check the box asking for a decision within 72 hours. Either way, be sure to return the form to the IRE at the address or toll-free fax number specified on the form.

You can request a reconsideration at any time within 60 calendar days of receiving your plan's redetermination denial, but I recommend doing so as quickly as possible, if you can. Sending the form by fax rather than mail speeds up the process. If you have supporting documents (such as a statement from your doctor saying you need an expedited decision), attach copies to the form.

Your Part D plan may refer your case to the IRE automatically if it's failed to give you a redetermination in good time, as explained in the previous section. If so, the plan must notify you that it's done so and explain what you should do next. If you originated the appeal, the IRE asks the plan to send copies of all the documents in your case file, quickly enough for the IRE to receive them within 24 hours (for an expedited review) or 48 hours (standard review).

The IRE will send you (or your representative) a letter saying that it has received your case file and will give you a reference number for the case. If English isn't your first language, you have the right to ask the IRE to send you letters written in the language you best understand. You also have the right to ask the IRE for a copy of every document in your case file (which includes information sent by your plan).

During the review process, if you obtain additional information you want the IRE to consider, fax it in immediately. Be sure to write your name and case number on each sheet. The review process moves quite fast after it's begun, so acting quickly is essential. If the IRE wants more details, it may contact you (and/or the prescribing doctor) by phone or mail.

After reviewing your case — according to Medicare rules and the information sent by you and your plan — the IRE must make a decision within 72 hours (expedited) or 7 days (standard). Here's what happens next:

✔ If the IRE decides in your favor, the plan must cover the drug(s) in question within 24 hours (expedited) or 72 hours (standard) of the decision. If you're appealing a payment issue, the plan should pay you the disputed amount within 30 days of the decision.

✔ If the IRE agrees with the plan and not you, you have the right to challenge its decision at the third level of appeal, an administrative law judge, under certain conditions.

Level 3: Hearing with Administrative Law Judge

An *administrative law judge (ALJ)* is a lawyer authorized to conduct hearings on disputes between a government agency and anyone affected by the agency's actions. ALJs are required to give impartial decisions according to the facts of the case and the law.

At the ALJ level of appeal, it may be best to get professional help from one of the sources listed later in this chapter. Someone who is experienced in Part D appeals can guide you through the process and act on your behalf in making the appeal if you want. If your appeal involves obtaining an exception for your plan to cover a drug, it may also help if your doctor — the one who prescribed the med(s) in question — agrees to take part in the hearing to speak on your behalf. However, your doc's presence is by no means essential.

The ALJ level introduces a new requirement that doesn't exist at lower levels of appeal. This requirement is the *amount in dispute* (sometimes called the *amount in controversy*) — a specified dollar minimum that represents the cost to you of having your drug or payment denied. In 2008, the amount is $120 (it goes up slightly each year). If your likely cost is less than this amount, you can't appeal to an ALJ. But bear in mind that

- ✔ If you're trying to get your plan to cover a drug, you can calculate the amount in dispute as what it will cost you out of pocket *for the whole year* if the plan doesn't help pay for the drug.

- ✔ You can submit more than one claim to the same ALJ hearing, and the combined claims may raise the amount in dispute over the threshold level. This can happen if, for example, you're asking the plan to cover more than one drug or your plan refused to reimburse you for the cost of a drug purchased for good reason at an out-of-network pharmacy on more than one occasion.

- ✔ If you're appealing because your plan hasn't reimbursed you for extra payments you made between the time you applied for Extra Help (or for Medicaid, SSI, or state-paid Part B premiums) and the date when you became eligible, all of those surplus payments count toward the amount in dispute. They include the difference between what you *should* have paid under Extra Help (premiums, deductibles, and co-pays) and what you *actually* paid under the regular Part D program.

You (or your representative) must request an ALJ hearing in writing within 60 calendar days of receiving the IRE's decision (see the preceding section for more on this level of appeal). Make this request on the form the IRE sends you and mail it to the address given in the IRE's notice. If you have a good reason to miss the 60-day deadline (such as sickness or a family crisis), you can ask for a deadline extension. You can also ask for a translator or interpreter for your own language (including sign language) if you need to.

Send copies of any written evidence that supports your case, either with your request for a hearing or within 10 days of receiving a notice that specifies the date and time of your hearing. This evidence may include copies of claim denial documents, supporting statements or other records from your doctor, pharmacy receipts, the dated form on which you applied for Extra Help, and so on, according to the circumstances.

You have the right to ask the ALJ to conduct a hearing just on the written evidence, without you taking part, but it's usually best to participate. You can ask to take part in an ALJ hearing in one of three ways:

- ✔ **In a telephone conference:** You talk with the judge on the phone and, if you want, you can have your representative (or anyone else helping you) join the conversation, no matter how far away she may be.

- ✔ **In a video conference:** You (and your representative, if desired) talk with the judge through a video link so you can see each other on television screens. A video conference can often be set up in a location near your home.

✔ **In person in a hearing room before the judge:** In-person hearings are held in only four places in the country — Irvine, California; Miami, Florida; Cleveland, Ohio; and Arlington, Virginia. (To find out which of these offices serves your home area, call Medicare at 800-633-4227 or go to www.hhs.gov/omha/offices.html.) This type of hearing is granted only to claimants who can show "special and extraordinary circumstances" for arguing their case in person.

You can call the ALJ's office to find out who else will be giving evidence at your hearing. *Note:* Somebody representing your Part D plan will likely participate. You can ask the ALJ's office to send you copies of any evidence that has been submitted by anyone besides you.

ALJ hearings are more informal than a civil court case, and judges are usually understanding and easy to talk to. Just be yourself and give your side of the story in your own words. Remember, though, that you, your representative, the person representing your Part D plan, and any other witnesses are under oath to tell the truth when giving evidence.

Often, the ALJ makes a decision within 90 days of your hearing, but this process may take longer if the judge decides that more evidence is needed. (However, Medicare proposed a new rule in mid-2008 that would allow fast ALJ decisions in some circumstances. By the time you read this book, that rule may be in effect.)

Here's what to do next based on the outcome of your appeal to the ALJ:

✔ If the judge decides in your favor, your plan must cover the drug(s) in question within 72 hours of receiving the decision. For payment issues, the plan should pay you the disputed amount within 30 days of the decision. However, the plan also has the right to take the case to the next level of appeal, the Medicare Appeals Council.

✔ If the judge decides against you, you have the right to appeal against the decision to the Medicare Appeals Council.

Level 4: Review by Medicare Appeals Council

The *Medicare Appeals Council (MAC)* is a section of the U.S. Department of Health and Human Services. If you want to take your case to this stage — the fourth level of appeal — I recommend you have an advocate or lawyer who has experience with the procedure represent you. The MAC review often focuses on a question of law (for example, whether the ALJ interpreted Medicare law correctly), a question of fairness (such as whether the ALJ considered all the evidence), or a question of Medicare policy (when there's a dispute about how Medicare interprets the law). Most people are way out of their depth here without an advocate preparing their case.

At this level of appeal, the MAC decides a case simply by reviewing the written evidence. No hearing is required, and the amount in dispute (see the preceding section for more info) doesn't matter.

To request an MAC review, you or your representative must write directly to the MAC within 60 days of receiving the ALJ's notice of denial. Follow the instructions included in the notice. If you have new or updated evidence that supports your case, you or your representative can submit it to the MAC at this time.

If the MAC decides

- **In your favor:** Your plan must give you what you were asking for within the same time frames as those given for the ALJ.

- **Against you or denies your request for a review:** You have the right to take your case to the fifth level of appeal in a federal court. The MAC notice tells you how to file for a federal court hearing.

Level 5: Hearing in federal court

If you go to this stage, you really want to be represented by a professional. (I explain how to find free legal help later in this chapter.) You can file for a judicial review in a U.S. district court if both of these circumstances apply:

- The MAC decides not to review your case _or_ decides against you (in other words, it upholds the ALJ's decision).

- The amount in dispute is more than a certain sum — $1,180 in 2008. This sum increases slightly every year.

The amount in dispute at this level of appeal is almost ten times higher than at the ALJ level, but the suggestions on ways to meet the amount that I present in the earlier section on ALJ hearings apply here, too. Also, if an advocacy organization is helping you appeal, it may be able to combine other Medicare beneficiaries' claims with yours. The rules allow appeals to be heard together if they satisfy certain conditions of similarity, and their claims can be added together to meet the required amount in dispute.

To request this review, you must file within 60 calendar days of receiving the MAC decision. The federal court judge first decides whether to review your case. If the case proceeds to court, it's heard under normal court procedures. Should the judge decide

- **In your favor:** Your plan must comply with your request within the same time frames as those given for the ALJ earlier in this chapter.

- **Against you:** Typically this is the end of the road for the Medicare appeals process. But the judge may offer possibilities for further appeals in the federal court system, depending on the legal issues of your case.

Coping with delays

Some of the appeals processes covered in this chapter can take months to decide. That's one kind of delay. Another is when the case has been decided in your favor, but the plan delays paying the money it owes you.

Handling delays in getting your drugs covered

When you've asked the plan to cover a drug you need, your priority is to get it as quickly as possible. Filing for a coverage determination, a redetermination, or an IRE reconsideration can bring relatively fast decisions. At higher appeals levels, however, the process is much more drawn out. If you move into the fourth level of appeal, you may have to decide whether continuing is worth it. Just bear the following in mind:

✔ The ability to afford to buy the drug(s) out-of-pocket for a while doesn't stop your right to continue the appeals process. If you win your case, the plan must cover the drug(s) retroactively, meaning it must reimburse you for all the excess payments you've made for your medicine during the appeals process. (So be sure to keep your receipts.) However, be aware that if you do pay for the drug, you can't ask for an expedited decision when requesting a coverage determination, redetermination, or reconsideration.

✔ If you're receiving Extra Help (see Chapter 5) or living in a nursing home (see Chapter 18), you have the right to switch Part D plans at any time of the year. So enrolling in a plan that *does* cover your drugs may be better than pursuing higher levels of appeal against your current plan.

✔ If your appeal to an IRE is turned down, you may consider asking it to *reopen* (take another look at) your case instead of appealing to the next level (ALJ). You can make this request if you think the IRE's denial was based on a definite error or if you have new medical evidence to support your case. Requests for a reopening can be tricky, so taking advice from a legal advocate before proceeding with this course of action is wise.

✔ The situation may change. As this book goes to press, Medicare has proposed new rules that should speed up the appeals process. These proposals include requiring ALJs (the third level of appeal) to decide a case within 90 days and allowing expedited appeals at the ALJ level.

Taking action if your plan has been told to pay up — but doesn't

Instances of plans not paying due reimbursements within the required 30 days abound. In fact, sometimes they don't pay for months after losing a payment case on appeal. If you're in this situation, consumer advocates suggest that you complain to Medicare. If necessary, continue complaining to Medicare until you receive your money.

Here are some suggestions for making your problem heard:

✔ **Call the Medicare help line at 800-633-4227 (or 877-486-2048 if you're a TDD user).** If the customer representative tells you to call the plan, you should specifically say: "I want this complaint entered into the complaint tracking module." Using this bit of jargon should ensure that Medicare logs the complaint and may speed up getting your money back.

✔ **File a written grievance with Medicare (as I explain earlier in this chapter) and ask that it be forwarded to the plan manager at your regional Medicare office.** The *plan manager* is the area Medicare official responsible for overseeing individual Part D plans. Enclose a copy of the appeal decision to show that more than 30 days have passed since the appeal was granted in your favor.

✔ **Consider reporting the plan's failure to repay you within the required time frame to your regional Medicare Drug Integrity Contractor (MEDIC).** This organization is responsible for investigating fraud and abuse in Part D, including legal and administrative violations by plans. To report a complaint, call 877-772-3379 or download a complaint form from MEDIC's Web site at www.healthintegrity.org.

✔ **Consider writing to your member of Congress.** Alert him or her that this part of the Part D appeals process isn't working as it should.

Consumer complaints are fed into Medicare's quality ratings system, which are displayed on Medicare's online Prescription Drug Plan Finder. If enough people complain about this problem, Medicare may lean on plans more heavily to guarantee they send payments within the required period.

Getting Help in Making an Appeal

Anyone can help you file for a coverage determination or an appeal — a relative, friend, doctor, consumer advocate, or lawyer. If you want any of these individuals to *represent* you — that is, prepare and present your arguments — that person must fill out a form provided by your plan or one of the appeal bodies (IRE, ALJ, MAC, or federal court). Free legal help from professionals who are experienced in Part D appeals is available from

✔ **The Medicare Rights Center:** A national not-for-profit consumer service, the Medicare Rights Center offers free counseling and representation with Part D appeals. Call the Center's appeals hot line toll-free at 888-466-9050. To download its guide to navigating the system, "Medicare Part D Appeals," go to www.medicarerights.org.

✔ **State advocacy groups:** Several states have organizations that offer residents free legal advice and representation with Part D appeals:

- **California:** Call the Health Insurance Counseling and Advocacy Program (HICAP) at 800-434-0222 or go to www.cahealthadvocates.org/HICAP/index.html.

- **Connecticut:** Call the Center for Medicare Advocacy at 860-456-7790 or visit www.medicareadvocacy.org.

- **Maine:** Call Legal Services for the Elderly at 800-750-5353 or go to www.mainelse.org.

- **Massachusetts:** Call the Medicare Advocacy Project at Greater Boston Legal Services at 800-323-3205 or visit www.gbls.org/map/index.htm.

✔ **State Health Insurance Assistance Programs:** All states have SHIPs that give free help and counseling to people with Medicare. If your state program doesn't directly provide legal help with Part D appeals, it can put you in contact with a local service that can. To find your local SHIP's phone number, see Appendix B.

Part V
The Part of Tens

The 5th Wave
By Rich Tennant

"Heartburn? I like the medication that shows 2 people in a rowboat having a picnic, but Cliff likes the one with 2 people on Roman holiday eating lasagne."

In this part . . .

Earlier chapters of this book deal with the daily business of Medicare Part D prescription drug coverage — all the practical things you need to know to get the most out of the program. The two chapters in this part veer off in a different direction. The first assumes you're a boomer not yet on Medicare but helping an older person — most likely a parent — deal with Part D. It suggests ten ways to manage that process effectively while helping yourself at the same time.

The second chapter alerts you to ten proposals to change Part D that have been put forward by members of Congress and others. These suggestions range from specific improvements to overhauls of the entire program. None may happen any time soon, or even at all. But Part D is a creation of politics, so it's good to know what's in the air.

Chapter 20

Ten Ways Boomers Can Help Loved Ones with Part D

. . . .

In This Chapter

▶ Offering to help your relative with Part D

▶ Thinking about the future — for your relative and yourself

. . . .

A lot is said about baby boomers — born between 1946 and 1964 — but one characteristic is unique: Boomers, much more than any previous generation, are (or will be) caring for elderly parents. Now that people commonly live into their 80s, 90s, and even 100s, often with chronic conditions that impair daily activities, their adult children are mostly the ones who care for them. Today, caregiving usually includes coping with Part D. So in this chapter, I suggest ten ways that you, as a boomer (or perhaps someone even younger), can help an older relative with Part D in the short term, and also prepare for the future when you too will become eligible for Medicare and face Part D.

Helping with Tact

Every family is different, of course. Your relationship with an aging relative may be close, strained, at loggerheads, or even a bit of all three at different times. Perhaps you're living in the same house or 3,000 miles away — spending a lot of time together or much less than you'd like. So generalizing is impossible. And I'm not about to lecture you on family relationships.

What I can tell you is that helping a relative, especially a parent, with Part D requires sensitivity and tact. Implying that Dad's incapable of figuring the program out for himself may not go down too well. (*"What do you think I am — senile?"*) Remember that it's not his age that makes him find Part D confusing. It's because Part D *is* confusing! So figuring it out together — or at least giving the impression of doing so, even if you're doing most of the heavy lifting — may bring about a sense of closeness (think "us versus the bureaucracy") that goes far beyond picking a Part D plan.

Identifying the Insurance Your Loved One Has Now

When helping a relative with Part D, you may first need to step back and ask some basic questions about what kinds of health and drug insurance she already has. And don't be surprised if she doesn't know! Her mind isn't going mushy. Seniors often have a perplexing patchwork of different kinds of insurance (not their fault) and aren't always sure which plan covers what.

For example, your relative may simply say, "I have Medicare." But does that mean traditional Medicare? Or a Medicare private health plan? Or both Medicare and Medicaid? Or Medicare plus a retiree health plan? And does she get her prescription drugs from a Medicare health plan, a stand-alone drug plan, or a retiree plan — or possibly some combination of these? Then again, she may say, "I have Blue Cross." But does that mean a Medigap policy, a Medicare private health plan, a stand-alone drug plan, or a retiree plan? Large insurers like Blue Cross sell all of these plans.

Here's how to find what type of medical insurance your relative currently has:

- ✔ **Find the paperwork for each plan.** If you're lucky, it may be neatly filed and accessible. If not, prepare for some hunting around: *"Would it be in a kitchen drawer, Mom, or your dresser? Please, not the attic!"*

- ✔ **Look for the Evidence of Coverage booklet(s).** Every private plan (but not traditional Medicare) sends this document annually to enrollees. The EOC may describe a retiree plan, a Medicare health plan, a stand-alone Part D plan, or Medigap insurance. Make sure the EOC you find is for the current year and not one that's expired.

- ✔ **Look to see what each plan is.** Your relative's EOB booklet and plan membership card should clearly identify what kind of plan she has. If you're still not sure what kind of plan it is, call the plan's customer service number to find out.

- ✔ **Check if your relative has health and drug insurance outside of Medicare.** She may have coverage from a previous employer or union, veterans or military benefits, or COBRA insurance. Or she may be enrolled in a State Pharmacy Assistance Program (SPAP). (Chapter 6 covers how these benefits fit in with Part D.)

- ✔ **Ask if your relative has a Medicaid card if you know or suspect that her income is limited.** Medicaid beneficiaries are automatically entitled to Part D's low-cost Extra Help program, covered in Chapter 5. (***Remember:*** Medicaid, a state program that provides healthcare for low-income people who qualify, is different from Medicare, as explained in Chapter 1.)

Doing Your Homework

You'll be much more confident (and competent) about helping your relative if you have a broad understanding of how Part D works. Good thing you picked up this book, huh? Reading the pertinent bits that fit in with your relative's situation can help you evaluate the insurance he already has and aid you both in deciding which Part D plan most suits his needs or if switching to a different plan may be worthwhile.

Without rehashing the information in the rest of this book, here are a few important points to keep in mind:

✔ If your relative has any kind of retiree benefits, don't let him sign up for a Part D plan (or persuade him to do so) without carefully investigating the consequences. Some retiree plans automatically disenroll anyone who signs up for Part D. (Chapter 6 has details.)

✔ Switching to a Medicare private health plan has consequences, especially in regard to choosing doctors and hospitals (see Chapter 9), that your relative should know about if he currently has traditional Medicare.

✔ If your relative has a limited income and few savings, check out if he qualifies for Extra Help (see Chapter 5). Many eligible people don't apply for this Extra Help and miss out on big savings on their medicines.

✔ Scams are out there, and sometimes sales agents persuade Medicare beneficiaries to buy plans that aren't right for them. If you think your relative is vulnerable, try to make sure he doesn't sign anything until after you've checked it out. (See Chapter 11 for red flags to look for.)

Offering Your Skills

You (yes, you!) have skills that can be of enormous help to a relative trying to figure out Part D. Of course, many older people are quite able to brave the Part D waters themselves, thank you very much, and don't need any help. On the other hand, some people can use help but don't want to admit it. You'll have to be the judge of that. But you may discover that offering your skills — on the computer, phone, or both — to find a suitable Part D plan for her or to troubleshoot problems will be very warmly received.

One great advantage of the Internet and toll-free phone numbers is that you can use your skills remotely, even if you don't live anywhere near the person you're helping. In some families, sorting out Medicare and Part D issues has become part of shared caregiving for a frail or sick parent — a way for the sibling who lives far away to lift at least one responsibility off the shoulders of a brother or sister who lives in the area and is on standby all the time.

Helping to Pick a Plan

If your relative doesn't have Internet access, or just doesn't feel up to doing a Web search personally, you can offer to compare Part D plans for him. Using the online Medicare Prescription Drug Plan Finder at www.medicare.gov is the most effective way of comparing plans and choosing the one that's most suitable. In Chapter 10, you can find a step-by-step guide to walk you through the process. Or you can call the Medicare help line at 800-633-4227 for similar information, also explained in Chapter 10. After you have a shortlist of the two or three plans that seem the most suitable, you and he can discuss the options to make a final choice.

For a relative enrolling in a Part D plan for the first time, you may need to talk with him about how the program works. For example, you may need to explain that drug coverage is offered through many private insurers, not by Medicare directly, and that he needs to pick one plan. If you're helping a couple, you may need to explain that the same plan probably won't be right for both of them.

Following Up

After your relative is in a Part D plan, your help isn't necessarily at an end. Asking her from time to time how the plan's working out is a wise precaution. Check that she's getting the prescriptions she needs. If the plan imposes restrictions on any of her drugs, find out if she needs help asking the plan for an exception (covered in Chapter 4) or filing an appeal (explained in Chapter 19). If so, suggest that she contact one of the help organizations listed in the last section of Chapter 19 or, if necessary, call one yourself.

Another time when your help may be needed is if your relative moves away from her present home. She may need to change her plan if she moves outside of her current plan's service area (covered in Chapter 17) or into a nursing home or other institutional facility (described in Chapter 18).

Making Part D an Annual Event

Everyone groans at the idea of comparing Part D plans all over again each year, but I strongly urge doing so if you want to make sure your relative continues to be in the plan that best meets his needs. Why? Because every plan can change its costs and benefits every calendar year, and usually they all do. At the very least, make sure your relative reads the Annual Notice of Change that his current plan mails out in October (as explained in Chapter 17), or read it yourself if necessary.

Some families make Part D plan comparisons an annual event — most often when they get together for Thanksgiving, which conveniently falls smack in the middle of open enrollment. It may not seem a task that fits perfectly with a mood of celebration, let alone the general lethargy that follows a big dinner, yet it can be a genuine moment of family connection. What's more, if you do a plan comparison for your parent(s) every year, the process becomes familiar and easy, taking maybe no more than half an hour on a computer after the remains of the turkey have been cleared away.

Looking to Your Loved One's Future

No one likes to think about the possibility of loved ones developing dementia or undergoing other medical events, like severe strokes, that rob them of the power to make decisions or even communicate. Yet this scenario happens with tragic frequency. According to the Alzheimer's Association, more than 19 million Americans are estimated to have a family member with Alzheimer's disease alone, and nearly one in two Americans who live beyond 85 are likely to have at least some of its symptoms.

Experts on aging suggest that long before anything like this happens, adult children need to talk with their parents and find out their wishes on what should be done in the case of incapacity. Certainly this isn't the easiest discussion topic in the world, but early planning makes for easier decision making should a crisis occur.

One of the most important questions to ask is who makes medical and legal decisions on behalf of your parent if and when she can no longer make her own. (These include decisions about her Part D coverage, especially if she needs to go into a nursing home, which I cover in Chapter 18.) This is a question that requires expert guidance. The process for becoming a legal guardian or obtaining *durable power of attorney* — the right to make legal decisions on behalf of someone else — depends on your state's laws.

For information on advance healthcare directives — in which your parent can specify who should make which decisions if she becomes incapacitated — and other legal instruments, go to the Web site of the American Bar Association's Commission on Law and Aging at www.abanet.org/aging/publications/home.shtml. (Click "Online Publications for Consumers" to access a list of helpful resources.) AARP also has a wealth of information about advance planning, including "Prepare to Care: A Planning Guide for Families," at www.aarp.org/family/caregiving.

Remembering That Your Time Will Come

Boomers, stereotypically, have never wanted to grow old. (Well, who does?) Many of you have already succeeded in redefining old age: "Fifty is the new thirty! Sixty is the new forty!" Nonetheless, just as you'll look in the mirror one morning and suddenly see your parent or grandparent staring back, so too will you one day confront at least some of the problems your elders face now.

One benefit of helping older relatives navigate Part D is perceiving what's in store not too many years down the road and, in a way, getting into training. The first boomers turn 65 — and become eligible for Medicare — in 2011. Will you be panicking about how to sign up? Will you be totally baffled by the complexities of Part D? Not if you've already been there, done that on behalf of Mom or Dad.

"Working with aging parents is a voyage of discovery," wrote psychologist Mary Pipher (author of *Another Country: Navigating the Emotional Terrain of Our Elders*) in her introduction to the AARP guide *Caring For Your Parents* (Sterling, 2005). "As we travel, we learn about us, about them, and about our relationship. We learn about caregiving and care receiving. And we learn how we want to handle our own old-old age."

Being a Bona Fide Boomer by Making Part D Better

So you've confronted Part D, navigated it, and emerged — with what thoughts? That it's a good program? Better than nothing? In need of major improvements? Boomers traditionally never accept the status quo and believe that anything can be made better, especially if it affects them personally. So you may take a very different view from today's generation of seniors who are the first to experience Part D and have in recent memory the bad old days when Medicare didn't cover outpatient prescription drugs at all.

Part D is a creature of politics. So if you don't like parts of it, don't blame Medicare. Congress writes the law, and only Congress can change it. Senators and representatives listen when enough of their constituents make a fuss (especially in election years). You can find their contact information at www. senate.gov or www.house.gov.

So if your generation lives up to its reputation, how will Part D evolve? Will future Medicare beneficiaries one day wave a not-so-fond farewell to the doughnut hole? Over to you, guys.

Chapter 21

Ten Proposed Changes to Part D You Should Know About

In This Chapter

▶ Improving Part D coverage as you know it

▶ Overhauling Part D completely

*P*art D has always been a political hot potato. Over time, it's tended to scorch the fingers of folks who support it and those who oppose it. Why? Because it's an imperfect, overcomplicated benefit that's hard to support wholeheartedly. Yet it's allowed millions of Medicare beneficiaries to buy prescription drugs more affordably than they ever could before, which makes it very hard to oppose wholeheartedly, too.

But of course, anything can be improved. In this chapter, I present ten proposals with the potential to change Medicare prescription drug coverage either in small or more sweeping ways. At the time I'm writing this book, these proposals are only suggestions put forward by consumer groups, policy experts, and/ or members of Congress. But they're worth keeping an eye on.

Simplifying Plan Choices

Having a multitude of choices supposedly allows people to choose the Medicare private health or drug plan that fits them best. But in practice, it doesn't necessarily work out that way. Faced with a dizzying number of plans, all with different costs and benefits, people are often too overwhelmed to make careful comparisons. As a result, many Medicare beneficiaries don't make informed choices at all.

What can improve this situation, while still keeping the principle of choice? One idea that's gained traction among some lawmakers and consumer advocates is to standardize and simplify plan choices. Medicare beneficiaries would be offered a certain number of standard plans — maybe ten or fewer — that each provide a different benefit package. Each plan would be sold by competing insurance companies for different premiums, according to the level of benefits. Sound familiar? It's modeled on Medigap supplementary insurance, which supporters of the proposal point to as a precedent. The Medigap market was a free-for-all until 1992, when Congress reformed it by introducing ten standardized policies. Choice and competition were preserved, but consumers were able to compare benefits more easily.

Standardization may well simplify choices among Medicare health plans' medical services, but it's difficult to see how it'd work on the prescription drug side. One snag is that the best drug plan for consumers depends less on its design and premium and much more on the specific prescription drugs that each person takes. Part D has far more variables in it than Medigap.

Abolishing the Asset Test for Extra Help

More than 2.5 million Americans with limited incomes would qualify for Part D's Extra Help benefit if it weren't for the asset test, which takes savings as well as income into account when determining eligibility. Consumer groups protest that the test penalizes individuals who've managed to save a little for their old age when they'll be living on low, fixed incomes. The chances of abolishing the asset test entirely aren't high, because doing so would add billions of taxpayer dollars to the cost of Part D. But bills have been introduced in the House and the Senate to raise the asset limits to a degree that would allow many more people whose incomes qualify them for Extra Help to actually get it. Some of these bills would also exclude individual retirement accounts and 401(k)s from being counted as assets.

Allowing Medicare to Negotiate Prices

It was obvious from the get-go that a prescription drug benefit in Medicare would eat up a lot of taxpayer money, so you'd think Congress would've done everything possible to keep drug prices in check. Yet the 2003 Medicare Modernization Act specifically prohibited the government from negotiating Part D drug prices directly with the manufacturers. Instead of using Medicare's huge bargaining clout to keep costs down, negotiation was left to individual Part D insurers. Proposals to reverse the ban have many powerful supporters (like AARP and the American Medical Association) and opponents (like the pharmaceutical industry and, latterly, the Bush administration).

In January 2007, the House of Representatives overwhelmingly passed a bill to allow direct negotiation for drugs in Medicare, but a similar bill failed in the Senate. Look for more attempts — and big controversy — in the future.

Eliminating the Doughnut Hole

For consumers, the doughnut hole (also known as the coverage gap) is the most unpopular aspect of Part D. But although many lawmakers have railed against it, no one has seriously tried to move legislation to fill in the gap and give year-round coverage to everyone enrolled in Part D. That's because doing so would cost an estimated $450 billion over ten years. Abolishing the doughnut hole is a popular enough cause for many lawmakers to continue proposing it. But given the hard choices of raising taxes, cutting benefits in other programs, or keeping Part D's doughnut hole, eliminating it in reality seems remote unless the whole program is overhauled.

Improving Access to Needed Drugs

Allowing plans to impose restrictions on some drugs (through cost-cutting measures such as prior authorization, quantity limits, and step therapy), and requiring consumers to go through the hoops of the exceptions and appeal process to get those drugs, burdens people unduly and discourages many from requesting the drugs they need, according to many consumer groups. No concrete proposals to simplify this system have been advanced. But one suggestion, for Medicare to require plans to inform enrollees at the point of sale why a drug isn't covered and how they can request coverage, would lessen many customers' bewilderment at the pharmacy and may encourage them to file for an exception more quickly.

Cutting Medicare Advantage Subsidies

The 2003 law that created Part D gave Medicare health plans large subsidies to persuade private insurers into the Medicare fold. The extra payments, in turn, allow the plans to offer richer benefits to their enrollees than traditional Medicare offers — an average value of $1,100 more in 2008 for each enrollee. The plans defend this lopsidedness as a boon to people who can't afford Medigap, whereas critics condemn it as a stealth agenda for essentially privatizing Medicare. Certainly, the extra payments add to Medicare's overall costs and therefore increase the Part B premium for everyone in Medicare, not just beneficiaries in the plans. In 2008, many members of Congress called for a halt to the subsidies and succeeded in reducing them slightly. But abolishing them would probably cause many Medicare Advantage plans to raise costs, reduce benefits, or withdraw from the market — a tricky political issue for lawmakers with constituents in the plans. Many in Congress still eye the subsidies — estimated to cost $54 billion over five years — as a pot of gold to pay for other priorities. So stay tuned: This issue isn't going away.

Legalizing Drug Imports from Abroad

Bills making it legal for American consumers to buy prescription drugs from Canada for their own use have been signed into law twice in the past decade. But in each case, the legal language required that the Secretary of Health and Human Services guarantee the safety of drugs imported from other countries, which no secretary has so far been willing to do, so the laws never went into effect. With many supporters on both sides of Congress, the issue will continue to be pressed. But drug pricing is complex, and experts say competition from abroad may not significantly push down prices in the U.S.

Creating a Government-Run Plan

One proposal floated by some Democrats is to create a government-run Part D plan to compete with private plans on a not-for-profit basis. It would allow Medicare to negotiate drug prices for its enrollees and provide "a consistent, uniform drug benefit" available to anyone, according to the House Ways and Means Committee chairman, Rep. Pete Stark. Just as people can choose between traditional Medicare and a private plan, Stark said, they "could remain in the Medicare drug plan or choose to switch to a private option."

Throwing Out Part D and Starting Over

For the severest Part D critics, getting rid of the program and starting over has been a dream since it first became law. But unless a general election throws up a Democratic president and huge Democratic majorities in Congress, it ain't gonna happen. Even so, overhauling the system would be a huge challenge in the face of Part D's established infrastructure and opposition from the health insurance industry. More likely, changes to Part D will be made bit by bit over many years.

Bringing in Universal Health Insurance

With 44 million Americans uninsured, and costs rising even for those who have insurance, the need to make health coverage affordable for everyone is a huge political issue. Of course, there's no consensus on how universal health coverage can be achieved. A wholly government-run health system? A mix of public and private systems? A kind of Medicare for all? Tax breaks for folks who buy health insurance? Who knows? We'll have to wait to see if whatever system is decided upon (if any) has an impact on Medicare and Part D.

Part VI
Appendixes

The 5th Wave   By Rich Tennant

"I think I'm having side effects from my new
prescription medication. I'm feeling nauseous
and disoriented all day."

In this part . . .

Appendix A contains three worksheets that are useful when you're choosing a Part D plan. The first helps you create your master list of the prescription drugs you take now, plus their dosages and how often you take them. You can use the second and third worksheets to help compare drug plans and Medicare health plans point by point.

Appendix B is the place to go for contact information for many sources of help. Here you find phone numbers and Web site addresses for the key government agencies (Medicare and Social Security), every State Health Insurance Assistance Program, and many consumer organizations. This appendix also suggests ways of getting updates on Medicare and Part D so you can stay informed on changes that come down the track.

Appendix C is a guide on how to get prescription drugs *safely* if you purchase them by mail order from Canada, where they generally cost less. It explains how to avoid scams and counterfeit meds, how to assess pharmacies for safe and ethical service, and how to find prescreened licensed pharmacies you can trust.

Appendix A

Worksheets

*F*inding the best drug plan among scores of possibilities — when each one has its own costs and benefits and is different from the next — can be a nightmarish prospect. But it doesn't have to be a nightmare in practice. In Part III, I explain how you can whittle those choices down to a manageable few — by first deciding whether you want to receive your healthcare from traditional Medicare or from a Medicare Advantage plan and then by comparing Part D plans head-to-head according to what they charge for the drugs you take (and other factors that may be important to you).

Using checklists and notes of point-by-point comparisons to track the info you're compiling can help you more clearly see the differences between the plans you're considering so you can make that final cut — down to one. This appendix has three worksheets designed to help you do just that.

✔ **Worksheet 1** is essentially your master list. It provides an organized way of jotting down complete information on all the prescription drugs you take. This is the list you need to make before you can compare Part D plans properly, as explained in Chapter 10.

✔ **Worksheet 2** is the tool to use after you've searched the online Medicare Prescription Drug Plan Finder (or had someone do this for you), as explained in Chapter 10, and reduced your number of drug-plan options to a shortlist of three or four that seem best. You can use this worksheet to finalize your choice among either stand-alone prescription drug plans (PDPs) or Medicare Advantage health plans that cover drugs (MAPDs).

✔ **Worksheet 3** is a checklist to use when considering Medicare Advantage plans for their health costs and benefits, as explained in Chapter 9, after you've reduced these plans to a shortlist of the three or four that seem best for you.

Worksheet 1 is the essential list you must make before comparing Part D plans, as explained in Chapter 10. For each of the drugs you take, write down its exact name together with any other words or letters that follow the name (for example, verapamil HCR ER), its dosage (120 mg, 2.50 ml, and so on), and how often you take it (one pill a day, one bottle a month, and so on).

Worksheet 1	Your Personal List of Prescription Drugs		
	Full Name of Prescription Drug	*Dosage*	*How Often You Take Drug*
1			
2			
3			
4			
5			
6			
7			
8			
9			
10			
11			
12			
13			
14			
15			
16			
17			

Worksheet 2 is designed to be used with the online Medicare Prescription Drug Plan Finder, found at www.medicare.gov. The plan finder tool provides answers to the following questions, as I describe in Chapter 10.

Worksheet 2	Comparing Part D Plans Point by Point			
Suggested Questions to Answer for Each Plan	Plan 1	Plan 2	Plan 3	Plan 4
Does this plan cover all of my drugs? (Yes or no)				
What will be my total estimated out-of-pocket costs over the year at *retail pharmacies* under this plan? (Dollar amount)				
What will be my total estimated out-of-pocket costs over the year under this plan's *mail-order service?* (Dollar amount or N/A if mail order not offered)				
What will my total estimated out-of-pocket costs be over the year under this plan if I choose available *lower-cost drugs?* (Dollar amount)				
How many of my drugs come with any restrictions: prior authorization, quantity limits, step therapy? (for example, 1 PA, 2 QL, 0 ST)				
Will I fall into the coverage gap under this plan? (Yes or no)				
Does this plan cover any of my drugs in the gap? (Yes or no)				
Does this plan use pharmacies that are convenient for me? (Yes or no)				
What are this plan's ratings for customer service? (**P**oor, **F**air, **G**ood, **V**ery **G**ood, **E**xcellent)				
Will this plan cover my prescriptions when I'm away from home? (Yes or no)				

You can use Worksheet 3 to compare Medicare Advantage health plans *after* you've decided to receive medical benefits from an MA plan rather than traditional Medicare (as explained in Chapter 9). This worksheet focuses only on medical care. You can get most of the answers by comparing Medicare health plans online at `www.medicare.gov`. You may have to ask plans or providers for answers the online tool can't provide. (To compare these plans' drug benefits, use Worksheet 2.)

Worksheet 3	Comparing Medical Benefits in Medicare Advantage Plans			
Suggested Questions to Answer For Each Plan	*Plan 1*	*Plan 2*	*Plan 3*	*Plan 4*
Will the providers (doctors, hospitals) that I prefer accept this plan? (Yes or no)				
Will this plan allow me to go to out-of-network providers for a higher co-pay? (Yes or no)				
Will this plan cover my nonemergency health-care needs outside of its service area? (Yes or no)				
What will my fixed costs (monthly premium, annual deductible) be in this plan? (Dollar amounts)				
Does this plan put a limit on my out-of-pocket expenses in a year? (Dollar amount) Are any services excluded from this limit? (Yes or no)				
What will I pay to visit my primary care doctor in this plan? (Dollar amount or percentage)				

Suggested Questions to Answer For Each Plan	Plan 1	Plan 2	Plan 3	Plan 4
What will I pay to visit a specialist in this plan? (Dollar amount or percentage)				
What will I pay to stay in a hospital in this plan? (Dollar amount or percentage)				
What are this plan's ratings for quality of care? (**P**oor, **F**air, **G**ood, **V**ery **G**ood, **E**xcellent)				
Does this plan offer benefits for vision, hearing, or dental care? (Yes or no for **V, H,** or **D**)				
Does this plan offer preventive care (screenings, scans, tests) that meets my needs? (Yes or no)				
Does this plan cover physical exams? (Yes or no)				

Appendix B

Sources of Help

*V*ery often, the help you need to deal with Part D plan issues is only a toll-free phone number or a Web site away. In these pages, I give contact information for government help lines and online resources; independent organizations that offer direct help; where to go for updated info on Medicare and Part D and for ways to save money; and advocacy organizations that work on behalf of people in Medicare. Throughout, I note special help provided for people whose first language isn't English.

Government Help Lines and Web Sites

The go-to sources for help provided by federal and state governments are the Centers for Medicare & Medicaid Services (CMS), the Social Security Administration (SSA), the State Health Insurance Assistance Programs (SHIPs), and the Eldercare Locator.

The Centers for Medicare & Medicaid Services

CMS is the federal agency that runs Medicare and Medicaid (under the umbrella of the U.S. Department of Health and Human Services) and is responsible for overseeing the Part D drug coverage program. It provides updated information and direct help to consumers in English and Spanish.

✔ The *Medicare & You* handbook is sent to everyone on Medicare every October. This basic overview of Medicare services also includes brief details of the Medicare private health plans and Part D stand-alone drug plans that will be available in your area for the following year.

✔ Medicare's toll-free help line at 800-633-4227 is available 24 hours a day, 7 days a week. (TDD users should call 877-486-2048.) The folks on the other end of the line can answer your questions, send you free fact sheets, and give you help on many Medicare and Part D issues. If neither English nor Spanish is your first language, you can ask for an interpreter — more than 70 languages are available.

✔ Medicare's Web site, www.medicare.gov, offers a huge amount of information. Go to this site to compare Part D plans, Medicare private health plans, nursing homes, and hospitals.

The Social Security Administration

SSA is the federal agency that administers Social Security benefits. Call SSA toll-free at 800-772-1213 (TDD: 800-325-0778) or go to its Web site at www.ssa.gov for information on Social Security, enrolling in Medicare Part A and/or B, and applying for Part D's Extra Help program.

 The SSA Web site can be read in Arabic, Armenian, Chinese, Farsi, French, Greek, Haitian-Creole, Italian, Korean, Polish, Portuguese, Spanish, Russian, Tagalog, and Vietnamese, as well as English. To choose a language, click the "Other Languages" button at the top of the home page. You can also ask for an interpreter in any language when you call the help line (press 2 for Spanish or 1 for any other language) or when you arrange to visit a local Social Security office.

State Health Insurance Assistance Programs

SHIPs are valuable resources for anyone who needs help with Medicare issues, especially Part D. They offer free, expert, personal counseling when you want to find a Part D plan that fits your needs, apply for Extra Help, get help making an appeal, or resolve a variety of other problems. If English isn't your first language, the program can provide interpreters or refer you to local organizations that offer counseling in your own language.

SHIPs, which are funded by the federal and state governments, are available in every state, the District of Columbia, Guam, Puerto Rico, and the U.S. Virgin Islands. The programs have different names in some states (for example, HICAP in California; SHINE in Florida). The following list includes every program, its name, the state agency that runs it, a toll-free telephone number (except for D.C. and the territories, which have local numbers), and the Web address. If the number you call isn't working, call the Eldercare Locator at 800-677-1116 or go to www.shiptalk.org or www.hapnetwork.org/ship-locator for an updated number. (Find out more about the Eldercare Locator in the next section.)

Alabama
SHIP, Department of Senior Services
Montgomery, AL
Phone 800-243-5463
Web site www.ageline.net/ship.cfm

Alaska
SHIP, Department of Health and Senior Services
Anchorage, AK
Phone 800-478-6065
Web site www.hss.state.ak.us/dsds/shipMedicare.htm

Arizona
SHIP, Aging and Adult Administration
Phoenix, AZ
Phone 800-432-4040
Web site www.azdes.gov/aaa/

Arkansas
SHIIP, State Insurance Department
Little Rock, AR
Phone 800-224-6330
Web site www.insurance.
arkansas.gov/seniors/
homepage.htm

California
HICAP, Department of Aging
Sacramento, CA
Phone 800-434-0222 (TDD
800-735-2929)
Web site www.cahealthadvocates.
org/HICAP/index.html

Colorado
SHIP, Division of Insurance
Denver, CO
Phone 888-696-7213 (TDD
303-894-7880)
Web site www.dora.state.co.us/
insurance/senior/senior.htm

Connecticut
CHOICES, Department of Social
Services
Hartford, CT
Phone 800-994-9422
Web site www.ct.gov/aging
services/site/default.asp

Delaware
ELDERinfo, Insurance Department
Dover, DE
Phone 800-336-9500
Web site delawareinsurance.gov

District of Columbia
Health Insurance Counseling Project,
George Washington University
Washington, D.C.
Phone 202-739-0668
Web site www.law.gwu.edu/
Academics/Clinical+Programs/
Health+Rights+Law+Clinic.htm

Florida
SHINE, Department of Elder Affairs
Tallahassee, FL
Phone 800-963-5337 (TDD
800-955-8771)
Web site www.floridashine.org

Georgia
GeorgiaCares, Division of Aging
Services
Atlanta, GA
Phone 800-669-8387 (TDD
404-657-1929)
Web site aging.dhr.georgia.
gov/portal/site/DHR-DAS

Guam
Division of Senior Citizens,
Department of Public Health and
Social Services
Hagatna, Guam
Phone 671-735-7388 or 671-735-7393
(TDD 671-734-7415)

Hawaii
SAGE Plus, Executive Office on Aging
Honolulu, HI
Phone 888-875-9229 (TDD
866-810-4379)
Web site www4.hawaii.gov/eoa/
programs/sage_plus

Idaho
SHIBA, Department of Insurance
Boise, ID
Phone 800-247-4422
Web site www.doi.state.id.us/
shiba/shibahealth.aspx

Illinois
SHIP, Department of Insurance
Springfield, IL
Phone 800-548-9034 (TDD
(217-524-4872)
Web site www.idfpr.com/DOI/
Ship/ship_help.asp

Indiana
SHIIP, Department of Insurance
Indianapolis, IN
Phone 800-452-4800
Web site www.in.gov/idoi/
2399.htm

Iowa
SHIIP, Insurance Division
Des Moines, IA
Phone 800-351-4664 (TDD
800-735-2942)
Web site www.shiip.state.ia.us

Kansas
SHICK, Kansas Department on Aging
Topeka, KS
Phone 800-860-5260
Web site www.agingkansas.org

Kentucky
SHIP, Division of Aging Services
Frankfort, KY
Phone 877-293-7447 (TDD
888-642-1137)
Web site chfs.ky.gov/agencies/
os/dail/ship.htm

Louisiana
SHIIP, Department of Insurance
Baton Rouge, LA
Phone 800-259-5301
Web site www.ldi.state.la.us/
Health/SHIIP/index.htm

Maine
HICAP, Bureau of Elder and Adult
Services
Augusta, ME
Phone 800-262-2232 (TDD
800-606-0215)
Web site www.state.me.us/dhs/
beas/hiap/purpose.htm

Maryland
SHIP, Department of Aging
Baltimore, MD
Phone 800-243-3425 (TDD
800-637-4113)
Web site www.mdoa.state.md.us/
ship.html

Massachusetts
SHINE, Executive Office of Elder
Affairs
Boston, MA
Phone 800-243-4636 (TDD
800-872-0166)
Web site www.mass.gov/elders

Michigan
MMAP, Medicare/Medicaid
Assistance Project
Lansing, MI
Phone 800-803-7174
Web site www.mymmap.org

Minnesota
SHIP, Minnesota Board on Aging
St. Paul, MN
Phone 800-333-2433
Web site www.mnaging.org/
advisor/SLL.htm

Mississippi
MICAP, Division of Aging and Adult
Services
Jackson, MS
Phone 800-948-3090
Web site www.mdhs.state.ms.us/
aas_info.html#MICAP

Missouri
CLAIM, Patient Care Review
Foundation
Columbia, MO
Phone 800-390-3330
Web site www.missouriclaim.org

Montana
SHIP, State Office on Aging
Helena, MT
Phone 800-551-3191 (TDD
406-444-2590)
Web site www.dphhs.mt.gov/
sltc/services/aging/ship.
shtml

Nebraska
SHIIP, Department of Insurance
Lincoln, NE
Phone 800-234-7119 (TDD
800-833-7352)
Web site www.doi.ne.gov/shiip

Nevada
SHIP, Division of Aging Services
Las Vegas, NV
Phone 800-307-4444
Web site www.nvaging.net/ship/
ship_main.htm

New Hampshire
NH ServiceLink Resource Center
Laconia, NH
Phone 866-634-9412 (TDD
800-735-2964)
Web site www.nh.gov/service
link

New Jersey
SHIP, Division of Senior Aging and
Community Services
Trenton, NJ
Phone 800-792-8820
Web site www.state.nj.us/
health/senior/ship.shtml

New Mexico
Health Insurance Benefits Assistance
Corps
Santa Fe, NM
Phone 800-432-2080
Web site www.nmaging.state.
nm.us/benes.html

New York
HIICAP, State Office for the Aging
Albany, NY
Phone 800-701-0501
Web site www.hiicap.state.
ny.us

North Carolina
SHIIP, Department of Insurance
Raleigh, NC
Phone 800-443-9354 (TDD
800-735-2962)
Web site www.ncshiip.com

North Dakota
SHIC, Insurance Department
Bismarck, ND
Phone 888-575-6611 (TDD
800-366-6888)
Web site www.nd.gov/ndins

Ohio
OSHIIP, Department of Insurance
Columbus, OH
Phone 800-686-1578 (TDD
614-644-3745)
Web site www.ohioinsurance.gov

Oklahoma
SHICP, Insurance Department
Oklahoma City, OK
Phone 800-763-2828
Web site www.oid.state.ok.us/
www2.oid.state.ok.us/
divisions/shicp.asp

Oregon
SHIBA, Division of Insurance
Salem, OR
Phone 800-722-4134 (TDD
800-735-2900)
Web site www.oregon.gov/DCBS/
SHIBA/index.shtm

Pennsylvania
APPRISE, Department of Aging
Harrisburg, PA
Phone 800-783-7067
Web site www.aging.state.
pa.us/aging/cwp/view.
asp?a=553&q=253802

Puerto Rico
Governor's Office of Elderly Affairs
San Juan, PR
Phone 787-725-4300

Rhode Island
SHIP, Department of Elderly Affairs
Cranston, RI
Phone 401-462-4000 (TDD
401-462-0740)
Web site adrc.ohhs.ri.gov

South Carolina
I-CARE, Office on Aging
Columbia, SC
Phone 800-868-9095
Web site www.aging.sc.gov/
Seniors/ICARE.htm

South Dakota
SHIINE, Center for Active Generations
Sioux Falls, SD
Phone 800-536-8197
Web site www.shiine.net

Tennessee
SHIP, Commission on Aging &
Disability
Nashville, TN
Phone 877-801-0044 (TDD
615-532-3893)
Web site www.state.tn.us/
comaging/ship.html

Texas
HICAP, Department of Aging
Austin, TX
Phone 800-252-9240 (TDD
800-735-2989)
Web site www.dads.state.tx.us/
services/dads_help/aaa/
hicap.html

Utah
SHIIP, Division of Aging and Adult
Services
Salt Lake City, UT
Phone 800-541-7735
Web site www.hsdaas.utah.gov/
insurance_programs.htm

Vermont
Area Agency on Aging
St. Johnsbury, VT
Phone 800-642-5119
Web site www.medicarehelpvt.net

Virgin Islands
VI SHIP
Christiansted, VI
Phone 340-772-7368 (St. Croix);
340-714-4345 (St. Thomas/St. John)
Web site ltg.gov.vi/vi-ship-
medicare.html

Virginia
VICAP, Department for the Aging
Richmond, VA
Phone 800-552-3402 (TDD
800-552-3402)
Web site www.vda.virginia.gov/
vicap2.asp

Washington
SHIBA, Office of the Insurance
Commissioner
Olympia, WA
Phone 800-562-6900 (TDD
360-586-0241)
Web site www.insurance.wa.gov/
shiba/index.shtml

West Virginia
SHINE, Bureau of Senior Services
Charleston, WV
Phone 877-987-4463
Web site www.wvseniorservices.
gov

Wyoming
SHIIP, Wyoming Senior Citizens Inc.
Riverton, WY
Phone 800-856-4398
Web site www.wyomingseniors.
com/WSHIIP.htm

Wisconsin
SHIP, Bureau of Aging and Long Term
Resources
Madison, WI
Phone 800-242-1060 (TDD
866-796-9725)
Web site www.dhfs.state.wi.us/
aging/SHIP.htm

The Eldercare Locator

The Eldercare Locator is a free public service run by the U.S. Administration
on Aging. It acts as a national clearinghouse for Americans age 60 and over to
find help and resources in their own communities. It can connect you to local
agencies and organizations that provide many different kinds of services and
assistance programs, typically those that help people continue to function at
home or in their communities as they age.

- ✔ **Phone:** 800-677-1116 (toll-free), Monday through Friday, 9 a.m. to 8 p.m.
  Eastern Time. The Language Line can handle 150 languages.

- ✔ **Web:** www.eldercare.gov. (For a list of links to home- and community-
  based services, go to www.n4a.org/locator/el_hcbs.cfm.)

Independent Sources of Direct Help

The following agencies are nonprofit organizations that are very similar to the
SHIPs I list earlier. They offer free direct help to consumers on Part D issues, but
are national and sometimes provide more specialized services. They also act as
advocates on behalf of Medicare beneficiaries in Congress and state legislatures.

The Medicare Rights Center

The Medicare Rights Center (MRC) is an independent, New York-based organization that offers information and free legal help and representation on Medicare
issues to consumers throughout the country. It also acts as a consumer watchdog and advocate for improving Medicare benefits (including Part D).

✔ **Consumer hot line:** Call 800-333-4114 (toll-free), Monday through Friday between 9 a.m. and 6 p.m. Eastern Time, to talk to a counselor about health insurance options, Medicare rights and protections, billing problems and payment denials, and complaints and appeals.

✔ **Medicare appeals hot line:** Call 888-466-9050 (toll-free) Monday through Thursday, noon to 2 p.m. Eastern Time to leave a message. This service provides free help with appeals if your Medicare health plan or Part D plan has denied you care or coverage that you need.

✔ **LINCS hot line:** Call this program *only* if you're a low-income New Yorker. LINCS (Linking Individuals in Need to Care and Services) can help you apply for Extra Help in Part D and/or connect you to other programs in New York that may reduce your prescription drug costs. Call 888-795-4627 (toll-free).

✔ **Online information:** For consumer guides on Medicare and the option of receiving free newsletters by e-mail or joining online seminars on Medicare topics, go to www.medicarerights.org.

The National Alliance for Hispanic Health

The National Alliance for Hispanic Health (NAHH) promotes the health and well-being of Hispanics through community programs that reach more than 14 million Hispanics throughout the country. It provides written information and free counseling services in English and Spanish on health programs for consumers of all ages, including direct help on Part D drug coverage. Based in Washington, D.C., NAHH is also a leader in advocacy and research for Hispanic health.

✔ **Phone:** You can call the National Hispanic Family Health Helpline (Su Familia) at 866-783-2645 toll-free Monday through Friday, 9 a.m. to 6 p.m. Eastern Time, for free one-on-one counseling on any health issue. A popular part of this service is personal help with Part D, including finding a drug plan and applying for Extra Help.

✔ **Web:** The NAHH Web site at www.hispanichealth.org has a wealth of health information and publications in English and Spanish. For Medicare information, click "Community" and then "Medicare."

The National Asian Pacific Center on Aging

The National Asian Pacific Center on Aging (NAPCA) promotes the health and well-being of senior Asians and Pacific Islanders throughout the U.S. through advocacy, education, and direct help. It provides details on a range of aging issues and free counseling to help navigate Part D drug coverage.

✔ **Phone:** The NAPCA National Toll-free Multilingual Helpline Center specifically deals with Part D issues, offering personal bilingual counseling on any aspect of the program — choosing a plan, helping with enrollment, applying for Extra Help, and troubleshooting problems. Call 800-582-4218 (Chinese); 800-582-4259 (Korean); 800-582-4336 (Vietnamese); or 800-336-2722 (English).

✔ **Web:** The NAPCA Web site at `www.napca.org` has information for Asian Americans and Pacific Islanders on healthcare and long-term care, employment, education, welfare reform, and many other issues.

Resources for Saving Money

The following resources can help you save money on prescription drugs through various public and private programs for people with limited incomes:

✔ **BenefitsCheckUp (`www.benefitscheckup.org`):** This Web site, a service of the National Council on Aging, allows you to find national, regional, state, or local programs that provide benefits you may qualify for without realizing it — or perhaps never knew existed. It has helped more than 2 million users find more than *$6 billion* in benefits. Online, you're asked about your zip code, age, health status, family circumstances, and income. You do *not* give your name, address, or any other identifying information. You can search for benefits that will help pay for prescriptions and/or other benefits to reduce your living expenses. You can also search the Senior Housing Locator to find housing options, including assisted living, residential and nursing home care, and independent-living retirement communities.

✔ **The Health Resources and Services Administration:** This federal agency, a division of the U.S. Department of Health and Social Services, provides a Web site, `ask.hrsa.gov/pc`, that allows you to locate clinics in your area for free or low-cost healthcare and medications.

✔ **The National Council on Aging:** This nonprofit organization sponsors many programs designed to help older Americans stay healthy and independent, find jobs and community service opportunities, and link them to benefits and resources. It provides consumer information and invites questions through its Web site at `www.ncoa.org`. If you don't have Internet access, you can call its Washington headquarters or four regional offices to ask for the phone numbers of resources in your community: Washington, D.C., 202-479-1200 (TDD 202-479-6674); San Francisco, California, 415-982-7007; Lakewood, New Jersey, 732-367-7111; Steubenville, Ohio, 740-283-2182; Nashville, Tennessee, 615-834-4900.

✔ **The Partnership for Prescription Assistance:** This organization gives a single access point for getting information on more than 475 public and private assistance programs — including 180 offered by pharmaceutical manufacturers — that provide free or low-cost prescription drugs to people with limited incomes. To see whether you qualify for any programs, go to the Web site at www.pparx.org or call toll-free 888-477-2669. You'll be asked to list your prescription drugs and give some information about yourself, including approximate income and savings — but not your name or any other identifying information. Any program you qualify for is identified, with instructions on how to apply. In many cases, you can download application forms from the Web site, fill them out, and take them to your doctor to send in. This Web site can be read in Spanish by clicking the "Español" button at the top of the home page.

Consumer Information and Advocacy Organizations

The nonprofit organizations listed in this section are leading sources of information on Medicare and act as advocates on behalf of Medicare beneficiaries within Congress and state legislatures. They want to hear about people's first-hand experiences with Medicare (including Part D), and they welcome volunteers to help their efforts.

✔ **AARP** uses the power of its membership (nearly 40 million members in 2008) to promote the interests of people age 50 and over. These interests include improving Medicare and Part D, preserving Social Security, and promoting legislation to achieve health insurance access for all Americans. A nonpartisan organization with headquarters in Washington, D.C., AARP has offices in every state (plus the District of Columbia, Puerto Rico, and the U.S. Virgin Islands) and advocates in Congress and all state legislatures. Through the AARP Foundation, attorneys litigate court cases of special importance to older Americans. Among other publications, its news magazine *Segunda Juventud* is for Spanish-speaking members. Toll-free phone 888-687-2277 (TDD 877-434-7598), Monday through Friday, 7 a.m. to midnight Eastern Time; Web site www.aarp.org.

✔ The **Center for Medicare Advocacy** promotes the interests of people on Medicare nationally and is staffed by policy experts, attorneys, researchers, and information specialists. Based in Connecticut, with an office in Washington, D.C., the nonpartisan center advocates to improve

Medicare services and other healthcare rights, litigates court cases, and publishes policy documents and consumer information. It invites consumers to send in questions to its Web site and responds to about 7,000 telephone and e-mail inquiries each year. Phone 860-456-7790 (Connecticut) or 202-293-5760 (Washington); Web site (with e-mail link) www.medicareadvocacy.org. This site can be read in Spanish by clicking the "Español" button at the top of the home page.

✔ **California Healthcare Advocates** is the leading consumer watchdog organization for Californians on Medicare. Based in Sacramento, with offices in Los Angeles, Oakland, and Santa Ana, CHA conducts public policy research and community outreach; promotes recommendations for improving Medicare services and rights at the federal and state level; and provides up-to-date consumer information on its Web site, including the publication *California Medicare News*. Phone 916-231-5110 (Sacramento); Web site www.cahealthadvocates.org.

✔ **Families USA** is a grassroots, nonpartisan organization that promotes quality healthcare for all Americans from the consumer perspective. Based in Washington, D.C., it serves as a consumer watchdog on govern-ment actions related to health coverage, including Medicare and Part D. It also provides updates on developments in the pharmaceutical indus-try and regularly publishes surveys of drug prices. Phone 202-628-3030; Web site www.familiesusa.org.

Sources for Updates on Medicare and Part D

Although the bulk of information in this book is likely to remain current, new regulations and some new Medicare services are introduced from time to time. Also, payment requirements (for example, Part B premiums), Part D coverage levels, and Extra Help out-of-pocket expenses change annually. You can find ongoing updates from these sources:

✔ **Medicare Interactive Counselor:** This free, searchable, comprehensive consumer guide, developed and regularly updated by the Medicare Rights Center (which I introduce earlier in this appendix) provides hundreds of answers to questions about Medicare. Go online to www.medicareinteractive.org or to www.medicareinteractive.org/aarp.

✔ **Ask Ms. Medicare:** You can e-mail questions about Medicare to me (the author of this book) through the *AARP Bulletin's* Web site, `bulletin.aarp.org`. Click the "Ask Ms. Medicare" link on the home page to view past questions and answers and (if you can't find what you're looking for) submit a new question.

✔ **AARP Medicare information:** You can find news, consumer guides, articles, and discussion boards about Medicare and other forms of health insurance (such as Medigap and COBRA) online at `www.aarp.org/health/insurance`.

Appendix C

Buying Prescription Drugs Safely from Abroad

*I*n Chapter 16, I mention the possibility of buying prescription drugs from abroad by mail order as a way to lower expenses in Part D's doughnut hole (formally called the coverage gap). You need to weigh the pros and cons, but if you decide to go this route, your chief concern is to make sure you order from a legitimate, licensed pharmacy that sends you the drugs your doctor prescribed.

Importing prescription drugs from abroad is still illegal in the United States. (Congress has passed legislation to legalize the practice, but it has never been put into effect, for reasons explained in Chapter 21.) However, no American has ever been prosecuted for importing drugs for his own personal use, and it's extremely unlikely that anybody would be. For the millions of otherwise law-abiding citizens who've ordered prescription drugs from abroad — mostly senior citizens before Medicare drug coverage began in 2006 — it's a no-brainer. The same meds that cost a fortune without insurance in the U.S. can often be bought from Canada and other countries, where drug prices are nationally regulated, for much less.

Certainly, getting drugs from abroad can be risky — unless you're careful. Unscrupulous sellers who lurk behind anonymous Web sites peddle counterfeit and other harmful drugs. Scammers will take your money without sending you any meds. The U.S. Food and Drug Administration regularly cites these reasons in warning Americans against buying drugs from abroad.

But many reputable online pharmacies sell bona fide prescription drugs to Americans safely and ethically. This appendix shows you how to find those that offer quality services and how to avoid the ones that are dubious. It also suggests ways of locating pharmacies that have been prescreened for safety and service by state governments or organizations that give seals of approval to online pharmacies that meet certain standards.

In these pages, I focus on ordering drugs from licensed Canadian pharmacies. The Canadian federal and provincial governments regulate pharmacy practices and drug safety as rigorously as American health authorities do, and after nearly a decade of experience in the cross-border trade, these pharmacies have an established track record. They operate mail-order services because that's the only way most Americans can buy drugs from Canada, although many people living in the northern-most states physically cross the border to fill prescriptions in regular drugstores. The mail-order pharmacies maintain Web sites that state their drug prices and policies and allow you to order online.

What if you don't have Internet access? You can order meds by phone from a mail-order pharmacy, but first you'll usually need someone to go online to look for a reputable one (by using the suggestions in this chapter) and find its phone number. Or you can call one of the state-operated services that provide links to prescreened Canadian pharmacies, as described later in this chapter.

Distinguishing the Good Guys from the Bad

Just because an online pharmacy *says* it's based in Canada doesn't mean it is. And just because it has a Canadian address doesn't mean it necessarily provides good service. Here are ways to evaluate legitimate pharmacies and avoid dubious sellers so you can be more confident that the medications you'll receive are the ones your doctor prescribed.

Assessing safe and ethical service

American and Canadian pharmacy experts recommend that you choose an online pharmacy that uses the following best practices of

- ✔ **Displaying on its Web site its license number and the name of the Canadian regulatory agency that granted it.** This means you can check that it's an authentic pharmacy. As an American, you have the same right to complain about a pharmacy to its licensing agency as a Canadian does.

- ✔ **Displaying on its Web site the approval seals of organizations that set standards for safety and service and accredit pharmacies that meet the standards.** See the next section for details of these organizations and how to ensure that the seals posted on pharmacy Web sites are genuine.

✔ **Requiring a prescription from your doctor.** This isn't a hassle — it's your best safety protection. Some reputable pharmacies may allow you to fax in the prescription, but will then phone your doctor to confirm the prescription or wait until they receive the original one in the mail before filling your order.

✔ **Requiring you to have taken the drug for at least one month before you order by mail so you and your doctor know it's working well for you.**

✔ **Requiring you to submit details of your medical history, usually through an online questionnaire.**

✔ **Stating its policy for ensuring your medical and personal privacy in clear language on its Web site.**

✔ **Sending drugs in the manufacturer's original container with seals intact.** This is normal practice among reputable Canadian pharmacies. In some cases, though, they may send drugs in regular pharmacy bottles if the manufacturer's own containers hold different quantities than you order.

✔ **Sending drugs with labeling written in English that includes strength, dosing directions, expiration date, appropriate warnings, and a Drug Identification Number (DIN) that shows the drug has been approved by the Canadian government health authorities.**

✔ **Explaining differences between American and Canadian drug names and labeling.** The same drugs sometimes have different names in other countries.

✔ **Explaining why it can't provide certain drugs.** Reputable pharmacies don't sell drugs that are regarded as controlled substances under American law (like narcotics), or drugs that can't be sent safely through the mail (such as some that require careful handling or refrigeration).

✔ **Providing a full mailing address and a toll-free phone number on its Web site so you can call the pharmacist with questions, check on the status of an order, or order by phone instead of online if you prefer.**

✔ **Displaying on its Web site full information about shipping fees, payment policies, and refunds.** Reputable pharmacies offer encrypted (that is, secure) online payment for credit cards, alternative payment options (such as electronic fund transfers and regular checks), and don't charge any separate fees except for shipping.

✔ **Charging the cost of drugs to your credit card only when they've been shipped to you — and not when the order is first placed.**

✔ **Refunding your money or shipping replacement drugs immediately if your order doesn't arrive.** Reputable pharmacies will do this even if your shipment is intercepted and confiscated by U.S. Customs, a practice that has happened in the past but has become much rarer in recent years since Congress condemned it.

Avoiding scams and dubious sellers

The snake oil salesmen are still out there and thriving — though these days they're usually peddling fake Viagra and other drugs that folks feel too shy to ask their doctors about. These are basic guidelines for avoiding unscrupulous sellers and counterfeit drugs:

- **Never use an online pharmacy that offers to sell you a prescription drug without a doctor's prescription.** This is the number-one no-no — a clear sign of unethical and potentially dangerous practices.

- **Never use an online pharmacy that sends you an uninvited e-mail.** Those unwanted e-mails that pop up so frequently in your in-box should always be seen as outright attempts to scam you. Delete them!

- **Don't trust an online pharmacy that doesn't display a customer service number on its Web site.** If there's no phone number, you can't contact the pharmacy — so how can you know it actually exists?

Finding a Pharmacy You Can Trust

The best way to find reputable licensed pharmacies that give quality service is to use some kind of filter — that is, a system that has already identified pharmacies that operate according to the best practices listed in the "Assessing safe and ethical service" section. In the following sections, I suggest two types of filters:

- Programs set up by state governments to link consumers to prescreened Canadian pharmacies

- Organizations that give seals of approval to online pharmacies that meet their standards

Using state links to Canadian pharmacies

In 2003–04, two state governors lost patience waiting for the federal government to legally allow people access to low-cost prescription drugs from Canada. Both governors created Web sites offering links to Canadian pharmacies that state health officials have prescreened and regularly inspect to ensure safety and quality service.

✔ **Minnesota RxConnect:** This program, set up by Minnesota Governor Tim Pawlenty in 2003, offers links to four prescreened Canadian pharmacies. Some other states (and the District of Columbia) direct their residents to this program, but residents of any state can use it. Go to `rxconnect.dhs.state.mn.us` and click "Order Your Medicine from Canada." Or call 800-333-2433.

✔ **Illinois I-SaveRx:** This program, created by Illinois Governor Rod Blagojevich in 2004, offers a link to one prescreened Canadian pharmacy. The program is open to residents of Illinois, Kansas, Missouri, Vermont, and Wisconsin. Call 866-472-8333 or go online to `www.i-saverx.net`.

Looking online for seals of approval

Hundreds of advertisements for low-cost prescription drugs litter the Internet, aimed at Americans who are trying to save money on their prescriptions. Every time you go online to search for any medical topic, these ads pop up on-screen in profusion. Some are legitimate, and some are total rip-offs. How can you tell which are which? You can't. However, you can play it safe. Ignore the ads. Instead, look for licensed pharmacies that display, on their Web sites, the seals of approval awarded by organizations that have screened them to meet certain safety and service standards.

Here's where those seals of approval come from:

✔ **Internet and Mail-Order Pharmacy Accreditation Commission (IMPAC):** IMPAC was founded in 2003 in Vermont by an independent group of doctors and pharmacists to promote consumer safety and quality service among licensed mail-order pharmacies in the U.S. and other countries. A pharmacy must meet rigorous standards during a two-day on-site inspection every two years to receive and retain IMPAC accreditation. To see a list of the currently accredited pharmacies, go to `www.impacsurvey.org` or call 800-677-7019.

✔ **Canadian International Pharmacy Association (CIPA):** CIPA was formed in 2002 to represent licensed Canadian pharmacies that sell prescription drugs to Americans by mail order and that meet its safety, service, and ethical standards. The group has testified before Congress and state legislatures to address safety issues and to promote U.S. legalization of the cross-border trade for consumers buying prescription drugs from Canada for their personal use. To verify that a pharmacy is currently accredited by CIPA, go to `www.ciparx.ca`.

✔ **Better Business Bureau (BBB):** The BBB awards its BBBOnline seal of approval to Web sites that meet its standards for ethical service, trustworthy business practices, and truth in advertising. You can check out BBB records for an online pharmacy, including whether the BBB has received consumer complaints about it, at www.bbbonline.org. If you go to a pharmacy Web site that displays the BBB seal, clicking the seal will take you straight to the BBB report on that pharmacy.

✔ **PharmacyChecker.com:** This Web site, run by an independent American consumer research group, provides ratings and drug price comparisons for about 30 online pharmacies in the US. and abroad (mainly Canada). It gives its "verification" seal to those that meet five service standards — it's licensed, requires a doctor's prescription, displays its address and phone number, offers secure online financial transactions, and promises privacy for medical information. The site also posts names of "rogue" pharmacies that it considers unethical or unsafe. It compares prices for more than 1,000 drugs at verified pharmacies and posts customers' comments on quality of service. Check it out at www.pharmacychecker.com.

Approval seals awarded by these organizations provide a useful guide for consumers looking for a legitimate online pharmacy. However — wouldn't you know? — some scam artists use these seals too to cheat customers by posting copies of them on their own rogue Web sites. The copies are good — you wouldn't know the difference just by looking at them. However, you can verify whether the displayed seals are genuine or fraudulent. Clicking the image of a seal on a pharmacy Web site should take you straight to the Web site of the organization that awarded it, whether IMPAC, CIPA, BBB, or PharmacyChecker. If nothing happens, you can be sure that the seal isn't genuine. Or you can go directly to the organization's Web site and enter the name of the pharmacy. This will tell you whether the pharmacy is entitled to display the seal.

Index

● *T* ●

BUSINESS, CAREERS & PERSONAL FINANCE

Accounting For Dummies, 4th Edition*
978-0-470-24600-9

Bookkeeping Workbook For Dummies†
978-0-470-16983-4

Commodities For Dummies
978-0-470-04928-0

Doing Business in China For Dummies
978-0-470-04929-7

E-Mail Marketing For Dummies
978-0-470-19087-6

Job Interviews For Dummies, 3rd Edition*†
978-0-470-17748-8

Personal Finance Workbook For Dummies*†
978-0-470-09933-9

Real Estate License Exams For Dummies
978-0-7645-7623-2

Six Sigma For Dummies
978-0-7645-6798-8

Small Business Kit For Dummies, 2nd Edition*†
978-0-7645-5984-6

Telephone Sales For Dummies
978-0-470-16836-3

BUSINESS PRODUCTIVITY & MICROSOFT OFFICE

Access 2007 For Dummies
978-0-470-03649-5

Excel 2007 For Dummies
978-0-470-03737-9

Office 2007 For Dummies
978-0-470-00923-9

Outlook 2007 For Dummies
978-0-470-03830-7

PowerPoint 2007 For Dummies
978-0-470-04059-1

Project 2007 For Dummies
978-0-470-03651-8

QuickBooks 2008 For Dummies
978-0-470-18470-7

Quicken 2008 For Dummies
978-0-470-17473-9

Salesforce.com For Dummies, 2nd Edition
978-0-470-04893-1

Word 2007 For Dummies
978-0-470-03658-7

EDUCATION, HISTORY, REFERENCE & TEST PREPARATION

African American History For Dummies
978-0-7645-5469-8

Algebra For Dummies
978-0-7645-5325-7

Algebra Workbook For Dummies
978-0-7645-8467-1

Art History For Dummies
978-0-470-09910-0

ASVAB For Dummies, 2nd Edition
978-0-470-10671-6

British Military History For Dummies
978-0-470-03213-8

Calculus For Dummies
978-0-7645-2498-1

Canadian History For Dummies, 2nd Edition
978-0-470-83656-9

Geometry Workbook For Dummies
978-0-471-79940-5

The SAT I For Dummies, 6th Edition
978-0-7645-7193-0

Series 7 Exam For Dummies
978-0-470-09932-2

World History For Dummies
978-0-7645-5242-7

FOOD, GARDEN, HOBBIES & HOME

Bridge For Dummies, 2nd Edition
978-0-471-92426-5

Coin Collecting For Dummies, 2nd Edition
978-0-470-22275-1

Cooking Basics For Dummies, 3rd Edition
978-0-7645-7206-7

Drawing For Dummies
978-0-7645-5476-6

Etiquette For Dummies, 2nd Edition
978-0-470-10672-3

Gardening Basics For Dummies*†
978-0-470-03749-2

Knitting Patterns For Dummies
978-0-470-04556-5

Living Gluten-Free For Dummies†
978-0-471-77383-2

Painting Do-It-Yourself For Dummies
978-0-470-17533-0

HEALTH, SELF HELP, PARENTING & PETS

Anger Management For Dummies
978-0-470-03715-7

Anxiety & Depression Workbook For Dummies
978-0-7645-9793-0

Dieting For Dummies, 2nd Edition
978-0-7645-4149-0

Dog Training For Dummies, 2nd Edition
978-0-7645-8418-3

Horseback Riding For Dummies
978-0-470-09719-9

Infertility For Dummies†
978-0-470-11518-3

Meditation For Dummies with CD-ROM, 2nd Edition
978-0-471-77774-8

Post-Traumatic Stress Disorder For Dummies
978-0-470-04922-8

Puppies For Dummies, 2nd Edition
978-0-470-03717-1

Thyroid For Dummies, 2nd Edition†
978-0-471-78755-6

Type 1 Diabetes For Dummies*†
978-0-470-17811-9

***** Separate Canadian edition also available
† Separate U.K. edition also available

Available wherever books are sold. For more information or to order direct: U.S. customers visit www.dummies.com or call 1-877-762-2974.
U.K. customers visit www.wileyeurope.com or call (0)1243 843291. Canadian customers visit www.wiley.ca or call 1-800-567-4797.

INTERNET & DIGITAL MEDIA

AdWords For Dummies
978-0-470-15252-2

Blogging For Dummies, 2nd Edition
978-0-470-23017-6

**Digital Photography All-in-One
Desk Reference For Dummies, 3rd Edition**
978-0-470-03743-0

Digital Photography For Dummies, 5th Edition
978-0-7645-9802-9

**Digital SLR Cameras & Photography
For Dummies, 2nd Edition**
978-0-470-14927-0

**eBay Business All-in-One Desk Reference
For Dummies**
978-0-7645-8438-1

eBay For Dummies, 5th Edition*
978-0-470-04529-9

eBay Listings That Sell For Dummies
978-0-471-78912-3

Facebook For Dummies
978-0-470-26273-3

The Internet For Dummies, 11th Edition
978-0-470-12174-0

Investing Online For Dummies, 5th Edition
978-0-7645-8456-5

iPod & iTunes For Dummies, 5th Edition
978-0-470-17474-6

MySpace For Dummies
978-0-470-09529-4

Podcasting For Dummies
978-0-471-74898-4

**Search Engine Optimization
For Dummies, 2nd Edition**
978-0-471-97998-2

Second Life For Dummies
978-0-470-18025-9

**Starting an eBay Business For Dummies
3rd Edition†**
978-0-470-14924-9

GRAPHICS, DESIGN & WEB DEVELOPMENT

**Adobe Creative Suite 3 Design Premium
All-in-One Desk Reference For Dummies**
978-0-470-11724-8

**Adobe Web Suite CS3 All-in-One Desk
Reference For Dummies**
978-0-470-12099-6

AutoCAD 2008 For Dummies
978-0-470-11650-0

**Building a Web Site For Dummies,
3rd Edition**
978-0-470-14928-7

**Creating Web Pages All-in-One Desk
Reference For Dummies, 3rd Edition**
978-0-470-09629-1

**Creating Web Pages For Dummies,
8th Edition**
978-0-470-08030-6

Dreamweaver CS3 For Dummies
978-0-470-11490-2

Flash CS3 For Dummies
978-0-470-12100-9

Google SketchUp For Dummies
978-0-470-13744-4

InDesign CS3 For Dummies
978-0-470-11865-8

**Photoshop CS3 All-in-One
Desk Reference For Dummies**
978-0-470-11195-6

Photoshop CS3 For Dummies
978-0-470-11193-2

Photoshop Elements 5 For Dummies
978-0-470-09810-3

SolidWorks For Dummies
978-0-7645-9555-4

Visio 2007 For Dummies
978-0-470-08983-5

Web Design For Dummies, 2nd Edition
978-0-471-78117-2

Web Sites Do-It-Yourself For Dummies
978-0-470-16903-2

Web Stores Do-It-Yourself For Dummies
978-0-470-17443-2

LANGUAGES, RELIGION & SPIRITUALITY

Arabic For Dummies
978-0-471-77270-5

Chinese For Dummies, Audio Set
978-0-470-12766-7

French For Dummies
978-0-7645-5193-2

German For Dummies
978-0-7645-5195-6

Hebrew For Dummies
978-0-7645-5489-6

Ingles Para Dummies
978-0-7645-5427-8

Italian For Dummies, Audio Set
978-0-470-09586-7

Italian Verbs For Dummies
978-0-471-77389-4

Japanese For Dummies
978-0-7645-5429-2

Latin For Dummies
978-0-7645-5431-5

Portuguese For Dummies
978-0-471-78738-9

Russian For Dummies
978-0-471-78001-4

Spanish Phrases For Dummies
978-0-7645-7204-3

Spanish For Dummies
978-0-7645-5194-9

Spanish For Dummies, Audio Set
978-0-470-09585-0

The Bible For Dummies
978-0-7645-5296-0

Catholicism For Dummies
978-0-7645-5391-2

The Historical Jesus For Dummies
978-0-470-16785-4

Islam For Dummies
978-0-7645-5503-9

**Spirituality For Dummies,
2nd Edition**
978-0-470-19142-2

NETWORKING AND PROGRAMMING

ASP.NET 3.5 For Dummies
978-0-470-19592-5

C# 2008 For Dummies
978-0-470-19109-5

Hacking For Dummies, 2nd Edition
978-0-470-05235-8

Home Networking For Dummies, 4th Edition
978-0-470-11806-1

Java For Dummies, 4th Edition
978-0-470-08716-9

**Microsoft® SQL Server™ 2008 All-in-One
Desk Reference For Dummies**
978-0-470-17954-3

**Networking All-in-One Desk Reference
For Dummies, 2nd Edition**
978-0-7645-9939-2

**Networking For Dummies,
8th Edition**
978-0-470-05620-2

SharePoint 2007 For Dummies
978-0-470-09941-4

**Wireless Home Networking
For Dummies, 2nd Edition**
978-0-471-74940-0